LEARNING TO CODE WITH CPT/HCPCS

LEARNING TO CODE WITH CPT/HCPCS

Thomas Falen, MA, RHIA, LHRM, CPUR/CPUM, EMT-B

Alice Noblin, MBA, RHIA, LHRM, CCS

Brandy G. Ziesemer, MA, RHIA, CCS

Wolters Kluwer | Lippincott Williams & Wilkins
Health

Philadelphia · Baltimore · New York · London
Buenos Aires · Hong Kong · Sydney · Tokyo

Publisher: Julie K. Stegman
Acquisitions Editor: Pete Sabatini
Editorial Manager: Eric Branger
Development Editor: Tanya Martin
Managing Editor: Amy Millholen
Marketing Manager: Zhan Caplan
Compositor: Aptara, Inc.
Printer: RR Donnelley – Willard

351 West Camden Street
Baltimore, Maryland 21201

530 Walnut Street
Philadelphia, Pennsylvania 19106

Printed in the United States of America

Library of Congress Cataloging-in-Publication Data

Falen, Thomas J.
  Learning to code with CPT/HCPCS / Thomas Falen, Alice Noblin, Brandy Ziesemer.
      p. ; cm.
  Includes bibliographical references and index.
  ISBN-13: 978-0-7817-8113-8
  ISBN-10: 0-7817-8113-2
  1. Nosology—Code numbers. 2. Medicine—Terminology—Code numbers. I. Noblin, Alice. II. Ziesemer, Brandy. III. Title.
  [DNLM: 1. Forms and Records Control—methods. 2. Delivery of Health Care—classification. 3. Health Services Administration—standards. 4. Insurance, Health, Reimbursement. 5. Terminology as Topic. W 80 F187La 2009]
  RB115.F354 2009
  651.5′04261—dc22

                    2008009414

To purchase additional copies of this book, call our customer service department at **(800) 638-3030** or fax orders to **(301) 824-7390**. International customers should call **(301) 714-2324.**

Visit Lippincott Williams & Wilkins on the Internet: http://www.LWW.com. Lippincott Williams & Wilkins customer service representatives are available from 8:30 am to 6:00 pm, EST.

09
1 2 3 4 5 6 7 8 9 10

Dedication

Tom Falen dedicates this book to his daughters Kristin and Molly, and his wife, Cindy, who bring meaning to his life; also, to his brother Steven Falen, MD, PhD, who inspired him to "catch up."

Alice Noblin recognizes her parents, Richard and Jane Brunet, for their emphasis on higher education and lifelong learning. Alice dedicates this book to her husband, Frank Noblin, RT (R)(N), for his understanding of the time required for this project. She also thanks him for providing expert knowledge of nuclear medicine and other imaging procedures.

Brandy Ziesemer recognizes her mentor in health information education, the late Laura A. Clark, whose achievements and love for the HIM profession inspired many people to reach for the stars. Brandy dedicates this book to her husband Thomas and son Alexander who constantly amaze her with wit, wisdom and love.

Preface

Health information has been very important to improving healthcare quality since the beginning of modern medical practice. Physicians have reported symptoms (described by the patient) and signs (observed by the physician) and documented remedies and outcomes for hundreds of years. Physicians shared this documentation and used different approaches to resolve a condition once they realized that some methods of treatment resulted in better patient outcomes than others. As populations increased and plagues wiped out significant numbers of people in a geographic location, healthcare professionals started keeping more formal records. It soon became evident that a standard vocabulary or medical terminology would increase the efficiency of researching medical cases to improve patient care. Early classification systems were developed that used numbers or codes to describe the causes of death or communicable diseases. Instead of long narrative descriptions of medical terms, coded information could be quickly recorded, communicated, and indexed to retrieve and study specific diseases. Some form of diagnosis coding has been used for epidemiological research throughout the world to track the incidence and prevalence of certain diseases in particular populations and areas. Also, medical coding has been used as a tool to locate medical data for various other studies.

Coding for reimbursement purposes is a much newer concept. In the past, physicians in the United States submitted brief descriptions of patient care (patient summaries) to private insurance companies to receive payment for the services they provided, such as consultations or surgeries. With the enactment of the federal Medicare and Medicaid programs in 1965, the American Medical Association (AMA) determined that a more consistent and efficient method of submitting bills to Medicare, Medicaid, and insurance companies was needed. In 1966, the AMA released the first version of Current Procedural Terminology (CPT). The current version used for procedural coding is CPT-4, and this version undergoes annual revisions to keep in step with progress in the medical and technological fields.

In the early 80s, the Federal Government negotiated with the AMA to use CPT as the official coding system for reporting physicians' professional services. Other national private insurance carriers soon followed this trend. Because the CPT system did not include codes for certain items or services payable under Medicare (e.g., durable medical equipment such as crutches and wheelchairs; supplies such as oxygen and drugs), the Health Care Finance Administration (now called the Center for Medicare and Medicaid Services or CMS) developed the Healthcare Common Procedure Coding System (HCPCS). HCPCS Level II (national codes) reimburse for items not adequately described in the CPT system, which is designated HCPCS Level I. Shortly thereafter, the federal government mandated an outpatient prospective payment system (OPPS) that resulted in medical coders assigning CPT codes for the technical services provided by hospitals.

The purpose of *Learning to Code with CPT/HCPCS* is to provide a practical and comprehensive approach to learning CPT and HCPCS coding and reimbursement concepts for future employment in healthcare as a professional coder, a reimbursement specialist, a quality analyst, or a manager. This book is best used by students studying medical coding in colleges and universities at both the undergraduate and graduate levels of health information management and health services administration. In addition, the book is ideal for students in vocational and technical schools who are being trained in CPT coding. After completing this book, students will gain a global understanding of how important precise coding is to the successful management of physicians' practices, hospitals, and other medical facilities.

This text offers an opportunity for beginning students to learn to code properly. It makes a clear distinction between the intricacies of CPT coding for physician offices versus CPT coding for facilities. We have collected samples of actual medical records from a variety of healthcare providers to assist you in developing the high-level coding skills needed to transition from school to work. That is, you will gain marketable coding skills by learning to code from real-world examples.

Healthcare providers want to be reimbursed for the services they provide in the care of each patient. It is important to be aware that each provider will create a unique medical record for each patient seen. Each medical record represents the story of the patient's episode of care, provides documented proof that the care was actually performed, and stands as the best evidence of the quality of the care provided. The medical record, in turn, will be coded so that an individual claim can be created and submitted to the patient's healthcare payer, whether government or private insurance, so that the provider of care is paid accurately for services provided. The codes, along with other data abstracted from the medical record, are used to create a database that will be used for future research, quality studies, and practice management purposes. One desired outcome of this research is to provide quality care at reduced cost through the development of standard treatment protocols called "best care practices."

We are delighted to have had this opportunity to work closely with our publisher, Lippincott Williams and Wilkins, and their competent and dedicated staff in developing a textbook that is both relevant to the needs of the health professions and critical in meeting the ever-increasing expectations of a watchful and wary public.

Note to Instructor: No two instructors approach teaching CPT coding in exactly the same manner. We have sequenced our chapters in what we believe is a logical order for a student to learn. The earlier chapters cover less complex material than the later chapters such as Evaluation and Management and Surgery. Therefore, the chapters do not match the order in which the topics are covered in the CPT Code Book. Everyone should feel free to teach the material in any order preferred.

Thomas Falen, MA, RHIA, LHRM, CPUR/CPUM, EMT-B
Alice Noblin, MBA, RHIA, LHRM, CCS
Brandy Ziesemer, MA, RHIA, CCS

User's Guide

This User's Guide introduces you to the many features of **Learning to Code with CPT/HCPCS**. Taking full advantage of these features, you'll quickly develop marketable coding skills. Moreover, it will help you become more productive and accurate, reducing the incidence of costly and time-consuming errors.

Each chapter is loaded with features that help you quickly gain essential coding skills and then test and strengthen those skills by putting them into practice.

Chapter Outline — beginning each chapter gives you a quick overview of what you'll find and be asked to do as you progress through the chapter.

Chapter Introduction — summarizes the key areas and skills covered in the chapter and helps you understand the importance of what you are about to learn.

Objectives help guide your studies by outlining what you'll know upon successful completion of the chapter.

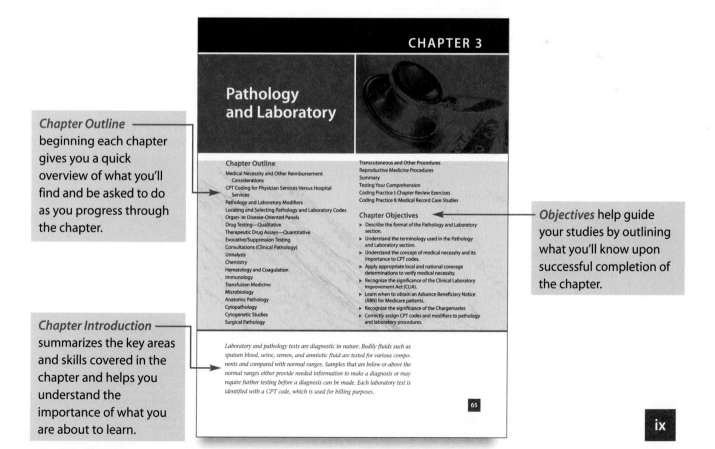

CHAPTER 3

Pathology and Laboratory

Chapter Outline

Medical Necessity and Other Reimbursement Considerations
CPT Coding for Physician Services Versus Hospital Services
Pathology and Laboratory Modifiers
Locating and Selecting Pathology and Laboratory Codes
Organ- or Disease-Oriented Panels
Drug Testing—Qualitative
Therapeutic Drug Assays—Quantitative
Evocative/Suppression Testing
Consultations (Clinical Pathology)
Urinalysis
Chemistry
Hematology and Coagulation
Immunology
Transfusion Medicine
Microbiology
Anatomic Pathology
Cytopathology
Cytogenetic Studies
Surgical Pathology

Transcutaneous and Other Procedures
Reproductive Medicine Procedures
Summary
Testing Your Comprehension
Coding Practice I: Chapter Review Exercises
Coding Practice II: Medical Record Case Studies

Chapter Objectives

► Describe the format of the Pathology and Laboratory section.
► Understand the terminology used in the Pathology and Laboratory section.
► Understand the concept of medical necessity and its importance to CPT codes.
► Apply appropriate local and national coverage determinations to verify medical necessity.
► Recognize the significance of the Clinical Laboratory Improvement Act (CLIA).
► Learn when to obtain an Advance Beneficiary Notice (ABN) for Medicare patients.
► Recognize the significance of the Chargemaster.
► Correctly assign CPT codes and modifiers to pathology and laboratory procedures.

Laboratory and pathology tests are diagnostic in nature. Bodily fluids such as sputum blood, urine, semen, and amniotic fluid are tested for various components and compared with normal ranges. Samples that are below or above the normal ranges either provide needed information to make a diagnosis or may require further testing before a diagnosis can be made. Each laboratory test is identified with a CPT code, which is used for billing purposes.

65

Examples interspersed throughout each chapter show you how specific procedures are correctly coded for reimbursement.

the actual time (in minutes) that the anesthesiologist spends providing the anesthesia service is required by Medicare and most other third-party payers. This is then factored into the payment to the provider. Anesthesia time starts when the anesthesia provider begins to prepare the patient for surgery and ends when the anesthesiologist has safely placed the patient under postoperative care (e.g., with the recovery room nurses) and is no longer in personal attendance of the patient. Many third-party payers may require the provider to report the total minutes as units of time based on an established formula.

> *Payers or providers may convert total time (in minutes) to units of time through the following formula: One unit of time is given for each 15 minutes of anesthesia time and fractions of it. Using this formula, a procedure requiring 120 minutes, converted to 15-minute intervals, results in 8 total time units. A procedure requiring 80 minutes, converted to 15-minute intervals, results in 5.33 total time units. Some carriers' guidelines may require coders to round up or round down fractions of anesthesia time units. Also, depending on the carrier, different unit intervals may be used.*   **EXAMPLE**

Anesthesia Modifiers

CPT was originally developed as a reimbursement system that provided a means for health-care providers to report their services to a payer. This understanding helps beginning coders appreciate the importance of assigning the correct modifiers to the anesthesia code in order for providers to receive fair reimbursement for the work they do. Patients who receive anesthesia are in various degrees of health, and the addition of modifiers helps to explain the overall clinical condition of the patient and, therefore, the extent of the work required by the anesthesiologist and other special circumstances that affect how payments to the provider are determined.

Anesthesia modifiers include:

▸ Physical status modifiers
▸ Qualifying circumstance codes (add-on codes that act as modifiers)
▸ CPT modifiers
▸ HCPCS Level II modifiers

Physical Status Modifiers

Physical status modifiers (P1–P6) are appended to the anesthesia codes to describe the various levels of complexity of the anesthesia services provided to the patient. The physical status modifiers are consistent with the American Society of Anesthesiologists (ASA) classification of patient health status, and these definitions are published in each annual edition of the ASA Relative Value Guide (RVG) and in the AMA's CPT manual. The ASA also provides a relative value description, called base or basic unit values, for each modifier. The physical status modifier class for the patient is assigned and documented in the medical report by the anesthesiologist (e.g., preanesthesia report or note). The following table outlines the physical status modifiers used with anesthesia codes.

Coders should read the guidelines carefully to ensure the correct code choice. If the physician is present at the time of vaccine administration and provides face-to-face counseling to the patient and family, codes 90465 or 90467 are assigned along with applicable add-on code(s). If the physician is not present to provide counseling, the proper code selection is 90471 for the first injection and 90472 for each additional vaccine or toxoid administration. To separately code for E/M services at the time of immunization administration, the -25 modifier is appended to the E/M code. Physician office visits must meet the documentation requirements for key components (see details in the Evaluation and Management chapter of this textbook).

> Some payers may not recognize the use of modifier -25. The E/M services should be documented thoroughly in the medical record. However, E/M service provided on the same day as an injection or infusion may not be reimbursable.

Hydration (90760–90761)

Hydration codes are used for reporting intravenous (IV) administration of prepackaged fluid and electrolytes. These codes are not applicable to infusion of drugs or other substances and should not be reported if concurrently administered with chemotherapy or infusions of other drugs. Hydration is typically not a high-risk procedure, and once the IV line is in place, the patient requires little monitoring. Documentation of start and stop times is needed to allow the

 TIP The initial hydration code of 90760 should not be used to report initial services if any other drug is administered. Even if hydration is listed as the first service received, the coder should report this service using 90761 with the drug administration code as the initial service.

EXAMPLE *A dehydrated patient is infused with one unit of a 5% dextrose/normal saline solution, which takes approximately 50 minutes: 90760, J7042. Alternatively, supply code 99070 can be used for the product administered if required by the payer (in place of J7042).*

coder to choose the correct code(s). The codes are based on time, with 90760 for the initial hour and an add-on code of 90761 used for each additional hour.

Supply codes (Substance/drug and amount admistered) for injections and infusions are documented using a "J" code from HCPCS Level II, such as J7030 for infusion of normal saline solution, 1,000 mL. Some commercial payers do not accept the HCPCS Level II supply codes and will not reimburse for them. In this case, CPT provides a general supply code, 99070, that is submitted along with the name(s) of the product(s) used. To avoid repeating the code for a particular products (e.g., drug), the number of units can be reported in an additional field on the billing form/abstract.

Red Flags alert you to and help you avoid common coding errors.

Tips draw attention to best practices, help make sense of confusing terms, and assist you in managing complex issues.

Positioning and Body Planes

Correct positioning of the patient is critically important in both diagnostic and therapeutic radiology for accuracy and to avoid repeating x-rays unnecessarily. Exposing healthy tissue to x-rays can be detrimental and should be kept to a minimum because prolonged exposure to x-rays can actually cause conditions such as cataracts or radiation colitis. For this reason, radiologic technologists (radiographers) and technicians wear badges that measure the amount of radiation to which they are exposed. Lead aprons or shields are used for technologists and patients to protect healthy tissue during diagnostic and therapeutic procedures.

The **anatomic position** (Fig. 4.2) refers to the patient standing, facing forward, toes pointed forward, and palms open with the thumbs pointing away from the body. While the patient stands in this position, x-rays may be taken from back to front, or **posteroanterior** (PA), with the film in the front. A chest x-ray is often taken in the PA position. **Anteroposterior** (AP) x-rays are taken from front to back, with the film in the back.

Key Terms are bolded within each chapter and defined in the glossary.

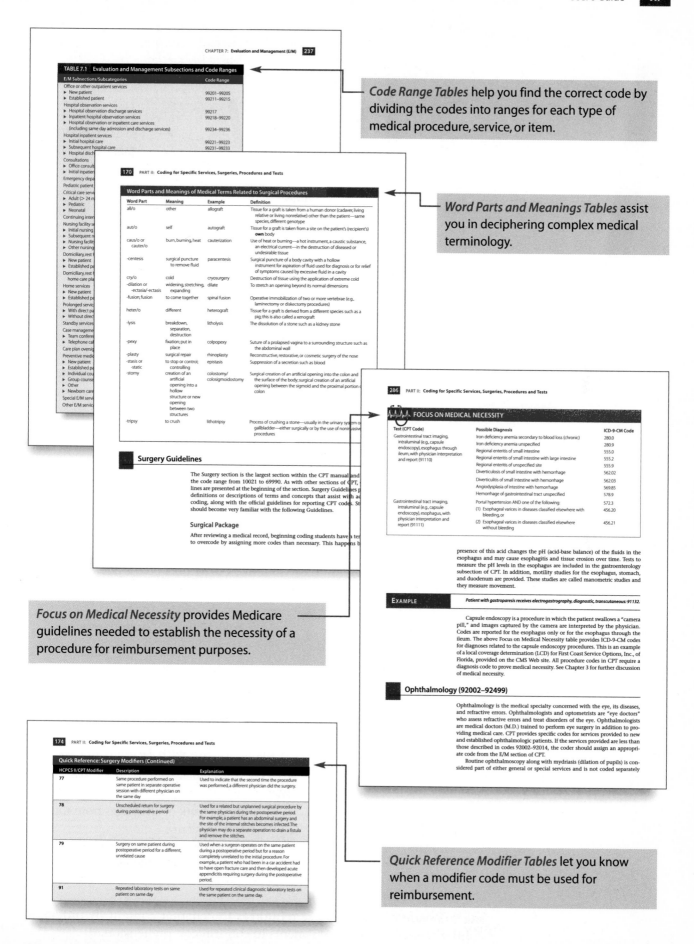

TABLE 7.1 Evaluation and Management Subsections and Code Ranges

E/M Subsections/Subcategories	Code Range
Office or other outpatient services	
▶ New patient	99201–99205
▶ Established patient	99211–99215
Hospital observation services	
▶ Hospital observation discharge services	99217
▶ Inpatient hospital observation services	99218–99220
▶ Hospital observation or inpatient care services (including same day admission and discharge services)	99234–99236
Hospital inpatient services	
▶ Initial hospital care	99221–99223
▶ Subsequent hospital care	99231–99233
▶ Hospital disch	
Consultations	
▶ Office consult	
▶ Initial inpatien	
Emergency depa	
Pediatric patient	
Critical care serv	
▶ Adult (> 24 m	
▶ Pediatric	
▶ Neonatal	
Continuing inten	
Nursing facility se	
▶ Initial nursing	
▶ Subsequent n	
▶ Nursing facili	
▶ Other nursing	
Domiciliary, rest	
▶ New patient	
▶ Established pa	
Domiciliary, rest i home care pla	
Home services	
▶ New patient	
▶ Established pa	
Prolonged servic	
▶ With direct pa	
▶ Without direc	
Standby services	
Case manageme	
▶ Team confere	
▶ Telephone cal	
Care plan oversig	
Preventive medic	
▶ New patient	
▶ Established pa	
▶ Individual cou	
▶ Group counse	
▶ Other	
▶ Newborn care	
Special E/M servi	
Other E/M servic	

Code Range Tables help you find the correct code by dividing the codes into ranges for each type of medical procedure, service, or item.

---

170 PART II: Coding for Specific Services, Surgeries, Procedures and Tests

Word Parts and Meanings of Medical Terms Related to Surgical Procedures

Word Part	Meaning	Example	Definition
all/o	other	allograft	Tissue for a graft is taken from a human donor (cadaver, living relative or living nonrelative) other than the patient—same species, different genotype
aut/o	self	autograft	Tissue for a graft is taken from a site on the patient's (recipient's) **own** body
caus/o or cauter/o	burn, burning, heat	cauterization	Use of heat or burning—a hot instrument, a caustic substance, an electrical current—in the destruction of diseased or undesirable tissue
-centesis	surgical puncture to remove fluid	paracentesis	Surgical puncture of a body cavity with a hollow instrument for aspiration of fluid used for diagnosis or for relief of symptoms caused by excessive fluid in a cavity
cry/o	cold	cryosurgery	Destruction of tissue using the application of extreme cold
-dilation or -ectasia/-ectasis	widening, stretching, expanding	dilate	To stretch an opening beyond its normal dimensions
-fusion; fusion	to come together	spinal fusion	Operative immobilization of two or more vertebrae (e.g., laminectomy or diskectomy procedures)
heter/o	different	heterograft	Tissue for a graft is derived from a different species such as a pig; this is also called a xenograft
-lysis	breakdown, separation, destruction	litholysis	The dissolution of a stone such as a kidney stone
-pexy	fixation; put in place	colpopexy	Suture of a prolapsed vagina to a surrounding structure such as the abdominal wall
-plasty	surgical repair	rhinoplasty	Reconstructive, restorative, or cosmetic surgery of the nose
-stasis or -static	to stop or control; controlling	epistasis	Suppression of a secretion such as blood
-stomy	creation of an artificial opening into a hollow structure or new opening between two structures	colostomy/ colosigmoidostomy	Surgical creation of an artificial opening into the colon and the surface of the body; surgical creation of an artificial opening between the sigmoid and the proximal portion of colon
-tripsy	to crush	lithotripsy	Process of crushing a stone—usually in the urinary system or gallbladder—either surgically or by the use of noninvasive procedures

Word Parts and Meanings Tables assist you in deciphering complex medical terminology.

Surgery Guidelines

The Surgery section is the largest section within the CPT manual and
the code range from 10021 to 69990. As with other sections of CPT,
lines are presented at the beginning of the section. Surgery Guidelines p
definitions or descriptions of terms and concepts that assist with ad
coding, along with the official guidelines for reporting CPT codes. St
should become very familiar with the following Guidelines.

Surgical Package

After reviewing a medical record, beginning coding students have a ter
to overcome by assigning more codes than necessary. This happens b

---

286 PART II: Coding for Specific Services, Surgeries, Procedures and Tests

FOCUS ON MEDICAL NECESSITY

Test (CPT Code)	Possible Diagnosis	ICD-9-CM Code
Gastrointestinal tract imaging, intraluminal (e.g., capsule endoscopy), esophagus through ileum, with physician interpretation and report (91110)	Iron deficiency anemia secondary to blood loss (chronic)	280.0
	Iron deficiency anemia unspecified	280.9
	Regional enteritis of small intestine	555.0
	Regional enteritis of small intestine with large intestine	555.2
	Regional enteritis of unspecified site	555.9
	Diverticulosis of small intestine with hemorrhage	562.02
	Diverticulitis of small intestine with hemorrhage	562.03
	Angiodysplasia of intestine with hemorrhage	569.85
	Hemorrhage of gastrointestinal tract unspecified	578.9
Gastrointestinal tract imaging, intraluminal (e.g., capsule endoscopy), esophagus, with physician interpretation and report (91111)	Portal hypertension AND one of the following:	572.3
	(1) Esophageal varices in diseases classified elsewhere with bleeding, or	456.20
	(2) Esophageal varices in diseases classified elsewhere without bleeding	456.21

presence of this acid changes the pH (acid-base balance) of the fluids in the
esophagus and may cause esophagitis and tissue erosion over time. Tests to
measure the pH levels in the esophagus are included in the gastroenterology
subsection of CPT. In addition, motility studies for the esophagus, stomach,
and duodenum are provided. These studies are called manometric studies and
they measure movement.

EXAMPLE *Patient with gastroparesis receives electrogastrography, diagnostic, transcutaneous: 91132.*

Capsule endoscopy is a procedure in which the patient swallows a "camera
pill," and images captured by the camera are interpreted by the physician.
Codes are reported for the esophagus only or for the esophagus through the
ileum. The above Focus on Medical Necessity table provides ICD-9-CM codes
for diagnoses related to the capsule endoscopy procedures. This is an example
of a local coverage determination (LCD) for First Coast Service Options, Inc., of
Florida, provided on the CMS Web site. All procedure codes in CPT require a
diagnosis code to prove medical necessity. See Chapter 3 for further discussion
of medical necessity.

Ophthalmology (92002–92499)

Ophthalmology is the medical specialty concerned with the eye, its diseases,
and refractive errors. Ophthalmologists and optometrists are "eye doctors"
who assess refractive errors and treat disorders of the eye. Ophthalmologists
are medical doctors (M.D.) trained to perform eye surgery in addition to providing medical care. CPT provides specific codes for services provided to new
and established ophthalmologic patients. If the services provided are less than
those described in codes 92002–92014, the coder should assign an appropriate code from the E/M section of CPT.
Routine ophthalmoscopy along with mydriasis (dilation of pupils) is considered part of either general or special services and is not coded separately

Focus on Medical Necessity provides Medicare guidelines needed to establish the necessity of a procedure for reimbursement purposes.

---

174 PART II: Coding for Specific Services, Surgeries, Procedures and Tests

Quick Reference: Surgery Modifiers (Continued)

HCPCS II/CPT Modifier	Description	Explanation
77	Same procedure performed on same patient in separate operative session with different physician on the same day	Used to indicate that the second time the procedure was performed, a different physician did the surgery.
78	Unscheduled return for surgery during postoperative period	Used for a related but unplanned surgical procedure by the same physician during the postoperative period. For example, a patient has an abdominal surgery and the site of the internal stitches becomes infected. The physician may do a separate operation to drain a fistula and remove the stitches.
79	Surgery on same patient during postoperative period for a different, unrelated cause	Used when a surgeon operates on the same patient during a postoperative period but for a reason completely unrelated to the initial procedure. For example, a patient who had been in a car accident had to have open fracture care and then developed acute appendicitis requiring surgery during the postoperative period.
91	Repeated laboratory tests on same patient on same day	Used for repeated clinical diagnostic laboratory tests on the same patient on the same day.

Quick Reference Modifier Tables let you know when a modifier code must be used for reimbursement.

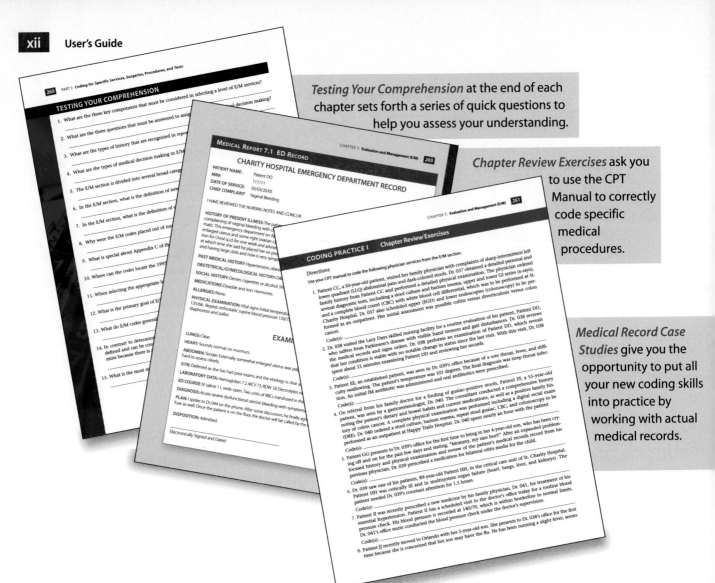

Testing Your Comprehension at the end of each chapter sets forth a series of quick questions to help you assess your understanding.

Chapter Review Exercises ask you to use the CPT Manual to correctly code specific medical procedures.

Medical Record Case Studies give you the opportunity to put all your new coding skills into practice by working with actual medical records.

STUDENT RESOURCES

The student CD-ROM and online resource center reinforce what you learn in the text with additional exercises for each chapter. Student resources include:

- ▶ additional coding practice questions
- ▶ extra case studies
- ▶ pdfs of the Medical Record Case Studies from the text
- ▶ appendices for the book
- ▶ links to helpful online resources

The Student Resource Center can be accessed at **http://thePoint.lww.com/FalenCPT09**.

INSTRUCTOR RESOURCES

The online instructor resources available for use with *Learning to Code with CPT/HCPCS* include a variety of helpful teaching tools that encourage active learning. Instructor resources include:

- ▶ PowerPoint presentations for each chapter
- ▶ lesson plans
- ▶ image bank of all images from the text
- ▶ test generator
- ▶ answer keys for text exercises and extra case studies

ONLINE COURSE

The companion online course reinforces the chapter content by providing additional exercises and assessments to confirm comprehension.

Acknowledgments

A special thank you to the following individuals for their positive input in improving the quality of this book:

Aaron Liberman, Ph.D.
Cynthia Falen, RHIT, CCS
Iching ("Iva") Chen
Brittney Draper

Reviewers

KAREN ALLEN ANDERSON, RHIT
Coding Specialist
Medical Data Services
Glens Falls Hospital
Glens Falls, NY

DARLENE BOSCHERT, BS, CPC-I. CPC-H-I, CMT. NCMA
Director
Allied Health Career Institute of Florida
St. Petersburg, FL

STACIE L. BUCK, RHIA, CCS-P, LHRM, RCC, CIC
Vice President
Southeast Radiology Management
Stuart, FL

BABS CERNA, CMA (AAMA)
Program Coordinator/Instructor
Medical Assisting Department
Highline Community College
Des Moines, WA

RASHMI GAONKAR, MS (POLYMER SCIENCE)
Senior Instructor
Department of Health Disciplines
ASA Institute
Brooklyn, NY

BEVERLEY GITELES, CPC, CMM, CCP
Professor
Gibbs College
Livingston, NJ

Illustration Sources

FIGURE 6.7   LifeART image copyright © 2008. Lippincott Williams & Wilkins. All rights reserved.

FIGURE 6.8   Image provided by Anatomical Chart Co.

FIGURE 6.9   From Nath JL. Using Medical Terminology: A Practical Approach. Baltimore: Lippincott Williams & Wilkins, 2006.

FIGURE 6.10   From Cohen BJ. Medical Terminology, 4th ed. Philadelphia. Lippincott Williams & Wilkins, 2003.

FIGURE 6.11   From Smeltzer SC and Bare BG. Brunner & Suddarth's Textbook of Medical-Surgical Nursing, 9th ed. Philadelphia: Lippincott Williams & Wilkins, 2000.

FIGURE 6.12   From Pillitteri A. Maternal and Child Nursing, 4th ed. Philadelphia: Lippincott, Williams & Wilkins, 2003.

FIGURE 6.13   From Cohen BJ. Medical Terminology, 4th ed. Philadelphia: Lippincott Williams & Wilkins, 2003.

FIGURE 6.14   From Cohen BJ. Medical Terminology, 4th ed. Philadelphia: Lippincott Williams & Wilkins, 2003.

FIGURE 6.15   From Bear MF, Connors BW, and Parasido, MA. Neuroscience: Exploring the Brain, 2nd ed. Philadelphia: Lippincott Williams & Wilkins, 2001.

FIGURE 8.1   LifeART image copyright © 2008. Lippincott Williams & Wilkins. All rights reserved.

FIGURE 8.2   LifeART image copyright © 2008. Lippincott Williams & Wilkins. All rights reserved.

FIGURE 8.3   From Cohen BJ. Medical Terminology, 4th ed. Philadelphia: Lippincott Williams & Wilkins, 2003.

FIGURE 8.4   From Bickley LS and Szilagyi P. Bates' Guide to Physical Examination and History Taking, 8th ed. Philadelphia: Lippincott Williams & Wilkins, 2003.

FIGURE 8.5   From Smeltzer SC and Bare BG. Textbook of Medical-Surgical Nursing, 9th ed. Philadelphia: Lippincott Williams & Wilkins, 2000.

FIGURE 8.6   From Cohen BJ. Medical Terminology, 4th ed. Philadelphia: Lippincott Williams & Wilkins, 2003.

FIGURE 8.7   From Willis MC. Medical Terminology: A Programmed Learning Approach to the Language of Health Care. Baltimore: Lippincott Williams & Wilkins, 2002.

FIGURE 8.8   From Goodheart HP. Goodheart's Photoguide of Common Skin Disorders, 2nd ed. Philadelphia: Lippincott Williams & Wilkins, 2003.

FIGURE 8.9   Reprinted with permission from Bear MF, Connors BW, and Paradiso MA. Neuroscience, 3rd ed. Baltimore: Lippincott Williams & Wilkins, 2007. Adapted from Horne, 1988.

FIGURE 9.1   From Oatis, CA. Kinesiology: The Mechanics and Pathomechanics of Human Movement. Baltimore: Lippincott Williams & Wilkins, 2004.

FIGURE 9.2   LifeART image copyright © 2008. Lippincott Williams & Wilkins. All rights reserved.

FIGURE 9.3   From Smeltzer SC and Bare BG. Textbook of Medical-Surgical Nursing, 9th ed. Philadelphia: Lippincott Williams & Wilkins, 2000.

FIGURE 9.4   From Smeltzer SC and Bare BG. Textbook of Medical-Surgical Nursing, 9th ed. Philadelphia: Lippincott Williams & Wilkins, 2000.

FIGURE 9.5   LifeART image copyright © 2008. Lippincott Williams & Wilkins. All rights reserved.

FIGURE 9.6   From Cohen BJ. Medical Terminology, 4th ed. Philadelphia: Lippincott Williams & Wilkins, 2003.

FIGURE 9.7   LifeART image copyright © 2008. Lippincott Williams & Wilkins. All rights reserved.

Contents in Brief

Expanded Contents

INTRODUCTION TO CPT CODING

Current Procedural Terminology and Healthcare Common Procedure Coding System

Chapter Outline

How CPT Codes Are Used

History of CPT

Coding and Reimbursement

Compliance Plans and Fraud and Abuse

The Process of Coding Using CPT

The CPT Coding Manual

Uniform Ambulatory Care Data Set

CPT and HCPCS Level II Modifiers

CPT-5

Summary

Testing Your Comprehension

Chapter Objectives

▶ Understand the history and purpose of the Current Procedural Terminology (CPT) coding system and Healthcare Common Procedure Coding System (HCPCS).

▶ Recognize the need for determination of medical necessity with ICD-9-CM diagnosis codes when using CPT.

▶ Be able to discuss the significance the inpatient prospective payment system had on outpatient services and on the use of CPT coding.

▶ Recognize the difference between the ASC, APG, APC, and RBRVS reimbursement systems.

▶ Define and understand the significance of upcoding and unbundling.

▶ Understand that CPT is a multiaxial system.

▶ Become familiar with the sections within the CPT manual and the symbols used within the coding system.

▶ Understand the importance of modifiers to maximum allowable reimbursement.

▶ Assign the correct CPT modifiers when appropriate.

Published and maintained by the American Medical Association (AMA), Current Procedural Terminology (CPT®) is a medical coding system that includes numbers that standardize descriptions of surgeries, procedures, and other types of medical services. By replacing long narrative names and descriptions of medical procedures with codes (numbers), CPT provides a fast and effective means for health-care providers to communicate their services to Medicare, Medicaid, and other third-party payers, which helps to expedite *payments to health-care providers for the work they do. A **third-party payer** is an organization or person (other than the patient) who furnishes the money to pay for the provision of health-care services.[1] For example, Medicare and Blue Cross/Blue Shield are third-party payers.*

How CPT Codes Are Used

Although CPT was originally designed by the AMA to serve as a reimbursement system for physicians, the use of coded medical information has since grown exponentially; it is now routinely transferred to other interested parties such as government agencies to help administer public health programs, and shared among health-care providers to coordinate care for their patients. Medical codes can be communicated quickly through electronic data interchange (EDI) for billing purposes and through standard billing forms, such as the CMS 1500 claim form used primarily by physicians and the UB-92 and newer version UB-04 claim form used by hospitals (copies of these standard forms are shown in Figs. 1.1, 1.2, and 1.3.). As of May 23, 2007, all eligible facility paper claim filers were required to submit bills using the UB-04, and Medicare will no longer accept the UB-92. Most providers now routinely submit claims electronically using EDI and no longer submit paper claims.

Medical codes are also used to improve the efficiency of providing health-care services. For example, coded data are transferred through computer networks used by managed care organizations (MCOs) and **Regional Health Information Organizations** (RHIOs) that serve a particular population of health-care consumers to coordinate, manage, and improve patient care.

Because CPT is strictly a procedural coding system, a separate coding and classification system, the *International Classification of Diseases, 9th Revision, Clinical Modification* (ICD-9-CM), is widely used in conjunction with CPT to describe patient diseases. Essentially, ICD-9-CM diagnosis codes describe the medical reasons for the procedures coded in CPT. For example, ICD-9-CM code 211.3 represents the diagnosis of a benign colon polyp, and CPT code 45384 represents the procedure colonoscopy, flexible, proximal to splenic flexure; with removal of tumor(s), polyp(s), or other lesions(s) by hot biopsy forceps or bipolar cautery. ICD-9-CM diagnosis codes help providers explain to third-party payers the **medical necessity** for the procedures performed and reported in CPT. Because this textbook presents CPT concepts and principles, it is highly recommended that the coder also obtain and study a textbook that covers the principles of ICD-9-CM. Together, the CPT and ICD-9-CM coding and classification systems provide a standardized and effective way of telling the important story of each patient's episode of medical care. In essence, coded patient data:

▶ Expedite payments to health-care providers from third-party payers.
▶ Allow for the timely sharing of medical information among providers to promote the continuity of patient care.

1500

HEALTH INSURANCE CLAIM FORM

APPROVED BY NATIONAL UNIFORM CLAIM COMMITTEE 08/05

CARRIER

| | PICA | | | | | | | | PICA | |

| 1. MEDICARE | MEDICAID | TRICARE CHAMPUS | CHAMPVA | GROUP HEALTH PLAN | FECA BLK LUNG | OTHER | 1a. INSURED'S I.D. NUMBER | (For Program in Item 1) |

(Medicare #) (Medicaid #) (Sponsor's SSN) (Member ID#) (SSN or ID) (SSN) (ID)

2. PATIENT'S NAME (Last Name, First Name, Middle Initial)

3. PATIENT'S BIRTH DATE
MM | DD | YY   SEX
M [ ]   F [ ]

4. INSURED'S NAME (Last Name, First Name, Middle Initial)

5. PATIENT'S ADDRESS (No., Street)

6. PATIENT RELATIONSHIP TO INSURED
Self [ ] Spouse [ ] Child [ ] Other [ ]

7. INSURED'S ADDRESS (No., Street)

CITY | STATE

8. PATIENT STATUS
Single [ ] Married [ ] Other [ ]

CITY | STATE

ZIP CODE | TELEPHONE (Include Area Code)
(   )

Employed [ ] Full-Time Student [ ] Part-Time Student [ ]

ZIP CODE | TELEPHONE (Include Area Code)
(   )

9. OTHER INSURED'S NAME (Last Name, First Name, Middle Initial)

10. IS PATIENT'S CONDITION RELATED TO:

11. INSURED'S POLICY GROUP OR FECA NUMBER

a. OTHER INSURED'S POLICY OR GROUP NUMBER

a. EMPLOYMENT? (Current or Previous)
[ ] YES   [ ] NO

a. INSURED'S DATE OF BIRTH
MM | DD | YY   SEX
M [ ]   F [ ]

b. OTHER INSURED'S DATE OF BIRTH
MM | DD | YY   SEX
M [ ]   F [ ]

b. AUTO ACCIDENT?
PLACE (State)
[ ] YES   [ ] NO

b. EMPLOYER'S NAME OR SCHOOL NAME

c. EMPLOYER'S NAME OR SCHOOL NAME

c. OTHER ACCIDENT?
[ ] YES   [ ] NO

c. INSURANCE PLAN NAME OR PROGRAM NAME

d. INSURANCE PLAN NAME OR PROGRAM NAME

10d. RESERVED FOR LOCAL USE

d. IS THERE ANOTHER HEALTH BENEFIT PLAN?
[ ] YES   [ ] NO   *If yes,* return to and complete item 9 a-d.

READ BACK OF FORM BEFORE COMPLETING & SIGNING THIS FORM.
12. PATIENT'S OR AUTHORIZED PERSON'S SIGNATURE I authorize the release of any medical or other information necessary to process this claim. I also request payment of government benefits either to myself or to the party who accepts assignment below.

SIGNED _____ DATE _____

13. INSURED'S OR AUTHORIZED PERSON'S SIGNATURE I authorize payment of medical benefits to the undersigned physician or supplier for services described below.

SIGNED _____

PATIENT AND INSURED INFORMATION

14. DATE OF CURRENT:
MM | DD | YY
ILLNESS (First symptom) OR
INJURY (Accident) OR
PREGNANCY(LMP)

15. IF PATIENT HAS HAD SAME OR SIMILAR ILLNESS.
GIVE FIRST DATE MM | DD | YY

16. DATES PATIENT UNABLE TO WORK IN CURRENT OCCUPATION
MM | DD | YY   MM | DD | YY
FROM _____ TO _____

17. NAME OF REFERRING PROVIDER OR OTHER SOURCE

17a. |
17b. NPI |

18. HOSPITALIZATION DATES RELATED TO CURRENT SERVICES
MM | DD | YY   MM | DD | YY
FROM _____ TO _____

19. RESERVED FOR LOCAL USE

20. OUTSIDE LAB? $ CHARGES
[ ] YES   [ ] NO

21. DIAGNOSIS OR NATURE OF ILLNESS OR INJURY (Relate Items 1, 2, 3 or 4 to Item 24E by Line)

1. |___.___| 3. |___.___|

2. |___.___| 4. |___.___|

22. MEDICAID RESUBMISSION
CODE   ORIGINAL REF. NO.

23. PRIOR AUTHORIZATION NUMBER

24. A. DATE(S) OF SERVICE		B. PLACE OF SERVICE	C. EMG	D. PROCEDURES, SERVICES, OR SUPPLIES (Explain Unusual Circumstances)		E. DIAGNOSIS POINTER	F. $ CHARGES	G. DAYS OR UNITS	H. EPSDT Family Plan	I. ID. QUAL.	J. RENDERING PROVIDER ID. #
From	To			CPT/HCPCS	MODIFIER						
MM DD YY	MM DD YY										
1										NPI	
2										NPI	
3										NPI	
4										NPI	
5										NPI	
6										NPI	

25. FEDERAL TAX I.D. NUMBER   SSN EIN
[ ] [ ]

26. PATIENT'S ACCOUNT NO.

27. ACCEPT ASSIGNMENT?
(For govt. claims, see back)
[ ] YES   [ ] NO

28. TOTAL CHARGE
$

29. AMOUNT PAID
$

30. BALANCE DUE
$

31. SIGNATURE OF PHYSICIAN OR SUPPLIER INCLUDING DEGREES OR CREDENTIALS
(I certify that the statements on the reverse apply to this bill and are made a part thereof.)

SIGNED _____ DATE _____

32. SERVICE FACILITY LOCATION INFORMATION

a. NPI   b.

33. BILLING PROVIDER INFO & PH # (   )

a. NPI   b.

PHYSICIAN OR SUPPLIER INFORMATION

NUCC Instruction Manual available at: www.nucc.org

APPROVED OMB-0938-0999 FORM CMS-1500 (08-05)

FIGURE 1.1 ■ Health Insurance Claim Form CMS-1500 is the standard billing form used by physicians. (Reprinted courtesy of U.S. Department of Health and Human Services, Centers for Medicare and Medicaid Services.)

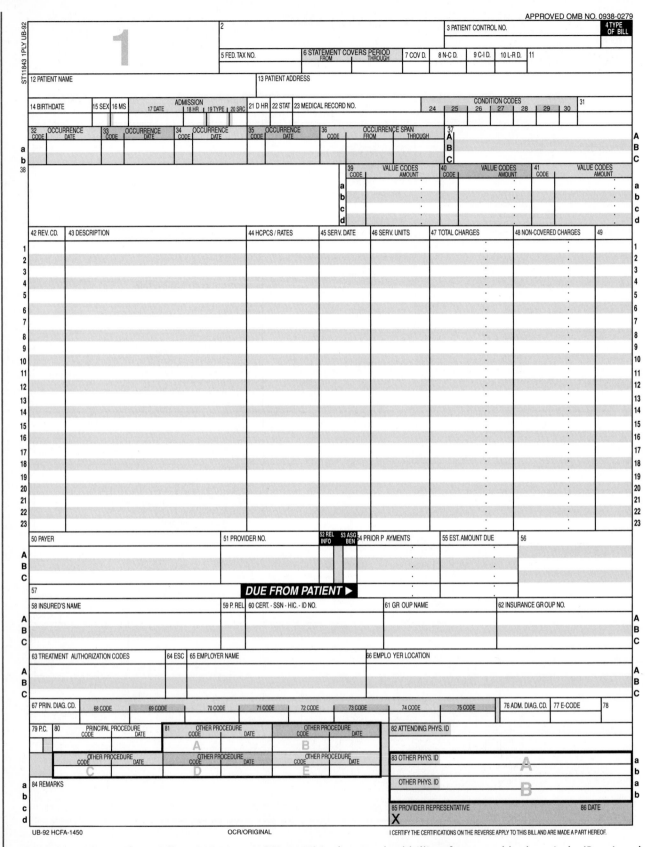

FIGURE 1.2 ■ Uniform Bill 92 (UB-92, or HCFA-1450) is the standard billing form used by hospitals. (Reprinted courtesy of U.S. Department of Health and Human Services, Centers for Medicare and Medicaid Services.)

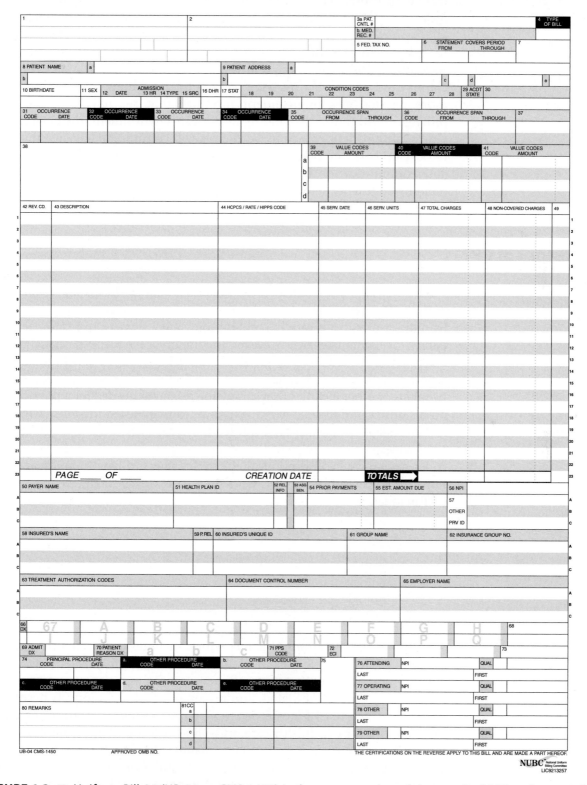

FIGURE 1.3 ■ Uniform Bill 04 (UB-04, or CMS 1450) is the newer version of the standard billing form used by hospitals. (Reprinted courtesy of the U.S. Department of Health and Human Services, Centers for Medicare and Medicaid Services.)

▶ Provide a mechanism for researchers to locate, collect, and study specific types of conditions to find new ways to improve patient care.

Studying particular types of medical cases helps to advance standard treatment protocols to represent the most recent, efficient, and effective means of treating diseases such as pneumonia, congestive heart failure, heart attacks, and strokes. These improved treatment protocols are often referred to as **best care practices.** With no doubt, ever-increasing health-care costs have resulted in increasing public and governmental scrutiny of providers' claims, and payers of care have reacted to these high costs by imposing more restrictive reimbursement formulas that set payment limits for providers. Within this demanding health-care environment, the need to provide quality patient care at reduced costs will continue to advance the need to develop best care practices far into the future; **medical coding** is a valuable communication tool used to locate the data needed to support this ongoing endeavor.

History of CPT

When the AMA first published the *Physicians' Current Procedural Terminology* (CPT) in 1966, it consisted mainly of surgical codes. It was a system developed by and for physicians to report their professional services to insurance companies for reimbursement. However, the use of CPT has substantially grown, and it is now widely used by physicians as well as nonphysician providers to report professional and technical services. Technical services are provided by hospitals or other facilities that supply the resources needed for a physician to do his or her professional work. What was initially titled the *Physicians' Current Procedural Terminology* is now titled *Current Procedural Terminology* because of its widespread use by providers other than physicians. Over the years, CPT codes have increased from four digits to five digits in length, and many sections have been added to CPT. Currently, there are six main sections in the CPT manual:

1. Evaluation and Management
2. Anesthesia
3. Surgery
4. Radiology
5. Pathology and Laboratory
6. Medicine

The AMA's CPT Editorial Panel, which includes physicians from many specialties, is responsible for annual updates to the CPT manual (effective January 1) by adding codes that represent new procedures, deleting codes for procedures that become outdated, and revising code descriptions as necessary. Annual revisions to CPT are needed to keep pace with the new treatments and technologies used in health care, as well as to support the complex reimbursement formulas and mechanisms mandated by health-care payers. The AMA is responsible for developing and publishing the official guidelines for CPT. It publishes *CPT Assistant,* a monthly newsletter, and offers CPT Information Services, a telephone service that provides users with expert advice on code use.[2]

As you begin the study of CPT, it is important to always keep in mind that the system is strictly procedural. The medical necessity for reported procedures is established by linking CPT codes to diagnoses that must be reported through the ICD-9-CM system.

The ICD-9-CM *Tabular List of Diseases* (volume 1) and the *Alphabetic Index to Diseases* (volume 2) represent a clinical modification (CM) of the World Health Organization's (WHO) publication *International Classification of Diseases*, 9th revision (ICD-9), that was adopted for use in the United States. Together, CPT and ICD-9-CM codes are assigned and reported by medical coders to record what is happening in health care. Physicians (billing for professional services) and nonphysician providers (billing for professional or technical services) use both ICD-9-CM (volumes 1 and 2) to code diagnoses and the CPT system to report procedures and services in health-care settings that include hospital-based and free-standing outpatient departments, ambulatory care medical clinics, and surgical centers, and the professional component of long-term care and inpatient procedures and services.

In some cases, a physician's services may be reported using codes that are outside his or her specialty. For example, codes from the Evaluation and Management section of CPT are generally used to bill for a family physician's services such as routine check-ups. That same physician may also excise a patient's mole during an office visit, and the excision procedure would be reported using a code from the Surgery section of CPT.

Coding and Reimbursement

In 1965, federal amendments to the 1935 Social Security Act established Title 19 Medicare, Health Insurance for the Elderly; and Title 18 Medicaid, the Medical Assistance Program for the Indigent. With this legislation, the federal government became a large health-care payer and insurer for a substantial segment of the United States population. After the initial passage of Medicare and Medicaid legislation, the federal government became interested in establishing **prospective payment systems** (PPS) to contain health-care costs. A prospective payment system limits reimbursements to health-care providers by assigning fixed-payment rates that are based on the average cost of treating the patient's condition or providing a specific service. In PPS, the provider's payment amount is established in advance of the services rendered based on the medical codes that are reported. Notwithstanding the initial federal interest in prospective payment systems, but up through the early 1980s, health-care providers continued to be paid for their services based on the prevailing charge for rendering the service. This was referred to as retrospective reimbursement. In **retrospective reimbursement systems,** the provider's payment is determined after the services are rendered based on the provider's **usual and customary charge.** For decades, under the retrospective payment methodology, health-care costs spiraled out of control, driven by what the market would bear, and far exceeded the general rate of inflation. It soon became evident that the ever-increasing and high costs of health care added to the numbers of medically uninsured or underinsured individuals in the United States.

TIP

It is important for new coders to be aware that a procedure being included in CPT does not guarantee payment by a third-party payer. CPT codes are available for plastic surgery that may be excluded for payment under the enrollee's health insurance plan. For example, Medicare will not pay for cosmetic procedures such as hair transplants, face-lifts, or tummy tucks.

Because the skyrocketing costs of health care could no longer be tolerated, in the 1980s, the federal government, as the largest payer of health-care bills, started the first major initiative to develop and implement a PPS for its Medicare population. In 1982, Congress passed the Tax Equity and Fiscal Responsibility Act (TEFRA), which required the development of a prospective payment system to reimburse hospitals for inpatient services provided to Medicare beneficiaries.

Beginning in 1983, and phased in over 3 years, the federal government implemented **diagnosis-related groups** (DRGs) as an **inpatient prospective payment system** (IPPS) to determine the amount of payment to the hospital in advance of the services rendered. The ICD-9-CM coding and classification system (volumes 1 through 3) is used to report both diseases and procedures for inpatient stays to assign the DRG for the hospital to receive payment. A software application called a **grouper** assigns the DRG based on reported diagnosis and procedure codes and sometimes other variables such as the presence of secondary diagnoses that represent complications and comorbidities, the patient's sex, and discharge status (e.g., discharged to home or transferred to a skilled nursing facility). A **complication** is a condition that occurs after admission that affects the patient's care or length of stay, and a **comorbidity** is a preexisting condition that affects the patient's care or length of stay. For example, if after admission the patient develops a urinary tract infection, that would be a complication; if the patient is admitted for pneumonia with preexisting chronic left heart failure, the heart failure would be a comorbidity. For the 2008 federal fiscal year (FY), the DRG system was renamed **Medicare Severity DRG** (MS-DRG). The new MS-DRG program was implemented by the Centers for Medicare and Medicaid Services (CMS) to better account for the differences in patient severity so that hospitals will be paid more for treating complicated cases. Hospital payment is contingent on reporting the medical codes to a regional fiscal intermediary for Medicare. A **fiscal intermediary**, or **carrier**, is an agency that contracts with the CMS to process Medicare claims.

It became clear to the federal government that the cost controls applied through the IPPS and through DRGs were effective at reducing hospital inpatient costs. A trend occurred in which health-care services began to dramatically shift to outpatient settings. In outpatient or ambulatory care settings, the patient's length of stay is typically less than 24 hours. The reasons for this shift from inpatient to outpatient services included the following:

▸ Providers were able to avoid the payment limits imposed under the inpatient DRG system.
▸ Utilization review organizations and programs (both federally contracted and commercial) denied payments for inpatient stays when it was determined that appropriate treatment could have been performed in a less-expensive outpatient setting.

▶ Consumers were driving demand for shorter hospital stays.

▶ Advances in technology in which less-invasive procedures were performed became available that reduced the length of patient stays. For example, more laparoscopic procedures such as appendectomies and cholecystectomies are performed today because they are less invasive, do not involve large incisions, and promote a shortened recovery time.

In response to the growing outpatient volumes, the federal government developed and initiated an **Outpatient Prospective Payment System** (OPPS) to control the costs of patient care received in these ambulatory care settings, and CPT was selected as the standard coding system for outpatient and ambulatory care procedural coding for reimbursement.

Healthcare Common Procedure Coding System (HCPCS)

In 1983, the CMS (formerly called Health Care Finance Administration or HCFA) signed a limited copyright agreement with the AMA allowing CMS to use CPT in a new coding system called the Healthcare Common Procedure Coding System (HCPCS). HCPCS was developed by CMS to meet the needs of the federal Medicare and Medicaid reimbursement programs. HCPCS has two levels, including Level I (published by the AMA as CPT) and Level II (national codes). HCPCS Level II, consisting of alphanumeric codes (starting with A–V), was developed by the CMS for providers to report and bill for Medicare and Medicaid services not found in CPT, such as nonphysician services and medical supplies.

HCPCS Level II code for ambulance service, BLS, emergency transport: A0302 *Injection, ampicillin sodium, up to 500 mg: J0290*	**EXAMPLE**

Originally, HCPCS included Level III (local codes), in which regional Medicare carriers were allowed some latitude by CMS to assign temporary alphanumeric codes (starting with W–Z) to describe procedures unique to the carrier's geographic area that should be payable under Medicare. The Level III codes could not substitute for existing Level I or II codes, but were used to create a billing record for Medicare and evaluated by the CMS to determine whether a regional procedure should be incorporated into Level II for national use. However, beginning in December 2003, CMS phased out the use of HCPCS Level III codes.

In ambulatory settings that primarily include hospital-based and freestanding outpatient surgery departments, physicians' offices, and ambulatory medical clinics and centers, providers use ICD-9-CM and CPT/HCPCS codes to report patients' diseases and the procedures and services performed to receive reimbursement from Medicare and Medicaid, commercial insurance companies and plans, and other third-party payers.

It is through CPT/HCPCS that the federal government has been able to establish a standard coding system to initiate the outpatient prospective payment system (OPPS). In addition, although the federal government initiated the use of PPS to control health-care costs, most other private third-party payers now use medical coding systems to structure prospective payment rates to health-care providers based on the federal PPS models. Current OPPS in use today include the following settings, described below.

AMBULATORY SURGICAL CENTER (ASC)

The Balanced Budget Act (BBA) of 1986 authorized CMS to implement an outpatient prospective payment system for hospital-based outpatient surgical services provided to Medicare patients. Based on the types and number of surgeries performed, ASC-approved procedures were reimbursed at fixed payment rates according to one of eight payment groups. If more than one ASC procedure was performed, the highest paying procedure was reimbursed at 100% of the ASC rate. Each additional (concurrent) covered procedure was reimbursed at 50% of the ASC rate. The applied payment method acknowledged that in instances in which more than one surgery was being performed during a single operative episode, the additional procedures would not require the additional expenses that would be incurred if the patient were returned to the operating room for each separate surgical procedure. Using the ASC formula, the payments for the additional procedures were reduced. The ASC system is currently used to reimburse state-licensed and Medicare-certified free-standing ambulatory surgery centers. However, as of 2000, hospital-based ambulatory surgeries are now paid under the Ambulatory Payment Classification (APC) system.

AMBULATORY PATIENT GROUPS (APG)

After the ASC, the next step in the evolution of OPPS was the APG. APGs were originally developed by 3M® Corporation for CMS and are currently used by some state Medicaid agencies and commercial insurance plans such as Blue Cross/Blue Shield, but the CMS did not adopt APGs for the Medicare system. Although ASCs only apply to surgical cases, APGs establish fixed payment rates to providers for both medical and surgical outpatient services. The basis of the APG formula is that if a patient has a *surgical service,* a global fee or packaged fee for all the services performed is assigned. For example, a lung biopsy procedure would include the payment for a preoperative chest x-ray. If a patient has a *medical service,* the diagnosis is used to assign a global payment fee. For example, a diagnosis of pneumonia would include the payments for commonly occurring or routine ancillary tests such as a chest x-ray and sputum culture.

AMBULATORY PAYMENT CLASSIFICATION (APC)

Implemented by CMS in 2000, the most current OPPS is the APC. APCs apply predetermined payment rates to hospitals for both medical and surgical outpatient services. The ASC payment rates are based on the CPT/HCPCS codes reported. Although ICD-9-CM diagnosis codes do not establish the APC payment rate, a provider's claim can be denied for payment if the reported diagnosis codes do not establish the medical necessity for the procedures coded in CPT/HCPCS. Several APCs may be assigned for one patient visit for each CPT/HCPCS code submitted. Accurate and timely charge entry (at the point of patient service) and procedure and diagnosis coding are crucial for a hospital to receive the full payment for each claim. APCs use a very complicated discounting formula that groups multiple APCs together to calculate a single reimbursement to the hospital. The OPPS using APCs is conceptually comparable to the IPPS program using DRGs. However, unlike the inpatient DRG system in which a single DRG is assigned at patient discharge, multiple APCs may be assigned to a single outpatient visit.

RESOURCE-BASED RELATIVE VALUE SCALE (RBRVS)

Authorized under the Omnibus Reconciliation Act (OBRA) of 1989 and 1990, implemented in 1992, and phased in over 5 years, RBRVS uses a fixed payment system or Medicare fee schedule that reimburses physicians' practice expenses based on the relative value for the physician's work, practice expense (overhead), and malpractice expense. RBRVS is not specifically an outpatient prospective payment system because it reimburses physicians for the work they do in both outpatient and inpatient settings. However, RBRVS does represent a PPS because the Medicare fee schedule establishes predetermined payment rates to physicians for the work they do. Payments to physicians are dependent on reporting CPT/HCPCS procedure or service codes to receive reimbursement under Medicare and Medicaid. Based on the federal model, most third-party payers or commercial insurers also use fee schedules to assign payments to physicians.

Compliance Plans and Fraud and Abuse

Compliance entails making a good faith effort to abide by the laws, regulations, and guidelines that govern a facility and having documented proof of that ongoing effort. Most health-care provider investigations, settlements, sanctions, and judgments with the federal government have involved some issue of improper coding of services. Many fraud and abuse investigations involve **upcoding,** which is the selection of a code to maximize provider reimbursement when the code is not the most accurate descriptor of the service performed.

CMS implemented the **National Correct Coding Initiative** (NCCI) in 1996 to develop correct coding methodologies to improve the appropriate payment of Medicare claims. Portions of the NCCI are incorporated into the **outpatient code editor** (OCE) against which all ambulatory claims are reviewed. Billing issues result from these CCI/OCE edits often result in claim denials.[3] Typically, NCCI edits reveal procedures and services that would not usually be billed on the same day of service. For example, edits can reveal mutually exclusive codes (codes that would not occur together) or the **unbundling** of codes. Unbundling occurs when components of a packaged procedure or service (bundled) are coded separately to receive a higher reimbursement than warranted. For example, code 58150 for total abdominal hysterectomy specifies with or without removal of tubes(s) and ovary(s); therefore, you would not add the code for the removal of the tubes and ovary(s) separately. Unbundling of codes is an unethical and fraudulent practice. Parties who are interested in pursuing fraud and abuse claims against providers include the Federal Office of Inspector General (OIG), the Department of Justice, commercial health insurance policy carriers, State Medicaid Fraud Control Units, and Medicare fiscal intermediaries and carriers.

Based on the physician's documentation in the patient's medical record, coding compliance derives from the correct assignment and precise sequencing of ICD-9-CM diagnoses codes and CPT/HCPCS procedures codes within established rules that ensure the appropriate reimbursement to the provider. This process requires competent individuals working within the coding process. In the following chapters, students will learn that medical coders must understand the rules and conventions of CPT/HCPCS and follow federal coding guidelines for reporting. They will need to apply CPT coding rules published through the AMA's newsletter *CPT Assistant* and follow the rules for assigning and sequencing ICD-9-CM diagnoses for ambulatory care as published in *Coding Clinic,* a quarterly publication of the American

Hospital Association. Prudent employers would provide these invaluable resources. Ultimately, students will learn to interpret a medical record for the process of coding and to assign and sequence codes according to the established and legal rules for reporting. At all times, the medical coding process must be practiced ethically within an organizational culture that supports this conduct.

The Process of Coding Using CPT

The process of medical coding can be thought of as putting the pieces of a puzzle together. The puzzle is the patient's medical record, and the medical coder searches documentation in the medical record for the puzzle pieces or information that reveals the patient's conditions and the procedures that were performed. When the puzzle pieces are collected, the medical coder has the information needed to assemble the puzzle and to correctly assign and properly sequence the medical codes that complete the patient's story.

TIP As you begin the process of coding, be sure to review the Guidelines at the beginning of each section of the CPT manual. The Guidelines provide important supplemental information to aid in correct code selection specific to the section.

CPT codes consist of five digits, such as 45378: colonoscopy with biopsy. HCPCS Level II consists of alphanumeric codes, such as A0429: ambulance service, emergency service with basic life support. Two-digit, two-alphanumeric code modifiers are available that can be appended to HCPCS codes that do not change the basic meaning of the code but help explain a special circumstance that affected the service in some way. An example is 50: bilateral procedure.

To locate the proper code for a procedure, a coder would first look in the alphabetic index of CPT. CPT is a **multiaxial system,** meaning you can look up procedures in different ways within the index. This allows more flexibility in the search to locate the correct code. In the alphabetic index, procedure codes may be located under the following:

- ▶ Name of the procedure (e.g., bypass graft)
- ▶ Name of the service (e.g., cardiology)
- ▶ Eponym (e.g., Mayo procedure)
- ▶ Anatomic site (e.g., heart)
- ▶ Medical abbreviation (e.g., PTCA)
- ▶ Diagnosis (e.g., carpal tunnel syndrome)

Within the alphabetic index, often a range of codes is offered, such as *see* Repair, Hernia, Inguinal, 49491-49521. The coder must then go to the tabular list of CPT, which is in numeric order, to select the most appropriate code according to the descriptions provided. Note that each code has a precise meaning, and CPT codes are often described as being stand-alone codes. This means that each code description includes sufficient detail to stand alone or be unique.

For both the CPT and the ICD-9-CM systems, a universal coding rule states that a *coder must never code directly from the index*. Critical to precise coding, indexes only serve to point to the tabular listings, where more information can always be found about the code.

It is helpful to remember the beginning number(s) for the codes contained within each major section. When assigning codes, this helps in quickly recognizing what part of the CPT manual contains the code. For example, codes beginning with the number 7 are from the Radiology section, and codes beginning with the number 8 are from the Pathology and Laboratory section. Note the following sections and their respective code ranges:

Evaluation and Management (<u>99</u>201–99499)
Anesthesia (<u>0</u>0100–01999)
Surgery (<u>1</u>0021–<u>6</u>9990)
Radiology (<u>7</u>0010–79999)
Pathology and laboratory (<u>8</u>0048–89356)
Medicine (<u>9</u>0281–99607; sometimes the first two digits "99" coming
    from the E/M and Medicine sections overlap)

CPT codes are arranged in numeric order in the tabular list. However, you will note that Evaluation and Management (E/M) codes (beginning with 99) are at the front of the CPT manual, an exception to this rule. Because Evaluation and Management codes are extensively used by physicians to receive reimbursement for patient visits in various health-care settings, such as offices and hospitals, the E/M section is placed first for easy accessibility.

The CPT Coding Manual

Although the CPT manual is published with permission of the AMA, certain other publishers may print the manual in different formats, such as Ingenix®. The format is generally the same (E/M codes will come first in the tabular list). However, some CPT manuals provide the alphabetic index before the tabular listing, and some provide the tabular listing first. Either way, an important first step to become familiar with the CPT manual is to read the table of contents (TOC). The TOC provides an overview of all the sections and categories at a glance. Each section begins with a set of Guidelines. These Guidelines serve as a "how-to" for assigning codes in that section. Additional Guidelines are also often provided within categories to give further specific directions in correct code assignment.

TIP

Before starting to use codes from any of the six sections in CPT, thoroughly review the Guidelines for each section. This will alert you to any special issues and help you in correctly assigning the codes.

In the tabular listing, each of the six sections contains subsections, which are also called categories. A subsection or category is a grouping of related codes and may include subcategories. For example, within the Surgery section, the respiratory subsection is further divided into subcategories. The subcategories are further divided into headings, and the headings lead to the correct procedure.

EXAMPLE			
	Section	*10021–69990*	*Surgery*
	Subsection (category)	*30000–32999*	*Respiratory System*
	Subcategory	*30000–30999*	*Nose*
	Heading	*30100–30160*	*Excision*
	Procedure	*30100*	*Biopsy, intranasal*

With each step, the code range narrows down from the section to the procedure. Fewer and fewer codes are available as the progression moves toward the specific procedure.

> **TIP** Always begin your search for a CPT code by locating the name of the procedure (or its synonym) within the alphabetic index. Occasionally, you may not be successful with this approach. A physician may provide a procedure name that is not easily accessed in the alphabetic index. If you remember the tabular organization, you can work your way backward through the tabular listing to locate the correct code. As always, it is important to confirm that the subheading and category for the procedure are correct.

Unlisted Codes

Many subcategories end with an unlisted code. These codes end in 9. Unlisted codes are used when a more specific CPT code is not available for a procedure and are considered the code choice of last resort. They act as a catchall for procedures not identified in the CPT code listing. Unlisted codes may not be assigned if a Category III code is available for a procedure.

EXAMPLE	
	Unlisted anesthesia procedure(s): 01999
	Unlisted procedure, hands or fingers: 26989
	Unlisted chemistry procedure: 84999

If a coder, after an exhaustive search, cannot find a code to match the procedure described in the medical record, the appropriate unlisted code should be assigned. Third-party payers will usually require additional documentation, such as an operative report or a laboratory report, when an unlisted code is assigned.

> **TIP** Assignment of an unlisted code requires additional documentation of the procedure when the insurance claim is filed.

Evaluation and Management Section (99201–99499)

The E/M section contains numerous categories that represent various settings in which a physician may work or the type of work performed. An important starting point for proper E/M code assignment is answering the following question regarding the health-care setting from the perspective of the provider or physician: *Where am I?* If the physician treats a patient in his or her office, a code from the office or other outpatient services category will be appropriate.

Subcategories within this category require the answer to a second question, again from the perspective of the provider or physician: *What am I dealing with?* The codes given are for New Patients and Established Patients. Different levels of codes are provided within each subcategory to allow the physician to charge for the level of service provided (levels 1–5). Detailed definitions and requirements are given for each level of service. An important factor in assigning these E/M codes is the documentation provided by the physician to establish medical necessity.

E/M codes are also assigned for physician visits to patients seen in hospitals, critical care units, nursing homes, and assisted living facilities, among other settings. Codes for additional services, such as prolonged services, telephone calls, preventive medicine services, and newborn care, are also provided. A new coder is encouraged to read through all the codes within each category to become familiar with the variety of codes available to report different service locations and situations.

New patient, office or other outpatient visit, with expanded problem-focused history, expanded problem-focused examination, and straightforward medical decision making: 99202

EXAMPLE

Anesthesia Section (00100–01999)

The Anesthesia section follows Evaluation and Management. These codes start with 0, and each category is quite broad. The categories are arranged anatomically (by body site). Most anesthesia codes cover numerous procedures. General, regional, epidural, and most other forms of anesthesia are included in the codes.

Anesthesia for procedures on salivary glands, including biopsy: 00100
Anesthesia for all procedures on the integumentary system, muscles and nerves of head, neck and posterior trunk, not otherwise specified: 00300

EXAMPLE

Surgery Section (10021–69990)

The largest section of the CPT manual is the Surgery section. Each body system is assigned a category (e.g., integumentary) with multiple subcategories (e.g., skin). Codes in the Surgery section begin with 1 through 6. Detailed Guidelines and general notes are provided throughout this section.

TIP You must be careful to choose the code that most correctly describes the procedure performed by the physician. Be sure to read the Surgery Guidelines and notes carefully. Also, read the code descriptions above and below the code you believe is correct to double-check that you have selected the right code.

EXAMPLE

Tonsillectomy and adenoidectomy; younger than age 12: 42820
Tonsillectomy, primary or secondary; younger than age 12: 42825
Adenoidectomy, primary; younger than age 12: 42830
Adenoidectomy, secondary; younger than age 12: 42835
If both tonsils and adenoids are removed in the same operative episode: 42820
If only the tonsils or only the adenoids are removed, one of the other codes must be
*   assigned.*

Radiology Section (70010–79999)

The Radiology section follows the Surgery section. Radiology codes begin with 7 and are divided by modality, such as diagnostic radiography, ultrasonography, mammography, magnetic resonance imaging (MRI), and nuclear medicine. Subcategories are further divided anatomically. Radiologic guidance codes are assigned when imaging procedures are used to provide a visual guide for placement of needles for biopsies or localization of a lesion, aspiration of fluid, and injections. Radiation oncology codes (assigned for patients undergoing radiation therapy as part of cancer treatment) are also included in the Radiology section.

EXAMPLE

Radiologic examination, hip, unilateral; one view: 73500

Interventional radiology procedures require codes from both the Surgery and Radiology sections. These procedures involve introduction of a catheter into a blood vessel and manipulation of the catheter into different blood vessels with contrast (dye) injected and imaging to allow detailed visualization of vascular anatomy. Surgical codes are needed to describe the introduction and manipulation of the catheter, and Radiology codes are needed for the imaging phase of the procedure.

Pathology and Laboratory Section (80048–89356)

The Pathology and Laboratory section follows Radiology. These codes begin with 8. The categories in this section are divided by type of laboratory test. Body fluids such as urine, blood, and amniotic fluid are tested by urinalysis, hematology, chemistry, and cytogenetic studies. Surgical specimens removed during operative interventions are tested for diagnostic purposes. A code from the surgical pathology category is used for services provided by a pathologist who examines a specimen.

EXAMPLE

Autopsy, gross and microscopic; with brain: 88025

Medicine Section (90281–99607)

The Medicine section is the last section. (Category II and Category III codes follow the Medicine section.) Medicine codes begin with 9 and cover a wide variety of services. This section is a virtual potpourri of specialty services that do not fit neatly into the other CPT sections such as dialysis, ophthalmology, cardiac catheterization, chemotherapy administration, electroencephalography, acupuncture, chiropractic therapy, and home infusion.

Acupuncture, one or more needles; with electrical stimulation: 97781	**EXAMPLE**

Appendices A-E

The appendices are organized as follows:

- ▶ Appendix A—modifier descriptions for CPT codes.
- ▶ Appendix B—"at-a-glance" summary of the annual CPT code additions, deletions, and revisions that includes a listing of the new codes and codes with changes in their descriptions that have occurred since the previous year. Category II and III codes that have been deleted or added are also listed.
- ▶ Appendix C—listing of clinical examples that help clarify E/M code assignments. Several patient scenarios are provided to assist the coder in selecting the proper E/M code to describe the physician's service.
- ▶ Appendix D—summary of CPT add-on codes.
- ▶ Appendix E—listing of the CPT codes exempt from modifier -51.

Common Coding Conventions and Symbols Used in the CPT Manual

SEMICOLONS (;)

When you see a semicolon in a CPT code description, you should immediately STOP. The information preceding the semicolon serves as a common stem or root for the information that follows. Each indented code after the root or stem will provide specific information to complete the stem.

 TIP Remember, STOP at the semicolon and use that common root or stem information for each indented code listed below.

The semicolon is a convention used in the CPT manual to prevent repeating the information contained in the stem for every code description. The semicolon makes the book appear less busy and reduces reader fatigue. The indented information may change an anatomic site or may describe a different technique used in the procedure. However, it is important to remember that the information that precedes the semicolon (the stem or root) does not change.

25100	*Arthrotomy, wrist joint; with biopsy*	**EXAMPLE**
25101	*with joint exploration, with or without biopsy, with or without removal of loose or foreign body*	
25105	*with synovectomy*	

An arthrotomy with biopsy could be coded either 25100 or 25101. The coder should verify in the report whether joint exploration was also done. If so, the correct code assignment is 25101. The code 25105 would be indicated if arthrotomy of the wrist was performed with synovectomy.

BULLETS (•)

Bullets signify the new codes added to CPT each year. The AMA provides a formal process for physicians to apply for new codes, with extensive justification

required. The bullet will only remain by the new code for the year it is introduced.

TRIANGLES (▲)

Triangles indicate a change in the code description from the previous year.
This alerts coders to read the description carefully for possible changes that
might affect the code selection.

FACING TRIANGLES (▶ ◀)

Facing triangles are used to indicate new or revised text not included in the
code description. These additional instructional notes may clarify correct
code usage. Facing triangles are also used to give notice that a code has been
deleted. As with bullets and triangles, these changes are only highlighted with
facing triangles in the year they take effect.

PLUS SYMBOLS (+)

Plus symbols indicate add-on codes. Add-on codes cannot be used alone. They
are included as additional codes with primary procedures to explain the full
extent of the surgery. Often these add-on codes are repeated as many times as
necessary to document the complete procedure.

EXAMPLE	*Biopsy of skin, subcutaneous tissue and/or mucous membrane (including simple closure), unless otherwise listed; single lesion: 11100*

*Each separate/additional lesion (list separately in addition to code for primary procedure):
+11101*
*In this example, a separate code is assigned to each lesion. Remember, the physician wants
to get paid for all services performed. Coding each lesion individually ensures that the
physician receives fair reimbursement for all the services provided.*

CIRCLED BULLETS (⊙)

A circled bullet by a procedure indicates that conscious sedation or anesthesia
is packaged or included in the payment for the procedure. Conscious sedation
allows the physician to communicate with the patient while the patient is in
an altered state of consciousness. This type of anesthesia does not require
intubation and is commonly used with colonoscopies, upper endoscopies,
biopsies, and bone marrow aspiration.

NULL SYMBOL (⊘)

The null symbol indicates that a code must not have a modifier -51 added to
the code. The -51 modifier indicates multiple procedures were performed during a single operative episode. This modifier is used only to report services of
physicians or surgeons.

PENDING SYMBOL (〃)

The pending symbol indicates that a vaccine is pending US Food and Drug
Administration (FDA) approval.

Uniform Ambulatory Care Data Set

ICD-9-CM diagnostic and procedural coding conforms with the Uniform
Hospital Discharge Data Set (UHDDS) as a guideline for assigning principal

and other diagnoses and significant procedures for inpatient reporting. For outpatients, the Uniform Ambulatory Care Data Set (UACDS) provides a standard, consistent set of data elements. This standard data set enables providers to compare data on different patients based on common definitions. Although the UACDS is not required for reimbursement, its use is recommended for the National Health Information Network (NHIN). The NHIN is an essential element in RHIOs, which share clinical information about patients in an area. The goals of RHIOs and the NHIN include improving the quality of patient care, increasing safety, and reducing errors in medical care.[4]

The UACDS data elements include a national provider identifier (NPI) (formerly UPIN), the location of the health-care **encounter,** the patient's chief complaint or symptoms presented at the time of the encounter, diagnostic and therapeutic procedures, the diagnosis, and planned follow-up care. The UPIN (unique physician identification number) was phased out and replaced with the NPI on May 23, 2008.

For inpatient stays, conditions documented by the physician as "possible," "probable," "questionable," "rule out," and "suspected" are coded as if the condition existed. This rule is not true for outpatient encounters, which are only coded to the **highest level of certainty.** The reason for this difference is that inpatients are admitted to the hospital and have a more prolonged episode of care than outpatients. This includes time for the physician to perform diagnostic and therapeutic modalities, in which, after study, a more definitive diagnosis is established. This additional time allows the physician to incorporate more information into the diagnostic formulation. The inpatient "after study" concept does not apply to short outpatient visits or encounters, in which physicians often do not have all the results of tests or workups before patient discharge and the assignment of diagnoses. The highest level of certainty concept allows outpatient coders to use signs and symptoms or abnormal test results (as interpreted by a physician) as a diagnosis. Signs and symptoms are discouraged for inpatient coding.

Diagnosis: Cough and fever, rule out pneumonia.
For an outpatient encounter, the diagnosis is cough and fever. For an inpatient visit, the diagnosis is pneumonia.

EXAMPLE

Primary diagnosis is a term commonly used to describe the first diagnosis sequenced for outpatient reporting. The primary diagnosis should represent the main reason the patient received outpatient care during a particular stay, visit, or encounter. For example, if the visit is for a therapeutic intervention, such as chemotherapy, a V code is assigned that denotes "Admission for chemotherapy" (code V58.11). In the case of an encounter for surgery, if the preoperative diagnosis differs from the postoperative diagnosis, the postoperative diagnosis should be assigned as the primary diagnosis. After the primary diagnosis, additional diagnosis codes may be added for other conditions that affected the overall care of the patient during the encounter.

The CMS 1500 billing form, used to report physician services, provides spaces for up to four diagnoses and six procedures (see Fig. 1.1, fields 21 and 24D). An additional field (24E Diagnosis Pointer) is provided to link the CPT procedure code to the related diagnosis (diagnosis 1, 2, 3, or 4).

CPT and HCPCS Level II Modifiers

In English, there are words that modify other words. For example, a fence is still a fence even when a modifier is added to specify it is a tall fence or a wooden fence. Such is the case with CPT and HCPCS Level II modifiers. Modifiers do not change the basic description of the code, but help explain to Medicare or other third-party payers special circumstances that increase or decrease the amount that should be reimbursed for the service. Modifiers are also used to describe a body location on which a procedure was performed, such as the right index finger. Modifiers are always two characters and can be numeric, alphabetic, or alphanumeric.

Modifiers are indicated on billing forms by adding the appropriate modifier to either a CPT code or to a HCPCS Level II code without a space or a hyphen. The use of hyphens in this text is for emphasis only.

EXAMPLE

1. *CPT code 69020 = drainage, external auditory canal, abscess*
   CPT modifier 50 = bilateral (used when the term bilateral is not listed in the procedure code description)
   Therefore, 69020-50 = drainage, external auditory canal, abscess, bilateral or both ears.
2. *HCPCS Level II modifier LT = left side*
   Therefore, 69020-LT = drainage, external auditory canal, abscess, left ear only.
3. *HCPCS Level II code A0832 = basic life support mileage*
   HCPCS Level II modifier QM = ambulance service provided under arrangement by a provider of service
   Therefore, A0832-QM 5 basic life support mileage for an ambulance service provided under arrangement by a provider of service (versus QN, which describes ambulance services furnished directly by a provider of service).

TIP

General rule to decide whether or not to use a modifier:

1. START with a CPT/HCPCS CODE.
2. ASK:
   a. Are there unusual circumstances?
   b. Is there more specificity in documentation than in the code description?
   c. Is increased or decreased time involved?
   d. Are there increased or decreased resources than intended by the code?
3. YES to any of these? Look for the applicable modifier.
4. NO? Modifier is unnecessary.

Each year, CPT lists all available modifiers in Appendix A of the manual (see Appendix A for full definitions of each code). Modifiers that are unique to a section of CPT are listed in the Guidelines for that section. The following chart presents an overview of modifiers and examples of how they are used.

Quick Reference: Overview of CPT Modifiers

Modifier Number and Description	Example and Correct Code Plus Modifier
21—Prolonged Evaluation and Management Services Used only on the highest level of E/M code within certain subsections. Usually added when the length of time spent on an E/M service exceeds the typical amount of time for that level of service by at least 15 minutes. NOT a guarantee of higher reimbursement: Medicare does not pay more when this modifier is used. A special report detailing the time and reason for the prolonged services may be required by the payer. NOT used with critical care or neonatal intensive care, as these codes are already based on units of time. Also not used with the prolonged service add-on codes (99358 and 99359), which are reserved for cases in which a physician spends extended time, other than direct face-to-face time, on the care of a patient (such as in research or consultation with other professionals).	Physician conducts a comprehensive history and physical on an established patient who presents in the physician's office 30 days status post several surgeries for internal and external injuries suffered in a car accident. Patient is experiencing abdominal cramping, headaches, nausea, shortness of breath, and general malaise. Medical decision making is moderate. Physician spends 60 minutes performing diagnostic procedures and reviewing the hospital records from the surgeries to help narrow the possible cause of patient's signs and symptoms and to determine a treatment plan. Typical time for this level of service is 40 minutes. 99215-21
22—Unusual Procedural Services Indicates a service required significantly more resources than is typical. A report that clearly describes the procedure is required by Medicare or third-party payer for additional reimbursement to be considered. If the special circumstances are not fully documented in the medical record, most likely the physician will not receive additional payment.	Surgeon removes a 2-pound cyst from the pancreas of a morbidly obese patient. The surgery was complicated because of a poor visual field attributed to the patient's obesity. Excision of lesion of pancreas (Cyst, adenoma) with unusual circumstances. 48120-22
23—Unusual Anesthesia Used only for codes in the Anesthesia section; indicates that a special circumstance required a general anesthesia to be administered (under normal circumstances, would not have been given). Used only by physician administering the anesthesia. Medicare and other third-party payers require a report from the medical record fully describing the reason for the administration of anesthesia before reimbursement will be considered.	Patient with bipolar disorder sustains a closed fracture of the ankle during a panic attack. Patient becomes agitated when the physician prepares to set the fracture and does not respond to efforts to calm him. Anesthesia is administered so the fracture can be reduced without the patient causing himself further injury. Anesthesia for all closed procedures on lower leg, ankle and foot. 01462-23
24—Unrelated Evaluation and Management Service by the Same Physician During a Postoperative Period Only used in conjunction with E/M codes. If a physician performs a surgical procedure that requires postoperative follow-up, the E/M code for the follow-up service is not reimbursed separately from the surgical code because the follow-up is covered under a global fee for the surgery. If the same physician, following a patient postoperatively, performs an E/M service unrelated to the surgery, the -24 modifier indicates the E/M service is eligible for separate reimbursement. A special report from the medical record clearly documenting the service as unrelated to the surgery must be sent to the payer for reimbursement to be considered.	Patient recovering from a C-section with complication presents to her OB/GYN's office complaining of a vaginal yeast infection. 99212-24
25—Significant Separately Identifiable E/M Service by the Same Physician on the Same Day of the Procedure or Other Service* Only used in conjunction with E/M codes. Allows the physician to submit charges for an E/M service that was distinctly separate from an office procedure that was performed. Medical necessity must be documented in the record.	Physician repairs a laceration on a patient who also is experiencing severe asthma symptoms. Simple repair of superficial wounds of scalp; 2.5 cm or less with separately identifiable E/M service. 12001 99212-25

(continued)

Quick Reference: Overview of CPT Modifiers *(Continued)*

Modifier Number and Description	Example and Correct Code Plus Modifier
26—*Professional Component* Used with some radiological procedures and other diagnostic tests (e. g., pulmonary function) to indicate that only the professional component is applicable (e. g., reading and interpreting an x-ray only). Physicians with their own radiography equipment and radiology technician on staff submit the appropriate code without a modifier.	Physician reads and interprets an x-ray of the ankle for one of his patients. Radiologic examination, ankle, 2 views physician interpretation and report only 73600-26
32—*Mandated Service* Used only when an official entity such as a governmental agency, worker's compensation company, or law enforcement agency requires that a service be performed. Often pays the service at 100% without applying deductibles or coinsurance under the patient's coverage. NOT appropriate to represent a request for a second opinion.	After determining the patient's willingness to cooperate, police ordered a local psychotherapist to perform hypnotherapy on a witness to a hit-and-run car accident to see whether the witness could recall more details, such as license plate number, under hypnosis. Hypnotherapy 90880-32
47—*Anesthesia by Surgeon* Appended to a surgery code in the rare situation in which the surgeon administers general or regional (never local) anesthesia to the patient in addition to performing the surgery. Along with the surgical report, the surgeon must determine and document the amount of time spent administering the anesthesia and submit the report for reimbursement consideration.	After the initial preparation, patient complained of extreme pain, and a decision was made that a general anesthesia would be used. Surgeon administered general anesthesia and performed the colonoscopy on patient. Colonoscopy, flexible, proximal to splenic flexure; diagnostic, with or without collection of specimen(s) by brushing or washing, with or without colon decompression; general anesthesia administered intraoperatively by surgeon 45378-47
50—*Bilateral Procedures** Indicates that a procedure code does not include the term "bilateral" or imply both as in "ovary or ovaries" in the description but was performed on both sides of the body, a paired organ or a single organ (right nostril and left nostril). Depending on payer preference, can be used as either a single procedure code appended with the -50 modifier or by listing procedure twice with -50 appended to the second code.	Patient presents with an abscess in both the right and left ear canals, and physician performs a drainage procedure to eliminate each abscess. Drainage, external auditory canal, abscess as a bilateral (both ears) procedure 69020-50
51—*Multiple Procedures* Used when more than one procedure is performed during a single operative episode. The most definitive or significant procedure is listed first without a modifier, and each additional procedure is appended with the modifier. Should not be appended to add-on codes denoted by plus symbols (+). If a procedure code is exempt from modifier −51, it is denoted by the null symbol (⊘) in the tabular listing.	Patient has stab wounds to the neck and chest. Physician performs an exploration of a deep penetrating wound of the neck and a lesser wound of the chest 20100 20101-51
52—*Reduced Services** Used when the full service described by the CPT code was not performed, and a code that more accurately describes the reduced procedure or service is not available. Requires that a report be sent to the payer describing the reason for the reduced service.	Physician performs a screening test, pure tone, air only on a patient's right ear (only) status post right ear infection. 92551-52
53—*Discontinued Procedure* Used only for the physician's claim and then only when a surgical or diagnostic procedure is started but discontinued. Procedures are usually discontinued by the physician during or after the anesthesia administration owing to a contraindication such as the patient's health status changes. NOT used when patient elects to cancel the procedure before it is started.	Surgeon begins the procedure for a ureteroureterostomy. After the incision has been made, patient experiences anaphylactic shock from an unknown allergy to the anesthetic. The procedure is immediately discontinued. 50760-53

(continued)

Quick Reference: Overview of CPT Modifiers *(Continued)*

Modifier Number and Description	Example and Correct Code Plus Modifier
54—Surgical Care Only Used only when the surgeon does not manage the patient's postoperative care. Indicates a reduced reimbursement amount is warranted for the surgical procedure because the preoperative or postoperative management will be carried out by another physician.	Specialist performs a ureteroureterostomy at a hospital 200 miles away from the patient's residence. Patient is discharged with instructions to have his own physician manage the postoperative care. 50760-54
55—Postoperative Management Only Reimbursement for postoperative care is generally included in the global reimbursement amount for the surgeon. If the surgeon does not provide postoperative management, the physician who assumes the patient's postoperative care would use this modifier.	In the example for modifier -54, the patient's primary care physician would code the follow-up care under the most appropriate level of E/M service with this modifier appended. 99212-55
56—Preoperative Management Only Reimbursement for preoperative care is generally included in the reimbursement amount for the surgeon. If the surgeon does not provide preoperative management, the physician who provides the patient's preoperative care would use this modifier.	One surgeon performed the preoperative tests and management and another surgeon from a different practice performed the surgery. The first surgeon would bill an appropriate E/M level with the modifier appended. 99202-56
57—Decision for Surgery Appended to the appropriate level of E/M code or general ophthalmology service code to indicate that during the encounter, a decision to perform surgery was made.	In the example for modifier -56, the surgeon conducted an office consultation based on a referral from the patient's primary care physician and made the decision that resulted in surgery. 99241-57
58—Staged or Related Procedure or Service by the Same Physician During the Postoperative Period* Used after an initial procedure when it is determined or planned that a second (staged) procedure is needed, and the second surgery occurs within the postoperative period for the first surgery. NOT used for an unscheduled return to the operating room.	Patient with a wound to the neck has an initial surgery to repair the wound and returns within the postoperative period for a flap graft of the neck (the graft would have this modifier appended). Delay of flap or sectioning of flap (division and inset); at forehead, cheeks, chin, neck, axillae, genitalia, hands or feet 15620-58
59—Distinct Procedural Service* Under certain circumstances, the physician may need to indicate that a procedure or service was distinct or independent from other services performed on the same day.	Patient has a diagnostic arthroscopy of both the left elbow and left shoulder during the same session with an orthopedic surgeon 29805-59, LT and 29830-59, LT
62—Two Surgeons When two surgeons work together as primary surgeons with each performing distinct parts of a procedure, the same procedure is coded for each surgeon appended with modifier 62. NOT used if the co-surgeon for the main procedure acts as an *assistant* in the performance of any additional procedures during the same surgical session. In that case, the additional procedure codes should have modifier -80 or -82 appended.	A neurosurgeon and orthopedic surgeon work together to perform separate parts of a surgical laminectomy with section of spinal accessory nerve. 63191-62

(continued)

Quick Reference: Overview of CPT Modifiers *(Continued)*

Modifier Number and Description	Example and Correct Code Plus Modifier
63—Procedures Performed on Infants Less than 4 kg Used for any surgical procedure for an infant or neonate whose body weight is less than 4 kg, except for procedures coded from the integumentary system in CPT.	Surgeon performs an inguinal hernia repair as soon as a neonate is stable. The neonate weighs less than 3.5 kg. Repair, initial inguinal hernia, preterm infant, performed from birth up to 50 weeks postconception age, with or without hydrocelectomy 49491-63
66—Surgical Team Complex procedures may require several physicians working as part of a team. Services for each physician participating on the surgical team should be coded with the correct procedure code plus modifier -66.	Three specialists perform emergency repair of a thoracoabdominal aortic aneurysm with graft and with cardiopulmonary bypass surgery. The same surgical CPT code is used for all three specialists, with the surgical team modifier 33877-66
76—Repeat Procedure by Same Physician* Used to distinguish that the same procedure is performed twice, by the same physician, on the same patient, on the same day. Without the -76 modifier, third-party payers will assume duplicate submission of a single procedure. Requires that a special report detailing the circumstances be submitted to the payer.	Patient had a closed reduction of a simple tibia fracture with casting performed. Immediately after casting, patient fell on the same bone, causing a second closed fracture to occur. A second reduction procedure was performed by the same physician. Original procedure 27530-LT Second procedure 27530-76, LT
77—Repeat Procedure by Another Physician* Serves the same function as modifier -76 except that it identifies that the same procedure was performed a second time by a different physician. Usually occurs because the first physician is not available at the time the repeat procedure is necessary.	Per the example for modifier -76, but with a different physician reducing the second fracture. Original procedure 27530-LT Second procedure 27530-77, LT
78—Return to the Operating Room for a Related Procedure During the Postoperative Period* Used when a patient is returned to the operating room for unplanned surgery to resolve a complication related to the first surgery. A report detailing the circumstances is generally required.	Patient is returned to the operating room during the postoperative period for an abdominal paracentesis as a result of a complication from the surgery. 49080-78
79—Unrelated Procedure or Service by the Same Physician During the Postoperative Period* Used to indicate that an unforeseen and completely unrelated surgical procedure was performed during the postoperative period of the original surgery. A separate diagnosis and special report must detail the circumstances that resulted in the unrelated procedure.	Surgeon removed patient's appendix. During the postoperative period, patient experienced severe abdominal pain and was diagnosed with gallstones. The same surgeon performed a second surgery to remove the gallbladder laparoscopically. Cholecystectomy 47562-79
80—Assistant Surgeon Used when a surgeon is asked to assist the primary surgeon. A special report is required, and some payers do not reimburse for an assistant at surgery. Services of the primary surgeon are coded without a modifier; those for the assistant append modifier –80.	Surgeon A asks Surgeon B to assist in a subtotal pancreatectomy with transplantation of pancreatic islet cells. Surgeon A = 48160 Surgeon B = 48160-80
81—Minimum Assistant Surgeon Used when a second surgeon provides minimal assistance to the primary surgeon during an operative procedure. Requires a special report to explain why an assistant was needed. NOT used when someone other than a physician is assisting the primary surgeon.	Surgeon C is asked to assist co-surgeons A and B in a pancreatectomy, distal, near-total with preservation of duodenum at a hospital that does not have a residency program. Co-surgeons A and B = 48146-62 Surgeon C = 48146-81

(continued)

Quick Reference: Overview of CPT Modifiers *(Continued)*

Modifier Number and Description	Example and Correct Code Plus Modifier
82—Assistant Surgeon When Qualified Resident Surgeon Not Available Used when a facility has an affiliation with a medical school for residency programs. If a surgeon finds it medically necessary to have an assistant, and a resident is not available, another qualified surgeon is eligible to assist. A special report verifying the reason a resident was not available must be submitted to the payer. (Medicare does not usually reimburse for this situation if the hospital has a residency program, but other payers may.)	Per the example for modifier -81, except surgery occurs at a hospital that has a residency program. Co-surgeons A and B = 48146-62 Surgeon C = 48146-82
90—Reference (Outside) Laboratory Used for codes in the Pathology and Laboratory section of CPT when the services of an outside laboratory were used. Note: Medicare does not allow the physician to bill for outside laboratory services and then reimburse the laboratory from his or her payment—the outside laboratory must bill Medicare directly. Other payers may allow physicians to bill for the service.	Physician collects a urine sample from patient and prepares it for pick-up and analysis by an outside laboratory. Physician bills a third-party payer (non-Medicare) for the collection and handling and the work of the outside laboratory and then pays the laboratory directly. Urinalysis 81000-90
91—Repeat Clinical Diagnostic Laboratory Test* Used only when a laboratory test is performed twice on the same day to measure a specific laboratory result that may change at different times during the day. Cannot be used when the laboratory test is repeated for any other reason, such as contaminated sample or malfunctioning laboratory equipment, or for a series of tests such as a repeated chemistry panel.	Patient who has undergone a blood transfusion has a complete blood cell count, automated at noon and 6:00 PM. Noon reading = 85049 6:00 PM reading = 85049-91
99—Multiple Modifiers Certain payers do not allow the submission of more than one modifier. If multiple modifiers are needed to adequately describe the circumstances, modifier -99 is appended to the procedure. A special report is sent to the payer describing the multiple conditions that require the use of multiple modifiers.	The third-party payer does not accept more than one modifier per CPT code. Surgery was an unusual circumstance complicating eye surgery, performed by co-surgeons on both eyes at the same operative session. Orbitotomy with bone flap and removal of foreign body 67420-99
P1—P6-Anesthesia Physical Status Modifiers Used to distinguish various levels of complexity of the anesthesia service provided. The appropriate level must be appended to each code used from the Anesthesia section. P1 designates a normal healthy patient, and P6 is a patient who has been declared brain-dead whose organs are being removed for donor purposes. (See Appendix A and the Guidelines to the Anesthesia section for detail on all the levels.)	Patient with a mild systemic disease has anesthesia administered in preparation for a percutaneous liver biopsy. 00702-P2 Same patient's procedure is discontinued because of heart palpitations after the anesthesia has been administered but before the actual surgery has begun. 00702-P2, 53

*Indicates modifiers that are approved for use by hospital-based ambulatory surgery centers (ASCs).

Quick Reference: Modifiers Used Exclusively by Hospital-Based ASCs

Modifier Number and Description	Example and Correct Code Plus Modifier
27—Multiple Outpatient Hospital E/M Encounters on the Same Date Used by the hospital to indicate that multiple E/M services were performed by different physicians in different service departments on the same day. Must be added to each E/M code.	Patient is seen in the emergency department of the local hospital with abdominal pain. Later in the day, patient returns for simple laceration repair from cutting herself with a paring knife while fixing dinner. 99282-27 99281-27
73—Discontinued Outpatient Procedure Prior to the Administration of Anesthesia Used when surgery is contraindicated by the patient's health status before the administration of anesthesia. (Cannot be used when the patient elects to cancel the procedure.)	Patient is in the hospital-based ASC and has been prepped for a laparoscopic cholecystectomy. Patient has a severe panic attack, so the anesthesia was not administered and the planned procedure is not performed. 47562-73
74—Discontinued Outpatient Procedure After Administration of Anesthesia Added to the CPT code for the intended surgery when owing to special circumstances, a decision is made to cancel the procedure after anesthesia has been administered.	Patient is in the hospital-based ASC and has been prepped for a laparoscopic cholecystectomy and anesthesia has been administered. The surgeon became suddenly ill and cannot proceed. 47562-74

HCPCS Level II Modifiers

The following chart lists those modifiers that are used with either CPT codes or HCPCS Level II national codes required by Medicare. These modifiers are increasingly being used by other third-party payers. Specific examples of modifier usage and opportunities to practice their application will be presented in subsequent chapters.

Quick Reference: Modifiers That Identify Body Location for a Procedure

Modifier	Description
E1	Upper left, eyelid
E2	Lower left, eyelid
E3	Upper right, eyelid
E4	Lower right, eyelid
F1	Left hand, second digit
F2	Left hand, third digit
F3	Left hand, fourth digit
F4	Left hand, fifth digit
F5	Right hand, thumb
F6	Right hand, second digit
F7	Right hand, third digit
F8	Right hand, fourth digit
F9	Right hand, fifth digit

(continued)

Quick Reference: Modifiers That Identify Body Location for a Procedure (Continued)

Modifier	Description
FA	Left hand, thumb
T1	Left foot, second digit
T2	Left foot, third digit
T3	Left foot, fourth digit
T4	Left foot, fifth digit
T5	Right foot, great toe
T6	Right foot, second digit
T7	Right foot, third digit
T8	Right foot, fourth digit
T9	Right foot, fifth digit
TA	Left foot, great toe
LT	Left side (procedures performed on the left side of the body)
RT	Right side (procedures performed on the right side of the body)
LC	Left circumflex coronary artery
LD	Left anterior descending coronary artery
RC	Right coronary artery

Quick Reference: Modifiers That Designate Special Reimbursement Circumstances for Mammograms and Ambulance Services

Modifier	Description
GG	Performance and payment of a screening mammogram and diagnostic mammogram on the same patient, same day
GH	Diagnostic mammogram converted from screening mammogram on same day
QM	Ambulance service provided under arrangement by a provider of services
QN	Ambulance service furnished directly by a provider of services

CPT-5

Beginning in 2000, the AMA initiated a CPT-5 project to ensure that the coding system continues to meet the individual needs of many physician and nonphysician users. The goals of this project included to continue to support provider reimbursement systems, to continue to provide the data needed to promote medical research, and to evaluate and develop best clinical care practices. The CPT-5 project also included improvements to comply with the electronic data interchange (EDI) and electronic health record (EHR) standards required under the administrative simplification section (Title II) of the 1996 Health Insurance Portability and Accountability Act (HIPAA). The intent of Title II of HIPAA is to reduce the administrative costs of health care by promoting the standardized electronic transfer of health-care transaction data. Under CPT-5, enhancements to the previous CPT-4 structure included new code categories as follows:

- ▶ Category I: The traditional five-digit codes. These codes make up the majority of the CPT manual and are included in the six (6) major sections: Evaluation and Management, Anesthesia, Surgery, Radiology Services, Pathology and Laboratory, and Medicine.
- ▶ Category II: Performance measures and tracking codes. Category II codes comprise alphanumeric characters such as 4050F, hypertension plan of care documented as appropriate. The use of these codes by health-care providers is optional. These codes can be used to track compliance with quality standards recognized by the AMA, National Committee for Quality Assurance (NCQA), Joint Commission, and other professional associations or societies. Category II codes are located after the Medicine section in the CPT manual.
- ▶ Category III: Temporary codes for new procedures and technologies that may or may not receive permanent placement in the CPT book as Category I codes. If a Category III code is not adopted as a permanent code within 5 years, the AMA will discontinue it. Category III codes comprise alphanumeric characters, such as 0051T, implantation of a total replacement heart system (artificial heart) with recipient cardiectomy. Category III codes are located after the Medicine section in the CPT manual.

SUMMARY

The CPT medical coding system is a communication tool that provides valuable information that translates data from a patient's medical record into numbers that tell the important story of a patient's health-care encounter. Medical codes expedite payments to providers from third-party payers, allow for the timely sharing of medical information among providers to promote the continuity of patient care, and provide a mechanism for researchers to study specific conditions and treatments to find new ways to improve disease management and patient care.

In response to growing outpatient volumes, the federal government developed and initiated an outpatient prospective payment system (OPPS) to control the costs of patient care received in ambulatory care settings. Subsequently, CPT was selected as the standard coding system for outpatient and ambulatory care procedural coding for reporting provider services to receive reimbursement under the federally funded health-care programs Medicare and Medicaid. Although the federal government initiated the use of PPS to control health-care costs, most other private third-party payers now use the CPT/HCPCS and ICD-9-CM medical coding systems to structure prospective payment rates to health-care providers based on the federal PPS models.

TESTING YOUR COMPREHENSION

1. Who publishes the CPT?

2. Which coding system provides information for medical necessity?

3. For whom was CPT originally developed?

4. Which coding system is used for coding inpatient diagnoses and procedures?

5. Name the reimbursement system that determines predetermined, fixed-rate payments to providers.

6. CPT codes are included in which level of HCPCS?

7. Which level of HCPCS codes has been phased out?

8. How many payment groups are used under the ASC system?

9. Under the APC system, which coding system is payment based on?

10. Which payment system reimburses physicians based on their work, practice experience (overhead), and malpractice insurance expense?

11. Name the term that describes the unethical and illegal practice of selecting a code to maximize provider reimbursement, even though the code is not the most appropriate descriptor of the services performed.

12. What is the range of codes for Radiology?

13. Why are E/M codes at the front of the CPT book?

14. What is the important first step for a student to take to become familiar with the CPT manual?

15. Which section of the CPT manual contains the subsection Office or Other Outpatient Services?

16. What number do anesthesia codes begin with?

17. Which section contains modalities such as computer tomography and nuclear medicine?

_____

18. Which symbol is used to indicate that conscious sedation is included in a code?

_____

19. How many add-on codes can be assigned to a CPT code?

_____

20. Which form is required for billing physician's services?

_____

21. What is the data set recommended for outpatient encounters?

_____

22. Which two sections of the CPT manual must be used to correctly code an interventional radiology procedure?

_____

23. What are the notes provided in the CPT that serve as a how-to for assigning codes?

_____

24. Where in the CPT manual is the complete list of all modifiers that can be used with CPT codes?

_____

25. List two places in the CPT manual in which a list of patient status modifiers for anesthesia CPT codes can be found.

_____

26. For any procedure that can be performed on a part of the body that is a pair (eyes, ears, knees, and so forth), which modifier must be used if the procedure was carried out on both sides?

_____

27. Some payers prefer that bilateral procedures be appended with a modifier that is specific to the side, such as right eye or left eye. What modifiers are used for these sides?

_____

28. Of the following (alpha, alphanumeric, or numeric), what format can modifiers be?

_____

29. If a modifier is appropriate for use by a physician seeking reimbursement for professional services, would the same modifier always be used by the hospital coder on that CPT code when coding for facility reimbursement?

_____

30. If two surgeons work equally on a case, performing different parts of a procedure with equal level of difficulty, what modifier should be appended to the surgical code submitted for each surgeon's work?

_____

CHAPTER 2

Medical Records: The Basis for All Coding

Chapter Outline

Introduction to Medical Records

Format and Content of Hospital Outpatient and Professional Medical Records

Technical Component: CPT Coding for Hospital Outpatient Facility Services

Professional Component: CPT Coding for Physician Services

Ten Steps for Coding the Technical Component From Hospital-Based Outpatient Medical Records

Five Steps for Coding the Professional Component from Physician-Based Medical Reports and Records

Summary

Testing Your Comprehension

Coding Practice I: Chapter Review Exercises

Coding Practice II: Medical Record Case Study—Coding for the Technical and Professional Components

Chapter Objectives

▶ Identify the most common medical reports important to the CPT coding process.

▶ Identify administrative and clinical data contained in medical records that are important to the coding process.

▶ Describe the basic steps taken to review a hospital outpatient medical record or professional reports within a medical record for CPT coding.

▶ Demonstrate coding for the technical component with a real-world hospital outpatient surgery medical record using the 10-step method.

▶ Demonstrate coding for the various professional components with a real-world hospital outpatient surgery medical record using the 5-step method.

▶ Demonstrate coding for the professional component for various providers in locations other than a hospital outpatient surgery department.

▶ Demonstrate the use of a Coder/Abstract Summary Form and a Physician/Coder Query/Clarification Form.

*The coding process begins with a thorough review of the **medical record (MR)**. It is most important that the coder perform a strategic review of the MR to find the information needed to accurately code each record. Whether it describes inpatient or outpatient services, the MR tells a story of each patient's care and provides the best evidence of what physicians, hospitals, and the health-care team are doing.*

Introduction to Medical Records

There is a common understanding in health care, "If it isn't documented, it didn't happen." This rule is important in all aspects of health-care management but is of special significance to coders. The MR is not only a detailed chronicle of every patient's encounter with any health-care provider, but it is also the source document on which precise coding is dependent.

This chapter explains and illustrates a real-world example of a hospital outpatient surgery MR and its importance to coders. It then presents a traditional step-by-step approach to strategically reviewing and interpreting the MR for accurate coding of the **technical component** (hospital-based) of care. Additionally, the chapter presents how to review and interpret the various reports within the medical record for accurate coding of the **professional component** (physician-based) of care. Finally, a cross section of individual real-world medical reports is included that represents coding the professional component from settings other than a hospital outpatient surgery center. This basic step-by-step approach serves as a framework on which the coder can build as he or she becomes more adept at coding.

Regardless of the source of a particular type of report, the report may be formatted or look different, but it will contain similar data or information that is needed for coding. For example, an operative report from Hospital A may look different from an operative report from Hospital B, but the coder will still find the information needed to code the diagnosis that justifies the medical necessity of the procedure or service. This information includes the name of the procedure, and a detailed enough description to select the most appropriate CPT code or codes to accurately reflect the work that was done. Likewise, an entire MR may or may not look similar among facilities; however, the content will remain constant because much of the content of each type of MR is defined by laws and accrediting standards. However, from provider to provider (facility or professional) there is no requirement for reports to be formatted in a consistent manner. Over time, information requirements have been standardized through accrediting agencies such as the Joint Commission (formerly JCAHO), Medicare's Conditions of Participation (COP), and state licensure laws. Health-care providers also want to collect and share data to improve their patient services by determining how some institutions can do certain things better than others (i.e., benchmarking to improve performance). This book uses real-world examples of medical reports to present different formats from various health-care providers as part of each chapter's coding exercises.

Format and Content of Hospital Outpatient and Professional Medical Records

The formatting of an MR, whether paper or electronic, can change from one facility, including physicians' offices, to another, but the contents or data remain consistent. Similar information is usually found, although it can be found in different places within MRs from different providers. To ensure correct coding, the coder should search for data first. Knowledge of MR formatting, although helpful, is of secondary concern.

The various medical record formats include the following:

▸ *Problem-oriented MR*—contains four main parts: database, problem list, initial plans, and progress notes. This format allows a physician to focus on the whole patient in the context of addressing all problems. Writing progress notes in the problem-oriented MR is referred to as *SOAPing*, which follows all problems through a structured approach of <u>S</u>ubjective (data), <u>O</u>bjective (data), <u>A</u>ssessment (of diagnoses), and <u>P</u>lan (for care).

▸ *Source-oriented MR*—organizes forms by departments or units (for example, laboratory, x-ray, nurses' notes, and physician's progress notes are separated).

▸ *Integrated MR*—integrates various forms and caregiver notes, arranging them in strict chronologic order to allow for a quick assessment of the patient at any particular moment in time.

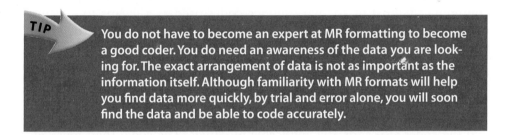

TIP You do not have to become an expert at MR formatting to become a good coder. You do need an awareness of the data you are looking for. The exact arrangement of data is not as important as the information itself. Although familiarity with MR formats will help you find data more quickly, by trial and error alone, you will soon find the data and be able to code accurately.

Complete MRs contain administrative and clinical data critical to the process of coding. Administrative data include routine patient identification: the patient's name, age, sex, date of birth, address, religious preference, insurance data, and consent for treatment. Clinical data include diagnoses, procedures, and results of tests such as laboratory work, x-ray studies, and operations.

Although most registration data (administrative) contribute to accurate coding, the key information for coding is clinical (for example, diagnosis of hepatitis or alcohol abuse and procedures such as cardiac pacemaker insertions or bowel resections).

Technical Component: CPT Coding for Hospital Outpatient Facility Services

Every provider of health-care services wants to be reimbursed fairly for the services provided to patients. (Reimbursement methods based on CPT codes are presented in more detail in Chapter 10.) Hospitals are reimbursed by Medicare, Medicaid, and other third-party payers using a prospective rather than retrospective payment system or methodology (see Chapter 1). For inpatient services, an acute-care hospital is reimbursed for the utilization of its resources (the technical component) using the inpatient prospective payment system based on Medicare severity diagnosis-related groups (MS-DRGs). This system uses only ICD-9-CM diagnoses (volumes 1 and 2) and procedures (volume 3), not CPT codes.

For the technical component of a hospital outpatient episode of care, the facility uses the outpatient prospective payment system (OPPS) based on ambulatory patient classifications (APCs). To establish a single payment to the hospital, APCs combine or group certain facility services together based on the CPT codes that reflect any particular outpatient episode of care. Hospitals must capture all outpatient services using CPT codes, which, in turn, are supported by justification for the services rendered using volumes 1 and 2 of ICD-9-CM codes. For example, if a patient is at the hospital for ambulatory surgery or an emergency department visit, all laboratory, pathology, radiology, medicine, evaluation and management (E/M), anesthesiology, and surgery services supplied by the hospital to a patient must be coded and/or validated by the hospital-based coder. The coder must use at least one ICD-9-CM diagnosis code to justify why all the services (procedures) provided were medically necessary.

At the hospital, certain CPT codes for ancillary services such as radiology, pathology, laboratory, and conscious sedation procedures are keyed into the Charge Description Master (CDM), also called a Chargemaster, by personnel in the department providing the service. A Chargemaster is a computerized comprehensive list of ancillary service codes used as a means to expedite claims to third-party payers. A Chargemaster automatically links the hospital's charge for a procedure to the CPT/HCPCS code for that same procedure. A more detailed description of how the Chargemaster works, along with examples, is provided in Chapter 3.

When the patient leaves the facility, the hospital coder must verify that the CPT codes generated from the Chargemaster are all captured accurately, and the coder also adds any applicable modifiers. The coder then must add ICD-9-CM codes for each diagnosis that was relevant to the total episode of care as well as the codes and modifiers for the surgical procedures, general anesthesia, and any services from the medicine chapter of CPT that were performed. Unlike the codes for ancillary services automated by the Chargemaster, codes from other sections of the CPT manual require interpretive analysis by the coder. This analysis often involves reviewing dictated reports and handwritten physician's progress notes. Trained professional coders must stay current on changing codes and guidelines to assign all applicable ICD-9-CM diagnoses codes, all relevant modifiers (including those appended to ancillary codes automatically generated by the Chargemaster), and all of the codes from the following sections: Anesthesiology, Surgery, and most Medicine codes.

In the case of an emergency department visit, the coder also selects and/or validates an appropriate evaluation and management CPT procedure code. Medicare regulations include one exception to this process. When a hospital outpatient visit results in an inpatient admission within 72 hours, the outpatient services are combined with the inpatient services. The entire episode of care is captured for the technical component as an inpatient record with the assignment of a MS-DRG.

Professional Component: CPT Coding for Physician Services

Coding for the professional component enables each physician involved in the care of a patient to be reimbursed the full amount to which he or she is legally and ethically entitled, regardless of the location in which services were provided. This concept is important for coders to understand. The technical component for the use of a facility is coded based on the full medical record with consideration of every diagnosis and procedure code relevant to the patient's entire episode of care (ICD-9-CM only for inpatient admissions and both ICD-9-CM and CPT-4 for outpatient encounters). The physician's coder must use the medical reports only to assign appropriate codes for the diagnoses and services that directly represent the care that physician provided.

EXAMPLE

A patient is admitted through the emergency department of a hospital and undergoes emergency surgery as a hospital inpatient. Claims from the following providers would be coded by individual coders using ICD-9-CM diagnostic codes and CPT-4 procedure codes:

> *Emergency department physician*
> *Attending physician*
> *Surgeon*
> *Assistant surgeon*
> *Anesthesiologist*
> *Specialists or consultants*
> *Radiologist*
> *Pathologist*

The rate that each physician is reimbursed for his or her professional component of services by Medicare and other third-party payers is based on the Medicare Fee Schedule (MFS), a national physician fee schedule updated annually on April 15. The fee schedule is determined by a combination of the relative value units for each CPT code, a geographic adjustment factor (which takes into consideration differences in the cost of doing business in different regions of the country), and a national conversion factor (converts relative weight to dollars). (The details of physician reimbursement are presented in Chapter 10.)

A hospital-based coder is able to code from the entire medical record for the technical component of care. The physician-based coder is able to code accurately from individual reports with significantly fewer steps for the professional component.

Ten Steps for Coding the Technical Component from Hospital-Based Outpatient Medical Records

Before beginning the process of coding any hospital outpatient or professional medical record, it is important to make sure that basic materials are in place, including up-to-date ICD-9-CM, CPT, and HCPCS Level II manuals, a medical dictionary, and reference books for drugs, human anatomy, the American Medical Association's *CPT Assistant,* and the American Hospital Association's *Coding Clinic.* It is wise to have a scratch pad available to take notes. An optimal environment includes a quiet place to work and plenty of desk space. Various software products are available to help in coding and are used by many hospitals. However, the basics are best learned starting with the coding manuals. The Office of Inspector General's Model Hospital Compliance Plan also prescribes not relying 100% on computerized encoders and indicates that staff must have access to coding books.[1]

Most hospitals use hundreds of different medical report forms. This chapter does not illustrate every possible report found within a medical record, but it does introduce those most important for beginning the process of CPT coding for the technical component.

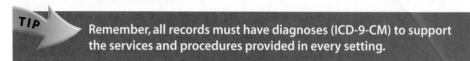

TIP Remember, all records must have diagnoses (ICD-9-CM) to support the services and procedures provided in every setting.

The following 10 steps provide a framework for coding the CPT codes from hospital outpatient MRs. Sample MRs referenced within the steps are included at the end of the chapter.

Step 1: Review Face Sheet or Registration Record

The Face Sheet or Registration Record (Medical Report 2.1) is the front page of the MR. It contains basic patient identification data, insurance information, and sometimes clinical data such as the diagnosis that reflects the primary reason for the encounter.

What to look for:

▶ The type of encounter and the reason for the encounter. Most hospitals require the coder to abstract or verify the accuracy of basic data elements from the MR that are included on the electronic form. This face sheet is used to reflect the summary and coded data necessary to create a claim for reimbursement and various databases used for research, such as an index of procedures. The type of encounter documented in Medical Report 2.1 is hospital-based ambulatory surgery. Another type of hospital outpatient encounter is a visit to the emergency department.

▶ Prospective payment system payers (e.g., Medicare), which may raise compliance and reimbursement issues.

Step 2: Review History and Physical, Emergency Department Report, and Consultant's Report

The History and Physical (H&P) Report (Medical Report 2.2) for hospital encounters can be dictated or handwritten by the attending physician as a separate report, or incorporated into the emergency room or consultant's record. In the case of hospital-based ambulatory surgery, the original H&P is often dictated by the surgeon before the date of the surgery. Another H&P is dictated or handwritten on the day of surgery and contains a brief summary including the planned procedure and the reason the surgery is being done.

For example, in Medical Report 2.2, the original H&P was performed in November by the surgeon during a consultation, and the surgery was scheduled for a date in January. The surgery actually takes place in February. The hospital medical record contains both the original H&P (Medical Report 2.3, Consultation) plus the updated H&P from the surgeon on the actual date of the surgery. The report dictated on the date of the surgery refers to the fact that the surgery was originally scheduled for January, but the patient had to cancel because of the flu. The H&P refers back to the original report in

November and states that other than the flu in January, there have been no significant changes.

The H&P is extremely important for coding all applicable ICD-9-CM diagnostic codes and for selecting the most appropriate evaluation and management code, when applicable. This report contains subjective data collected from the patient to begin the process of diagnosis by the physician. The physical examination includes a system-by-system examination by the provider to collect objective data on the patient's condition. In general, the history uncovers:

▶ The patient's chief complaint.
▶ History of the present illness.
▶ Review of systems (from the patient's perspective, based on physician questions regarding each body system).
▶ Personal, family, and social history.

An emergency department report captures the reason or reasons for the emergency encounter, a history and physical, and the following information:

▶ List of tests ordered and the results of those tests.
▶ List of medications ordered.
▶ Description of any procedures performed in the emergency room, such as laceration repair.
▶ Notes on the patient's progress.
▶ Patient instructions and status on discharge.

The coder uses all of the information on the emergency department report to code and/or validate the Evaluation and Management (E/M) service and any surgical procedures and to verify codes from the CDM (Chargemaster) as appropriate. The report would also indicate information required to assign appropriate modifiers to the CPT codes. (The matrix used by hospitals to select an appropriate level of E/M CPT code is explained in detail in the Evaluation and Management chapter.)

Consultant's Report (Medical Report 2.3) contains a history and physical along with an expert opinion requested by the attending physician to aid in the patient's diagnosis and treatment. A consultant may be brought to the emergency department for an expert opinion on treatment options or to determine whether the patient should be admitted. In the case of an admission from emergency, the record is coded as an inpatient admission rather than an outpatient hospital encounter. In some cases, for outpatient hospital surgery, there may be a consultation report from a second physician or from an anesthesiologist. More commonly, however, the surgeon's previous consultation with the patient (at the time the patient was referred to the surgeon by his or her primary care physician) is included in the hospital's medical record, but a consultation is not done on the day of the ambulatory surgery encounter.

Step 3: Review Operative Reports, Special Procedure Reports, Anesthesia, and Pathology Reports

The Operative Report is usually dictated by the surgeon or physician and then transcribed. If applicable, go to the operative report to note operations or procedures and the preoperative and postoperative diagnoses (Medical Report 2.4, Part I). Depending on whether it is a major operation or a minor procedure, it is best to recognize that MR forms related to operations or special procedures usually exist as a set of linked forms. This operative set includes the operative report itself, the anesthesia record (Medical Report 2.4, Part II), special consents for surgery, the recovery room record, and pathology reports for specimen analysis (Medical Report 2.4, Part III).

Coders must review the reports of procedures such as cardiac catheterizations, colonoscopies, and bronchoscopies, with or without biopsies. This review is necessary to properly code both the diagnostic codes and the CPT codes. Appropriate modifiers from any section of CPT are included. Verification of codes and assignment of modifiers for codes reflected on the CDM is also part of the review.

TIP If more than one procedure is performed, remember to sequence the most work- or resource-intensive procedure code before other codes. Be aware of any applicable modifiers that need to be assigned and append them to the appropriate CPT code(s).

Step 4: Review Physician's Progress Notes

Physician's progress notes (Medical Report 2.5) are recorded as often as the patient's condition warrants. Progress notes include information that relates to the patient's condition and progress, any complications that occur, the patient's response to treatment(s), and a final note. Progress notes are important to recording diagnoses. They are used to assign proper E/M codes for emergency encounters and to determine whether modifiers are needed to indicate unusual anesthesia or surgical procedures.

Step 5: Review Laboratory, Radiology, and Special Test Reports

Laboratory work (Medical Report 2.6) includes several types of chemistry tests, analyses, cultures, and other examinations of body fluids or substances such as blood, urine, stool, and pus. Coders should review laboratory, x-ray, and special tests to note any abnormal results and clarify treatments given through physician documentation. Although the codes will be entered by the laboratory staff into the CDM, coders are responsible for verifying the accuracy and assigning modifiers for these laboratory and pathology procedures. Query the physician for added documentation if necessary to clarify the precise code selection.

Radiology reports (Medical Report 2.7) include x-ray studies, computed tomographic scans, nuclear medicine studies, magnetic resonance imaging, arteriograms, and other radiologic findings. These reports are reviewed to note any abnormal findings and to clarify the information through additional physician documentation within the MR (such as physician's progress notes). These codes will be entered into the CDM by radiology staff, but coders are responsible for verifying the accuracy and assigning modifiers to all radiology procedures.

Special Test Reports (Medical Report 2.8) include electrocardiograms, echocardiograms, cardiac stress tests, and other tests. Most of these tests require CPT codes selected from the Medicine section of the CPT manual.

Step 6: Review Physician's Orders

Physician's orders (Medical Report 2.9) are written or oral orders to nursing or ancillary personnel that direct all treatments and medications to be given to the patient. Review the doctor's written orders to help determine the appropriate level of E/M code for an emergency encounter plus codes for any treatments given. In some cases, a physician may prescribe treatments without documenting the corresponding diagnoses or conditions. Coders may need to query the physician to clarify a diagnosis and ask the physician to add supporting documentation to the patient's MR through an addendum. Diagnosis codes establish the medical necessity for services—an important compliance issue.

Step 7: Review Medication Administration Record

The Medication Administration Record (MAR) is valuable for ICD-9-CM diagnosis coding, and it may provide more data to accurately select the most appropriate level of E/M code from CPT for an emergency encounter. For example, through review of the MAR and the progress notes, a coder finds that the physician ordered Bactrim for a urinary tract infection. In this case, the E/M code will most likely be a low-level service.

Step 8: Review Final Progress Note

For an outpatient encounter, final progress notes generally provide physician's notes that are helpful in determining whether any unusual circumstances may require a higher level of E/M code or modifier. For example, a final progress note by an emergency department physician may indicate that the patient was discharged after prolonged but successful treatment of an allergic reaction to anesthetic used. This may justify adding a modifier 21 for prolonged E/M service.

Step 9: Assign Codes

The Coder/Abstract Summary Form shown in Figure 2.1 is a form typically used by coders to summarize their MR review and assign the codes. All codes and modifiers should be assigned by following all CPT Guidelines, *CPT Assistant*, and OPPS rules.

Step 10: Submit Physician/Coder Query/Clarification Form if Necessary

The Physician/Coder Query/Clarification Form shown in Figure 2.2 is typically used as a good-faith communication tool between coders and physicians to clarify proper code assignment for a patient care episode. Physician's/Coder Query/Clarification Forms become part of the permanent hospital outpatient MR, and the physician must add supporting documentation to the body of the MR as appropriate. For example, if a physician fails to give sufficient detail to describe the technique used to remove polyps during a colonoscopy, the coder uses the query form to ask the physician to describe the technique used to assign the correct code (e.g., removal of polyps by hot biopsy forceps is a different CPT code than removal by snare technique). For CPT codes, this form is generally used to clarify a surgical approach or some other aspect of a

CODER/ABSTRACT SUMMARY FORM
XYZ COMMUNITY MEDICAL CENTER

Medical Record #   Acct. #:   Name:

Admit Date/Time: Encounter Type: Outpatient
Discharge Date/Time: Origin:
Birthdate: Primary Payor:
                                              Sex:
Admission Type:
Admission Source:
Discharge Disposition:

Admit Physician:
Discharge MD:
Consultant:

	CODE(S)	SHORT DESCRIPTION(S)
Admit Diag		
Primary Diag		
Other Diag		
Other Diag		
Other Diag		
Other Diag		
Other Diag		
Other Diag		
Other Diag		
Other Diag		

	CODE(S)	SHORT DESCRIPTION(S)
Major Proc		
Other Proc		
Other Proc		
Other Proc		
Other Proc		
Other Proc		

I certify that the narrative description of the primary and secondary diagnoses and major procedures performed are accurate and complete to the best of my knowledge.

_____   _____
            SIGNATURE   DATE

FIGURE 2.1 ■ The Coder/Abstract Summary Form is typically used by coders to summarize their MR review and assign and sequence the patient's codes.

PHYSICIAN/CODER QUERY/CLARIFICATION FORM

Date: _____ / _____ / _____

Dear Dr.:

We need your help. Per the documentation in the medical record, the following has to be clarified in order to correctly code the patient's medical record. The fact that a question is asked does not imply that we expect or desire any particular answer. Please exercise your independent judgment when responding. We sincerely appreciate your clarification on this issue.

Coder's Name / Phone Extension #: _____

Patient Name: _____

Admit / Discharge Date: _____

MR.#: _____

The medical record reflects the following clinical findings per the following source forms:

_____

_____

_____

Please respond to the following question:

_____

_____

_____

PHYSICIAN RESPONSE:

☐ YES – If yes, please document your response in the space below and be sure to include the
       clarification in your documentation within the body of the medical record (i.e.- progress notes, dictated
       report or as an addendum to a dictated report)

_____

_____

_____

_____   _____
            PHYSICIAN SIGNATURE   DATE

☐ NO – If no, please check the box, and sign and date below.

☐ UNABLE TO DETERMINE – If so, please check the box, and sign and date below.

_____   _____
            PHYSICIAN SIGNATURE   DATE

This form is a part of the Permanent Medical Record

FIGURE 2.2 ■ The Physician/Coder Query/Clarification Form is typically used as a good-faith communication tool between coders and physicians to clarify proper code assignment for a patient care episode.

procedure when there is more than one CPT code from which to choose to fully describe the procedure.

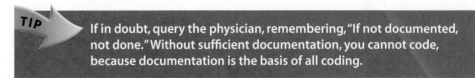

TIP If in doubt, query the physician, remembering, "If not documented, not done." Without sufficient documentation, you cannot code, because documentation is the basis of all coding.

There has been some concern expressed by the CMS that questions from coders are at times inappropriately asking physicians to add diagnoses and procedures that lead to a higher payment than is ethically merited. Nonetheless, Physician Query Forms are still in use, but coders must now communicate within the form that:

1. They are neither seeking nor expecting any particular response from the physician.
2. The physician must add documentation to the body of the medical record.
3. The query form itself will be labeled as part of the permanent medical record.

Five Steps for Coding the Professional Component from Physician-Based Medical Reports and Records

Coding for the professional (i.e., physician) component is based on specific reports rather than the medical record as a whole. A brief review of the E/M section of the CPT manual reveals the various health-care settings and the types and levels of E/M services a coder must be familiar with to assign the codes for correct reimbursement for the particular physician who performed the service(s). Regardless of the location or type of service, each professional provider has some format of medical report as a **source document** so the coder for that physician is able to assign accurate codes. It is rare for a professional coder to have more than one or two related reports to code services rendered to one patient on any given day. Physicians do, however, maintain ongoing medical records for each service provided to a patient, beginning with the first encounter.

For every hospital inpatient or outpatient medical record, individual medical reports are used by each physician's coder to submit a claim for reimbursement. The following five steps provide a framework for coding the CPT codes from physician-based medical reports and records.

Step 1: Review Face Sheet or Registration Record

All coders must abstract key demographic information to submit a claim for reimbursement. For physicians' services and procedures, if the patient was treated at the hospital and the physician has never seen the patient in the medical office, the coder must obtain the face sheet from the hospital for this information. If the patient has been seen in the medical office before the hospital-based service, the coder will also have access to the registration record in the patient's office medical record.

Step 2: Review the Appropriate Report for the Current Professional Services

This step is based on the location of the service, the specialty of the physician, and the service or procedure provided. For example, for an outpatient hospital-based surgery, the surgeon would obtain a copy of the operative report from the facility where the services were rendered. On the other hand, the primary care physician who referred the patient for hospital-based surgery would have a copy of the history and physical along with any notes pertaining to the office visit during which the referral was made in the office's copy of the patient medical record. If the services being coded were the evaluation and management services provided by the primary care physician for an inpatient admission, subsequent daily care, and discharge, the coder would need to obtain the history and physical, discharge summary, and progress notes from the facility and then ask the physician for any additional notes regarding each daily visit to the patient during the hospital stay.

Step 3: Review Supporting Documentation From Patient's Medical Record

For example, to code the surgery for excision of a malignancy, the coder may need to obtain a copy of the laboratory report to further specify the exact location and morphology of the lesion.

Step 4: Assign Codes

Most coders for physicians key the codes directly into a practice management computer system without having to generate a Coder/Abstract Summary Form.

Step 5: Submit Physician/Coder Query/Clarification Form if Necessary

Most coders for physicians do not use an official query form because the physician is easily accessible. When the coder needs more specific information, he or she generally has a procedure in place so that the physician makes a dated, initialed notation directly on the medical record or as an addendum to the medical record.

SUMMARY

Coders must become familiar with the common contents and formats of medical records. Coders use both the administrative and clinical data contained in MRs as part of the coding process. A 10-step method can be used for CPT coding of the technical component. A 5-step method for CPT coding of the professional component (physician services) is based on review and analysis of specific reports rather than on the entire medical record.

TESTING YOUR COMPREHENSION

1. What are the four parts of a problem-oriented medical record?

   _____

2. What is unique about the source-oriented medical record?

   _____

3. What is the unique element of the integrated medical record?

   _____

4. The Face Sheet (Registration Record) of the clinical record customarily contains what information?

   _____

5. What medical report is defined as an expert opinion requested by a physician to aid in the diagnosis and treatment of a patient?

   _____

6. In a typical hospital outpatient surgery encounter, list the different professionals who would most likely have their services coded and submitted for reimbursement separately from the technical component?

   _____

7. What is used as a good-faith communication tool between the coder and the physician?

   _____

8. What reports are typically considered to be linked when a significant procedure is performed?

   _____

Chapter Review Exercises

CODING PRACTICE I

Directions

Using your CPT manual, code the following procedures and services. (Remember, in the real world, CPT codes would not be assigned without at least one diagnosis to reflect the reason for the service or services.)

	PROCEDURE/SERVICE	CODE
1	Evaluation and management services provided to a patient in the emergency department requiring a problem-focused history and physical examination and straightforward medical decision-making. (Alpha Index, main term Evaluation and Management, subterm Emergency Department, range 99281–99288. Go to range in tabular listing. Look at the bulleted criteria delineating the key components for the codes in the range and select the code that meets all three of the key components because all three must be met to select the proper level of code in this category.)	
2	A consultation provided to a patient in the hospital (inpatient) with an expanded problem- focused history and examination and straightforward decision making. (Consultation, Inpatient—go to range.)	
3	General anesthesia provided during a corneal transplant. (Anesthesia, Corneal Implant and then always verify the code in the tabular listing, even when there is only one code listed in index).	
4	Simple repair of a superficial facial wound 2.6 cm in length along the cheekbone. (Repair, Wound, Simple)	
5	Simple excision of two nasal polyps in the physician's office. (Excision, Polyp, Nose, Simple)	
6	Laparoscopic repair of an initial inguinal hernia. (Repair, Hernia, Inguinal, Initial)	
7	Blepharotomy to drain an abscess of the right lower eyelid. (Blepharotomy)	
8	Single frontal view chest x-ray. (X-ray, Chest)	
9	Computed tomography guidance for needle placement for biopsy, radiologic supervision, and interpretation. (CT Scan, Guidance, Needle, Placement)	

	PROCEDURE/SERVICE	CODE
10	Radiation treatment management, five treatments. (Radiation Therapy, Treatment Management, Weekly).	
11	Laboratory test to determine level of bilirubin; total. (Bilirubin, Blood)	
12	Automated differential white blood cell count. (Blood Cell Count, Differential, WBC)	
13	Testing for West Nile virus, IgM. (West Nile Virus, Antibody)	
14	Chemotherapy administration into pleural cavity, requiring and including thoracentesis. (Chemotherapy, Pleural Cavity)	
15	Thirty-minute psychotherapy session in the psychologist's office to assist with smoking cessation including medical evaluation and management services. (Psychiatric Treatment, Individual, Insight-Oriented, Office or Outpatient)	

Medical Record Case Study

CODING PRACTICE II

Instructions

This is an exercise to give you practice in coding from a real-life medical record.

1. Refer to the 10 steps for coding from hospital outpatient medical records for the technical component presented in this chapter.

2. Follow each step and carefully review Medical Reports 2.1 through 2.10; these are all part of this patient's medical record.

3. At Step 9, begin filling in the correct codes on the Coder/Abstract Summary Form (Fig. 2.1). HINTS: Main term for principal procedure is Excision, Skin, Malignant; for the second procedure, see main term Skin, Grafts, Free; for the surgical pathology code, see Pathology, Surgical, Gross and Micro, and then go to tabular to see which level is most appropriate for skin. For the Anesthesia, main term Anesthesia, Integumentary System, Head. For laboratory, there are two panels, both under main term Blood Tests, Panels, then one for Lipids and one for Metabolic, Total Calcium. The third laboratory test is found under main term, Complete Blood Count. The x-ray main term is X-ray, Chest. The ECG is under Electrocardiography.

4. If necessary, complete a Physician/Coder Query/Clarification Form (Fig. 2.2) to clarify the physician's documentation and ensure more precise coding. Remember not to suggest a specific procedure, but if a more specific detail would assist in selecting the most accurate code, it is acceptable to use this form. For example, if a physician did a series of biopsies during a colonoscopy, but did not specify which locations of lesions were removed by hot biopsy versus cold, and none of the other reports in the record such as anesthesia or surgical pathology provided this delineation, the coder could ask the physician for clarification.

MEDICAL REPORT 2.1

REGISTRATION RECORD

MR#:   123456
ACCT#: 432165

SUNSHINE HEALTH SYSTEMS INC.   SHSI, SUN HOSPITAL AMBULATORY SURGERY

ADMIT DATE/TIME: 2/2/20XX 0700

NAME: Patient A

PT. TYPE: Ambulatory Surgery

DISCHARGE DATE/TIME: 2/2/20XX 1400

VISIT TYPE: Oncology Services

Coder reviews demographic and payer informa-tion. Administrative data such as the patient's age and sex can provide insight for correct coding. For example, an 82-year-old man could not have a hysterectomy.

PATIENT INFORMATION

PATIENT ADDRESS:	111 Oak St.	DOB: 1/1	
ADDRESS LINE 2:		AGE: 31Y	
CITY:	Anywhere	SEX:	M
STATE:	FL	M/S:	Married
ZIP:	33222	RACE:	Latino
HOME PH:	999-999-9999	RELIGION:	Methodist
WORK PH:	999-999-8888	SSN:	123-12-1234
EMP. STATUS:	Employed Full Time	LMP:	N/A
OCCUPATION:	Landscaper	ONSET OF ILLNESS:	11/01/XX
EMPLOYER:	Southern Yard & Garden	INSURANCE:	Blue Cross/Blue Shield
EMPLOYER ADD:	777 7th Ave	POLICY:	1111111
CITY:	Anywhere	INSURANCE ADD:	555 Hwy 11
STATE:	FL		Elsewhere, FL 33333
ZIP:	33222		

ADV. DIRECTIVE:	No	2ND INS:	N/A		
GUARANTOR NAME:	Patient A	SSN:	RELATIONSHIP TO PATIENT: Self		
ADDRESS:	CITY:	ST:	ZIP:		PH:
NEXT OF KIN:	Patient A's wife	SSN: 222-22-2222	RELATIONSHIP TO PATIENT: Wife		
ADDRESS:	Same as Patient	CITY:	ST:	ZIP:	PH:

PHYSICIAN/DIAGNOSIS INFORMATION

ATTENDING: Dr. 001   ADMITTING: Dr. 002   REFERRING: New Care

ADMITTING DIAGNOSIS: 173.3 Basal Cell Carcinoma, Forehead

MEDICAL REPORT 2.2

Dr. 002 Surgeon
PREOPERATIVE HISTORY & PHYSICAL

MR#:   123456

ACCT#:   432165

PATIENT: Patient A

DATE: 2/1/20XX

SURGERY

DATE: 2/2/20XX

Coder obtains this report from the surgeon's copy of the patient's record.

The patient was originally scheduled for surgery last month but had to cancel because he was ill.

HISTORY OF PRESENT ILLNESS: The patient is a 32-year-old Latino gentleman who has a biopsy-proven basal cell carcinoma of the right forehead, measuring at least 4 × 5 cm in diameter. He was originally scheduled for surgery last month, thought the patient had the flu at that point and had to cancel. He now presents to the hospital for treatment of this extremely large cancer. We are planning on wide excision with split-thickness skin graft reconstruction. The procedure has been thoroughly detailed to the patient, and he expresses understanding, including the potential cosmetic deficits that will result from this type of reconstruction.

I have reviewed his past medical history, and other than the flu that he had in January of this year, nothing much has changed.

The E/M service is included in the global fee or surgical package and would not be coded separately from the assigned surgical code.

Physical exam, again, remains overall unremarkable. The patient is scheduled for surgery tomorrow, 2/2/20XX at Sunshine Health Systems, Inc., ambulatory surgery center.

Please refer to the originally dictated H&P for additional details as necessary.

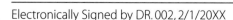

Electronically Signed by DR. 002, 2/1/20XX

MEDICAL REPORT 2.3

Dr. 002
PREOPERATIVE CONSULTATION

MR#:   123456

ACCT#:   432165

PATIENT: Patient A

DATE: 2/1/20XX

SURGERY

DATE: 2/2/20XX

This is a 32-year-old Latino male who was referred by New Care with a biopsy-proven basal cell carcinoma of the right forehead. This is a large lesion which has been present for at least 6 or 7 years, according to the patient. He says he felt it began with a small laceration to the region, though he is out in the sun quite a bit, too. There is no family history of melanoma or any past history of other previous skin cancer. This large lesion has grown to 4 × 5 cm, however. He was treated through the New Care program with a biopsy, actually performed last March, and I am unsure where the delay was in getting him seen, though he is seen today in regard to this previous biopsy.

PAST MEDICAL HISTORY: The patient claims to have mild shortness of breath, though this may be related to his smoking. He otherwise states he is healthy. He uses Dr. 003 at New Care Clinic for primary care.

PAST SURGICAL HISTORY: No prior surgeries.

MEDICATIONS: Zoloft 100 mg orally daily for anxiety.

DRUG ALLERGIES: No known drug allergies.

SOCIAL HISTORY: Married. He just changed jobs but is still a professional landscaper. He smokes one pack of cigarettes daily. He drinks alcohol rarely. He denies use of drugs. He currently lives with his wife and 6-year-old son.

FAMILY HISTORY: No melanoma. Family history of diabetes.

REVIEW OF SYSTEMS: Denies weight loss or gastrointestinal disturbance. He claims some occasional shortness of breath but this appears to most likely be related to smoking. He gets some exertional chest pain in the muscles only, and has no evidence of actual cardiac pain on thorough discussion. He denies additional skin lesions.

PHYSICAL EXAMINATION

GENERAL: Well-developed, well-nourished appearing Latino male in no acute distress.

VITAL SIGNS: Pulse approximately 80, respirations approximately 14, blood pressure not taken at time of initial examination.

HEENT: There is a large plaquelike lesion on the right forehead with distinct borders measuring 4 × 5 cm in greatest diameter. This is the only obvious skin lesion present. There is no evidence of major sun damage. Pupils are equally round, reactive to light and accommodation. Sclerae are clear. Extraocular muscle motion is intact. Jaw function is good. He does have multiple decayed teeth with multiple missing teeth.

NECK: Supple without adenopathy.

CAROTID UPSTROKES: 2+ bilaterally without bruits.

LUNGS: Clear to auscultation and percussion.

HEART: Regular rate and rhythm without murmur.

ABDOMEN: Benign on this examination. No hepatomegaly, splenomegaly, or other masses.

EXTREMITIES: Normal range of motion and function for age.

SKIN: No additional skin lesions detected clinically.

NEUROLOGICAL: Grossly intact with cranial nerves II–XII functioning.

LABORATORY DATA: Pending.

IMPRESSION: Large basal cell carcinoma of right forehead.

PLAN: I have discussed this lesion thoroughly with the patient. I have discussed basal cell carcinoma as well as additional skin cancers, their prevention and expectations from this particular lesion. I have recommended excision of it, though due to its large size, excision with clear margins is going to require a fairly major reconstruction. This could be accomplished with either major rotation flap or skin graft, though even the major rotation flaps are going to leave quite a bit of scarring present, and I think his best option at this time is to cover this with a split-thickness skin graft. This would allow some retraction, and hopefully color would blend it fairly well. It should not look any worse than the current lesion does, as far as aesthetic appearances, though I did tell him that skin grafts on the forehead region do not always give the best final aesthetic appearance and that he may require some scar revision or other treatments to try to maximize the aesthetic appearance, though this would not be covered by his insurance. I told him that the major goal here is to remove the cancer, however, and he says he is in agreement with that. Excision with skin grafting would be my recommendation.

The surgeon's coder would have previously assigned the appropriate E/M code for this office consultation. This report would be part of the office copy of the patient's medical record.

In addition to this consultation, the PCP's coder would select the appropriate level of E/M office code for the visit during which the PCP referred the patient to the surgeon for consultation.

I had a full discussion with the patient about potential risks, benefits and goals, limitations, and potential complications of this surgery to make sure he had a good understanding. Surgery is scheduled after the holidays at the patient's request.

The lesion is mobile, above the adventitial plane and should not require any bony resection; therefore, we can leave periosteum in place to support the skin graft most likely.

MEDICAL REPORT 2.4   OPERATIVE REPORT

PART I

Dr. 002, Surgeon
OPERATIVE REPORT

MR#:   123456

ACCT#:   432165

PATIENT: Patient A

DATE: 2/2/20XX

DATE OF OPERATION: 2/2/20XX

PREOPERATIVE DIAGNOSIS: Very large basal cell carcinoma of forehead.

POSTOPERATIVE DIAGNOSIS: Very large basal cell carcinoma of forehead.

OPERATION PERFORMED: Excision of large basal cell carcinoma of forehead with split-thickness skin graft (45 sq cm).

SURGEON: Dr. 002

ANESTHESIA: General via endotracheal tube.

COMPLICATIONS: None apparent.

ESTIMATED BLOOD LOSS: Less than 25 mL.

FLUID REPLACEMENT: See anesthesia record.

SPECIMEN: Wide excision, originally sent for frozen section, but converted to permanent section only.

DRAINS: None.

> *The surgeon's coder selects the appropriate CPT code from the Surgery section. In this case, there are no assistants or co-surgeons involved. If there were, that physician's coder would use the same CPT code as the surgeon but with a modifier indicating assistant or co-surgeon.*

FINDINGS: The patient had a large biopsy-proven BCCa of the forehead, measuring approximately 5 cm. The patient originally was seen in December and scheduled for surgery, though he got the flu and had to cancel an early January surgery. He is now back on the operating schedule for this procedure, which has been thoroughly discussed with him previously.

PROCEDURE: The patient was placed on the operating table in the supine position, anesthetized, prepped, and draped in a sterile fashion. I marked out approximately 1 cm borders around all areas of this extensive basal cell carcinoma which left a good sized overall defect. I injected 1% Xylocaine with epinephrine locally, and then excised the area, tagging at the 12 o'clock superior margin. I tried to take the lesion as thin as possible, yet still maintain good margins, although there were many areas, due to the difficulty in removing skin from galea in this region, that I actually did have essentially just adventitial tissue present. There were some areas where it did appear that nerve fibers were present and required sacrifice. I did feel, however, that I had good clear margins around the entire lesion. We sent the lesion to pathology, though due to some confusion, the lesion was not received in pathology in a timely fashion. Rather than keep the patient on the operating table for a prolonged period of time, we elected to forego the frozen section and simply go with permanent section margins based on the nature of the basal cell. A split-thickness skin graft of 14 one-thousandths of an inch was harvested from the right thigh, and the donor site covered with epinephrine-soaked gauze. The graft was used as a sheet graft, placed into the defect, and trimmed to size. It was sewn into place with #4-0 silk sutures, tails left long. The tails were subsequently used to construct a tie-down bolster of Xeroform and wet cotton balls. The epinephrine-soaked sponge was removed from the donor site, this area air dried, and then covered with a Tegaderm dressing. I left the bolster open on the forehead. The patient overall tolerated the procedure well. Sponge and needle counts were correct at the end of the procedure. He was escorted in stable condition back to the recovery room.

MEDICAL REPORT 2.4   OPERATIVE REPORT

PART II
ANESTHESIOLOGY REPORT

CLINICAL DIAGNOSIS: Basal cell carcinoma of forehead.

PREMEDICATIONS: Versed IV

OP PROPOSED: Excision of large basal cell carcinoma of forehead with split-thickness skin graft (45 sq cm)

PHYSICAL STATS (ASA) 1-X 2-__ 3-__ 4-__ 5-__ E-__

Date	2/2/20XX
N2O / O2	3
VERSED	4 mg
DIPRIVAN	20/20/30
	50×
TIME (Surgery)	10:35-10:47a
TIME (Anesthesia)	10:23-10:52a
Technique	General via endotrach
BP	From 160/80 to 119/55
ECG	Monitored
SpO2	97 & 99
FiO2	1.5 & 1.0

ANESTHESIA EQUIPMENT

CHECKED-PER-LIST

VENTILATOR-ALARMS-SET

XO2-ANALYZER

PATIENT-ID/CHART

CORONARY MONITOR

BP TO RECOVERY 128/59

INTAKE&OUTPUT

CRYSTALLOID: 100

The anesthesiologist's coder selects the correct code from the Anesthesiology section of CPT. The anesthesiologist indicates the patient status on the report, and the coder must add the appropriate modifier to the CPT code.

OPERATION: As proposed

POST-OP DX: Same as Pre-op Clinical Dx

CRNA/MDA ELECTRONIC SIG: Dr. 004 and 005 Surgeon(s): Dr. 002

PATIENT:
MR#:   123456
ACCT#:   432165
PATIENT: Patient A

MEDICAL REPORT 2.4   OPERATIVE REPORT

PART III
SURGICAL PATHOLOGY REPORT

PATIENT: Patient A
MR#: 123456 ACCT# 432165

PHYSICIAN: Dr. 002
ACCESSION #: S05-5555
TAKEN: 2/2/20XX
RECEIVED: 2/2/20XX
REPORTED: 2/3/20XX
LOCATION: ASU

Specimen(s) Received
EXCISION FOREHEAD

FINAL DIAGNOSIS

Skin, Forehead, Excision:

Basal Cell Carcinoma

Margins Appear Free of Tumor

Report Electronically Signed: Dr. 006

MICROSCOPIC DESCRIPTION:
A microscopic examination is performed and incorporated in the final diagnosis.

CLINICAL DIAGNOSIS & HISTORY
Basal Cell Carcinoma Forehead

The pathologist's coder selects the correct code from the Pathology and Laboratory section of CPT.

GROSS DESCRIPTION
Received fresh labeled "excision forehead": is a 5.5 × 4.0 cm ellipse of skin with maximal depth of 0.5 cm. There is a suture at one pole of the short axis designated as 12:00. The specimen is inked yellow over the 12:00 aspect, blue over the 6:00 aspect, serially sectioned perpendicular to the long axis and submitted completely as follows:

A1–A3—3:00 half of specimen

A4–A6—9:00 half of specimen

MEDICAL REPORT 2.5

PROGRESS NOTES

MR#:   123456
ACCT#:   432165
PATIENT: Patient A

LAB RESULTS: See Report—all values within normal range
ALLERGIES: NKDA
CURRENT MEDS: Zoloft 100 mg orally daily for anxiety

In general, progress notes for an attending physician for an inpatient justify the level of hospital E/M code.

2/2/20XX 10:47: *Patient tolerated the procedure well. He is on his way to the recovery room with the anesthesiologist. Blood pressure is returning to normal.*

002

10:55: *Patient is awake. He is groggy but not in any distress.*

002

11:30: *Patient is able to sit up and drink 3 oz. apple juice.*

002

11:55: *Orally gave patient and his spouse discharge instructions and discharged him home with script for pain (see orders).*

002

Surgeon's progress notes are included in the surgical package; therefore, a code is not assigned.

MEDICAL REPORT 2.6

LABORATORY REPORT

MR#:   123456

ACCT#:   432165

PATIENT: Patient A

DATE: 2/1/20XX

(Pre-op labwork)

COLLECTED: 2/1/20XX 8:00a

RECEIVED: 2/1/20XX 9:15a

REPORTED: 2/1/20XX 10:30a

The pathologist's coder would be responsible for coding any laboratory services.

TEST NAME	IN RANGE	OUT OF RANGE	REFERENCE RANGE
LIPID PANEL			
Triglycerides	106		<150 mg/dL
Cholesterol (Total)	189		<200 mg/dL
HDL	72		>or = 40 mg/dL
LDL	96		<130 mg/dL (CALC)
Chol/HDLC Ratio	2.6		<4.4 (CALC)
AST	31		2–35 U/L
ALT	17		2–40 U/L
BASIC METABOLIC PANEL			
Glucose	91		65–99 mg/dL
BUN	10		7–25 mg/dL
Creatinine	0.7		0.5–1.2 mg/dL
BUN/Creatinine Ratio	14		6–25 (CALC)
Sodium	142		135–146 mmol/L
Potassium	4.6		3.5–5.3 mmol/L
Chloride	104		98–110 mmol/L
Carbon Dioxide	26		21–33 mmol/L
Calcium	9.1		8.5–10.4 mg/dL
HEMOGRAM/PLT			
White Blood Cell Ct	5.8		3.8–10.8 THOUS/mcL
Red Blood Cell Ct	4.18		3.80–5.10 MILL/mcL
Hemoglobin	13.0		11.7–15.5 g/dL
Hematocrit	39.0		35.0–45.0%

Electronically Signed by Dr. 006

MEDICAL REPORT 2.7

RADIOLOGY REPORT

MR#:   123456
ACCT#:   432165
PATIENT: Patient A
DATE: 2/2/20XX

CHEST PA AND LATERAL: Views of the chest reveal several scattered granuloma from previous granulomatous disease. The heart and mediastinum are normal. The lungs are well-expanded and clear.

IMPRESSION: No acute abnormality in the chest.

> *The radiologist's coder selects the correct code from the Radiology section of CPT. Remember that modifiers may take on special significance in radiology procedures. For example, modifiers are sometimes used to differentiate between the professional and the technical component of the service.*

Electronically Signed by Dr. 007

MEDICAL REPORT 2.8

ELECTROCARDIOGRAM REPORT

MR#: 123456

ACCT#: 432165

PATIENT: Patient A

DATE: 2/2/20XX

> The coder for the physician who read and completed the ECG report selects the correct code from the Medicine section of CPT.

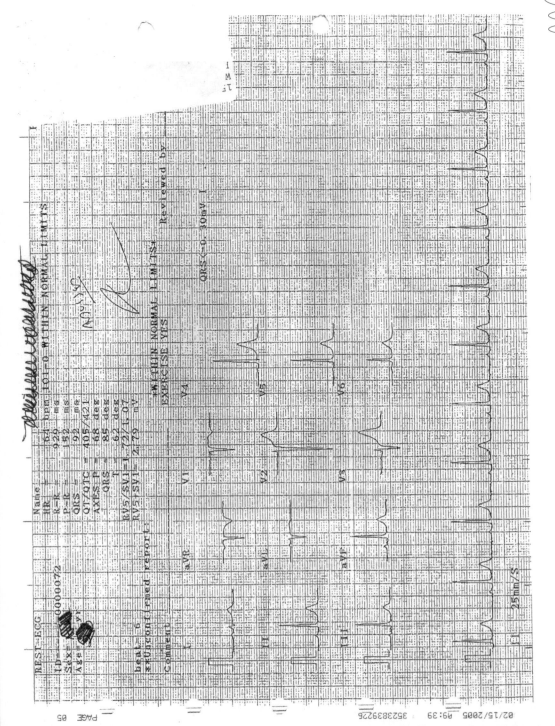

MEDICAL REPORT 2.9

PHYSICIAN'S ORDERS

MR#:   123456
ACCT#:   432165
PATIENT: Patient A
DATE: 2/2/20XX

Physician's orders are included in the surgical package. Attending physician's orders help the coder select the correct E/M code for a hospital visit.

1. Discharge home.
2. Dressing may be removed in 1–2 days.
3. 1–2 tabs Darvocet N-100 po prn for pain.
4. 50–75 mg Demerol with 25 mg Vistaril IM for severe pain.
5. Follow-up in office in 1 week.

Electronically Signed: Dr. 002

MEDICAL REPORT 2.10

OFFICE NOTES

MR#:	22222
ACCT#:	44444
PATIENT:	Patient B
DATE:	3/20/20XX

SUBJECTIVE: The patient is in my office today to review her recent progress on metformin. This medication has been well-tolerated at the current 850 mg/day po b.i.d. dose. Unfortunately, the patient has experienced some insomnia and low-energy levels since her Prempro was discontinued approximately 1 month ago.

OBJECTIVE: Fasting insulin on Feb 19 was 8.3. This compares favorably with the measurement in November, which was essentially unchanged. It will be recalled that her baseline fasting insulin was nominally elevated at 11. Weight today = 182 lbs. LMP = 6 years ago.

ASSESSMENT: Relative hyperinsulinemia (251.1).

PLAN: A prescription for 0.625 mg Prempro is provided to the patient today. Additionally, refills for 850 mg metformin is provided for her. We will see her back in approximately 6 months. A repeat fasting insulin and glucose level will be obtained at that time along with a fasting lipid panel. Her general questions were answered and she will be in contact with me as needed.

PART II

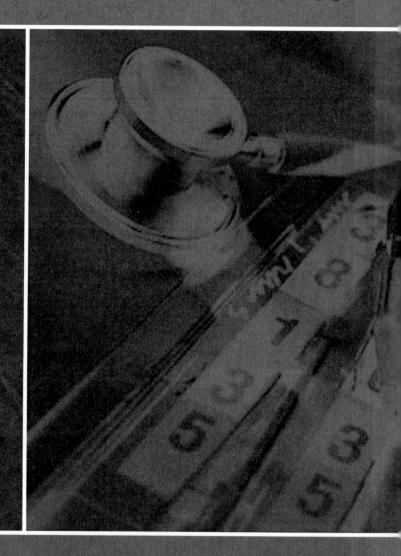

CODING FOR SPECIFIC SERVICES, SURGERIES, PROCEDURES, AND TESTS

Pathology and Laboratory

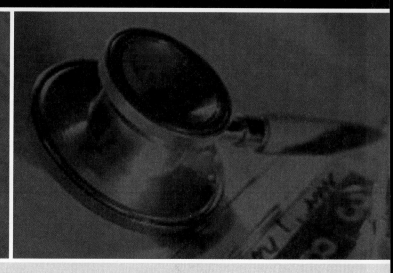

Chapter Objectives

▶ Describe the format of the Pathology and Laboratory
  section.
▶ Understand the terminology used in the Pathology
  and Laboratory section.
▶ Understand the concept of medical necessity and its
  importance to CPT codes.
▶ Apply appropriate local and national coverage
  determinations to verify medical necessity.
▶ Recognize the significance of the Clinical Laboratory
  Improvement Act (CLIA).
▶ Learn when to obtain an Advance Beneficiary Notice
  (ABN) for Medicare patients.
▶ Recognize the significance of the Chargemaster.
▶ Correctly assign CPT codes and modifiers to pathology
  and laboratory procedures.

*Laboratory and pathology tests are diagnostic in nature. Bodily fluids such as
sputum blood, urine, semen, and amniotic fluid are tested for various components and compared with normal ranges. Samples that are below or above the
normal ranges either provide needed information to make a diagnosis or may
require further testing before a diagnosis can be made. Each laboratory test is
identified with a CPT code, which is used for billing purposes.*

Word Parts and Meanings of Medical Terms Related to Pathology and Laboratory			
Word Part	Meaning	Example	Definition
agglutin/o-	clumping	agglutination	Process of cells clumping together
amyl/o	starch	amylase	Enzyme that breaks down starch
erythr/o	red	erythrocyte	Red blood cell
glycos/o	sugar	glycosuria	Sugar in the urine
hemat/o	blood	hematuria	Blood in the urine
kary/o	nucleus	karyotype	Chromosome characteristics of an individual cell
leuk/o	white	leukocyte	White blood cell
path/o	disease	pathology	The study of disease from the perspective of structural and functional changes in tissues and organs
phleb/o, ven/o	vein	phlebotomy or venipuncture	Incision (puncture) of a vein
thromb/o	clot	thrombocyte	Clotting cell (platelet)
-uria	urine condition	pyuria	Pus in the urine

Medical Necessity and Other Reimbursement Considerations

All laboratory and pathology tests within this section require proof of medical necessity in the form of an ICD-9-CM diagnosis code that justifies the performance of each individual procedure or panel. Medicare does not pay for tests performed without a minimum of a sign or symptom code to justify the test. To help coders know what diagnosis justifies a laboratory test, Medicare provides national coverage determinations (NCD), and the local carrier (in each state) provides local coverage determinations (LCD).

> **TIP**
> To better understand coverage determinations, go to www.cms.hhs.gov and see the Medicare Coverage Database. Within the database, choose national or local coverage. Include your state to access specific information for your local area. You can search the database in a number of ways, including keywords or CPT codes. For example, if you enter 80076 for a hepatic function panel, a listing of more than 180 ICD-9-CM codes that support medical necessity for CPT code 80076 are shown.

It is important to note that it is fraudulent to choose one of these diagnoses to support the billing of the panel unless the patient has that condition or disease and it is documented in the medical record. For example, if a Medicare-eligible patient has malnutrition (ICD-9-CM code 263.9), it is appropriate to do a test for albumin. Albumin is included in the hepatic function panel; however, the test can also be performed individually. The coder would select the procedure code for the individual test and not the panel.

Advance Beneficiary Notice

In the preceding example, if the physician feels it is important to perform the entire panel for malnutrition, and the diagnosis does not justify the medical necessity of the full panel and will not be covered by Medicare, the patient would be informed before the test is performed and asked to sign an **Advance Beneficiary Notice** (ABN). This form states that the patient is responsible for payment if denied by Medicare, and it may only be obtained for specific services. Without a signed ABN (which is designated on the claim form by using a -GA modifier), a Medicare patient cannot be billed for a test. The only valid ABN is the form approved by the Centers for Medicare and Medicaid Services (CMS). If the CMS-approved form is not used, the ABN is not valid. (CMS standardized the form in 2002, and a proposed revised version is currently under review.) An approved form must be used that includes the statement: "Medicare probably will not pay for laboratory tests listed below for the following reasons." Space is also provided on the form to show the estimated cost of the tests. The patient is given two options: "Yes, I want to receive these laboratory tests," or "No, I have decided not to receive these laboratory tests."

Clinical Laboratory Improvement Act

Providers performing the laboratory tests listed in the Pathology and Laboratory section of the CPT manual must be federally certified. The **Clinical Laboratory Improvement Act** (CLIA) of 1967 mandated government regulation of laboratories providing more than 100 commercial laboratory tests per year across state lines. Revised legislation, the CLIA of 1988, broadened the scope and required *all* providers to have CLIA certification to perform any laboratory tests. Tests are rated by complexity, and laboratories are given a rating for the level of tests they can perform. The CLIA Certificate Number must be included on the CMS 1500 billing form. A waiver can be obtained for tests cleared by the U.S. Food and Drug Administration (FDA) for home use. Examples of tests included under the waiver are stool guaiacs, blood glucose, and urine pregnancy tests. To obtain moderate or high complexity certification, the laboratory must pass proficiency testing. This quality testing is performed every 6 months for each laboratory test provided by the facility.

CPT Coding for Physician Services Versus Hospital Services

Codes may be applied differently depending on the billing entity (physician versus hospital), and coders must keep in mind for *whom* they are billing. Hospitals may use a **Chargemaster**, also known as a charge description master (CDM), which is a computerized comprehensive list of service codes for laboratory, pathology, radiology, and other services used to expedite claims to third-party payers. Physician offices often use an encounter form, also known as a **Superbill**, which contains a checklist of tests, for the same purpose. (See Fig. 3.1 for an example of a Superbill.) Both billing formats require ongoing review to assure that new CPT codes (updated annually on January 1) and periodic coding updates (called Bulletins or transmittals) from insurance carriers or Medicare have been entered correctly.

Chargemaster

A Chargemaster expedites claims to payers, helps the institution assess financial profits or losses, and provides a mechanism to audit services. It does this by automatically linking the hospital's charge for a procedure to the CPT/HCPCS code for that procedure (see Table 3.1 for an example of a laboratory Chargemaster).

Please return form to Receptionist

@ = ABN may be needed; see policy

NEW	✓	OFFICE VISIT	✓	ESTAB	FEE	CPT	✓	OFFICE PROCEDURES	FEE	CPT	✓	LABORATORY – OUT	FEE	CODE	✓	INJECTIONS	FEE
99201		Focused		99212		46600		Anoscopy		84460		ALT/SGPT @		95115		Allergy (Own Med.)	
99202		Expanded		99213		93000		EKG @		82150		Amylase (Blood)		95117		Allergy - Multiple Inj.	
99203		Detailed		99214		20600		Joint Injection (Small) @		84450		AST/SGOT @		90782		I.M. Inj.	
99204		Compre.		99215		20605		Joint Injection (Inter) @		80048		Basic Metabolic Panel @		90788		IM Antibiotic	
99205		Complex				20610		Joint Injection (Major) @		84520		BUN		J3420		B-12 1000	
		Follow up to Proc.		99024	N/C	94640		Nebulizer Treatment		82465		Cholesterol @		J0702		Celestone 3mg x ____	
		Minimal – Nurse		99211		94150		Peak Flow		82550		CK (Creatine Kinase) @		J2175		Demerol 50mg x ____	
		CONSULT / PRE-OP				94010		Pulmonary Func. Test		80053		Comp. Metabolic Panel @		J1040		Depo-medrol 80mg	
99241		Problem Focused				94760		Pulse Oximetry		82565		Creatinine @		J1055		Depo-Provera	
99242		Expanded				69210		Remove Impacted Cerum (MD)		87070		Culture, any other source		J3301		Kenelog each 10mg x ____	
99243		Detailed				93040		Rhythm Strip		87086		Culture, Urine @		J2550		Phenergan up to 25mg x ____	
99244		Comprehensive				45330		Sigmoidoscopy, Flex @		80051		Electrolyte Panel		J0696		Rocephin 250mg x ____	
99245		High Complexity				G0104		Sigmoid Screening (Mcare Only)		82728		Ferritin @		J1885		Toradol 30mg x ____	
PREVENTATIVE MEDICINE - NEW PATIENT						20550		Tendon Sheath/Trig. Pt. Inj.		82746		Folate @		IMMUNIZATIONS			
99381		Physical, Age under 1				29580		Unna Boot LT/RT		82947		Glucose/FBS @		90471		Immun. Adm. Single	
99382		Physical, Age 1-4								85027		Hemogram & Platelet		90472		Immun. Add'l	
99383		Physical, Age 5-11						OFFICE LABS		85025		Hemogram c̄ Auto (Comp.) Diff. @		G0008		Adm. of Flu (Medicare Only)	
99384		Physical, Age 12-17				82962		Glucose/Accuck		85024		Hemogram c̄ Auto (Partial) Diff. @		G0009		Adm. of Pneumo (Medicare Only)	
99385		Physical, Age 18-39				83036		Glycohemoglobin (A1C)@ QW		85014		Hematocrit @		90700		DTAP	
99386		Physical, Age 40-64				86677		H. Pylori @		80061		Lipid Panel c̄ Cardiac Risk @		90701		DTP	
99387		Physical, Age 65 & over				85018		Hemoglobin @ QW		80076		Liver Profile @		90658		Flu Vaccine > 3 yrs.	
PREVENTATIVE MEDICINE - ESTAB. PATIENT					82044		Microalbumin @		86308		Mono		90744		HEP B Ped	
99391		Physical, Age under 1				85610		Prothrombin Time/PT @ QW		84132		Potassium @		90746		HEP B Adult	
99392		Physical, Age 1-4				87880		Quick Strep QW		84153		PSA @		90707		MMR	
99393		Physical, Age 5-11				82270		Stool, Guiac @		85651		Sed Rate (Non Auto) @		90645		Hib	
99394		Physical, Age 12-17				G0107		Stool, Guiac, Medicare Only @		84295		Sodium, Serum @		90713		Polio Virus Inj.	
99395		Physical, Age 18-39				81002		Urinalysis (Dip Stick) @		84479		T3 @		90732		Pneumovax	
99396		Physical, Age 40-64				81025		Urine Pregnancy Test		84436		T4 @		86580		PPD Intradermal	
99397		Physical, Age 65 & over				G0001		Venipuncture/Medicare		84443		TSH @		90703		Tetanus Toxoid	
99499		BCBS Well Woman (CAP)				36415		Venipuncture		84550		Uric Acid @		90720		Tetramune	
Q0091		Pap Handling-Mcare @				87229		Wet Smear/KOH		81000		Urinalysis c Micro (Price)		90716		Varicella	
G0101		Breast/Pelvic Exam-Mcare								81003		Urinalysis s̄ Micro (Auto) @		90669		Prevnar	
CPT	✓			OFFICE SURGERY	FEE					82607		Vitamin B-12 (Cyano) @		SUPPLIES			
17000		Destruction (Any Method) 1 Lesion								85048		WBC		A4460		Ace Bandage	
17003		Destruction (Any Method) 2 to 14 Lesions # ____												L1906		Ankle Support	
17004		Destruction (Any Method) 15 or More Lesions # ____												L0120		Cervical Collar	
10060		I & D Simple @										X-RAY		L1830		Knee Splint	
10061		I & D Complex								76075		Bone Density @		E1805		Wrist Brace	
		Excision Lesions: Size ____ Site ____ ☐ Path Sent								71010		Chest 1 View @		L3908		Wrist Support	
		Lac. Repairs: Size ____ Site ____								71020		Chest 2 View (PA & LAT)		L3260		Surgical Boot	
11200		Removal of Skin Tags, Multiple up to 15 lesions								72100		Lumbar Spine		E0112		Crutches	
11201		Each Additional 10 Lesions															
17110		Destruction of Flat Warts (Any Method) up to 14 Lesions															
17111		Destruction of Flat Warts (Any Method) 15 or More Lesions															

Patient Information

Encounter# 999999
Pat# Mike Michaelson
Chart# 333333
Diagnoses:
380.4 Cerumen
462 Pharyngitis

☐ Medical Records

Return With:

Dr. 1   Dr. 2   Dr. 3   Dr. 4   RN   PA

Return

____ Days   ____ Weeks   ____ Months   OV   RC   Pap   Labs   MS30   CPE   PT ____

Date	Group	Dept.	Doctor	Time	Today's Charge
Patient			D.O.B. Sex Soc. Sec. #		Prior Balance

Responsible Party

Location   Patient
Insurance

Reason for Visit

Referring Doctor

Copay Due

Today's Payment

Current	Over 30 Days	Over 60 Days	Total Due

Insurance Company   BA   SCT   Policy ID#

☐ Cash
☐ Check   Ck#
☐ CC

Authorization #

X ____
Physician's Signature

FIGURE 3.1 ■ Example of a Superbill—physician encounter form.

TABLE 3.1	Sample Laboratory Chargemaster			
Price File Code	**Rev**	**Description**	**CPT/HCPCS**	**Total Charges**
3150188–324	301	Urea nitrogen	84540	$11.00
3150188–899	301	Urea nitrogen	84540	$23.00
3150188–934	301	Urea nitrogen	84540	$23.00
3150188–935	301	Urea nitrogen	84540	$42.00
3150189–324	301	Creatinine Serum	82565	$6.00
3150189–899	301	Creatinine Serum	82565	$21.00
3150189–934	301	Creatinine Serum	82565	$21.00
3150189–935	301	Creatinine Serum	82565	$42.00

324 = PHYS–LAB, 899 = ER, 934 = OUTPT, 935 = IP

It is interesting to note the difference in hospital charges between an outpatient and inpatient for the same test (e.g., urea nitrogen). This is attributable to differences in expenses between outpatient and inpatient care.

After a test is ordered by a physician, a requisition for the test is sent to the department performing the test. After the test is performed, a price file code is entered for the service under the patient's account. The price file code links to the type of patient (or originating department), a short narrative description of the service, the CPT/HCPCS code, a revenue code (a service code required by insurance carriers), and the institutional charge for the service. This plays an important part in the revenue cycle, in which charges can be totaled and evaluated against provider payments to assess financial profits and losses. It also plays a key role in the internal and external auditing of health-care services. Although the Chargemaster is an efficient process, it presents a serious problem if data (including CPT codes) are entered incorrectly. This is a high-volume, high-risk, and problem-prone process and is an area of special interest to the Office of Inspector General (OIG), a federal agency that investigates fraud and abuse in Medicare charges.

Physician Offices

Because of CLIA regulations, most physician offices will send patients to outside laboratories for testing. In some offices, the **specimen** is collected in the office, and then sent out to a reference laboratory. In this case, the collection of the specimen and its preparation for the outside laboratory are coded by the physician's office, and the laboratory receiving the specimen bills for the actual tests. Medicare only reimburses for services provided in the physician's office. Other third-party payers allow the physician's office to bill the patient for laboratory tests, and the physician's office pays the laboratory directly for these tests.

TIP To code for collection of a blood specimen, look up Venipuncture in the index and then see the appropriate tabular listing(s). Specimen handling for a reference laboratory is found in the index under Specimen Handling.

Hospitals and Pathologists

Hospitals and pathologists may have different billing arrangements for non-Medicare patients. According to the 1999 *College of American Pathologists Professional Relations Manual*, "Professional component billing is one valid method of billing for the professional services of pathologists in the clinical laboratory. In many communities, the standard practice is for the pathologist to direct bill patients for the professional component of clinical laboratory services. When the pathologist bills a professional component to a non-Medicare patient, no payment is made by the hospital to the pathologist for this service. The hospital's bill for the technical component covers hospital costs for laboratory equipment, supplies and non-physician personnel—it does not include the professional services of the pathologist."[1]

Pathology and Laboratory Modifiers

The modifiers shown in the Quick Reference chart below are commonly used with pathology and laboratory codes.

Locating and Selecting Pathology and Laboratory Codes

Proper code selection requires review of all notes and specific directions in the CPT manual, including the Guidelines at the beginning of the Pathology and Laboratory section and the notes included under subsections and with code descriptions. The tabular listing for Pathology and Laboratory is divided into subsections based on the type of test performed. Table 3.2 shows the Pathology and Laboratory subsections and the code ranges that apply to each subsection.

Quick Reference: Pathology and Laboratory Modifiers

HCPCS II/ CPT Modifier	Description	Explanation
GA	Advance Beneficiary Notice has been obtained	Used when an ABN is obtained for a test the provider suspects Medicare will not cover and for which the patient may be billed.
26	Professional component	Used when the pathologist is billing for the professional component only (separate from the facility).
59	Same laboratory procedure is performed on a separate specimen on the same day	Used if the same laboratory test is run a second time on a distinctly separate specimen on the same day. This is appropriate when several blood cultures are performed on the same day in an effort to isolate a specific bacterium.
90	Specimen testing performed by reference laboratory	Used when a specimen is obtained in the physician's office and sent to a reference laboratory for testing.
91	Repeat clinical diagnostic test on same day	Used when a laboratory test is repeated on the same day to obtain multiple test results needed in the course of treatment. If a patient is undergoing replacement therapy, such as potassium, multiple blood samples may be obtained at various time intervals during the therapy to determine its success. NOT used to confirm initial results or if testing problems arise with the initial specimen.

TABLE 3.2 Pathology and Laboratory Subsections and Code Ranges	
Pathology and Laboratory Subsection	**Code Range**
Organ- or disease-oriented panels	80048–80076
Drug testing	80100–80103
Therapeutic drug assays	80150–80299
Evocative/suppression testing	80400–80440
Consultations (clinical pathology)	80500–80502
Urinalysis	81000–81099
Chemistry	82000–84999
Hematology and coagulation	85002–85999
Immunology	86000–86849
Transfusion medicine	86850–86999
Microbiology	87001–87999
Anatomic pathology	88000–88099
Cytopathology	88104–88199
Cytogenic studies	88230–88299
Surgical pathology	88300–88399
Transcutaneous procedures	88400
Other procedures	89049–89240
Reproductive medicine procedures	89250–89356

Organ- or Disease-Oriented Panels (80048–80076)

Before 1998, these laboratory tests were not grouped specifically as panels. A list of 19 tests identified as "frequently grouped" was given, and once the determination of the number of tests was made, the appropriate code was assigned. For example, 10 tests would be coded as 80010. This system was unmanageable and fraught with billing errors as the exact number of tests was often difficult to determine. With the 1998 CPT codes, panels were introduced. **Panels** are groups of laboratory tests commonly performed together and assigned one code. To use a panel code, ALL tests must be performed. No substitutions are allowed. If three of the four listed tests are performed, the panel code is not used; the three tests must be coded separately. Alternatively, it is incorrect to code each test separately if all tests in a panel are performed. If all the tests in a panel are performed and an additional test is performed, then the panel code is used along with the additional code for the one extra test.

 TIP To assign a panel code, ALL tests in the panel must be performed. No substitutions are permitted.

Focus on Medical Necessity

The Focus on Medical Necessity tables in this chapter will help you understand the concept of medical necessity. As noted previously, Medicare lists acceptable ICD-9-CM diagnosis codes that provide a valid reason for a laboratory test or panel of tests. As an example, the following table presents the

♒♒♒♒ FOCUS ON MEDICAL NECESSITY

Focus on Medical Necessity—Organ- or Disease-Oriented Panels—CPT Code 80076

Hepatic Function Panel— 80076 (ALL included)	Conventional Units	Possible Diagnoses	ICD-9-CM Code
Albumin	3.5–5.2 g/dL	Dehydration (H)	276.51*
		Hepatic disease (L)	573.9
		Malnutrition (L)	263.9*
		Nephritis (L)	581.9*
Total bilirubin	00.2–1.2 mg/dL	Hemolytic anemia (H)	283.9*
		Cirrhosis (H)	571.5
		Pernicious anemia (H)	281.0*
		Transfusion reaction (H)	999.8
Direct bilirubin	0.0–0.4 mg/dL	Biliary obstruction (L)	576.2
		Cirrhosis (H)	571.5
		Hepatitis (H)	573.3
Alkaline phosphatase	38–126 U/L (37°C)	Paget disease of bone (H)	731.0*
		Viral hepatitis (H)	070.9
		Hypophosphatasia (L)	275.3*
		Protein deficiency (L)	260*
Total protein	6.4–8.3 g/dL	Polyneuritis (H)	356.9*
		Liver damage (H)	571.9
		Kidney damage (H)	593.9*
Alanine aminotransferase	Male: 13–40 U/L (37°C)	Hepatitis (H)	573.3
	Female: 10–28 U/L (37°C)	Mononucleosis (H)	075*
		Cholecystitis (H)	575.10
		Acute myocardial infarction (H)	410.90*
Aspartate aminotransferase	10–59 U/L (37°C)	Hepatitis (H)	573.3
		Liver cell necrosis (H)	570*

(H) = above normal level; (L) = below normal level.

*Denotes an ICD-9-CM code that supports medical necessity for the individual test but *not for the entire panel.*

ICD-9-CM codes that support medical necessity for each individual test as well as the entire hepatic function panel. This panel, also known as the liver function panel, is done to evaluate the baseline status of the liver. The CPT code for the panel may only be used if all of the tests in the panel are performed. Remember, only certain diagnosis codes will justify medical necessity of the full panel. Some of the ICD-9-CM codes given for the possible diagnoses for one or more individual tests within the panel are not listed on the LCD for the entire panel. Keep in mind that these blood tests may be performed individually for signs and symptoms other than those related to the liver. In these instances, the test or tests performed would be assigned the appropriate individual CPT code(s).

Drug Testing—Qualitative (80100–80103)

Qualitative testing denotes the presence or absence of a drug. This is often done as part of the legal system for prior users of illicit drugs to prove continued abstinence. Home kits are also available for common illicit drugs such as cannabis, cocaine, heroin, ecstasy, and angel dust. This is considered a screening test and is found in the index under Drug Screen.

Professional baseball players are now routinely tested for anabolic steroids. A result of present or absent is given, but not a quantity or level. A confirmatory test may then be performed using a second testing method, and a code is provided for this additional test. The codes assigned are 80101 and 80102.

EXAMPLE

Therapeutic Drug Assays—Quantitative (80150–80299)

An **assay** is the quantitative or qualitative evaluation of a substance to determine its components and their proportions. **Quantitative testing** determines the amount or concentration of a drug in numeric form. A drug level is measured and an amount determined. Generic drug levels are measured with this type of testing. Prescription amounts are adjusted up or down depending on the test result. Coders should reference the specific drug being tested for in the index.

An epileptic patient would periodically need to have phenobarbital levels tested. If the amount of the phenobarbital is out of the therapeutic range, this may trigger onset of a seizure. Reference Phenobarbital, assay in the index. The code assigned is 80184.

EXAMPLE

Evocative/Suppression Testing (80400–80440)

With **evocative/suppression tests**, component levels of a substance are measured after the administration of an evoking or suppressing agent. The results can confirm or rule out certain disorders. Additional codes from the Medicine section include supply and administration codes and an E/M code for prolonged service if applicable. At a minimum, two chemistry tests are performed: one *before* and one *after* administration of the evoking or suppressing agent. In most cases, three to five tests are performed.

TIP   The code for evocative/suppression testing represents a panel, and ALL the required tests must be included for assignment of the panel code. Reference the component being measured in the index, such as renin.

If a patient is hypothyroid, the thyrotropin-releasing hormone stimulation test (TRH) may be performed to pinpoint the defective tissue (hypothalamus or hypophysis). The 1-hour TRH stimulation panel must include three thyroid-stimulating hormone (TSH) levels including one baseline, one drawn at 30 minutes, and the final draw at 60 minutes. See the index under Thyrotropin Releasing Hormone for TRH stimulation panel. The code assigned is 80438. Coders cannot use modifier -91 with this code because the three tests are included in a series.

EXAMPLE

Consultations (Clinical Pathology) (80500–80502)

The clinical pathology consultation codes represent the pathologist's charge for a consultation or a second opinion. An interpretation is given by a pathologist who did not do the initial report on the specimen. A specific request from the attending physician or surgeon is required and a report is produced, just as with any other type of consultation by a specialist. If the patient is examined, refer to codes 99241–99255 for E/M Office or Other Outpatient Consultation codes. Reference Pathology in the index.

Urinalysis (81000–81099)

For correct code assignment, methodology must be determined, such as a dipstick. A **dipstick test** is commonly performed in a physician's office as part of an annual physical examination. Hematuria, pyuria, proteinuria, and glycosuria are some conditions that can be detected with a dipstick. A dipstick is a nonautomated test. An automated test, done by a machine, is coded differently, and both can include microscopy. Reference Urinalysis in the index.

EXAMPLE	*Pregnancy tests can be performed on blood or urine. A urine pregnancy test is assigned code 81025.*

Chemistry (82000–84999)

Chemistry tests are quantitative and specific component levels are measured. Blood, urine, feces, or other fluids are included. Reference the specific component being tested in the index.

EXAMPLE	*Amylase is an enzyme produced by the pancreas to help digest starch. An increased amount of amylase may indicate acute pancreatitis: 82150.*

The following Medical Necessity Table shows diagnosis codes that support medical necessity for various chemistry procedures.

Hematology and Coagulation (85002–85999)

Hematology is the medical specialty related to the blood and blood-forming tissues. A **complete blood count** (CBC) is a comprehensive test that includes the number of erythrocytes, leukocytes, and thrombocytes. A CBC is one of the most commonly ordered tests, and is routinely done if a patient is to undergo a surgical procedure. Specific clotting factors and clotting inhibitors are tested in patients with abnormal bleeding time. **Thrombocytes** are the clotting cells. **Erythrocytes** are red blood cells (RBC) that carry oxygen to body tissues. **Leukocytes** are white blood cells (WBC) that increase in number in the presence of an infection, inflammation, or allergic response. A WBC differential will give specific levels of the leukocytes affected (basophils, neutrophils, eosinophils, lymphocytes, and monocytes). See Figure 3.2 for an illustration of red blood cells, white blood cells, and platelets. See Figure 3.3 for an illustration of a hematocrit, a test that measures red blood cells as a percentage of whole blood.

FOCUS ON MEDICAL NECESSITY

Focus on Medical Necessity—Chemistry

Test (CPT code)	Conventional Units	Possible Diagnoses	ICD-9-CM Code
Sodium (84295)	135–145 mEq/L	Adrenal hyperfunction (H)	255.3
		Congestive heart failure (H)	428.0
		Syndrome of inappropriate secretion of ADH (L)	253.6
		Vomiting (L)	787.03
Potassium (84132)	3.5–5.1 mEq/L	Renal failure (H)	586
		Metabolic acidosis (H)	276.2
		Diabetic ketoacidosis (L)	250.10
		Cushing syndrome (L)	255.0
Blood urea nitrogen (84520)	6–20 mg/dL	Chronic glomerulonephritis (H)	582.9
		Pyelonephritis (H)	590.80
		Hepatic damage (L)	571.9
		Malnutrition (L)	263.9
Glucose (82947)	74–106 mg/dL	Diabetes mellitus (H)	250.00
		Hyperthyroidism (H)	242.90, 242.91
		Hyperinsulinism (L)	251.1
		Hypopituitarism (L)	253.2

(H) = above normal level; (L) = below normal level.

TIP In assigning codes for hematology and coagulation, you will need to know whether the test is automated or manual for correct code assignment. Reference Blood or the specific test in the index.

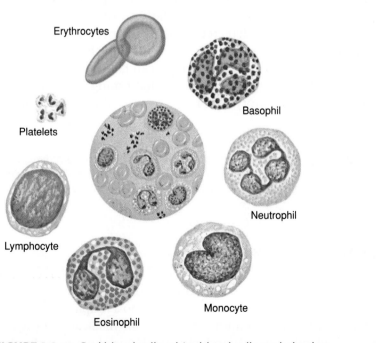

FIGURE 3.2 ■ Red blood cells, white blood cells, and platelets.

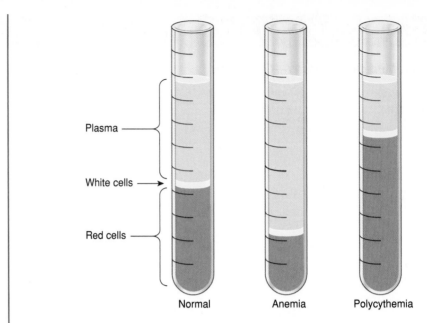

Plasma

White cells →

Red cells

Normal   Anemia   Polycythemia

FIGURE 3.3 ■ Hematocrit. The tube on the left shows a normal hematocrit. The center tube shows a low percentage of red blood cells, indicating anemia. The tube on the right shows a high percentage of red blood cells, indicating polycythemia.

The following Medical Necessity table lists some possible diagnoses if the RBC or WBC levels are abnormal. For example, a bacterial infection will result in an increased WBC count.

Immunology (86000–86849)

When a patient is exposed to an **antigen**, a substance that induces a state of sensitivity or immune response, the body will produce antibodies to fight the antigen. An **antibody** is a molecule the body produces in response to an antigen; the presence of antibodies indicates exposure to an antigen or disease. For example, HIV is detected by the presence of antibodies. Although the patient may not have a full-blown case, he or she may have been exposed to the disease and have the infection. It can take up to 6 months for a person to develop antibodies to the HIV virus; that timing may result in a delayed diagnosis because laboratory tests may not show the presence of antibodies in the earliest stages.

EXAMPLE

Chlamydia is the most common sexually transmitted disease. Although an active infection may not be diagnosed, an antibody can be detected that confirms exposure to the disease. Reference Antibody in the index. The code assigned is 86631.

Transfusion Medicine (86850–86999)

Blood usage is highly scrutinized in hospitals. All **transfusions** (the transfer of blood or blood components from a donor to a recipient) are reviewed by a Blood Utilization Review Committee to determine medical necessity. When a patient requires blood or blood products, the donor blood must be the correct blood

FOCUS ON MEDICAL NECESSITY

Focus on Medical Necessity—Hematology and Coagulation

Test (CPT code)	Conventional Units	Possible Diagnoses	ICD-9-CM Code
RBC count (manual = 85032, automated = 85041)	Male: 4.7–6.1 million Female: 4.2–5.4 million	Polycythemia (H) Dehydration (H) Iron deficiency anemia (L) Blood loss (L)	238.4 276.51 280.9 459.0
WBC count (manual = 85032, automated = 85048)	4,800–10,800	Bacterial infection (H) Leukemia (H) Viral infection (L) Chemotherapy	041.9 208.90 079.99 V58.11
Platelet count (manual = 85032, automated = 85049)	130,000–400,000	Polycythemia vera (H) Myeloproliferative disorders (H) Aplastic anemia (L) Leukemia (L)	238.4 238.79 284.9 208.90

(H) = above normal level; (L) = below normal level.

type. **Agglutination,** or clumping of the patient's blood cells, will result if a correct match is not done. **Cross match** is the comparison of donor erythrocytes to recipient **serum,** the fluid portion of the blood. As part of the cross match, acquired or naturally occurring antibodies in recipient serum are checked against donor erythrocytes. The transfusion procedure is coded in the Surgery section; the type and cross match of the blood is coded through Pathology and Laboratory. Reference Blood Typing in the index for some of these codes.

Microbiology (87001–87999)

Microbiology is the study of bacteria, fungi, parasites, and viruses. An important test included in this section is **culture and sensitivity,** in which a specimen is cultured and the isolated bacteria's susceptibility (sensitivity) to particular antibiotics is determined. For example, when a urinary tract infection is diagnosed, the physician needs to know the specific bacteria involved to prescribe the proper treatment. The type of infection dictates the treatment. An antibiotic is required to treat a bacterial infection; however, an antifungal is required for a fungus, and an antiviral is required for a virus. Reference Culture in the index.

Laboratories can help determine the efficacy of particular medications, thereby helping physicians ensure that patients receive proper and cost-effective treatment. Figure 3.4 is a sample microbiology report in which a wound culture identifies two bacteria: *Staphylococcus aureus* and *Acinetobacter lwoffi.* Eleven antibiotics are listed as either susceptible or resistant. Note that for both types of bacteria, trimethoprim/sulfasoxazole and levofloxacin are identified as antibiotics that are susceptible. One $ (dollar sign) is listed for trimethoprim/sulfasoxazole, which means its cost is in the $1 to $10 range. Two $$ are listed for levofloxacin, meaning its cost is in the $11 to $20 range. Therefore, if both medications are equally effective, the physician has the option of prescribing the less expensive antibiotic as treatment.

XYZ MEMORIAL HOSPITAL
MICROBIOLOGY

PAGE 1

PATIENT: MARK JONES	MRN:	BILLING#:
DOB:	AGE:	SEX:
DATE:		ORDERED BY:
SOURCE: Left lower extremity		COLLECTED:
ORDER#:		RECEIVED:
ANTIBIOTICS AT COLLECTION:		

WOUND CULTURE OF LLE

CULTURE WOUND
- Reincubating for more growth .
- M oderate growth of Staph species, coagulase POSITIVE.
- I dentification and sensitivity to follow .
- Light growth of gram negative rods .
- I dentification and sensitivity to follow .

Isolate 1 Staphylococcus aureus
Isolate 2 Acinetobacter lwoffi   i

Isolate ANTIBIOTIC S	Iso# 01 mcg/ml Intr	p	I so# 02 mcg/mg Intrp		Relative Cost
Trimeth/Sulfa	<2/38	S	<2/38	S	$
Erythromyci n	0.5	S			$
Cefazolin	<8	S			$
Clindamyci n	0.5	S			$$
Levofloxacin	<2	S	<1	S	$$
Ampicillin/Sulbact			<8/ 4	S	$$$
Ceftazidime			8	S	$$$
Cefotaxime			>32	R	$$$
Ticar/K Clavate			<16	S	$$$$$
Imipenem			<1	S	$$$$$$$$
Aztreonam			>16	R	$$$$$$$$

Relative Cost Key—($ = approx. $1–$10)

S = Susceptible   I = Intermediate   R = Resistant   B lac = beta-lactamase Positive
MS = Moderately Susceptible   B lank = Drug not tested or advisable
Gentamicin Synergy: S = synergy exists between Aminoglycosides and Beta Lactam Drugs, for the treatment of serious infections. Gentamicin Synergy: R = synergy DOES NOT EXIST between Aminogly-
conides and Beta Lactam drugs. Interpretations based on NCCLS most recent recommendations.

GRAM STAIN   - PLATED   Bite = B

FIGURE 3.4 ■ Microbiology medical report.

Anatomic Pathology (88000–88099)

An **autopsy** is a postmortem examination of the organs of the body, usually
to determine the cause of death. Autopsies are coded based on how extensive
a procedure was done and may or may not include the brain. Reimbursement
is based on the amount of the body that is examined. Thus, the higher codes
provide higher reimbursement. Gross examination would entail just a visual

examination. Autopsies on adults and infants are coded differently. This sub-section includes codes for medical examiner's and coroner's cases. Reference Autopsy in the index.

 ## Cytopathology (88104–88199)

Cytology is the study of cells, and **cytopathology** is the study of disease changes within individual cells or cell types. Pap smears and studies on fluids are tests in the Cytopathology section. Obtaining the specimen is a separate code for the physician or his designee. Preparation of the specimen for an outside reference laboratory is also a separate code reported by the physician's office. Technology for computer-assisted screening of specimens has resulted in additional CPT code choices for cervical and vaginal smears. Because of the large number of Pap smears performed and the resulting high-volume work-load, computer screening is used by laboratories. Cytotechnologists then review the abnormal specimens, approximately 10% to 20% of the total Pap smears, by preparing thin-layer slides. This preparation is an additional vari-able coders must know for correct code assignment. Reference Pap smear in the index.

The **Bethesda method** (also called the Bethesda system) requires labora-tories to determine whether there are enough cervical cells in the specimen to make an accurate evaluation and provides a consistent terminology for improved communication of cervical and vaginal cytopathology between lab-oratories and physicians. The quality of the specimen and categories for diag-noses are provided with this system. If a specimen is inadequate, the physi-cian is notified by the laboratory so that a new specimen can be obtained. Categories provided for abnormal specimens include abnormalities of epithe-lial cells and glandular cells.

Fine-needle aspiration is a technique used to collect fluid from many sources. One com-mon source is cysts in the breast. This method allows fluid to be removed without an invasive procedure being performed. Samples obtained by fine-needle aspiration are coded 88172 or 88173.

EXAMPLE

 ## Cytogenetic Studies (88230–88299)

Cytogenetic studies are complex tests used to identify genetic disorders through analysis of tissue, cells, or chromosomes. They usually require multi-ple CPT codes to fully explain the services rendered. Inherited disorders are tested for using chromosome analysis, and for accurate code assignment, cell numbers are required. Codes for cryopreservation (freezing) and thawing of cells are listed in this section, as are tissue culture codes. Reference Chromo-some Analysis in the index.

---

*It is common for pregnant women older than 35 to have **amniocentesis**, a test that examines amniotic fluid for fetal abnormalities, during the fourth month (see Fig. 3.5). Karyotyping after amniocentesis would include 88235; 88269; 88280; 88285; and 88291.*

EXAMPLE

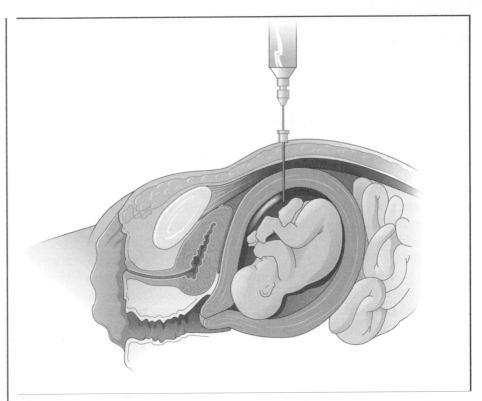

FIGURE 3.5 ■ Amniocentesis. A sample is extracted from the amniotic sac. Cells and fluid are tested to determine whether any fetal abnormalities are present.

Surgical Pathology (88300–88399)

A separate code is assigned for each tissue specimen. If specimens are submitted together, they should be labeled separately to be considered separate specimens. These codes are grouped by level, with Level I the lowest and Level VI the highest. The levels are assigned on the basis of how much work was required of the pathologist. Level VI represents larger and more complicated specimens that require more time on the part of the pathologist than a Level III code. Level I is gross examination only; the tissue is examined with the naked eye, without a microscope. Reference Pathology in the index.

Frozen section is performed during surgery, and the surgeon requests a pathologic opinion about the tissue removed. Usually performed on cancer patients, this procedure determines clean tissue margins, which indicate the surgeon has removed all diseased tissue. Two important terms used in the CPT manual are **block** and **section**. A block of tissue is a piece of tissue. A section is a thin slice of the tissue block that has been prepared for examination. A block of tissue may yield several sections.

EXAMPLE

A hysterectomy may be performed with removal of one or both ovaries. If the pathologist receives a request for consultation during surgery and performs frozen sections on two blocks of uterine tissue and one block of ovarian tissue, the codes assigned are 88331; 88332; and 88331-59.

Surgical pathology codes are assigned for each specimen submitted. Specimens submitted together should be labeled separately and considered separate specimens for multiple use of the 88331 code. For each specimen, the first tissue block and all associated sections are coded 88331. Any additional blocks from the same specimen are coded 88332. Attach modifier -59 to indicate the same procedure is performed on a separate specimen on the same day.

Mohs surgery, which includes microscopic examination of tissue by the surgeon, is reported using codes from the Surgery section, Integumentary System subsection (codes 17304–17310).

Transcutaneous and Other Procedures (88400–89240)

Transcutaneous is defined as through the skin. In transcutaneous bilirubin testing, a device is placed on the infant's forehead and a reading is taken through the skin. Transcutaneous bilirubin testing (code 88400) is used for jaundiced infants because it is more cost-effective and less traumatic than the previously used method, which required a needle stick in the infant's heel. Reference Bilirubin, Transcutaneous in the index.

Other procedures such as duodenal and gastric intubation and aspiration may require additional codes from the Radiology or Medicine sections.

Reproductive Medicine Procedures (89250-89356)

Advances in infertility treatment options have resulted in reproductive medicine procedures such as in vitro fertilization. The majority of insurance carriers do not reimburse for these services, and the patient is billed directly. Reference In Vitro Fertilization in the index.

The laboratory codes used for in vitro fertilization at a minimum would include 89250; 89254; 89255; and 89260.

EXAMPLE

SUMMARY

In this chapter, several administrative aspects of CPT coding were introduced. The concept of medical necessity is important to ensure proper reimbursement. Coders must always be aware of the link between the diagnosis and procedure codes. Laboratory and Pathology coding includes all specimens removed from the body. Separate codes are used by the phlebotomist to report obtaining a blood sample and by the surgeon to report removal of tissue (for testing) during a surgical procedure.

TESTING YOUR COMPREHENSION

1. What legislation mandated certification before performing laboratory tests?

   _____

2. Why is an ICD-9-CM diagnostic code required for laboratory tests?

   _____

3. What is another term for a basic metabolic profile?

   _____

4. What does quantitation test for?

   _____

5. What is another term for a postmortem examination?

   _____

6. Which blood test gives the number of erythrocytes, leukocytes, and thrombocytes?

   _____

7. What is the computerized system used by most hospitals to link laboratory procedures to the charges for the procedures?

   _____

8. What type of code is needed to provide medical necessity for CPT codes?

   _____

9. Why is it necessary to update Chargemasters and Superbills at least annually?

   _____

10. Sometimes laboratory tests must be performed more than once in the same day, for example, a morning and an evening bilirubin. What modifier is attached to indicate this necessity?

    _____

11. What type of testing measures generic drug levels?

    _____

12. What is the name of the form signed by Medicare patients to indicate they are aware that Medicare will probably not pay for a specific laboratory test and the patient is therefore financially responsible for the test?

    _____

13. Which modifier is used on the claim form to indicate that an ABN has been signed by the patient?

    _____

14. What is the name of the form that is a checklist of tests and other services provided in a physician's office used for billing purposes?

    _____

15. What is the method that provides a consistent terminology for improved communication of cervical and vaginal cytopathology between laboratories and physicians?

    _____

CODING PRACTICE I — Chapter Review Exercises

Directions

Using your CPT manual, code the following tests and scenarios or brief reports using codes from the Pathology and Laboratory section.

Tests

1. Total bilirubin. _____
2. Autopsy of the heart only. _____
3. Huhner test. _____
4. Lipid panel and triglycerides. _____
5. FSH gonadotropin test. _____
6. Cryopreservation of five cell lines. _____
7. Sputum culture. _____
8. Monospot test. _____
9. HIV confirmation with Western blot. _____
10. Automated thrombocyte count. _____
11. Digoxin level. _____
12. Gastric secretory study, 1 hour. _____
13. Glucose tolerance test, three specimens. _____
14. Stool guaiac. _____
15. Bone marrow smear interpretation. _____
16. TB skin test. _____
17. Prothrombin time. _____
18. Albumin, pleural fluid. _____
19. Vaginal smear with wet prep. _____
20. Arterial blood gases. _____
21. Triglycerides. _____
22. Prostate-specific antigen, total. _____
23. Prostate needle biopsy, surgical pathology. _____
24. Vitamin B-12. _____
25. Gram stain. _____

Scenarios and Brief Reports

1. Patient C reported to Dr. 008's office for a preoperative physical examination. She had the following tests performed as part of her physical: urinalysis (examined by dipstick in the office) and a CBC drawn by the office staff and sent out to a reference laboratory that will bill for the actual tests. What CPT code(s) will Dr. 008's office use for laboratory services for Patient C?

_____

2. Patient D was admitted to the hospital to have her gallbladder removed. Dr. 009 performed the cholecystectomy and a biopsy of the pancreas. Several gallstones were also submitted to pathology. What will the pathologist bill for examination of the tissue specimen(s)?

_____

3. Code the following laboratory report on Patient E in the spaces provided in the CPT code column on the far right.

TEST (REFERENCE RANGE)	RESULTS	LOW	NORMAL	HIGH	CPT CODE
Glucose (70–125 mg/dL)	85.0		X		
BUN (5–25 mg/dL)	14.0		X		
Creatinine (0.5–1.5 mg/dL)	1.0		X		
Alkaline phosphatase (30–115 U/L)	68.0		X		
Total bilirubin (0.1–1.2 mg/dL)	0.5		X		
AST (SGOT) (0–41 U/L)	22.0		X		
ALT (SGPT) (0–45 U/L)	27.0		X		
Total protein (6.0–8.5 g/dL)	6.9		X		
Albumin (3.0–5.5 g/dL)	4.4		X		
Cholesterol (75–260 mg/dL)	251.0		X		
Triglycerides (10–190 mg/dL)	209.0			X	
HDL cholesterol (31–56 mg/dL)	33.0		X		
LDL cholesterol (60–160 mg/dL)	176.0			X	
PSA (<4.0 ng/dL)	2.0	X			

4. Code the following laboratory report on Patient F in the spaces provided in the CPT column on the far right.

TEST (ACCEPTABLE RANGE)	PATIENT RESULTS	LOW	NORMAL	HIGH	CPT CODE
BUN (8–20 mg/dL)	10		X		
Albumin (3.5–5.0 g/kg)	3.9		X		
Potassium (3.5–5.0 g/kg)	6.6			X	
Phosphorus (4.5–6.0 mg/dL)	7.4			X	
Calcium (9.5–11.5 mg/dL)	9.5		X		
Glucose (80–120 mg/dL)	102		X		
Carbon dioxide (22–26 mmol/L)	25		X		
Chloride (97–107 mmol/L)	109			X	
Creatinine (0.5–1.5 mg/dL)	0.8		X		
Sodium (135–145 mEq/L)	152			X	

CODING PRACTICE II   Medical Record Case Studies

Directions

1. Carefully review the medical reports provided for each case study.
2. Research any abbreviations and terms that are unfamiliar or unclear.
3. Identify as many diagnoses and procedures as possible.
4. Because only part of the patient's total record is available, think about any additional documentation that you might need.
5. If appropriate, identify any questions you might ask the pathologist to code this case correctly and completely.
6. Complete the appropriate blanks below for each case study. Explain (in writing) questions 1 through 5 and assign the Pathology and Laboratory code(s) for question 6.

Case Study 3.1

Patient: **Patient G**

Patient documentation: **Read Medical Report 3.1**

1. What is the diagnosis (description) that supports the medical necessity of this procedure?

   _____

2. Are there any secondary diagnoses present that required additional procedures?

   _____

3. What was the main procedure, and were other secondary procedures performed on this patient?

   _____

4. Do you believe you need additional documentation to correctly assign the Pathology and Laboratory codes to this record? If so, what is the additional documentation that you need?

   _____

5. Do you have any additional questions for the pathologist?

   _____

6. What is(are) the procedure code(s) you would assign to this case study?

   _____

   _____

MEDICAL REPORT 3.1

COMMUNITY HOSPITAL
DEPARTMENT OF PATHOLOGY
CYTOLOGY REPORT

NAME:	Patient G
COLLECTION DATE:	5/30/XX
SURGEON:	Dr. 010
DOB:	2/27
AGE:	69
SEX:	F
PATH #:	0005672434
HOSP #:	1000156478
ACCT #:	047891
LOCATION:	Outpatient

SOURCE OF SPECIMEN(S)

RIGHT LUNG MASS CT-GUIDED BX (up to 5 slides)

FINAL CYTOLOGIC DIAGNOSIS

RIGHT LUNG MASS, CT-DIRECTED NEEDLE BIOPSIES: SMALL CELL CARCINOMA

CLINICAL HISTORY

RIGHT LUNG MASS

MICROSCOPIC DESCRIPTION

A microscopic examination is performed and incorporated in the final diagnosis.

GROSS DESCRIPTION

Received are two smears prepared as touch-preps of needle biopsy cores from CT-directed needle biopsy of a right lung mass. These are stained and submitted for immediate evaluation of specimen adequacy. The corresponding cores each have less than 0.05 cm external diameters and are approximately 0.8 cm in aggregate length. After fixation in formalin, these are submitted for histologic processing.

_____

Electronically Signed and Dated

Case Study 3.2

Patient: **Patient H**

Patient documentation: **Read Medical Report 3.2**

1. What is the diagnosis (description) that supports the medical necessity of this procedure?

   _____

2. Are there any secondary diagnoses present that required additional procedures?

   _____

3. What was the main procedure, and were other secondary procedures performed on this patient?

   _____

4. Do you believe you need additional documentation to correctly assign the Pathology and Laboratory codes to this record? If so, what is the additional documentation that you need?

   _____

5. Do you have any additional questions for the pathologist?

   _____

6. What is(are) the procedure code(s) you would assign to this case study?

   _____

   _____

MEDICAL REPORT 3.2

PATIENT NAME: Patient H		**ACCESSION #: S05-1746**	
MED. REC #: 095088		**ACCOUNT #:**	
DOB: 7/31		**TAKEN:** 2/23/XX	
GENDER: Female		**RECEIVED:** 2/23/XX	
SOC. SEC. #: XXX-XX-XXXX		**REPORTED:** 2/24/XX	
PHYSICIAN: Dr. 011		**LOCATION:** Outpatient	

SPECIMEN(S) RECEIVED

EXCISION FOREHEAD

FINAL DIAGNOSIS

SKIN, FOREHEAD, EXCISION:
    BASAL CELL CARCINOMA.
    MARGINS APPEAR FREE OF TUMOR.

REPORT ELECTRONICALLY SIGNED

Dr. 012
mbg 2/24/20XX

MICROSCOPIC DESCRIPTION

A microscopic examination is performed and incorporated in the final diagnosis.

CLINICAL DIAGNOSIS & HISTORY

BASAL CELL CARCINOMA FOREHEAD

GROSS DESCRIPTION

Received fresh labeled "excision forehead" is a 5.5 × 4.0 cm ellipse with maximal depth of 0.5 cm. There is a suture at one pole of the short axis designated as 12:00. The specimen is inked yellow over the 12:00 aspect, blue over the 6:00 aspect, serially sectioned perpendicular to the long axis, and submitted completely as follows:

    A1–A3—3:00 half of specimen
    A4–A6—9:00 half of specimen

Electronically Signed and Dated

Case Study 3.3

Patient: **Patient I**

Patient documentation: **Read Medical Report 3.3**

1. What is the diagnosis (description) that supports the medical necessity of this procedure?

   _____

2. Are there any secondary diagnoses present that required additional procedures?

   _____

3. What was the main procedure, and were other secondary procedures performed on this patient?

   _____

4. Do you believe you need additional documentation to correctly assign the Pathology and Laboratory codes to this record? If so, what is the additional documentation that you need?

   _____

5. Do you have any additional questions for the pathologist?

   _____

6. What is(are) the procedure code(s) you would assign to this case study?

   _____

   _____

MEDICAL REPORT 3.3

SURGICAL PATHOLOGY REPORT

PATIENT NAME: Patient I

MED REC #: 138977

DOB: 01/02

GENDER: M

SOC. SEC. #: XXX-XX-XXXX

PHYSICIAN: Dr. 013

COPY TO: Dr. 014

ACCESSION #: 1233389

ACCOUNT#: 019187765

TAKEN: (date) 4/2/XX

RECEIVED: (date) 4/2/XX

REPORTED: (date) 4/3/XX

LOCATION: Endoscopy

SPECIMEN(S) RECEIVED

Transverse Polyp

FINAL DIAGNOSIS

SPECIMEN SUBMITTED AS "TRANSVERSE POLYP":

> MILDLY CONGESTED, MILDLY EDEMATOUS COLONIC MUCOSA COMPATIBLE WITH BENIGN MUCOSAL EXCRESCENCE OR TAG.

SEE COMMENT

COMMENT

The above biopsy findings would be consistent with a benign mucosal excrescence or tag. The possibility that the biopsy may have missed a larger or more suspicious polyp cannot be excluded on the basis of this specimen alone. Clinical correlation is warranted in this regard.

REPORT ELECTRONICALLY SIGNED
DR NAME

MICROSCOPIC DESCRIPTION

A microscopic examination is performed and incorporated in the final diagnosis.

CLINICAL DIAGNOSIS & HISTORY

COLON SCREENING; POLYP, DIVERTICULOSIS

GROSS DESCRIPTION

Received in formalin labeled "transverse polyp" is a 0.2 cm aggregate of tan tissue which is submitted completely in one cassette.

Case Study 3.4

Patient: **Patient J**

Patient documentation: **Read Medical Report 3.4**

1. What is the diagnosis (description) that supports the medical necessity of this procedure?

   _____

2. Are there any secondary diagnoses present that required additional procedures?

   _____

3. What was the main procedure, and were other secondary procedures performed on this patient?

   _____

4. Do you believe you need additional documentation to correctly assign the Pathology and Laboratory codes to this record? If so, what is the additional documentation that you need?

   _____

5. Do you have any additional questions for the pathologist?

   _____

6. What is(are) the procedure code(s) you would assign to this case study?

   _____

   _____

MEDICAL REPORT 3.4

PATIENT NAME:	Patient J	ACCESSION #:	**C05**
MED REC #:	11122	ACCOUNT #:	
DOB:	2/5	TAKEN:	2/23/20XX
GENDER:	Female	RECEIVED:	2/23/20XX
SOC. SEC:	XXX-XX-XXXX	REPORTED:	2/24/20XX
PHYSICIAN:	Dr. 015	LOCATION:	Outpatient
COPY TO:	Dr. 016		

SOURCE OF SPECIMEN(S)

LT ABDOMINAL LYMPH NODE CT GUIDED BX (up to 5 slides)

PRELIMINARY CYTOLOGIC DIAGNOSIS

LYMPH NODE, LEFT ABDOMINAL, CT-DIRECTED NEEDLE BIOPSY:

MONOTONOUS INFILTRATE OF SMALL LYMPHOCYTES SUGGESTIVE OF LOW GRADE LYMPHOMA.

arm 2/24/20XX

CLINICAL HISTORY

LYMPH NODE ABD

MICROSCOPIC DESCRIPTION

A microscopic examination was performed and is incorporated in the final diagnosis.

GROSS DESCRIPTION

Received labeled "bx left lymph node ABD" are multiple cores of white tissue measuring 3.0 cm in aggregate length and less than 0.1 cm in average diameter obtained from CT-directed needle biopsy of left abdominal lymph node. Touch preps are stained and evaluated at the time of the procedure to assess specimen adequacy. The tissue cores are subsequently submitted completely in one cassette for routine processing and evaluation.

Electronically Signed and Dated

Radiology

Chapter Objectives

▶ Describe the format of the CPT Radiology section.

▶ Recognize terminology used in the Radiology section, including x-ray positions, modalities, and contrast media.

▶ Understand the difference between diagnostic and therapeutic radiology, including the need for supervision and interpretation and surgical code assignment.

▶ Recognize the significance of the Chargemaster and Superbill checklist forms for ordering and assigning codes.

▶ Correctly assign CPT codes and modifiers to radiology procedures.

Radiography procedures can be diagnostic or therapeutic. X-rays, using ionizing radiation or high-level energy, have particular qualities that are helpful to physicians to diagnose diseases and injuries and to treat certain diseases such as cancers. In most cases, an image is taken to verify the existence or absence of something (for example, a foreign body), to verify status (such as obstetric ultrasound checking for status of a fetus), or to check on patency (for example, fallopian tubes open versus closed). Radiation therapy is used to treat neoplasms; it may be the primary treatment or additional treatment with surgery or chemotherapy.

*A **radiolucent** substance or structure in the body (e.g., soft tissue) allows the passage of most of the x-rays. By allowing the x-rays to pass through, the*

Word Parts and Meanings of Medical Terms Related to Radiology

Word Part	Meaning	Example	Definition
angi/o	vessel	lymphangiography	Process of obtaining x-ray image of a lymph vessel
anter/o	front	anteroposterior	Pertaining to the front and the back
brachy-	near	brachytherapy	Therapy close to the lesion or tumor
cardi/o	heart	pericardiocentesis	Withdrawal of fluid from the sac surrounding the heart
chol/e	gall, bile	cholecystography	Process of obtaining x-ray image of the gallbladder
hyper-	excessive, above	hyperthermia	Increased temperature
ipsi-	same	ipsilateral	Same side
onc/o	cancer	oncology	Study of cancer
ultra-	above	ultrasound	Using high-frequency sound waves to obtain images
xer/o	dry	xeroradiography	Process of developing an x-ray with a dry powder instead of liquid chemicals

object(s) appear black on x-ray films. The lungs are an example of a radiolucent structure, with the air in the lungs not absorbing x-rays. Conversely, **radiopaque** *substances or structures (e.g., bones) absorb x-rays and thus produce distinct images on x-ray films. Bones absorb the x-rays, allowing only a small amount to pass through to the x-ray film. Another example of radiopacity occurs when fluid is present in the lungs, as in pneumonia. This causes the affected lung tissue to appear white on a chest x-ray. Figure 4.1 is a radiograph that was taken to verify the location of a foreign body (coin).*

To make radiolucent structures more visible, a contrast medium, such as dye, may be injected. This allows the target organ to be radiopaque. Often

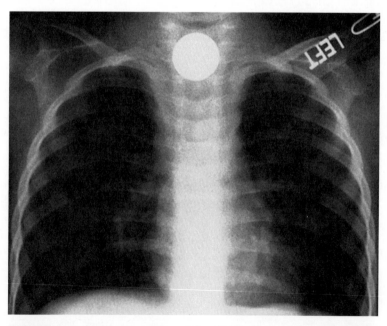

FIGURE 4.1 ■ Chest radiograph of swallowed foreign body, demonstrating impacted esophageal coin located at the thoracic inlet.

contrast media are used to provide a clearer picture, as in an arteriogram, when dye is introduced into the vasculature to provide a detailed outline of the internal surfaces of the blood vessels.

On completion of radiographic procedures, the radiologist is required to produce a written report. This report is dictated by the radiologist and transcribed into a final report. When voice-recognition software is used to create the report, it can be generated almost instantaneously if the radiologist edits while dictating. The resulting radiology report is an important **source document** *for the coder, who will use this report to assign CPT codes for radiologic procedures. Details of the procedure(s) are included, along with the diagnosis. Examples of actual radiology reports are included with the end-of-chapter coding practice exercises.*

Positioning and Body Planes

Correct positioning of the patient is critically important in both diagnostic and therapeutic radiology for accuracy and to avoid repeating x-rays unnecessarily. Exposing healthy tissue to x-rays can be detrimental and should be kept to a minimum because prolonged exposure to x-rays can actually cause conditions such as cataracts or radiation colitis. For this reason, radiologic technologists (radiographers) and technicians wear badges that measure the amount of radiation to which they are exposed. Lead aprons or shields are used for technologists and patients to protect healthy tissue during diagnostic and therapeutic procedures.

The **anatomic position** (Fig. 4.2) refers to the patient standing, facing forward, toes pointed forward, and palms open with the thumbs pointing away from the body. While the patient stands in this position, x-rays may be taken from back to front, or **posteroanterior** (PA), with the film in the front. A chest x-ray is often taken in the PA position. **Anteroposterior** (AP) x-rays are taken from front to back, with the film in the back.

When the x-ray is taken with the patient lying on his or her back (face up), the position is known as **supine.** Many x-rays are taken in this position, and in some modalities, such as magnetic resonance imaging (MRI), computed tomography (CT), and nuclear medicine, the machine moves around the supine patient to produce the images. X-ray images are also taken laterally from the side, or obliquely, which is from the side at an angle.

Body planes are imaginary lines that divide the body into sections. The **frontal plane** (also called coronal) divides the body vertically into anterior and posterior portions. The PA view of the chest is in the frontal plane. The **sagittal plane** divides the body vertically into right and left portions. The **midsagittal plane** divides the body vertically into halves. X-rays taken laterally are considered to be in the sagittal plane. The **transverse plane** is horizontal and divides the body into upper and lower portions. CT scans image the body in transverse "slices" to visualize internal organs.

Modalities for Imaging Services

A **modality** is a form of application or use of a therapeutic agent or regimen. The Radiology section of CPT is divided by modalities as follows:

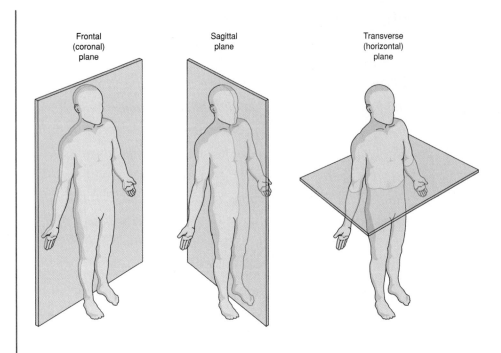

FIGURE 4.2 ■ Body planes (in anatomic position).

▶ Diagnostic Radiology
▶ Diagnostic Ultrasound
▶ Radiologic Guidance
▶ Mammography
▶ Bone and Joint Studies
▶ Radiation Oncology
▶ Nuclear Medicine

These sections are further divided anatomically and by types of procedures. Sections and subsections contain specific notes on how to assign the codes. Coders should read the information carefully before code selection. In the alphabetic index, first locate the appropriate modality, such as Nuclear Medicine, Radiation Therapy, X-ray, or Ultrasound, and then go to the tabular listing for detail. Table 4.1 shows the Radiology subsections and the code ranges that apply to each subsection.

TABLE 4.1 Radiology Subsections and Code Ranges	
Radiology Subsection	**Code Range**
Diagnostic radiology	70010–76499
Diagnostic ultrasound	76506–76999
Radiologic guidance	77001–77032
Mammography	77051–77059
Bone and joint studies	77071–77084
Radiation oncology	77261–77799
Nuclear medicine	78000–79999

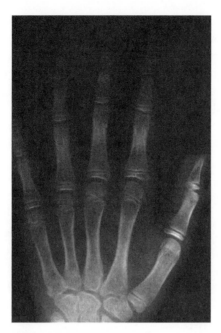

FIGURE 4.3 ■ Radiograph of a normal hand.

Diagnostic Radiology

Diagnostic radiology provides images of parts of the body to help establish a diagnosis. Plain x-rays are included in this section, including chest x-rays and those involving the spine and the upper or lower extremities (Fig. 4.3).

Invasive procedures such as hysterosalpingogram (HSG; Fig. 4.4) are also located in this section. Dye is introduced under slight pressure through the uterine cervix to provide an outline of the endometrium and the fallopian tubes. The resulting images are diagnostic, showing patency status. If one or

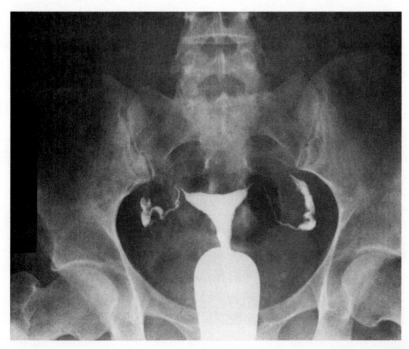

FIGURE 4.4 ■ Hysterosalpingogram.

both tubes are blocked (nonpatent), the HSG procedure itself may be therapeutic, resulting in opening of the tube(s).

Computed tomography, commonly known as a CT scan or CAT scan (computerized axial tomography), is also in this section. This modality uses a computer to form images called "slices" of the body around an axis. This process can be thought of as similar to the slices in a loaf of bread. CT scans can be performed with or without contrast. **Magnetic resonance imaging** (MRI) uses magnetic waves to produce images and, like CT scans, can be performed with or without contrast.

> **TIP** Many of the codes listed in the Vascular Procedures subsection are used in conjunction with one or more codes from the Surgery section. The radiologist's portion of the procedures is identified as "radiological supervision and interpretation." The additional surgery codes may be used by the radiologist or by a surgeon.

Diagnostic Ultrasound

Diagnostic ultrasound is a process in which sound waves are used to produce images. This type of imaging does not require the use of radiation, which makes it safe for everyone, including a developing fetus. Obstetric ultrasounds are commonly performed to monitor the progress of fetal development, by measuring structures such as the femur and the head (Fig. 4.5). Ultrasounds

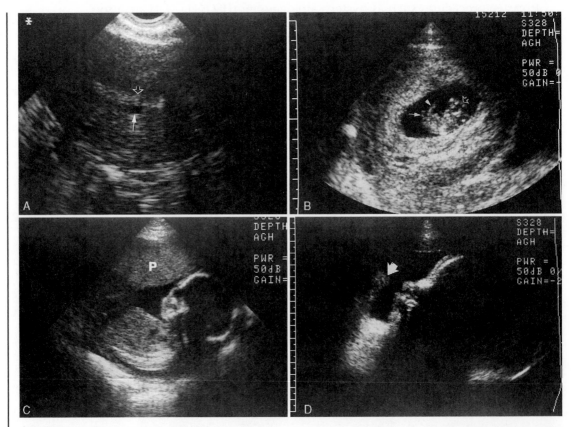

FIGURE 4.5 ■ Ultrasound images revealing the progressive growth and development of a normal embryo and fetus.

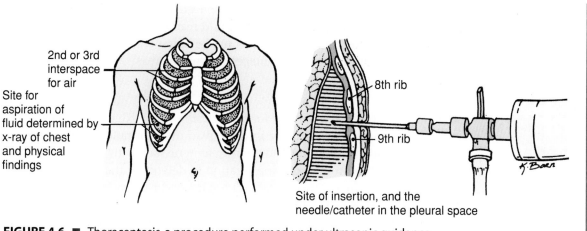

2nd or 3rd interspace for air

Site for aspiration of fluid determined by x-ray of chest and physical findings

8th rib

9th rib

Site of insertion, and the needle/catheter in the pleural space

FIGURE 4.6 ■ Thoracentesis, a procedure performed under ultrasonic guidance.

are useful for revealing fetal deformities or anomalies, as well. The physician is required to document all portions of the ultrasound procedure, so the coder should be able to provide the proper code to match the radiography report. CPT also provides nonobstetric codes for pelvic ultrasound, including procedures performed on male patients.

Radiologic Guidance

Ultrasonic guidance provides internal visualization during procedures such as pericardiocentesis, thoracentesis, and amniocentesis. Pericardiocentesis is performed to remove fluid from the sac surrounding the heart that occurs in a cardiac tamponade. Thoracentesis is performed to remove fluid from the chest that occurs in a pleural effusion (Fig. 4.6). Amniocentesis is performed to remove fluid from the amniotic sac to look for possible chromosomal abnormalities in a fetus. In each of these procedures, a needle is inserted into the body to withdraw fluid. Precision is required to avoid damage to internal structures such as the fetus or a lung. Other guidance procedures may be for biopsy, placement of radiation therapy fields, and aspiration of ova (for in vitro fertilization).

Radiologic guidance can also be accomplished with fluoroscopy, computed tomography, magnetic resonance, stereotactic localization, and mammographic guidance. A radiologic supervision and interpretation (S&I) code is assigned along with a surgical code. Additional information about S&I codes is provided later in this chapter.

Needle core biopsy of the breast: 19102, 76942

EXAMPLE

Mammography

Mammography is coded as screening or diagnostic. **Screening mammography** is routine periodic imaging, in most cases performed annually. If the patient or a physician detects a breast lump and a mammogram is ordered by the physician, this is **diagnostic mammography.**

Nuclear Medicine

Nuclear medicine imaging uses radioactive substances that emit gamma rays to produce images of different body parts. A gamma camera detects the gamma rays, and an image is produced. The resulting images show functionality of body parts or organs rather than just anatomy. This reveals both structure and function of an organ. The coder should read the descriptions carefully to ensure that the correct code choice is made. Some codes are for whole-body imaging, whereas others are for images of limited areas.

Radiation Oncology

Radiation oncology is treatment for cancer using either external beam radiation or **brachytherapy** (superficial or internal placement of radioactive elements). Services for patients requiring radiation treatment start with clinical treatment planning, which is an in-depth consultation to determine the proper treatment regimen for the patient. Treatments will usually occur several times a week for 3 to 4 months. To provide a focused entry point for the therapy and protect normal surrounding tissues, ports and shields (blocks) are used. Codes are assigned depending on the number of ports involved and the amount of radiation delivered in the treatment. (Detailed information about these topics may be found in the Radiation Therapy Coding portion of this chapter.)

Contrast Media

Many radiographic procedures can be performed with or without contrast media. Sometimes, when two body organs or parts are side by side, it is difficult to tell them apart radiographically because the density of the tissue is similar (e.g., kidney and liver). The advantage of a contrast medium is that body structures can be outlined and details visualized more readily.

The use of contrast media is particularly useful when trying to visualize blood vessels because they are inherently difficult to see and can be very tiny. **Angiography** is used for radiography of blood vessels after the injection of a contrast material. To be coded as "with contrast," a procedure must have contrast injected intrathecally (within the spinal cord), intra-articularly (within a joint), or intravascularly (within a blood vessel). Thecal refers to the sheath covering the spinal cord. Intrathecal contrast is used in CT, MRI, and magnetic resonance angiography (MRA) of the spine. The coder would assign additional codes 61055 or 62284 for the injection with these procedures.

EXAMPLE	*CT scan of the abdomen performed after oral ingestion of contrast medium: 74150*

Articular refers to joints. Intra-articular contrast is used in radiographic **arthrography** and may also be used with CT or MRI of a joint. The coder should look for terminology such as "with contrast" or "without contrast material followed by contrast material." If CT or MRI of a joint with contrast is performed without radiographic arthrography, three codes are required: one for the CT or MRI, a second code for the joint injection, and a third code for imaging guidance for the joint injection. Radiographic arthrography requires two codes: one for supervision and interpretation and one for the joint injection. In the latter case, fluoroscopic guidance for the joint injection is included in the S&I code. Vascular refers to blood vessels. Intravenous (IV) is the most common route of intravascular contrast medium injection, but intra-arterial can also be used. If the study is to be performed without and then with contrast, the noncontrasted study is performed first, followed by administration of the IV contrast and another study. This allows comparison of the images by the radiologist for a more accurate interpretation of the findings (Fig. 4.7).

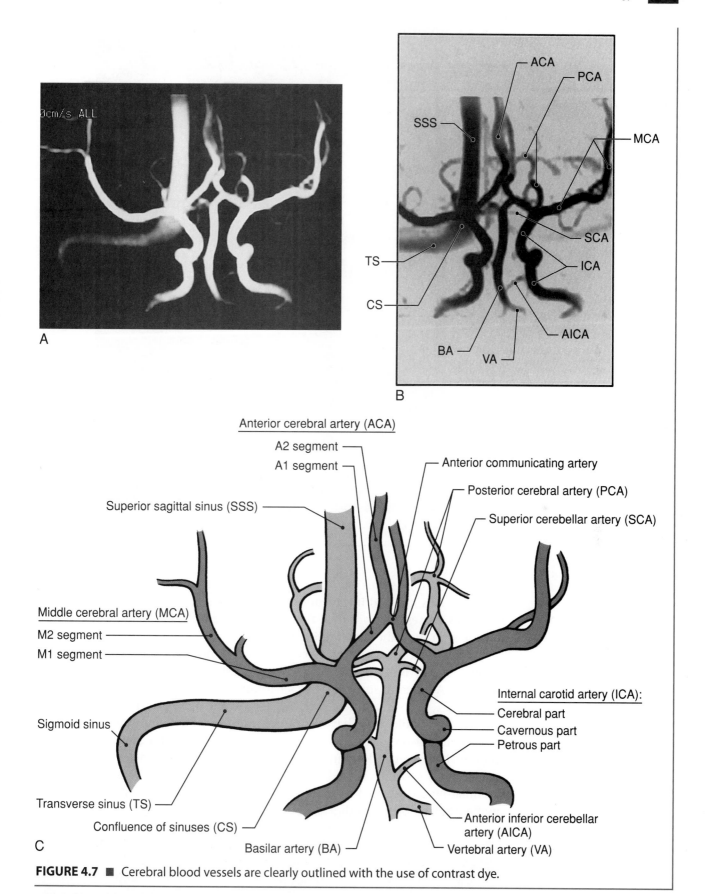

FIGURE 4.7 ■ Cerebral blood vessels are clearly outlined with the use of contrast dye.

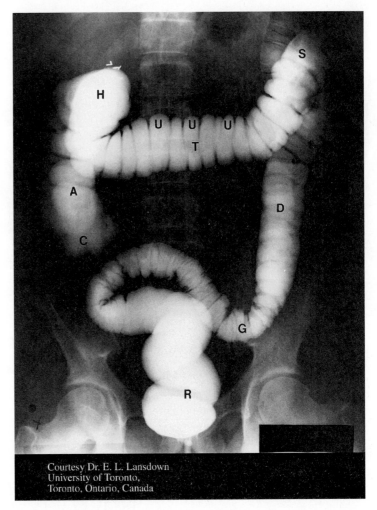

Courtesy Dr. E. L. Lansdown
University of Toronto,
Toronto, Ontario, Canada

FIGURE 4.8 ■ Barium enema examination of the colon.

Gadolinium is an IV contrast agent used only with magnetic resonance imaging. It is injected intravenously and collects at the area of abnormal tissue. This causes the abnormal tissue to be enhanced, and it appears brighter on the scan than the surrounding tissues.

Some procedures do not specify with or without contrast. For example, a barium enema (BE) uses barium, a white powder mixed with water, as a contrast medium. A different study is called a barium enema with air contrast, and a different CPT code is assigned for this test. Using these two types of contrast enables the radiologist to have a clearer picture of the internal structures, lumen or opening, of the colon. Barium enemas can be useful for diagnosing conditions such as diverticulosis and cancer. Figure 4.8 shows a single-contrast barium enema study (no air was used as an additional contrast). The barium swallow is a similar procedure used for imaging of the esophagus. Barium swallows can be useful for diagnosing conditions such as esophageal varices and cancer.

TIP When an abdominal x-ray such as a KUB (kidneys, ureters, bladder) is performed just before a BE, it is included in the BE (bundled) and is not coded separately. The radiologist may document this as a scout film in the written report.

Supervision and Interpretation

Some radiologic procedures have an invasive component (for example, interventional radiology). The radiologist's procedures are coded to signify "radiologic supervision and interpretation" if he or she performs supervision of the performance of the procedure and provides a written report of the findings. The radiologist may also perform the invasive component, which is usually represented by a code from the Surgery section of CPT. In this case, the radiologist's coder reports CPT codes for both components of the procedure, which will require at least two CPT codes. However, sometimes a surgeon will perform the surgical portion, and in that case, billing for the radiologist would only include the S&I code.

Cholecystectomy is surgical removal of the gallbladder, often performed laparoscopically because of the presence of gallstones. Before completing the surgical procedure, the surgeon would request a cholangiogram (Fig. 4.9) to ensure that no gallstones remain in the biliary tree. For the radiologist's billing, S&I code 74300 is submitted, and for the surgeon's billing, code 47563 is submitted.

EXAMPLE

Chargemaster and Superbill

Most hospitals use a Chargemaster to assign laboratory and radiology service CPT codes and charges. Chargemasters require ongoing review to assure that the new CPT codes and updates from insurance carriers have been entered correctly. Figure 4.10 shows an example of a radiology Chargemaster.

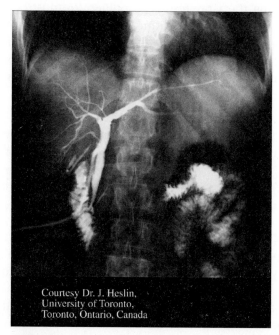

Courtesy Dr. J. Heslin, University of Toronto, Toronto, Ontario, Canada

FIGURE 4.9 ■ Cholangiogram.

General Radiology				
ChargeCode	Rev	ChargeCode Description	CPT/HCPCS	Charge
443500040	543	Orbit for foreign body	70030	$469.00
443500100	543	Mandible, limited	70100	$285.00
443500110	543	Mandible, complete	70110	$547.00
443500111	543	Optic foramina	70190	$347.00
443500120	543	Mastoid, limited	70120	$332.00
443500130	543	Mastoid, complete	70130	$572.00
443500140	543	Facial bones, limited	70140	$441.00
443500150	543	Facial bones, complete	70150	$525.00
443500160	543	Nasal bones, complete	70160	$371.00
443500200	543	Orbit, complete	70200	$459.00
443500210	543	Sinuses, paranasal, limited	70210	$277.00
443500220	543	Sinuses, paranasal, complete	70220	$484.00

FIGURE 4.10 ■ Sample radiology Chargemaster.

Some outpatient facilities or physician offices might use a Superbill (order form or encounter form) to check off procedures when they are requested. These forms are convenient for busy office staff, but need to be double-checked for CPT code updates at least annually or as required by CMS coding and billing policy changes/transmittals. Note that a diagnosis is required for medical necessity. An example of an Outpatient Radiological Order Form is shown in Figure 4.11.

Radiology Modifiers

Some radiology codes describe both a professional and technical component of the service. When the radiologist is only billing for his or her professional services (e.g., interpreting the x-ray results), modifier -26 must be used. Modifier -TC would be used by a free-standing clinic that is billing for the technical component of care (e.g., technicians, x-ray equipment and supplies). If neither modifier is used, it is assumed that the radiologist is billing for both professional and technical components (e.g., radiologist reads the films and owns the equipment).

TIP Separate codes are given for certain unilateral and bilateral procedures, such as mammograms, and a modifier should not be added. The -50 modifier should not be used if the code for the procedure is specified as "unilateral *or* bilateral."

Modifier -52 is used for reduced services. For example, a screening mammogram is only available as a bilateral procedure. If the procedure is performed unilaterally, a -52 modifier is appended to the 77057 code. There are some radiography codes that specify minimum views in the description. If one view is taken and no other code applies, the code for multiple views is used with -52 appended to signify that fewer views were taken. In addition, -52 is used if a scheduled procedure that does not require anesthesia is cancelled after preparation, but before initiation of the procedure.

Outpatient Radiological Order Form

Name: _____ Date of Birth: _____

Indication for Study/Medical Necessity:	ICD-9 Code

Special Instructions: _____

Physician Name: _____ Date: _____

General X-ray	CPT Codes	L	R
□ Abdomen AP	74000		
□ Abdomen obstruction series	74022		
□ Acromioclavicular joint	73050		
□ Ankle 2 View	73600		
□ Ankle 3+ View	73610		
□ Bone age Study	77072		
□ Bone Length Study	77073		
□ Chest 1 View	71010		
□ Chest 2 View	71020		
□ Chest 4+ View	71030		
□ Cervical Spine 2-3 view	72040		
□ Cervical Spine 4+ view	72050		
□ Cervical Spine with flexion/extension	72052		
□ Clavicle	73000		
□ Elbow 2 view	73070		
□ Elbow 3 view	73080		
□ Facial Bones 3 view	70150		
□ Femur	73550		
□ Fingers	73140		
□ Foot 2 view	73620		
□ Foot 3+ view	73630		
□ Forearm	73090		
□ Hand 2 view	73120		
□ Hand 3+ view	73130		
□ Heel/Calcaneus	73650		
□ Hip & Pelvis Child	73540		
□ Hip Unilateral 2 view	73510		
□ Hip bil 2 view w/Pelvis	73520		
□ Humerus	73060		
□ Hysterosalpingogram	74740		
□ Knee 1-2 view	73560		
□ Knee 3 view	73562		
□ Knee 4+ view	73564		
□ Lumbar Spine 2-3 views	72100		
□ Lumbar Spine 4+ views	72110		
□ Lumbar Spine flex/ext	72114		
□ Mandible 4 view	70110		
□ Nasal bones 3 view	70160		
□ Neck Soft Tissue	70360		
□ Orbits 4 view	70200		
□ Paranasal Sinuses complete	70220		
□ Pelvis 1 View AP	72170		
□ Rib Unilateral w/ PA chest	71101		
□ Ribs Bilateral w/PA chest	71111		
□ Sternoclavicular Joints	71130		
□ Sacroiliac joints	72202		
□ Sacrum & Coccyx	72220		
□ Scapula	73010		
□ Scoliosis	72090		
□ Scoliosis 36"	72069		
□ Shoulder 1 view	73020		
□ Shoulder 2+ view	73030		
□ Sinuses limited	70210		
□ Skeletal survey	77075		
□ Skull limited	70250		

General X-ray cont.	CPT Codes	L	R
□ Skull complete	70260		
□ Sternum	71120		
□ Thoracic Spine	72070		
□ Tibia & Fibula	73590		
□ Toes	73660		
□ Wrist 2	73100		
□ Wrist 3+ view	73110		
Mammography/Breast Imaging			
□ Mammography Screening	77057		
□ Mammography Diagnostic Bilateral	77056		
□ Mammography Diagnostic Unilateral	77055		
□ Breast Ultrasound	76645		
□ Breast Cyst Aspiration	19000		
□ Breast Cyst Aspiration additional	19001		
□ Breast Needle Core Biopsy	19102		
□ Review outside films for Breast core biopsy/aspiration	76140		
□ U/S guidance for needle placement	76942		
Bone Density			
□ (DXA) Bone Density	77080		
Ultrasound			
□ Thyroid	76536		
□ Abdomen complete	76700		
□ Abdomen limited	76705		
Retroperitoneal			
□ Kidney / Bladder	76770 / 76856		
□ Kidney / Aorta	76770		
□ Scrotum and Contents	76870		
□ Pelvis	76856		
□ Transvaginal Pelvis	76830		
□ Pregnancy >14 wks	76805		
□ Pregnancy <14 wks	76801		
□ Pregnancy ltd.	76815		
□ Pregnancy Transvaginal	76817		
□ Extremity for palpable abnormality	76880		
□ Venous Extremity Bilateral r/o DVT	93970		
□ Venous Extremity Unilateral r/o DVT	93971		
□ Abdomen Doppler / complete	93975		
□ Abd Doppler limited	93976		
□ Carotid Artery Bilateral	93880		
Fluoro			
□ Barium Swallow	74220		
□ Barium Enema w/ Air	74280		
□ Barium Enema w/o Air	74270		
□ Small Bowel	74250		
□ Upper GI w/Air	74247		
□ UGI Small Bowel	74249		

CT	With	W/O	Combined	CPT Codes
□ Abdomen include Pelvis if indicated				
□ Brain				
□ Cardiac Scoring				
□ Lower Extremity				
□ Pelvis				
□ Soft Tissue Neck				
□ Thorax				
□ Upper Extremity				
CT Maxillofacial				
□ Facial				
□ Orbits				
□ Sinuses				
□ Temporal Bone				
CT Spine				
□ Cervical Spine				
□ Lumbar Spine				
□ Thoracic Spine				

CT Angiography	With	W/O	Combined	CPT Codes
□ Abdomen				
□ Abdomen aorta & Bilateral runoff				
□ Chest				
□ Head				
□ Lower Extremity				
□ Neck				
□ Upper Extremity				

□ PT ALLERGIC – NO CONTRAST

MRI	CPT Codes
□ Abdomen MRA	74185
□ Abdomen	74181
□ Brain	70553
□ Brain MRI Circle of Willis	70554
□ Breast Rt □, Lt □,	77058
BiLat □	77059
□ Carotids Neck MRA	70547
□ Chest	71550
□ C-Spine	72141
□ Lower Extremity	73721
□ Lumbar Spine	72148
□ MRI Abd w/o & w/ contrast	74183
□ Neck	70543
□ Orbit, Face, Neck	70543
□ Pelvis	72196
□ Thoracic Spine	72146
□ TMJ Joint	70336
□ Upper Extremity	73221

FIGURE 4.11 ■ Sample radiological order form.

| EXAMPLE | *Radiographic examination of the hand, one view: 73120-52* |

HCPCS modifiers, -RT or -LT, may be used for specificity with extremities and other paired structures such as eyes, but some payers will not recognize these for right or left and payment is not affected.

Modifier -59 is used for a distinct procedural service. The modifier is appended to a CPT code representing a secondary procedure that was performed independent of the primary procedure. These may be bundled services, and as long as the service is performed separately from the primary service, it can be coded with the -59 modifier. Interventional radiology procedures would require -59 if a treated narrowed vessel requires a separate procedure for another narrowing (i.e., stenosis) that is not more accurately described by a different CPT code or modifier.

| EXAMPLE | *If the subclavian vein is involved with a second percutaneous transluminal angioplasty on the same day, 35476-59 and 75978-59 are assigned for the second procedure. The same codes without modifier -59 would be used for the first angioplasty performed on the subclavian vein that day.* |

Modifier -73 is used if a procedure is terminated after being prepped for surgery but *before* the induction of anesthesia. Modifier -74 is used if the procedure is terminated *after* induction of anesthesia. Used by hospitals for outpatient procedures, these two modifiers would most likely be used with interventional radiology procedures that require sedation. The physician assigns -53 for a discontinued procedure.

Modifier -76 is used if a procedure is repeated by the same physician on the same day. If a chest x-ray is performed multiple times in the same day (by the same physician), the initial procedure is coded 71010. The follow-up x-rays would be coded 71010-76. Modifier -77 is assigned if the repeated procedure is performed by a different physician.

The following chart provides a quick reference for modifiers used in coding radiology procedures.

Diagnostic Radiology and Mammography Coding

The Diagnostic Radiology section begins with the head and neck, and includes chest, upper extremities, lower extremities, and abdomen. Within these anatomic subsections are CPT codes for x-ray procedures, contrasted studies, CT scans, and MRI scans. The coder should be familiar with anatomy to ensure correct code selection. X-ray procedures, such as an ankle x-ray, are relatively straightforward. Many of these codes specify the number of views taken. Contrasted studies are invasive, and usually the code description includes the fact that the study uses contrast. Hysterosalpingogram and barium enema are examples of contrasted studies.

CT Scans

A CT scanner uses two-dimensional x-ray images taken around a single rotational axis to generate a three-dimensional image of internal structures. The

Quick Reference: Radiology Modifiers		
HCPCS II/ CPT Modifier	**Description**	**Explanation**
TC	Technical component	The technical component of a radiographic procedure includes all supplies, contrast media, equipment usage, and the technologist's time.
26	Professional component	Includes the radiologist's time in performing and interpreting the procedure(s).
50	Bilateral procedure	Used if the same procedure is performed bilaterally. It is not used if a separate code is available for a bilateral procedure or if the procedure is specified as "unilateral or bilateral."
52	Reduced services	If a procedure specified in a code as bilateral is performed unilaterally, a -52 modifier is appended to the code. This may also be used if a radiology code specifies minimum views in the description and fewer views are performed.
59	Distinct procedural service	Appended to a CPT code representing a secondary procedure performed independent of the primary procedure. These may be bundled services, but as long as the service is performed separate from the primary service, it can be coded with the -59 modifier.
73	Termination of procedure	Used if a procedure is terminated after being prepped for surgery but before the induction of anesthesia at the beginning of a procedure.
74	Termination of procedure	Used if the procedure is terminated after induction of anesthesia.
76	Repeated procedure	Used if a procedure is repeated by the same physician on the same day or during the postoperative period.
77	Repeated procedure	Used if a repeated procedure is performed by a different physician.

CT scanner emits x-ray pulses that take pictures of a thin slice of the body area being studied. The scanner can tilt to take pictures from different angles. The images are then saved on a computer. CT scans are often performed first without and then with contrast. Contrast is useful to make certain tissues stand out against other tissues. Doing both forms of the procedure provides a more detailed diagnostic scan for the radiologist to interpret.

MRI Scans

An MRI scanner sends magnetic radiowave forces many times stronger than the magnetic field of the earth through the body. The resulting effect on the body's atoms forces the nuclei to move into a different position. As they move back into place they send out radio waves that are picked up by the scanner. A computer turns the waves into a picture. As with CT scans, MRI scans may be performed with or without contrast. Figure 4.12 shows an MRI of the brain without contrast.

Mammography

Mammograms are categorized as screening or diagnostic. Screening mammograms are usually performed annually on asymptomatic patients and are coded as bilateral. If only one breast is imaged, the reduced services modifier, −52, is appended to the code. Typically two views of each breast are taken,

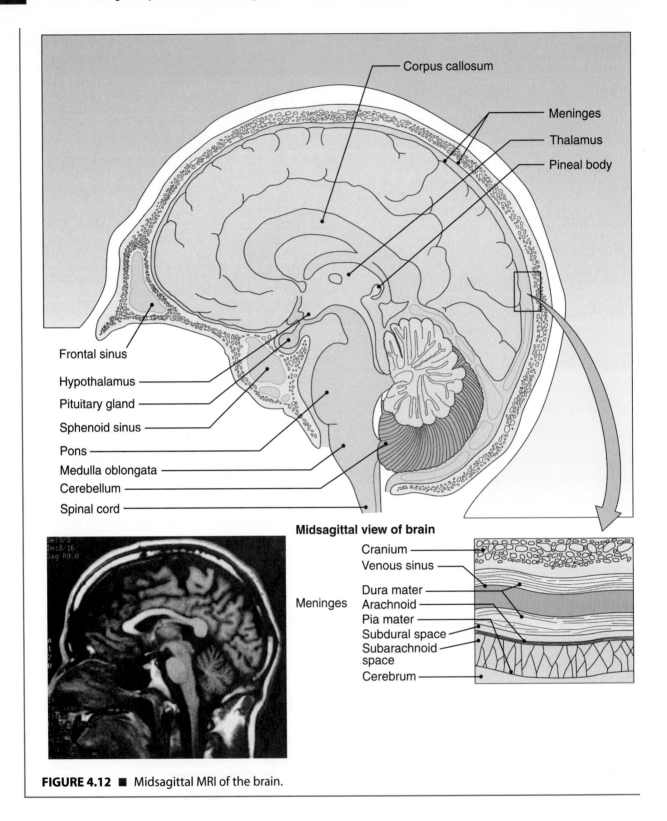

Frontal sinus

Hypothalamus

Pituitary gland

Sphenoid sinus

Pons

Medulla oblongata

Cerebellum

Spinal cord

Corpus callosum

Meninges

Thalamus

Pineal body

Midsagittal view of brain

Meninges

Cranium

Venous sinus

Dura mater

Arachnoid

Pia mater

Subdural space

Subarachnoid space

Cerebrum

FIGURE 4.12 ■ Midsagittal MRI of the brain.

but additional views can be obtained (Fig. 4.13). The number of views is not a determining factor in coding a mammogram as screening or diagnostic.[1]

Diagnostic mammograms are ordered when a physical examination reveals a suspicious mass or lump in the breast, the patient has an abnormal screening mammogram, or the patient has a history of benign or

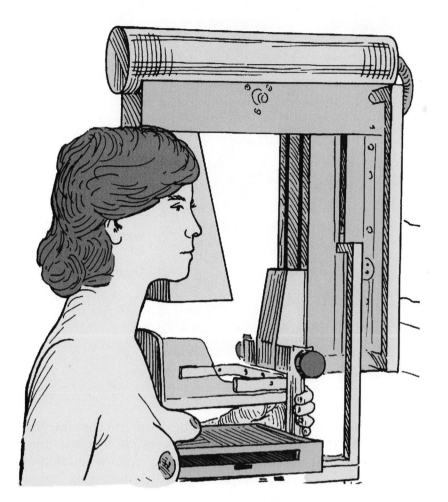

FIGURE 4.13 ■ Screening mammogram using a Lorad M-IV mammography machine.

malignant breast disease. Figure 4.14 shows an example of a normal mammogram. There are separate codes for bilateral or unilateral diagnostic mammograms. Computer-aided detection (CAD) codes are add-on codes. CAD produces a digitized image to be correlated with screening (77052) or diagnostic (77051) mammographic images. After correlating the mammogram images with the CAD, the additional information produced by the CAD may allow the radiologist to detect an abnormality at an earlier stage than without the CAD.

Focus on Medical Necessity

The concept of medical necessity and the importance of linking ICD-9-CM diagnosis codes with the CPT codes has been previously discussed. Medicare and other payers do not provide specific diagnosis codes for imaging procedures to prove medical necessity, but do offer guidelines. Medicare will not reimburse for tests not deemed medically necessary. The determination for payment eligibility should be made when the patient is scheduled for the test. If medical necessity for the procedure is not sufficient for payment, an Advance Beneficiary Notice (ABN) can be obtained if the patient wishes to proceed with the test. The ABN will allow the provider to bill the patient directly for the service.

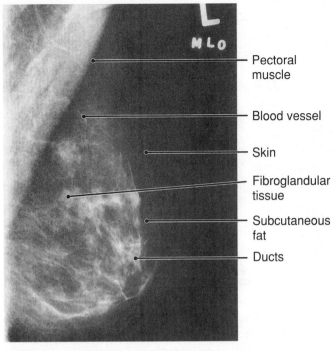

FIGURE 4.14 ■ Normal left breast mammogram.

For medical necessity of CT scans, the provider must determine that the test is necessary for the individual patient. CT scans can eliminate the need for other tests. However, the patient's presenting symptoms and initial diagnosis must be taken into consideration for medical necessity. Patterns of overuse of these scans may trigger an audit by the Centers for Medicare and Medicaid Services (CMS) to determine patterns of abuse.

For medical necessity of MRIs, Medicare specifically excludes blood flow measurement, imaging of cortical bone and calcifications, and procedures involving spatial resolution of bone and calcifications as indications for the scan. Similar to CT scans, the patient's signs and symptoms should be taken into account for medical necessity determinations for MRIs.

Medical necessity for a screening mammogram requires that several criteria be met. Screening mammograms are not reimbursed for a woman younger than age 35, and only one screening mammogram will be reimbursed during the 5 years between the ages of 35 and 40. After age 40, 11 months must pass after the month in which the prior screening mammogram was performed. Annual routine screening mammograms in asymptomatic women older than 40 are considered medically *appropriate,* but would not necessarily be covered by Medicare. Other payers may have different age guidelines for screening mammograms.

Medical necessity for a diagnostic mammogram requires that one of the following conditions be met:

▶ The patient has distinct indications for a mammogram, such as a breast mass discovered through a self-examination and confirmed by a physician.

▶ The patient has a personal history of breast cancer or biopsy-proven benign breast disease.

▶ The patient has an abnormal screening mammogram.

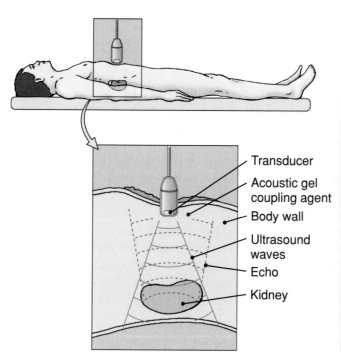

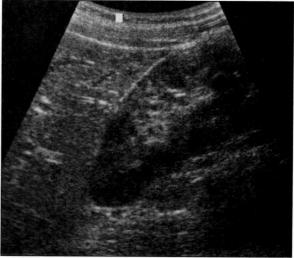

FIGURE 4.15 ■ Technique for producing an ultrasound scan of the upper abdomen. The image results from the echo of ultrasound waves from abdominal structures of different densities. The ultrasound image of the right kidney is displayed on a monitor.

Ultrasound Coding

Ultrasound uses sound waves to produce images of internal body structures (Fig. 4.15). The codes are described as limited or complete. The coder should read the notes within the Diagnostic Ultrasound subsection carefully to determine what constitutes a complete examination. If a complete examination is not carried out, then a limited examination code must be assigned.

Real-time ultrasound of the gallbladder with image documentation: 76705 **EXAMPLE**

One-dimensional ultrasounds can be A-mode or M-mode. A-mode refers to the amplitude of the sound waves being measured. Amplitude is the height reached on a graph corresponding to the strength of the sound wave. M-mode ultrasounds include recordings of body structures with amplitude and velocity. The display is shown by dots with the strength of the sound waves being given in brightness—the stronger the echo, the brighter the corresponding dot. The resulting image includes the motion of structures.

Two-dimensional ultrasounds are B-scans and real-time scans. Similar to M-mode, B-scans use brightness of dots determined by echo strength. The resulting image is a two-dimensional display of the anatomic structures. Real-time scans include display of both structure and motion with time in a two-dimensional image.

Nuclear Medicine Coding

Diagnostic nuclear medicine studies use specially formulated pharmaceuticals that emit gamma rays. Certain organs will take up the pharmaceuticals, and the resulting gamma rays are detected by a gamma camera and images are produced. Radiopharmaceuticals can be inhaled, ingested, or injected. Images show organ or tissue activity and viability. A common, well-known diagnostic nuclear medicine test is a bone scan (Fig. 4.16). This procedure is usually completed after cancer is diagnosed to determine whether there is bone metastasis.

Positron emission tomography (PET) and **single photon emission computed tomography** (SPECT) scanning measure certain functions of the body. PET scans of the heart are performed to assess viability of the heart muscle, metabolic activity of the heart, and perfusion of the heart muscle. Perfusion is the blood flow (circulation) that supports healthy cells. When the heart is injured or diseased, blood flow is inhibited, which damages the heart muscle cells and affects its function.

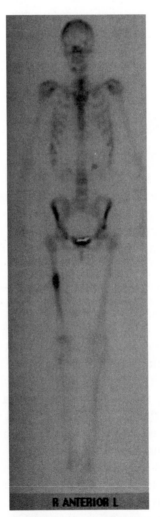
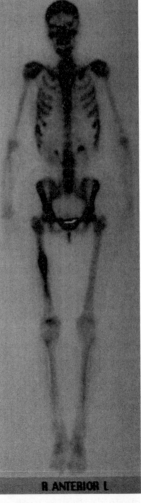

R ANTERIOR L

R ANTERIOR L

FIGURE 4.16 ■ Bone scan showing a lesion on the femur.

CPT codes for myocardial PET imaging are:

▶ *Metabolic evaluation 78459*

▶ *Single PET for perfusion 78491*

Brain evaluations with PET are coded:

▶ *Metabolic evaluation 78608*

▶ *Perfusion evaluation 78609*

SPECT scans provide three-dimensional (3D) computer reconstructed views or "slices" of an organ in varying depths. These 3D images are obtained by the gamma camera rotating 360 degrees around the patient, who is positioned on an imaging table. For heart tissue, the slices obtained can delineate myocardial tissue from nonmyocardial tissue. This is helpful in diagnosing small infarctions missed by other imaging techniques.

A **sentinel node scan** is a study to determine the first (closest) lymph node(s) to a cancerous tumor. This critical test can reveal possible spread (metastasis) of the disease. Under mammographic guidance (for breast cancer), a fine needle is placed in the tumor for localization, and the area surrounding the tumor is subsequently injected with a pharmaceutical. The radioactive tracer migrates to the sentinel node. Then a nuclear scan is performed to determine the location of the sentinel node. This enables the surgeon to remove only specifically affected lymph nodes and leave healthy nodes in place.

Sentinel node scan, including injection of radionuclide and scintigraphy imaging: 78195

Nuclear medicine can also be therapeutic. For example, iodine pills ingested by patients being treated for a hyperactive thyroid cause ablation (destruction) of thyroid tissue. Iodine is preferentially taken up by the thyroid to manufacture hormones important to our metabolism. Supply of radiopharmaceuticals is not included in the CPT codes. To receive payment for these supplies, the facility billing must include HCPCS Level II codes.

Interventional Radiology Coding

Interventional radiology procedures can be diagnostic, therapeutic, or both. The procedures begin with the introduction of a catheter into a blood vessel. A catheter is a tiny tube inserted into an artery or vein for various reasons, such as to withdraw or instill fluids or dye. This puncture is assigned a CPT code from the Surgery section. Other surgery codes are assigned for moving the catheter into additional vessel(s). Surgery codes may be reported by a radiologist or a surgeon. Interventional radiology procedures also require a supervision and interpretation (S&I) code from the Radiology section. All vessels injected with dye and areas imaged are coded and reported by the radiologist. The S&I code represents the effort involved in studying the visualized vessel.

If an additional puncture is required for access to vessels in a different location, the second puncture is also assigned a CPT code. Nonselective placements mean that the punctured vessel is the vessel to be studied, and the catheter is not moved. The only exception to this is the aorta, which is always considered nonselective regardless of the puncture site.

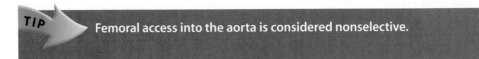

TIP   Femoral access into the aorta is considered nonselective.

Selective catheterization occurs when the catheter is moved into another vessel beyond the aorta or initially punctured vessel (Fig. 4.17). Catheter placements can also be described as contralateral or ipsilateral. Contralateral placements indicate that the catheter is moved to the opposite side of the body once introduced into the blood vessel. Ipsilateral placements advance only on the same side of the body.

In selective catheterization, the catheter is advanced into a vascular tree, known as a vascular family. As in a tree, the vascular family branches off the trunk into secondary and tertiary branches. First-order selective catheterization is the first branch studied, second-order selective catheterization is the secondary branch, and third-order selective catheterization is the tertiary branch. As each branch is traversed, this information must be documented in the report of the procedure for accurate coding. The coder codes only the highest order of selectivity for each branch of a vascular family, which is the final position of the catheter, because reaching the third order required traversing the first- and second-order branches. If additional second- or third-order selective catheter

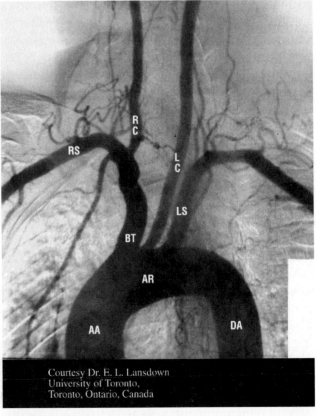

Courtesy Dr. E. L. Lansdown
University of Toronto,
Toronto, Ontario, Canada

FIGURE 4.17 ■ Aortic angiogram.

placements are performed within a vascular family (from the same first-order artery or vein), these procedures are coded 36012 (for venous system), 36248 (arterial system below the diaphragm), or 36218 (arterial system above the diaphragm). The latter two codes (36248 and 36218) are add-on codes used in addition to the initial second- or third-order vessel placements.

In addition to diagnostic catheter placements, therapeutic procedures can be performed, which require additional surgical codes. Angioplasty uses a balloon to dilate a narrowed vessel. Angioplasty codes are assigned per vessel treated, not per stenosis. Surgical codes are specific to the artery treated. Radiologic S&I codes for angioplasty are general, with three categories:

- ▶ Peripheral artery.
- ▶ Aorta, renal, or visceral artery.
- ▶ Venous.

Stent placement can be performed in conjunction with angioplasty. Codes are assigned per vessel treated, not per lesion. Catheter placement is coded as in diagnostic angioplasty. Angioplasty may be coded separately if:

- ▶ There is a suboptimal result.
- ▶ Treatment is of an area not treated by the stent.
- ▶ Treatment is for dissection or stent-induced stenosis.

Follow-up angiogram is not coded because it is bundled with the larger stent placement procedure.

Atherectomy is performed by shaving plaque from the inside of a blood vessel. The surgical codes are specific to the approach (percutaneous or open) and artery treated. S&I codes are delineated by peripheral and visceral arteries. A separate code is needed for catheter placement and diagnostic angiography done before the atherectomy, if there are no prior studies. Atherectomy codes are assigned per vessel treated, not per stenosis. Follow-up angiogram is not coded because it is bundled with the atherectomy.

Radiation Therapy Coding

Radiation therapy is treatment for cancer supervised by a radiation oncologist. This therapy can be delivered either externally or internally. In either case, the objective is to kill cancer cells while sparing surrounding healthy tissue. This is done with ports to direct radiation to a specific area and blocks to shield healthy tissue from the radiation. With external beam radiation, the high-energy rays are directed at the cancer.

Brachytherapy is the term for internal treatments. In this treatment, radioactive seeds are implanted into the diseased tissue. Both external beam radiation and brachytherapy may require multiple treatment sessions. A large radiation dosage may be divided into portions, and this is often referred to as fractionation. This technique results in the same amount of radiation, but in smaller divided doses, which causes less damage to the surrounding healthy tissues.

The patient's initial encounter with the radiation oncologist will allow for review of the patient's history and clinical picture to determine whether the patient is a candidate for radiation therapy. Codes for these consultations are assigned from the Evaluation and Management (E/M) section. Follow-up office visits for counseling and recommendations for care are also coded from the E/M section.

Radiation therapy codes begin with clinical treatment planning. These are assigned by the radiation oncologist based on whether the planning process for patient treatment is simple, intermediate, or complex. In planning for radiation therapy, the physician must take into account possible surgery and other therapy, tests to determine the size and depth of the tumor to be treated, calculation of the radiation dose to be delivered, and necessary ports for delivery of treatments.[2] After these factors have been considered, the physician determines a prescription for treatment.

Calculation of the radiation dose to be administered is called **dosimetry.** The dosage is calculated in units of absorbed radiation called rads and grays (Gy). One hundred rad units equals one Gy. This must be carefully calculated to ensure the correct depth and strength of therapy. During these calculations, the size and shape of ports is determined. Precise dose delivery is important for optimal patient treatment.

The next step in treatment is simulation. Simulation can be simple, intermediate, complex, or three-dimensional. It can be performed on a dedicated simulator, a radiation therapy treatment unit, or a diagnostic x-ray machine. Simulation always occurs before beginning the radiation therapy treatments. During simulation, the treatment area may be marked, the patient may be aligned with lasers, and additional aids may be developed to help with positioning of the patient for treatment.

Delivery of external beam radiation is coded according to the number of areas of treatment, the number of ports within the treatment area, and the number of megavolts (MeV) used in the treatment. External beam radiation therapy is usually given on consecutive days and may last weeks to months. The duration of treatment depends on tumor size and location in addition to other factors. Codes for the radiation oncologist's services should be assigned from the Radiation Treatment Management portion of the CPT manual. These codes cover multiple treatments and may include review of dosing, positioning of the patient, and patient evaluation.

EXAMPLE	*Code 77427 is assigned for each of five fractions or treatment sessions. It is possible that two distinct treatment sessions will occur in 1 day, and this would count as two sessions. These sessions are continually added for billing, and at the end of treatment, if there are at least three sessions, the 77427 code may be submitted for the final sessions.*

Brachytherapy involves the insertion of a radioisotope internally. The radiation sources can be implanted permanently (sources) or temporarily (ribbons). The corresponding codes are divided into simple, intermediate, and complex application. A simple application has one to four sources or ribbons; a complex application has more than 10. Codes are also given for the approach, being intracavitary, interstitial, or surface applications. In addition, CPT provides codes for high-intensity brachytherapy, depending on the number of source positions or catheters. Radiation therapy is administered through the catheters directly at the tumor being treated. Intracavitary brachytherapy is delivered into a cavity, such as the uterus in the treatment of cervical cancer. Interstitial brachytherapy is delivered into tissue, such as the prostate gland in the treatment of prostate cancer.

SUMMARY

Radiologic procedures such as x-rays and scans are important diagnostic tools. Some procedures can also be therapeutic, as in the case of radiation therapy for cancer treatment. An extensive evaluation process occurs before the initiation of radiation therapy. Coders should be aware of these steps, as well as the specific treatment plan, to properly code for all services provided. Certain therapeutic imaging services include codes from the Surgery section of CPT, along with a supervision and interpretation (S&I) code from the Radiology section. Accurate coding of interventional radiology procedures requires both the operative report and the radiology report.

Freestanding imaging clinics may bill separately for the technical component of imaging services, and a modifier –TC should be appended to the CPT codes. The physician's coder uses modifier -26 to explain that he or she is only billing for the professional component of the service.

TESTING YOUR COMPREHENSION

1. What is an example of a modality in imaging services?

   _____

2. Why are contrast media used in some imaging procedures?

   _____

3. What is another term for computed tomography?

   _____

4. What is the modifier used to indicate that fewer than the minimum number of images were obtained?

   _____

5. Which modality uses gamma rays to produce an image?

   _____

6. Which imaging procedure uses sound waves to produce images?

   _____

7. What is the modifier used for the professional component of a CPT code?

   _____

8. What is radiation therapy used to treat?

   _____

9. What modifier is used if an x-ray is repeated and reviewed on the same day by the same physician?

   _____

10. What are the required routes of administration for a procedure to be considered "with contrast"?

    _____

11. What is a sentinel node scan?

    _____

12. What is the difference between nonselective and selective catheter placement?

    _____

13. If a CPT code includes the terminology "unilateral or bilateral," is a modifier necessary to specify that it is a bilateral procedure? If so, which modifier?

    _____

14. Why might a woman have a diagnostic mammogram rather than a screening mammogram?

    _____

15. What is brachytherapy?

    _____

Chapter Review Exercises

CODING PRACTICE I

Directions

Use your CPT manual to code the following tests using codes from the Radiology section.

1. Shoulder x-ray, three views. _____
2. CT scan of the pelvis with contrast. _____
3. Schilling test. _____
4. Bilateral screening mammogram. _____
5. Nephrotomography. _____
6. Bilateral TMJ x-rays. _____
7. Transvaginal nonobstetrical ultrasound. _____
8. Nuclear medicine scan of the parathyroid. _____
9. Abdomen KUB. _____
10. Breast ultrasound. _____
11. Hysterosonography. _____
12. Gastric emptying study. _____
13. OB ultrasound, 17 weeks. _____
14. DXA scan for vertebral fracture assessment. _____
15. Chest x-ray, 5 views. _____
16. Neck MRA, without contrast followed by contrast material and further sequences. _____
17. Hysterosalpingogram, S&I. _____
18. Radiation therapy, 2 treatment areas, 3 ports, multiple blocks, 17 MeV. _____
19. PET myocardial imaging, metabolic evaluation. _____
20. CT guidance for placement of radiation therapy fields. _____
21. X-ray calcaneus, 3 views. _____
22. MRI scan, cervical spine, without contrast. _____
23. Thyroid ultrasound. _____
24. Whole body bone scan. _____
25. Complex therapeutic radiology treatment planning. _____

CODING PRACTICE II | Medical Record Case Studies

Directions

1. Carefully review the medical reports provided for each case study.
2. Research any abbreviations and terms that are unfamiliar or unclear.
3. Identify as many diagnoses and procedures as possible.
4. Because only part of the patient's total record is available, think about any additional documentation that you might need.
5. If appropriate, identify any questions you might ask the radiologist to code this case correctly and completely.
6. Complete the appropriate blanks below for each case study. Explain (in writing) questions 1–5 and assign the Radiology code(s) for question 6.

Case Study 4.1

Patient: **Patient K**

Patient documentation: **Read Medical Report 4.1**

1. What is the diagnosis (description) that supports the medical necessity of this procedure?

   _____

2. Are there any secondary diagnoses present that required additional procedures?

   _____

3. What was the principal or main procedure, and were other secondary procedures performed on this patient?

   _____

4. Do you believe you need additional documentation to correctly assign the Radiology codes to this record? If so, what is the additional documentation that you need?

   _____

5. Do you have any additional questions for the radiologist?

   _____

6. What is(are) the procedure code(s) you would assign to this case study?

   _____

   _____

GENERAL HOSPITAL
DEPARTMENT OF RADIOLOGY

PATIENT'S NAME:	Patient K
DATE OF BIRTH:	7/6
DATE EXAM PERFORMED:	9/9/20XX
HOSPITAL ROOM NO.:	645
RADIOLOGY FILE NO.:	2579811
REFERRING PHYSICIAN:	Dr. 017

PORTABLE CHEST 9-9 @ 2251

HISTORY: Chest pain.

There is a limited inspirational effort. This crowds the bronchovascular markings. Mild congestion is difficult to exclude. There are no focal infiltrates or effusions. The heart is at the upper limits of normal in size and there has been previous sternotomy.

IMPRESSION:

Limited inspirational effort. Mild congestion is difficult to exclude.

COMPUTERIZED TOMOGRAPHY OF THE BRAIN 9-10

HISTORY: Chest pain. Right-sided weakness and nausea.

There is an area of hypodensity involving the left frontal lobe. It is atypical in distribution, i.e., it does not follow a definite vascular distribution. Therefore, a contrast-enhanced exam is recommended for further evaluation in exclusion of underlying disease process. There is no hemorrhage. There is no extra-axial fluid collection. The ventricles and subarachnoid spaces appear normal.

IMPESSION:

Hypodensity left frontal lobe, though this could represent an infarct. Contrast-enhanced exam is recommended to evaluate for neoplasm or inflammatory process.

_____

Electronically Signed and Dated

Case Study 4.2

Patient: **Patient L**

Patient documentation: **Read Medical Report 4.2**

1. What is the diagnosis (description) that supports the medical necessity of this procedure?

   _____

2. Are there any secondary diagnoses present that required additional procedures?

   _____

3. What was the main procedure, and were other secondary procedures performed on this patient?

   _____

4. Do you believe you need additional documentation to correctly assign the Radiology codes to this record? If so, what is the additional documentation that you need?

   _____

5. Do you have any additional questions for the radiologist?

   _____

6. What is(are) the procedure code(s) you would assign to this case study?

   _____

   _____

GENERAL HOSPITAL
DEPARTMENT OF RADIOLOGY

PATIENT'S NAME:	Patient L	DATE OF BIRTH:	5/9
DATE EXAM PERFORMED:	11/7/20XX	HOSPITAL ROOM NO.:	502
RADIOLOGY FILE NO.:	2596621	REFERRING PHYSICIAN:	Dr. 018

BONE SCAN WHOLE BODY

INTERPRETATION REPORT

SCAN PERFORMED FOLLOWING INTRAVENOUS INJECTION OF 21 MS. TC. 99M-MDP

MULTIPLE AREAS OF INCREASED ISOTOPE UPTAKE SEEN IN MULTIPLE RIBS DUE TO OLD HEALED RIB FRACTURES. INCREASED ISOTOPE UPTAKE IN THE CLAVICLES DUE TO CLAVICULAR FRACTURES. INCREASED ISOTOPE UPTAKE IN THE LOWER CERVICAL SPINE DUE TO SEVERE DEGENERATIVE CHANGE. NO OTHER ABNORMAL AREA OF INCREASED ISOTOPE UPTAKE NOTED.

IMPRESSION

INCREASED ISOTOPE UPTAKE IN MULTIPLE RIBS AND CLAVICLES DUE TO OLD FRACTURES. INCREASED ISOTOPE UPTAKE IN THE LOWER CERVICAL SPINE DUE TO DEGENERATIVE CHANGE.

Electronically Signed and Dated

Case Study 4.3

Patient: **Patient M**

Patient documentation: **Read Medical Report 4.3**

1. What is the diagnosis (description) that supports the medical necessity of this procedure?

   _____

2. Are there any secondary diagnoses present that required additional procedures?

   _____

3. What was the main procedure, and were other secondary procedures performed on this patient?

   _____

4. Do you believe you need additional documentation to correctly assign the Radiology codes to this record? If so, what is the additional documentation that you need?

   _____

5. Do you have any additional questions for the radiologist?

   _____

6. What is(are) the procedure code(s) you would assign to this case study?

   _____

   _____

GENERAL HOSPITAL
DEPARTMENT OF RADIOLOGY

PATIENT'S NAME:	Patient M	**DATE OF BIRTH:**	7/22
DATE EXAM PERFORMED:	8/11/20XX	**HOSPITAL ROOM NO.:**	311
RADIOLOGY FILE NO.:	2295781	**REFERRING PHYSICIAN:**	Dr. 019

AP CHEST

Chest reveals a double festoon-type presentation with enlargement of the left atrium. The remaining cardiac silhouette appeared unremarkable. There does appear to be a slight accentuation of the vessels to the upper lobes as well as mild paucity of vessels to the lower lobes, which is characteristic of enlargement with a degree of mitral valvular involvement. Since there is no history of valvular heart disease we would suggest, without other changes noted, that the enlargement may well be due to either benign fibroma or benign myxoma of the left atrium. No calcification within this region is noted. We cannot exclude recent inflammatory mitral valvular disease.

IMPRESSION: Left atrial accentuation with minimal vascular findings as reported above without other cardiac changes which might suggest the possibility of a benign fibroma or benign myxoma of the left atrium. We cannot rule out inflammatory mitral valvular disease.

BARIUM SWALLOW

The barium swallow reveals no evidence of disease involving the oropharynx, hypopharynx, or esophagus. We do note, however, that the left atrium projects somewhat posteriorly due to enlargement, which may well be due to the previously suggested benign myxoma or fibroma of the left atrium.

IMPRESSION: Normal barium swallow except for enlargement of the left atrium as we stated above.

_____

Electronically Signed and Dated

Case Study 4.4

Patient: **Patient N**

Patient documentation: **Read Medical Report 4.4**

1. What is the diagnosis (description) that supports the medical necessity of this procedure?

    _____

2. Are there any secondary diagnoses present that required additional procedures?

    _____

3. What was the main procedure, and were other secondary procedures performed on this patient?

    _____

4. Do you believe you need additional documentation to correctly assign the Radiology codes to this record? If so, what is the additional documentation that you need?

    _____

5. Do you have any additional questions for the radiologist?

    _____

6. What is(are) the procedure code(s) you would assign to this case study?

    _____

    _____

GENERAL HOSPITAL
DEPARTMENT OF RADIOLOGY

PATIENT'S NAME:	Patient N	DATE OF BIRTH:	2/20
DATE EXAM PERFORMED:	9/8/20XX	HOSPITAL ROOM NO.:	344
RADIOLOGY FILE NO.:	2579899	REFERRING PHYSICIAN:	Dr. 020

IVP–IV PYELOGRAM

INTERPRETATION REPORT

Survey film reveals 8-mm calculus in the path of the proximal left ureter at the L3 level. Prominent excretion on the right. Normal right pyelocalyceal system and ureter. On the left, there is a prominent nephrogram. Delayed excretion. Moderate pyelocaliectasis and ureterectasis reaching the obstructing left ureteral stone at the L3 level at approximately 1 $\frac{1}{2}$ hours. Bladder is unremarkable. There is prostatic enlargement and calcification. Large post void residual.

_____

Electronically Signed and Dated

Case Study 4.5

Patient: **Patient O**

Patient documentation: **Read Medical Report 4.5**

1. What is the diagnosis (description) that supports the medical necessity of this procedure?

   _____

2. Are there any secondary diagnoses present that required additional procedures?

   _____

3. What was the main procedure, and were other secondary procedures performed on this patient?

   _____

4. Do you believe you need additional documentation to correctly assign the Radiology codes to this record? If so, what is the additional documentation that you need?

   _____

5. Do you have any additional questions for the radiologist?

   _____

6. What is(are) the procedure code(s) you would assign to this case study?

   _____

   _____

GENERAL HOSPITAL
DEPARTMENT OF RADIOLOGY

PATIENT'S NAME:	Patient O	**DATE OF BIRTH:**	8/6
DATE EXAM PERFORMED:	9/11/20XX	**HOSPITAL ROOM NO.:**	218
RADIOLOGY FILE NO.:	2579999	**REFERRING PHYSICIAN:**	Dr. 021

MRI OF THE BRAIN WITH CONTRAST

No previous films for comparison.

CLINICAL INDICATION: Left frontal brain lesion seen on CT scan. Patient has a history of ovarian cancer.

We performed multisequence, multiplanar images of the brain pre and post gadolinium enhancement. There is an area of increased signal intensity seen within the left parietal lobe involving both the gray and white matter in the region of the left centrum semiovale. This is seen as increased signal intensity on the T_2 weighted FLAIR and gradient-echo images. There is no evidence of enhancement within this region. It is having very little mass effect. On the diffusion-weighted images, there is increased signal in this region; however, I feel this is likely T_2 shine-through artifact. The ventricles are normal in size. No enhancing lesions are seen. There is no evidence of extra-axial collections. There is no evidence of hemorrhage.

IMPRESSION:

Infarct within the left parietal lobe as described above. This is likely subacute in nature. I would not favor a metastatic lesion as there is no evidence of enhancement on the post gadolinium images. I see no other enhancing lesions. A follow-up MRI would be helpful to confirm stability.

_____

Electronically Signed and Dated

Case Study 4.6

Patient: **Patient P**

Patient documentation: **Read Medical Report 4.6**

1. What is the diagnosis (description) that supports the medical necessity of this procedure?

   _____

2. Are there any secondary diagnoses present that required additional procedures?

   _____

3. What was the main procedure, and were other secondary procedures performed on this patient?

   _____

4. Do you believe you need additional documentation to correctly assign the Radiology codes to this record? If so, what is the additional documentation that you need?

   _____

5. Do you have any additional questions for the radiologist?

   _____

6. What is(are) the procedure code(s) you would assign to this case study?

   _____

   _____

GENERAL HOSPITAL
DEPARTMENT OF RADIOLOGY

PATIENT'S NAME:	Patient P	DATE OF BIRTH:	9/12
DATE EXAM PERFORMED:	1/6	HOSPITAL ROOM NO.:	222
RADIOLOGY FILE NO.:	2557921	REFERRING PHYSICIAN:	Dr. 022

FOLLOW-UP FETAL SONOGRAM

Patient referred for intrauterine pregnancy with no prenatal care; assess position, amniotic fluid, and fetal size.

There is a single fetus in breech presentation with an anterior placenta and normal-appearing amniotic fluid. Fetal measurements are as follows:

> Biparietal diameter = 7.1 cm
>
> Abdominal circumference = 24.0 cm
>
> Femur length = 5.6 cm
>
> Estimated fetal weight = 1,209 grams
>
> Average gestational age = 29 weeks

Fetal anatomic survey reveals a normal head shape with no evidence of intracranial anatomic disturbance. The neck appears normal with no evidence of cystic hygroma or encephalocele. The chest cavity appears normal with no evidence of intrinsic lung disease. The stomach is seen, as are both kidneys and urinary bladder. Umbilical cord insertion, four-chamber view of the heart, and spine were not fully visualized.

Biophysical profile score is 8/10. There is a nonreactive nonstress test. There is adequate fluid, good fetal breathing movement, tone, and movement.

IMPRESSION

Intrauterine pregnancy at 29.0 weeks with no evidence of amniotic fluid, gross fetal, or placental disorder.

_____

Electronically Signed and Dated

Case Study 4.7

Patient: **Patient Q**

Patient documentation: **Read Medical Report 4.7**

1. What is the diagnosis (description) that supports the medical necessity of this procedure?

   _____

2. Are there any secondary diagnoses present that required additional procedures?

   _____

3. What was the main procedure, and were other secondary procedures performed on this patient?

   _____

4. Do you believe you need additional documentation to correctly assign the Radiology codes to this record? If so, what is the additional documentation that you need?

   _____

5. Do you have any additional questions for the radiologist?

   _____

6. What is(are) the procedure code(s) you would assign to this case study?

   _____

   _____

MEDICAL REPORT 4.7

GENERAL HOSPITAL
DEPARTMENT OF RADIOLOGY

PATIENT'S NAME:	Patient Q	**DATE OF BIRTH:**	6/6
DATE EXAM PERFORMED:	9/13/20XX	**HOSPITAL ROOM NO.:**	321
RADIOLOGY FILE NO.:	25799654	**REFERRING PHYSICIAN:**	Dr. 023

ARCH AORTOGRAM, BILATERAL SELECTIVE CAROTID-CERVICAL AND CEREBRAL ARTERIOGRAMS

CLINICAL INDICATION: Carotid stenosis.

Informed consent was obtained after explanation of risks, benefits, and alternatives.

The right groin was prepped and draped in the usual sterile fashion. Using modified Seldinger technique, access is gained through the right common femoral artery. A 5 French vascular sheath was placed through the sheath and over the guidewire, a 5 French pigtail catheter was advanced in the position of the aortic arch. Arch aortogram in biplane projections was obtained. The catheter was exchanged for an H1H catheter, and the right common carotid artery is selectively catheterized. The right cervical and cerebral carotid arteriograms were obtained. The catheter was then removed. The sheath will be removed once the patient reaches the recovery room. The patient left the department in stable condition.

INTERPRETATION: Aortic arch is patent. There is normal branching pattern of the great vessels. Left vertebral artery is dominant.

Right common carotid artery is patent. There is approximately 50% stenosis of the proximal portion of the right internal carotid artery, slightly beyond the carotid bifurcation. There is also mild stenosis at the origin of the right internal carotid artery. The external carotid artery is patent. Remainder of the right ICA is patent. Intracranial flow is unremarkable.

Common carotid artery is patent. Carotid bifurcation is patent.

Approximately 1.5 cm beyond the origin, there is a short-segment stenosis of the left internal carotid artery, approximately 70% by NASCET criteria. The remainder of the left ICA is patent. External carotid artery is patent. Intracranial flow is unremarkable on the left. No significant cross-filling is seen.

IMPRESSION:

Moderate right and severe left external carotid stenosis.

_____

Electronically Signed and Dated

Case Study 4.8

Patient: **Patient R**

Patient documentation: **Read Medical Report 4.8**

1. What is the diagnosis (description) that supports the medical necessity of this procedure?

   _____

2. Are there any secondary diagnoses present that required additional procedures?

   _____

3. What was the main procedure, and were other secondary procedures performed on this patient?

   _____

4. Do you believe you need additional documentation to correctly assign the Radiology codes to this record? If so, what is the additional documentation that you need?

   _____

5. Do you have any additional questions for the radiologist?

   _____

6. What is(are) the procedure code(s) you would assign to this case study?

   _____

   _____

GENERAL HOSPITAL
DEPARTMENT OF RADIOLOGY

PATIENT'S NAME:	Patient R	**DATE OF BIRTH:**	4/28
DATE EXAM PERFORMED:	10/3/20XX	**HOSPITAL ROOM NO.:**	502
RADIOLOGY FILE NO.:	25824443	**REFERRING PHYSICIAN:**	Dr. 024

COMPUTERIZED TOMOGRAPHY OF THE THORAX

CLINICAL INFORMATION: Chest pain, rule out aortic dissection.

Axial images were obtained from the apices to just below the level of the diaphragm during the administration of intravenous contrast material. The scout image of the chest reveals some elevation of the right hemidiaphragm. The axial images reveal some calcifications of the thoracic aorta, but there is no evidence for thoracic aneurysm and there is no CT evidence for an aortic dissection. The aorta is well opacified. There are no effusions. There is no mediastinal or hilar adenopathy. When viewed at lung windows, there are no lung masses.

Images below the diaphragm reveal no adrenal masses. There are surgical clips in the gallbladder fossa. There is a tiny less than 1.0-cm cortical renal cyst on the right as well as 1.5-cm parapelvic cyst. There is a 1.2-cm cortical cyst involving the left kidney as well.

IMPRESSION:

1. No CT evidence for thoracic aneurysm or aortic dissection.
2. Previous coronary artery bypass graft.
3. No lung masses or pleural effusions.
4. Small bilateral renal cysts.

_____

Electronically Signed and Dated

Anesthesia

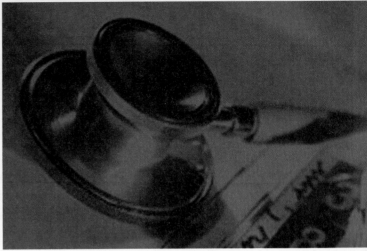

Chapter Outline

Types of Anesthesia
Locating Anesthesia Codes
Time Reporting for Anesthesia Services
Anesthesia Modifiers
Documentation Requirements
Special Reporting Requirements
Anesthesia Reimbursement
Summary
Testing Your Comprehension
Coding Practice I: Chapter Review Exercises
Coding Practice II: Medical Record Case Studies

Chapter Objectives

▶ Define types of anesthesia.
▶ Identify the modifiers used in the Anesthesia section.
▶ Explain the format of the Anesthesia section and subsections.
▶ Recognize terminology used in the Anesthesia section.
▶ Correctly assign CPT codes and modifiers to anesthesiology procedures.

Anesthesia procedure codes are included in section 00100 to 01999 and 99100 to 99140 of the CPT manual. **Anesthetics** *are drugs that reduce or eliminate body sensation.* **Anesthesiology** *is the medical specialty concerned with the pharmacologic, physiologic, and clinical bases of anesthesia and related fields, including resuscitation, intensive care, and the treatment of acute and chronic pain. An* **anesthesiologist** *is a physician (MD or DO) who specializes in anesthesiology and is legally qualified to administer anesthetics. A* **certified registered nurse anesthetist** *(CRNA) is also qualified to administer anesthetics. A CRNA is a licensed nurse who has completed additional specialized training in anesthesiology and passed a national certification examination.*

Word Parts and Meanings of Medical Terms Related to Anesthesia

Word Part	Meaning	Example	Definition
alges/o	sensitivity to pain	analgesia	No sensitivity to pain
-algesia	sensitivity to pain	hyperalgesia	Increased sensitivity to pain
-algia	pain	neuralgia	Nerve pain
esthesi/o	feeling, nervous sensation	anesthesia	No feeling
-esthesia	feeling, nervous sensation	paresthesia	Abnormal feeling (e.g., numbness and tingling)
par-	other than, apart from	parenteral	Drugs given by injection (apart from the digestive tract)
-logy	study of	anesthesiology	The study of anesthetics
-ist	specialist	anesthesiologist	A specialist (physician) in the use of anesthetic agents
-ic	pertaining to	anesthetic	A substance that reduces body sensation
-al	pertaining to	spinal	Pertaining to the spine. A spinal anesthetic
ven/o	vein	intravenous	Pertaining to within the vein

Types of Anesthesia

Types of anesthesia include:

▶ Local
▶ Regional
▶ General
▶ Monitored anesthesia care.

Local anesthesia affects a small part of the body (e.g., to suture a small cut or perform dental work). **Regional anesthesia,** using local anesthetic agents, affects a larger part of the body; an example is the epidural anesthetic administered in the lumbar area to relieve labor pain during delivery (Fig. 5.1). Local or regional anesthetics block sensory nerve impulses in the body area in which they are injected or applied. **General anesthesia** affects the whole body by depressing the central nervous system, producing a loss of consciousness. Like general anesthesia, **monitored anesthesia care** (MAC) uses sedatives and other agents, but the dosage is low enough that patients remain responsive and breathe without assistance. MAC is often used to supplement local and regional anesthesia, particularly during simple procedures and minor surgery to provide more comfort to the patient.[1] Additionally, MAC is used to monitor the patient's vital signs and physiologic progress during surgery in the event that an adverse response to the procedure requires conversion to a general anesthetic. MAC reimbursement is the same as with general anesthesia; however, the ICD-9-CM diagnosis code reported and supported by the anesthesiologist's documentation must establish the medical necessity for MAC.

Anesthetic agents may be injected into soft tissues, muscles, or veins; inhaled into the respiratory tract; or applied topically to the surface of skin or tissues. There are several types of regional anesthesia that are named after the area they are administered to that include spinal, caudal, **epidural,** peripheral nerve blocks, and **intravenous regional block** (Bier block; Figs. 5.2 and 5.3). Local and regional anesthetic agents include lidocaine (Xylocaine) and procaine (Novocaine), and general anesthetic agents include ether, halothane (Fluothane), nitrous oxide, and thiopental (Pentothal).

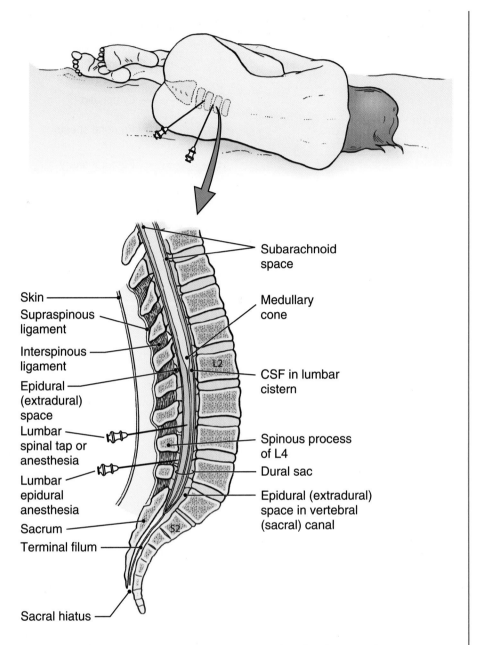

FIGURE 5.1 ■ Epidural anesthetic administered via lumbar spinal puncture.

Providers who can bill for anesthesia services include anesthesiologists, other physicians who perform anesthesia services, and certified registered nurse anesthetists (CRNA). Codes from the Anesthesia section of the CPT manual are specifically reported for the administration of regional and general anesthesia. The administration of local anesthesia for minor surgical procedures is usually not covered by payers because local anesthesia is paid under the global fee for the surgical procedure.

The following components, which must be clearly documented, are bundled into each anesthesia service code:

▶ Usual preoperative and postoperative visits
▶ Anesthesia care during the procedure

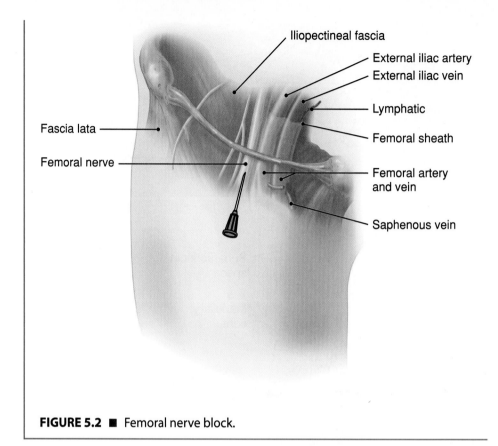

FIGURE 5.2 ■ Femoral nerve block.

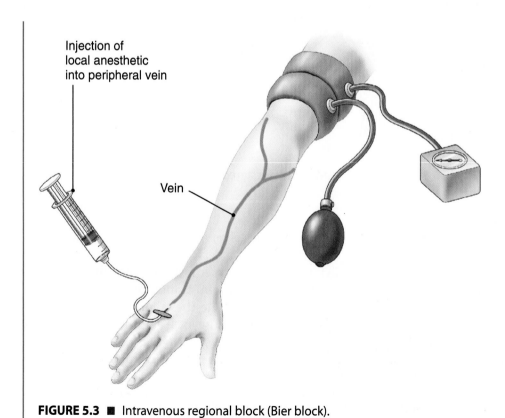

FIGURE 5.3 ■ Intravenous regional block (Bier block).

▶ Administration of fluids or blood products, as needed

▶ Usual monitoring services including:

    ▶ electrocardiogram (ECG to evaluate heart rhythm)

    ▶ monitoring vitals including temperature, blood pressure, respirations

    ▶ oximetry (administering oxygen)

    ▶ capnography (measuring carbon dioxide levels)

    ▶ mass spectrometry (used for respiratory gas analysis during surgery)

Unusual monitoring is not included in the anesthesia code and must be reported using separate codes. When the anesthesiologist bills for these services, the coder must append the modifier-59 to the procedure code. Modifier-59 describes that a distinct and separate service (apart from the anesthesia service) was performed.

Swan-Ganz catheter insertion (code 93503) to monitor the hemodynamic status of a critically ill patient or insertion of intra-arterial (code 36620) or central venous lines (codes 36555–36558) are documented and coded as unusual monitoring procedures.

EXAMPLE

Locating Anesthesia Codes

To locate an anesthesia code in the CPT manual, go first to the main term Anesthesia in the alphabetic index and search for the subterm that best describes the name of the anatomic site, specific procedure, or condition that relates to the anesthesia service provided. Note that anesthesia codes have five digits that begin with '0.' The subterm entries may provide a single code or range of codes for review. After locating the code(s) from the subterms in the alphabetic index, locate the code(s) within the tabular listing and carefully review all the notes to select the most precise code that describes the anesthesia service performed. As you begin the process of coding for Anesthesia services, be sure to review the Guidelines at the beginning of the Anesthesia section. The Guidelines provide important supplemental information to aid in correct code selection specific to anesthesia services.

Follow the universal coding rule to never code directly from the alphabetic index! Always check the notes provided in the tabular listing to prevent coding errors. Remember, indexes only serve as pointers to the correct information. The tabular listing contains the detailed information and descriptions you need for accurate code selection.

Locating the correct anesthesia code for a laparoscopic cholecystectomy procedure:

Step 1: Locate Anesthesia (main term) in the alphabetic index.

Step 2: Under Anesthesia, search for the subterm that best describes the name of a body (anatomic) site or specific procedure or condition that relates to the anesthesia service provided. The CPT manual is a multiaxial system, which means you can search for terms in different ways. Searching for gallbladder (the body site), gallstones or cholelithiasis (the condition), or laparoscopic cholecystectomy (the specific procedure), you will locate the subterm laparoscopic, with a range of codes to review that include 00790–00792, 00840.

EXAMPLE

Step 3: Locate the codes within the tabular listing and review the descriptions to find the correct code.

Step 4: You would choose code 00790 because it most closely describes the anesthesia service performed for a laparoscopic cholecystectomy.

00790 = Anesthesia for intraperitoneal procedures in upper abdomen including laparoscopy; not otherwise specified.

Note that the tabular listing for Anesthesia is divided into 19 subsections that describe anesthesia services provided to specific body sites (starting with the head and moving downward). The last four subsections provide anesthesia codes for radiological procedures, burn excisions or debridements, obstetrical procedures, and other procedures. An "unlisted anesthesia procedure," code 01999 is available at the end of the section. Generally, unlisted codes end in 99, and are only used when a more specific CPT code is not available for a procedure or service. They are considered the code choice of last resort, and act as a catchall for procedures not identified in the CPT or HCPCS Level II code listing. When using an unlisted anesthesia service code, a special report describing the medical necessity for the anesthesia service will need to be sent to the third-party payer (i.e., health-care plan or insurer) to substantiate reimbursement to the provider. Table 5.1 shows the Anesthesia subsections and the code ranges that apply to each subsection

Time Reporting for Anesthesia Services

The components of preanesthesia, intraoperative anesthesia and postanesthesia care are bundled into the each anesthesia service code. Also, reporting

TABLE 5.1 Anesthesia Subsections and Code Ranges	
Anesthesia Subsection	**Code Range**
Head	00100–00222
Neck	00300–00352
Thorax (chest wall and shoulder girdle)	00400–00474
Intrathoracic	00500–00580
Spine and spinal cord	00600–00670
Upper abdomen	00700–00797
Lower abdomen	00800–00882
Perineum	00902–00952
Pelvis (except hip)	01112–01190
Upper leg (except knee)	01200–01274
Knee and popliteal area	01320–01444
Lower leg (below knee, includes ankle and foot)	01462–01522
Shoulder and axilla	01610–01682
Upper arm and elbow	01710–01782
Forearm, wrist, and hand	01810–01860
Radiological procedures	01905–01933
Burn excisions or debridement	01951–01953
Obstetric	01958–01969
Other procedures	01990–01999

the actual time (in minutes) that the anesthesiologist spends providing the anesthesia service is required by Medicare and most other third-party payers. This is then factored into the payment to the provider. Anesthesia time starts when the anesthesia provider begins to prepare the patient for surgery and ends when the anesthesiologist has safely placed the patient under postoperative care (e.g., with the recovery room nurses) and is no longer in personal attendance of the patient. Many third-party payers may require the provider to report the total minutes as units of time based on an established formula.

> *Payers or providers may convert total time (in minutes) to units of time through the following formula: One unit of time is given for each 15 minutes of anesthesia time and fractions of it. Using this formula, a procedure requiring 120 minutes, converted to 15-minute intervals, results in 8 total time units. A procedure requiring 80 minutes, converted to 15-minute intervals, results in 5.33 total time units. Some carriers' guidelines may require coders to round up or round down fractions of anesthesia time units. Also, depending on the carrier, different unit intervals may be used.*

EXAMPLE

Anesthesia Modifiers

CPT was originally developed as a reimbursement system that provided a means for health-care providers to report their services to a payer. This understanding helps beginning coders appreciate the importance of assigning the correct modifiers to the anesthesia code in order for providers to receive fair reimbursement for the work they do. Patients who receive anesthesia are in various degrees of health, and the addition of modifiers helps to explain the overall clinical condition of the patient and, therefore, the extent of the work required by the anesthesiologist and other special circumstances that affect how payments to the provider are determined.

Anesthesia modifiers include:

▶ Physical status modifiers
▶ Qualifying circumstance codes (add-on codes that act as modifiers)
▶ CPT modifiers
▶ HCPCS Level II modifiers

Physical Status Modifiers

Physical status modifiers (P1–P6) are appended to the anesthesia codes to describe the various levels of complexity of the anesthesia services provided to the patient. The physical status modifiers are consistent with the American Society of Anesthesiologists (ASA) classification of patient health status, and these definitions are published in each annual edition of the ASA Relative Value Guide (RVG) and in the AMA's CPT manual. The ASA also provides a relative value description, called base or basic unit values, for each modifier. The physical status modifier class for the patient is assigned and documented in the medical report by the anesthesiologist (e.g., preanesthesia report or note). The following table outlines the physical status modifiers used with anesthesia codes.

Quick Reference: Physical Status Modifiers Added to Anesthesia Codes		
Physical Status Modifier	**Description**	**Example(s)**
P1	Normal, healthy patient	Patient in good health with no chronic conditions
P2	Patient with a mild systemic disease	Essential hypertension Adult-onset diabetes
P3	Patient with severe systemic disease	Type 1 insulin-dependent diabetic Severe coronary artery disease with unstable angina
P4	Patient with severe systemic disease that is a constant threat to life	End-stage heart, lung, or kidney disease
P5	Moribund patient who is not expected to survive without the operation	Flailed chest and massive hemothorax from a motor vehicle accident Ruptured aortic aneurysm
P6	Declared brain-dead patient whose organs are being removed for donor purposes	Organ harvesting from a donor declared brain-dead

Qualifying Circumstance Codes

Qualifying circumstance codes 99100–99140 are add-on codes that act as modifiers. They are found in both the Anesthesia Guidelines and in the Medicine section of the CPT manual. Qualifying circumstance codes are used to describe situations in which anesthesia services were provided under difficult circumstances. These codes indicate that the patient has a particular condition or conditions that pose unusual anesthetic risks. Qualifying circumstance codes are add-on codes and cannot be used alone. They must always be preceded by the anesthesia code and physical status code. The following table outlines the qualifying circumstance add-on codes used with anesthesia codes.

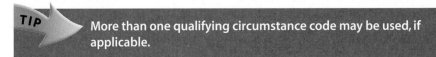

TIP More than one qualifying circumstance code may be used, if applicable.

Quick Reference: Qualifying Circumstance Codes	
Qualifying Circumstance Code	**Description**
+99100	Anesthesia for a patient of extreme age: younger than 1 year and older than 70
+99116	Anesthesia complicated by the utilization of total body hypothermia
+99135	Anesthesia complicated by the utilization of controlled hypotension
+99140	Anesthesia complicated by emergency conditions Emergency is defined as a situation in which the delay in treatment of the patient would lead to a significant increase in the threat to life or body part

CPT Modifiers

The following table shows CPT modifiers commonly used with anesthesia codes.

Quick Reference: Anesthesia Modifiers

CPT Modifier	Description	Explanation
22	Unusual procedural services	Reported to identify that the anesthesia service provided was greater than what would usually be required for the procedure. A special report will usually need to be submitted to the payer to justify the use of modifier-22.
23	Unusual anesthesia	Reported when the anesthesia administered (general or regional) is administered for a procedure that usually requires a local anesthetic only (such as a special circumstance for a child or elderly or disabled person). A special report will usually need to be submitted to the payer to justify the use of modifier-23.
32	Mandated services	Reported when payer mandates a service.
47	Anesthesia by surgeon	Physicians who provide anesthesia in addition to performing a procedure must add modifier-47 (anesthesia by surgeon) to the procedure code (10021–69990). Modifier-47 cannot be used with codes from the Anesthesia section (00100–01999).
51	Multiple procedures	Used to identify that multiple anesthesia services were provided on the same day or during the same operative episode. The first procedure listed should identify the main or most resource-intensive service provided. Secondary services should be appended with modifier-51.
59	Distinct procedural service	Used to identify that the procedure or service was distinct or separate from the other services provided on the same day.

Modifier-47 (anesthesia by surgeon) cannot be used with codes from the Anesthesia section.

HCPCS Level II Modifiers

The following table shows HCPCS Level II modifiers commonly used with anesthesia codes.

Quick Reference: HCPCS Level II Modifiers Used with Anesthesia Codes

HCPCS II Modifier	Description
AA	Anesthesia services personally performed by the anesthesiologist.
AD	Medical supervision: more than 4 concurrent cases by the physician.
G8	MAC for a deep, complex, or markedly invasive procedure.
G9	MAC for a patient with a history of severe cardiopulmonary condition.
QK	Medical direction of 2–4 concurrent anesthesia practices involving qualified individuals.
QS	Monitored anesthesia care (MAC). The QS modifier must be billed with an additional modifier to indicate whether or not the service was personally performed (AA, QZ) or medically directed (QK, QX, QY).
QX	CRNA service, with medical direction.
QY	Medical direction of one CRNA by an anesthesiologist.
QZ	CRNA service, without medical direction.

EXAMPLES

1 – *Under the medical direction of the anesthesiologist, a CRNA provides spinal anesthesia for a 66-year-old male patient who is undergoing a transurethral resection of the prostate as a result of urinary retention from benign prostatic hypertrophy. The patient has mild emphysema changes in the lungs from smoking, essential hypertension, and hypercholesterolemia. Assign code 00914-P2-QX.*

2 – *An otherwise healthy 65-year-old female patient receives general anesthesia services from a CRNA for a radical abdominal hysterectomy as a result of postmenopausal bleeding. Assign code 00846-P1-QZ.*

3 – *An anesthesiologist administers spinal anesthesia to a 71-year-old male patient for transurethral resection of bladder tumors as a result of bladder cancer. The patient has chronic atrial fibrillation (on Coumadin, an anticoagulant drug), has severe CAD (coronary artery disease), status post 5-vessel CABG (coronary artery bypass grafting), and previous AMIs (acute myocardial infarctions) X2. Assign codes 00912-P4-AA and 99100.*

TIP

When anesthesiologists use the -QK, -QX, and -QY modifiers to bill for medical direction of a CRNA or qualified individual, the patient's medical record must include sufficient documentation to substantiate that the physician was involved enough in the patient's care to support the payment of a medical direction fee. When billing for medical direction services only, the anesthesiologist's fee is typically discounted (e.g., 50% reimbursement from a full fee received for modifier -AA).

Documentation Requirements

All the components of anesthesia care must be clearly documented in the patient's medical record by the responsible anesthesiologist or nurse anesthetist to substantiate that the services actually occurred. When procedures require more than a local anesthetic, preanesthesia notes, an intraoperative anesthesia report, and postanesthesia notes are required.

Preanesthesia Notes

The anesthesiologist or CRNA must document a preanesthesia evaluation before surgery. The preanesthesia evaluation may be written on a special report or documented in the physician's progress notes. Preanesthesia notes must include:

▶ Type of anesthesia to be used
▶ Planned procedure(s)
▶ Patient's previous drug and health history
▶ Past or present anesthetic problems or risks
▶ Findings from a physical examination
▶ Summary of laboratory data
▶ Preanesthetic medication to be administered
▶ Assigned physical status level (ASA 1–6) based on the preanesthesia assessment.

Anesthesia Report

The report describes the patient's condition monitored throughout the entire procedure. The anesthesiologist or nurse anesthetist is responsible for recording the information and authenticating (signing) the anesthesia report. The anesthesia report must include:

▸ Preoperative medication given (concentration, time given, and effect)
▸ Anesthetic agent(s) administered during surgery (amount, route of administration, effect, and duration)
▸ Monitoring vitals (e.g., temperature, pulse, respirations, blood pressure)
▸ Record of blood loss, blood transfusions, and IV fluids given

Postanesthesia Notes

The anesthesiologist, CRNA, or other qualified personnel must document a postanesthesia evaluation after surgery. The postanesthesia evaluation may be written on a separate special form or documented in the physician's progress notes. Postanesthesia notes must include:

▸ Patient's condition after anesthesia, specifying the nature and extent of any anesthesia-related complications
▸ Postanesthesia visits, describing the presence or absence of anesthesia-related complications

The Joint Commission (formerly JCAHO) is a private, not-for-profit organization that evaluates and accredits hospitals and other health-care organizations based on their compliance with predefined quality performance standards. To evaluate compliance, a Joint Commission survey includes a review of documentation taken from medical records, including anesthesia notes and reports. According to Joint Commission standards, at least one postanesthesia visit must be documented in the patient's health record that confirms the presence or absence of anesthesia-related complications. A visit is usually considered to occur apart from the operative or recovery area, and should be completed within 24 hours after surgery. Notes must specify the time and date, with one visit occurring soon after surgery and another after the patient has completely recovered.[2]

Special Reporting Requirements

A code from the Anesthesia section followed by a physical status modifier (P1–P6) is exclusively mandated for reporting anesthesia services to Medicare. In contrast, other third-party payers may require the anesthesiologist to report anesthesia services using codes from the Surgery section of CPT that describe the procedure performed followed by a physical status modifier (P1–P6). For example, a healthy adult patient is admitted for an initial inguinal hernia repair under a general anesthetic. For Medicare billing, the coder would assign 00830-P1. For commercial insurance billing, the coder would assign 49505-P1. Some publishers (e.g., ASA, Ingenix) provide surgical code to anesthesia code crosswalks to help coders in this process (see examples below).

CPT surgery code to anesthesia code crosswalk

 EXAMPLES

Surgery Code	Description	Anesthesia Code	Description
10060	I & D of abscess; simple or single	00400, 00300	Anesthesia for procedures on the integumentary system; NOS (00400 extremities, anterior trunk and perineum)

Surgery Code	Description	Anesthesia Code	Description
			(00300 muscles and nerves of head, neck, and posterior trunk)
10061	*I & D of abscess; complicated or multiple*	*00400, 00300*	*Anesthesia for procedures on the integumentary system; NOS (00400 extremities, anterior trunk and perineum)*
			(00300 muscles and nerves of head, neck, and posterior trunk)
10080	*I & D of pilonidal cyst; simple*	*00300*	*(00300 muscles and nerves of head, neck, and posterior trunk)*
10081	*I & D of pilonidal cyst; complicated*	*00300*	*(00300 muscles and nerves of head,neck, and posterior trunk)*
10120	*Incision and removal of FB, subcutaneous tissues; simple*	*00300, 00400*	*Anesthesia for procedures on the integumentary system; NOS (00400 extremities, anterior trunk and perineum)*
			(00300 muscles and nerves of head, neck, and posterior trunk)
10121	*Incision and removal of FB, subcutaneous tissues; complicated*	*00300, 00400*	*Anesthesia for procedures on the integumentary system; NOS (00400 extremities, anterior trunk and perineum)*
			(00300 muscles and nerves of head, neck, and posterior trunk)

FB = foreign body
I&D = incision and drainage
NOS = not otherwise specified

Anesthesia Reimbursement

Reimbursement for anesthesia services is calculated based on units of time, called **base units.** Each year, the American Society of Anesthesiologists (ASA) publishes a Relative Value Guide (RVG) that assigns base unit values to the anesthesia services documented by the anesthesia codes and their modifiers. The Centers for Medicare and Medicaid Services (CMS) also releases Anesthesia Base Unit Values, which are available for downloading (see CMS Anesthesiologists' Center 2008 Anesthesia Base Units by CPT Code at http://www.cms.hhs.gov/center/anesth.asp). The ASA and CMS set standards in the United States for anesthesia base units, and these values help payers establish anesthesia service fees.

If more than one procedure is performed during the same operative episode (for example, the patient is in an automobile accident and sustains

TABLE 5.2   Anesthesia Code Base Value Units

CPT Anesthesia Code	Anesthesia Procedure	Base Units
00100	Anesthesia for procedure on integumentary system of head or salivary glands, including biopsy; not otherwise specified	5
00102	Plastic repair of cleft lip	6
00103	Anesthesia for procedures in eye, blepharoplasty	5
00104	Anesthesia for electroconvulsive therapy	4
00120	Anesthesia for procedures on external, middle, and inner ear, including biopsy; not otherwise specified	5
00124	Otoscopy	4
00126	Tympanotomy	4
00140	Anesthesia for procedures on eye; not otherwise specified	5
00142	Lens surgery	4
00144	Corneal transplant	6

chest and leg injuries that both require surgery), the anesthesia code with the highest ASA value, along with the total time for both procedures, would be reported. Tables 5.2, 5.3, and 5.4 show how CPT procedure codes, physical status modifiers, and qualifying circumstance codes translate into CMS anesthesia base unit values.

TIP When multiple surgical procedures are performed under a single anesthetic administration, the code for the most complex procedure (the procedure with the highest base unit value) is reported first.

TABLE 5.3   Physical Status Modifier Base Value Units

Physical Status Modifier	Description	Base Units
P1	A normal, healthy patient	0
P2	A patient with a mild systemic disease	0
P3	A patient with severe systemic disease	1
P4	A patient with severe systemic disease that is a constant threat to life	2
P5	A moribund patient who is not expected to survive without the operation	3
P6	A declared brain-dead patient whose organs are being removed for donor purposes	0

TABLE 5.4	Qualifying Circumstance Code Base Value Units	
Qualifying Circumstance Code	Description	Base Units
+99100	Anesthesia for patient of extreme age, younger than 1 year and older than 70	1
+99116	Anesthesia complicated by utilization of total body hypothermia	5
+99135	Anesthesia complicated by utilization of controlled hypotension	5
+99140	Anesthesia complicated by emergency conditions	2

Reimbursement formulas vary among third-party payers, as do base unit values and the conversion factors relating to the locality in which services are provided. Some modifiers may also be excluded for payment.

Reimbursement Calculation

Anesthesia reimbursement is commonly calculated using the following payment formula:

$$(B + T + M) \times (CF) = Payment$$
(**B**ase unit value for the CPT code + **T**ime units + base unit value for **M**odifiers) × (Conversion Factor for the specific locality) = **P**ayment for anesthesia services

A **conversion factor** (CF) is a number assigned to convert a relative value for the anesthesia service to the payment in dollars based on the geographic location in which services are provided. Conversion factors vary and are adjusted for the overhead, labor, and malpractice costs associated with particular geographic locations. Table 5.5 provides examples of conversion factors for various cities and regions.

TABLE 5.5	Locality Conversion Factors for Anesthesia Services (2008)		
Carrier	Locality Number	Locality Name	2008 Anesthesia Conversion Factor
00590	04	Miami, FL	22.73
00590	99	Rest of Florida	20.59
00511	01	Atlanta, GA	20.06
00511	99	Rest of Georgia	19.54
00833	01	Hawaii/Guam	19.86
05130	00	Idaho	18.93
00952	12	East St. Louis, IL	20.99
00952	15	Suburban Chicago, IL	21.42
00952	16	Chicago, IL	21.97

EXAMPLE

Calculating Anesthesia Reimbursement
At a hospital in Miami, Florida, an anesthesiologist begins anesthesia preparation at 1:00 PM
for an otherwise healthy 75-year-old Medicare patient who is having a corneal transplant
surgery. The case ends at 1:45 PM when the anesthesiologist safely releases the patient to
recovery room personnel. Coded: 00144-P1-AA and 99100.
Corneal transplant surgery (00144) Base Unit Value = 6
Time (45/15) = 3
Physical Status Modifier (P1) Base Unit Value = 0
Qualifying Circumstance (99100) Base Unit Value = 1
Conversion Factor for Miami, FL = $22.73
(6) + (3) + (1) = 10 × $22.73 = $227.30 payment to anesthesiologist or CRNA (without
medical direction by a physician).

SUMMARY

Anesthesia codes are used to report services provided by anesthesiologists or other physicians and CRNAs. To locate an anesthesia code, begin by looking under Anesthesia in the alphabetic index. After locating the code(s) in the alphabetic index, then locate the code(s) in the tabular listing and carefully review all the notes provided to ensure that the most precise code that describes the anesthesia service performed is selected. Anesthesia codes range from 00100 through 01999 (excluding qualifying circumstance codes).

An appropriate physical status modifier (P1–P6) is attached to codes from the Anesthesia section. The physical status modifiers are consistent with the American Society of Anesthesiologists classification of patient health status. Other CPT or HCPCS Level II modifiers may also be required.

Specific qualifying circumstance codes describe situations in which anesthesia services are provided under difficult circumstances. More than one of these may be selected, if applicable. These are add-on codes and cannot be used alone. Some third-party payers require anesthesiologists to bill using the appropriate code from the Surgery section with a physical status modifier appended. When multiple surgical procedures are performed under a single anesthetic administration, the code for the most complex procedure (the procedure with the highest base unit value) is reported first.

TESTING YOUR COMPREHENSION

1. What are the different types of anesthesia and how do they affect the body?

   _____

2. What components are bundled into the Anesthesia service code?

   _____

3. What is the first thing you do to locate a CPT Anesthesia code?

   _____

4. What is the second thing you do to locate a CPT Anesthesia code?

   _____

5. How are the subsections of the Anesthesia tabular listings arranged?

   _____

6. What are some common types of regional anesthesia?

   _____

7. What type of anesthesia is usually not covered by a payer but is part of a global fee for surgery?

   _____

8. In what way is MAC different from general anesthesia?

   _____

9. What is the formula for anesthesia reimbursement?

   _____

10. How is time described for anesthesia reporting?

    _____

11. How many subsections are in the tabular section for anesthesia?

    _____

12. What organization publishes an annual Relative Value Guide (RVG) that helps to establish payment fees for anesthesia services?

    _____

13. When can modifier-47 be used as part of documenting anesthesia services?

    _____

14. What providers can bill for anesthesia services?

    _____

15. What modifier must be attached to unusual monitoring services (e.g., Swan-Ganz catheterization) that are coded separately from the anesthesia code?

    _____

16. What is a conversion factor (CF)?

    _____

17. What is the main difference in reporting anesthesia codes to Medicare versus reporting to a commercial or private payer?

_____

18. Why is it advisable or not advisable to code directly from the CPT alphabetic index?

_____

19. How are total minutes of anesthesia time commonly converted to base units of time?

_____

20. What codes are used to describe that the anesthesia services were provided under difficult or extreme circumstances (i.e., high-risk patients)?

_____

CODING PRACTICE I   Chapter Review Exercises

Directions

Using your CPT manual, code the following anesthesia services for Medicare and non-Medicare claims. Include the anesthesia code, physical status modifier, and qualifying circumstance code, if applicable. Add HCPCS Level II modifiers to the Medicare cases only.

Medicare Claims

1. A 72-year-old woman trips and falls in a mall parking lot. She receives general anesthesia services from the anesthesiologist for an open treatment with pinning of a distal radial fracture. The patient has a history of type 2 diabetes and hypertension_____

2. A 69-year-old man receives general anesthesia services from the anesthesiologist for coronary artery bypass grafts × 4 vessels. The patient was admitted with acute myocardial infarction, severe coronary artery disease, chronic obstructive pulmonary disease, congestive heart failure, and essential hypertension. The anesthesiologist also inserts a Swan-Ganz catheter for monitoring during surgery _____

3. A 65-year-old man receives general anesthesia services from a CRNA under the medical direction of an anesthesiologist for an extracorporeal shockwave lithotripsy with water bath secondary to kidney stones. Patient also has hypercholesterolemia and hypertension _____

4. A 68-year-old man receives general anesthesia services from the anesthesiologist for a right lower lobe resection of the lung. The patient has RLL lung cancer, severe emphysema, coronary artery disease, and hypertension _____

5. A 73-year-old healthy woman receives general anesthesia services by a CRNA (without medical direction by a physician) for a needle biopsy of a thyroid nodule in the outpatient surgery clinic. The patient has a history of well-controlled type 2 diabetes and hyperlipidemia _____

6. A 75-year-old man receives general anesthesia services from the anesthesiologist for a left carotid endarterectomy. The patient has left carotid stenosis with 90% occlusion with a history of recurring transient ischemic attacks _____

7. A 66-year-old man receives general anesthesia services from the anesthesiologist for suture of an acute bleeding duodenal ulcer. The patient is status post cardiac pacemaker insertion for a 3rd-degree atrioventricular heart block, and has acute blood loss anemia associated with the ulcer, which requires a transfusion of 2 units of packed red blood cells _____

8. A 67-year-old woman receives general anesthesia personally from the anesthesiologist for a left hemicolectomy with temporary colostomy secondary to diverticulitis with bleeding. The patient also has acute blood loss anemia and is transfused with 2 units of packed red blood cells _____

9. A 68-year-old woman receives general anesthesia services from a CRNA, who is under the medical direction of an anesthesiologist, for a modified radical mastectomy with axillary lymph node dissection. The patient has left upper quadrant breast cancer with axillary node and liver metastases _____

10. A 78-year-old receives anesthesia services for a left above-knee amputation by the anesthesiologist, who is medically directing two other concurrent procedures by qualified individuals. The patient has arteriosclerosis of the left lower extremity with ulcer, coronary artery disease, hypertension, and type 1 insulin-dependent diabetes mellitus _____

Non-Medicare Claims

11. An otherwise healthy 12-year-old girl receives general anesthesia for laparoscopic appendectomy secondary to acute appendicitis _____

12. A 30-year-old woman receives general anesthesia services for a total abdominal hysterectomy secondary to dysfunctional uterine bleeding. The patient is mildly obese, has gastroesophageal reflux disease, and has a history of asthma _____

13. A 32-year-old woman receives general anesthesia services for a gastric stapling (gastroplasty) owing to morbid obesity. The patient is a type 1 diabetic and has hypertension and osteoarthritis in the knees

_____

14. A 6-year-old boy with Down syndrome with severe mental retardation and known severe congenital heart defects receives general anesthesia services for a tonsillectomy for chronic tonsillitis _____

15. A 51-year-old woman receives general anesthesia services for left-sided nephrectomy including removal of a section of the ureter. The patient has a history of recurrent urinary tract infections and newly diagnosed renal cancer _____

16. A 29-year-old man receives general anesthesia for a left-sided orchiectomy, inguinal approach for tumor removal. The patient has testicular cancer _____

17. A 45-year-old man receives general anesthesia services for an initial repair of a reducible right-sided inguinal hernia. The patient is mildly obese and has hypertension and hypercholesterolemia _____

18. A 37-year-old woman receives general anesthesia services for a partial thyroid lobectomy secondary to Grave's disease with a history of a recent thyrotoxic crisis _____

19. An otherwise healthy 42-year-old man receives general anesthesia services for an L2–3 laminectomy with diskectomy, anterior approach. The patient has lower back pain and radiculitis secondary to a herniated lumbar disk with myelopathy _____

20. A 35-year-old man receives general anesthesia services for right femoral-popliteal bypass. The patient has femoral-popliteal occlusive disease, right leg _____

CODING PRACTICE II   Medical Record Case Studies

Directions:

1. Carefully review the medical reports provided for each case study.
2. Research any abbreviations and terms that are unfamiliar or unclear.
3. Identify as many diagnoses and procedures as possible.
4. Because only part of the patient's total record is available, think about any additional documentation that you might need.
5. If appropriate, identify any questions you might ask the anesthesiologist to code this case correctly and completely.
6. Complete the appropriate blanks below for each case study. Explain (in writing) questions 1–5 and assign the anesthesia code(s) for question 6.

Case Study 5.1

Patient: **Patient S**

Patient documentation: **Medical Reports 5.1 through 5.6**

1. What is the principal or primary diagnosis for this patient?

   _____

2. What are the secondary or other diagnoses for this patient that present anesthetic risks, and what ASA class was assigned by the anesthesiologist?

   _____

3. What was the principal or main procedure, and were other secondary procedures performed on this patient?

   _____

4. Do you believe you need additional documentation to correctly assign the anesthesia codes to this record? If so, what is the additional documentation that you need?

   _____

5. Do you have any additional questions for the anesthesiologist?

   _____

6. What is (are) the anesthesia service code(s) you would assign to this case study?

   _____

   _____

MEDICAL REPORT 5.1

PRE-ANESTHETIC QUESTIONNAIRE
THIS PART TO BE FILLED OUT BY PATIENT OR FOR PATIENT BY RESPONSIBLE PERSON

The following questions have been designed for use by the Department of Anesthesia. They are to be completed prior to the operation. Please answer each question carefully and return the completed sheets to the nurse or anesthesiologist as soon as possible.

1. Have you ever had trouble with any of the following? Please circle—Heart, lungs, kidneys, stroke, diabetes, hiatal hemia, thyroid, high blood pressure, ulcers, communicable disease (e.g., Resistant Staphyococcus Aureus, ect.) and/or other medical problem (please explain):

    Asthma all her life – Lungs "not good." Angina
    Hypothyroid

2. List any other serious illnesses and dates of occurrence:

Illness	Date	Illness	Date

Illness	Date	Illness	Date

3. Please list all medicines used in the last six months:

    Toprol - XL   Heart patch
    Micro - K   Claritin
    Synthroid   Ibuprofen 600

4. List surgical operations and year.

    Hysterectomy

Appendix out	age 14	Bladder suspension	age 45
Surgery	Date	Surgery	Date
Gallbladder out	age 40	eye surgery	age 60
Surgery	Date	Surgery	Date

5. Do you smoke? __NO__ Did you ever smoke? __NO__ When did you stop? _____
    If yes, how much and how long? _____

6. your height __4'10"__ Your weight __Approx. 135__

7. To the best of your knowledge, do you have any loose, chipped, or capped teeth? Bridgework, full or <u>partial dentures</u>?		**(Yes)**	No
8. Have you had a <u>cold</u>, cough, flu, or fever in the last two weeks? Allergies		**(Yes)**	No
9. Have you taken any steroids, Cortisone or Prednisone in the last year?		Yes	**(No)**
10. Are you allergic to anything? If so, what is it and what reaction did you have?		**(Yes)**	No
Codeine, Penicillin, Iodine Dyes			
11. Have you or any member of your family ever had a bad reaction to local, general, or any anesthetic? If so, what kind? _____		Yes	**(No)**
12. Have you ever had a blood transfusion?		**(Yes)**	No
If yes, did you have any reaction to the blood?		Yes	**(No)**
13. Last time you had anything to eat or drink? __36 Hrs.__ Time ____ Date ____			
14. Is there any possibility that you could be pregnant? When was your last menstrual period? ____/____/____		Yes	**(No)**
Comment: _____			

Signature of M.D. Anesthesiologist reviewing history

__Dr. 025__

Signature of Patient or Responsible Person   __Patient S__

Time: __12:00__   Date: __8-8__

MEDICAL REPORT 5.2

CHARITY◊

Charity ◊ Hospital
Medical Center
Somewhere, Florida

THIS PART TO BE FILLED OUT BY YOUR ANESTHESIOLOGIST

Patient's previous anesthesia history discussed	☑ Yes ☐ No
NPO status verified	☑ Yes ☐ No
Patient accepts, understands and consents to _Spinal_ anesthesia.	☑ Yes ☐ No
Risk and benefits and possible complications, and alternatives explained.	☑ Yes ☐ No
Anesthesia care team approach may be utilized has been explained	☑ Yes ☐ No
Use and risk of anesthesia addressed	☑ Yes ☐ No
Questions answered and explained	☑ Yes ☐ No

Pertinent Diagnostic Findings

H/H – 15/48   ↑ WBC   A/W ↓ wheezing
Lyte – OK

CXR – cardiomegaly   Chest-Clear
EKG.   NSR

Pre Operative Remarks

Alert
Daughter Present

Physical Status (ASA)   1   2 ③ 4   5   E: ASHD, Asthma, elderly

Type of Anesthesia Planned: ___Spinal___

Pre-Op Evaluation: ___—___   Time: 16⁰⁵   ADDRESSOGRAPH
                                    Date: 8/8/20XX
___Dr. 025___
Signature of M.D.

PATIENT: Patient S
ACCT: 1234567   MR: 999999
ADM: 08/08 PHY: Dr. 025
RM: 210-B   SUR
DOB: 08/07/1941   066 F

Intra-Op MD: ___Dr. 025___   Time: 16²⁵
                                    Date: 8/8/20XX

MEDICAL REPORT 5.3

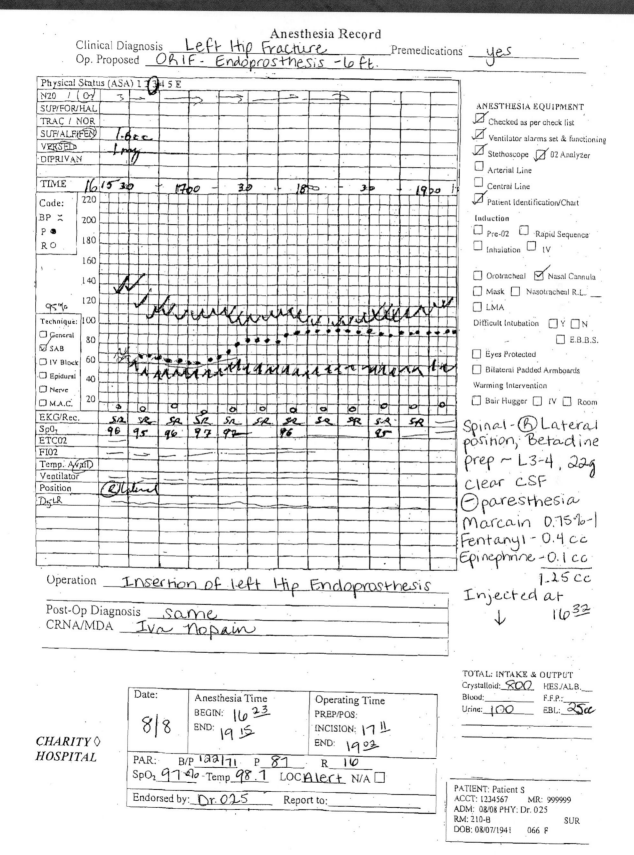

Anesthesia Record

Clinical Diagnosis Left Hip Fracture   Premedications yes
Op. Proposed ORIF - Endoprosthesis - Left.

Physical Status (ASA) 1 2 3 4 5 E

Operation Insertion of left Hip Endoprosthesis

Post-Op Diagnosis same
CRNA/MDA Iva Nopain

ANESTHESIA EQUIPMENT
☑ Checked as per check list
☑ Ventilator alarms set & functioning
☑ Stethoscope ☑ 02 Analyzer
☐ Arterial Line
☐ Central Line
☑ Patient Identification/Chart

Induction
☐ Pre-02   ☐ Rapid Sequence
☐ Inhalation ☐ IV

☐ Orotracheal ☑ Nasal Cannula
☐ Mask ☐ Nasotracheal R.L.
☐ LMA
Difficult Intubation ☐ Y ☐ N
                          ☐ E.B.B.S.
☐ Eyes Protected
☐ Bilateral Padded Armboards
Warming Intervention
☐ Bair Hugger ☐ IV ☐ Room

Spinal - ® Lateral
position, Betadine
prep ~ L3-4, 22g
clear CSF
⊖ paresthesia
Marcain 0.75% - 1
Fentanyl - 0.4 cc
Epinephrine - 0.1 cc
                1.25 cc
Injected at
  ↓   16³²

TOTAL: INTAKE & OUTPUT
Crystalloid: 800 HES./ALB.
Blood: F.F.P.:
Urine: 100   EBL: 25cc

**CHARITY ◊
HOSPITAL**

Date: 8/8

Anesthesia Time
BEGIN: 16²³
END: 19¹⁵

Operating Time
PREP/POS:
INCISION: 17¹¹
END: 19⁰²

PAR: B/P 122/71 P 81 R 16
SpO₂ 97% Temp 98.1 LOC Alert N/A ☐

Endorsed by: Dr. 025   Report to:

MEDICAL REPORT 5.4

CHARITY ◊ HOSPITAL
REPORT OF OPERATION

Patient Name: Patient S
Medical Record #: 999999
ATTENDING: Dr. 025
SURGEON: Dr. 026
Date of Procedure: 08/08/20XX
Date/Time Dictated: 08/08 1740
Page 1   Date/Time Transcribed: 08/09 1010

Patients

Date of surgery: 08/08/20XX

Preoperative Diagnosis: Fractured femoral neck

Postoperative Diagnosis: Fractured femoral neck

Surgeon: Dr. 026

Assistant:

Description of Procedure: Under satisfactory anesthesia, the patient was prepped and draped in the usual manner.

An incision was made and carried down through the subcutaneous tissue. Bleeders were bovied. The fascia was identified and split in the direction of its fibers. Retractor was placed. The external rotators were taken en masse. The capsule was opened. The formal neck fracture was identified.

The guide was placed one fingerbreadth above the lesser trochanter. The neck was cut. A jaws retractor was placed. We progressively reamed the shaft up to a 13.5, and we drove down to 13.5 broach, which fit quite nicely.

We then attempted to reduce the hip. The hip would not reduce using a 0 head. Prior to this, we had removed a 43 femoral head; using 0 neck and a 43 femoral head. We then released the iliopsoas. We still could not reduce the hip. We removed the broach and we recut the neck. At this point, though, the neck was too narrow in the mediolateral diameter to accept a 13.5 all the way down, so what we did was went back to the 12.0. We then reduced the hip, and the hip reduced quite nicely.

However, the 12.0 was not wide enough in the AP diameter, and was loose. So, therefore, we elected to go ahead and cement. A restrictor was placed. The shaft was copiously irrigated out with saline solution. Epinephrine soaked 4x4s, followed by dry 4x4s were packed on the shaft. A cement restrictor had been driven home prior to this. The cement was pressurized into the shaft. The prosthesis was driven home and held until the cement cured.

A 0 taper neck followed by a 43 femoral head was placed. The hip was taken through a range of motion and was totally stable. We then drilled two holes through the trochanter

MEDICAL REPORT 5.4 (CONTINUED)

Page 2

CHARITY ◊ HOSPITAL
REPORT OF OPERATION

and brought back the capsule and external rotators, and tied them back to the trochanter itself.

The fascia was closed with Vicryl. The subcutaneous tissue was closed with the same and the skin was closed with clips.

The patient left the operating room in satisfactory condition.

Electronically Signed and Dated

MEDICAL REPORT 5.5

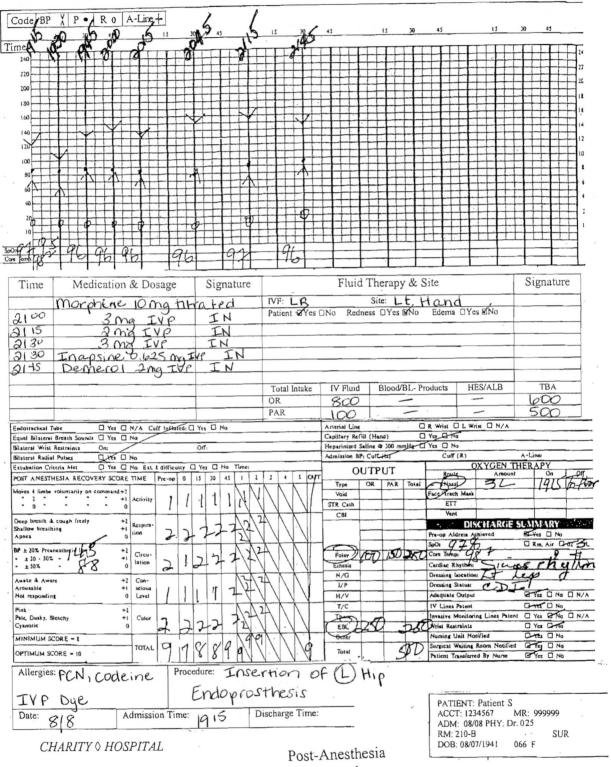

Time	Medication & Dosage	Signature	Fluid Therapy & Site				Signature
	Morphine 10 mg titrated		IVF: LR	Site: Lt. Hand			
2100	3 mg IVP	IN	Patient ☑Yes ☐No Redness ☐Yes ☑No Edema ☐Yes ☑No				
2115	2 mg IVP	IN					
2130	3 mg IVP	IN					
2130	Inapsine 0.625 mg IVP	IN					
2145	Demerol 2mg IVP	IN					

		IV Fluid	Blood/BL- Products	HES/ALB	TBA
	Total Intake				
	OR	800	—	—	600
	PAR	100	—	—	500

Procedure: Insertion of (L) Hip Endoprosthesis

Allergies: PCN, Codeine, IVP Dye

Date: 8/8   Admission Time: 1915   Discharge Time:

CHARITY ◊ HOSPITAL

Post-Anesthesia Record

PATIENT: Patient S
ACCT: 1234567   MR: 999999
ADM: 08/08 PHY: Dr. 025
RM: 210-B   SUR
DOB: 08/07/1941   066 F

MEDICAL REPORT 5.6

DATE:		POST ANESTHESIA RECOVERY ASSESSMENT AND NURSING NOTES		

#	TIME	Admission Assessment
①	1915	L.O.C. □ Unreacted ☑ Partially reacted □ Reacted
		Anes Type □ General ☑ S.A.B Moving lower extremities □ L □ R □ No □ IVB □ MAC □ EPI
		Position ☑ Supine □ Lateral □ L □ R HOB: *Flat Skin warm + dry*
		Cardiac Status: Rhythm: *NSR* Rate: *80's* Ectopy: *∅*
		Dressing: Site: *Lt hip* Types: *∅* Condition: *Stable*
		Drains: *c̄ Abductor pillow* Drainage Type: *∅*

Pulses are present by doppler. both feet are warm c̄ good capillary refill. No movement to feet ∂ this time.

	1930	*Dr. Bone ∂ bedside + ordered stat X-ray of the hip done.*
	1945	*X-ray done, Film was taken to Dr Bone in the O.R. who says everything is OK.*
	2000	*Pt states she feels confused + ∂ does not know what is going on. She was reassured.*
	2030	*Denies pain ∂ this time good movement to feet noted. Ted hose + Ice applied.*
	2100	*C/o pain Rx given.*
	2105	*Daughter allowed to visit, Pt does not appear confused ∂ this time.*
	2150	*To room 210 B.*

#	DIAGNOSIS	GOAL	EVALUATION (Goal achieved)	
			Yes	No
	(Circle any number of diagnoses made)	By the time of discharge from the PAR. The patient will:		
①	Alteration in neurological status	A. State person & place B. Exhibit no neurological deficit	1 ✓	
②	Alteration in comfort	Be relieved of pain	2 ✓	
3	Alteration in emotional status	Show no increased signs & symptoms of anxiety	3	
4	Alteration in fluid volume	Receive fluid volume as indicated by condition	4	
⑤	Alteration in mobility	Be able to move all unaffected extremities	5	
6	Alteration in respiratory status	Maintain O2 saturation of 95% or greater	6	
⑦	Alteration in circulation	A. Maintain vital signs ±20% of pre-po level B. Maintain adequate circulation to affected extremities	7 ✓	
8	Alteration in skin integrity	Develop no skin impairments	8	
9	Alteration in temperature	A. Be relieved of coldness & shivering B. Maintain core temperature between 95°F and 100°F	9	
10	Alteration in elimination	Maintain urine output ≧ 30cc/hour	10	
11	Alteration in gastrointestinal function	A. Be relieved of nausea B. Be relieved of vomiting	11	
⑫	Potential for presence of bleeding	Be free from excessive bleeding at operative site, dressings/drains	12 ✓	
13	Potential for injury	Remain free of bodily injury	13	
14	Alteration in hemodynamic status	Maintain hemodynamic stability	14	
15	Alteration in cardiac status	Asymptomatic or relieved of cardiac dysrhythmia(s)	15	
16	Other:		16	
17	Other:		17	
18	Other:		18	

Unresolved nursing diagnosis communicated: □ Yes   □ No   # *∅*

CHARITY ◊ HOSPITAL

PAR Nurse: *P. Ritchell*

Report To:

PATIENT: Patient S
ACCT: 1234567   MR: 999999
ADM: 08/08 PHY: Dr. 025
RM: 210-B   SUR
DOB: 08/07/1941   066 F

Case Study 5.2

Patient: **John Doe**

Patient documentation: **Medical Reports 5.7 and 5.8**

1. What is the principal or primary diagnosis for this patient?

   _____

2. What are the secondary or other diagnoses for this patient that present anesthetic risks, and what ASA class was assigned by the anesthesiologist?

   _____

3. What was the principal or main procedure, and were other secondary procedures performed on this patient?

   _____

4. Do you believe you need additional documentation to correctly assign the anesthesia codes to this record? If so, what is the additional documentation that you need?

   _____

5. Do you have any additional questions for the anesthesiologist?

   _____

6. What is(are) the anesthesia service code(s) you would assign to this case study?

   _____

   _____

MEDICAL REPORT 5.7

PLEASE ANSWER THESE QUESTIONS PRIOR TO YOUR OPERATION.

THIS WILL ASSIST THE ANESTHESIA DEPARTMENT IN MAKING YOUR PREANESTHESIA EVALUATION.

1. Please list any operations you have had and the dates.

_____
_____
_____

2. Please list any major illnesses you have had in your life.

_____
_____

3. Have you ever had any problem with a general anesthetic?_____ Yes ☐ No ☒
4. Have you ever had any problem with a spinal anesthetic? What?_____ Yes ☐ No ☒
5. Have any relatives had problems with anesthetics? (high fever or trouble breathing, etc) Yes ☐ No ☒
6. List any medications, pills, or injections you take(aspirin, aspirin compounds, birth control pills)_____
_____
7. Are you allergic to any medicines? What? __Feldene_____ Yes ☒ No ☐
8. Have you ever had high or low blood pressure? (Circle one)...................... Yes ☐ No ☒
9. Have you ever had trouble with your heart?................................ Yes ☐ No ☒
10. Have you ever had a heart attack? When?_____ Stroke? When?_____ Yes ☐ No ☒
11. Do you have angina chest pains? How often?_____ Yes ☐ No ☒
12. Do your feet or ankles swell?.. Yes ☐ No ☒
13. Do you have any problem with your breathing or lungs:
    Asthma   Wheezing   Emphysema   Cough up anything (Circle)
14. Do you smoke? How much? __'/2 pack__ How long? __45 yrs_____ Yes ☒ No ☐
15. Have you had a cold or flu in the last two weeks?........................... Yes ☐ No ☒
16. Does anyone in the family have a cold or flu?............................. Yes ☐ No ☒
17. Have you ever had any problem with your kidneys?............ __STONES__ Yes ☒ No ☐
18. Have you ever had any problem with your liver? Have you ever has hepatitis or yellow jaundice?............ Yes ☐ No ☒
19. How many drinks or beers do you have in an average week or day?___ __NONE__ _____
20. Do you have diabetes, arthritis, hiatal hernia, frequent heartburn, epilepsy, seizures, pass out?(Circle)..... Yes ☐ No ☐
21. Do you have any loose teeth, (false teeth) dentures, caps, bridges? (Circle)............ Yes ☐ No ☐
22. Do you wear contact lenses? If so please remove before surgery........... Yes ☐ No ☒
23. Have you taken prednisone, steroids, or ACTH in the past six months? Yes ☐ No ☐
24. Please check if you take any medicine, injections. Or pills for:
    Heart_____ Lungs_____ Diabetes_____ Kidneys_____ Blood pressure_____ .... Yes ☐ No ☒
25. Do you have any questions?_____

26. Height __5'7"__   Weight __148__

PRE-ANESTHESIA EVALUATION:

DATE __8/21__

☑GA   CXR-no pulm disease
☑SAB EKG-NSR, no acute
☐ REG   D's
Lungs clear |41 |104| 19
CV - WNL   4.0 |30 |1.3
ENT- WNL   10.9 15.7 ⟨188
                    41

ASA II

66 yowm for cysto, visual ureterotomy
PMH-NONE
PSH- GA-well tolerated
Meds- Zantac
All- Percodan- itch
     Feldene-swell
SO Hx-⊕Cigs-1/2 PPD x45 yrs ⊕dentures
       ∅ ETOH, OA, cataracts + asthma

Discussed SAB/advantages
& disadvantages -he
understands & agrees
to proceed.
              Iva
              nopain

_____
Signature of physician

POST-ANESTHESIA EVALUATION:

After reviewing the chart there appears
to have been no anesthetic complications

_____
Signature of physician

DATE __8/21__ TIME_____

MEDICAL REPORT 5.8

CHARITY◊HOSPITAL

Patient Name: John Doe   Hosp.Rm.No. 410-B   Med. Rec. No. 222222

OPERATIVE REPORT

Date of operation: 8/21

Preoperative Diagnosis: Difficulty with voiding with bladder neck obstruction versus urethral
stricture.

Postoperative Diagnosis: Bladder neck obstruction and no evidence of urethral stricture.

Operation: Cystoscopy, TUR of prostate

Surgeon: Yuri Retention, M.D.

Anesthesia: SAB

Indication: The patient is 66 years old and he has to sit to urinate and he has a large residual urine.

Procedure:

The patient was placed in the dorsal lithotomy position and prepped and draped in the usual standard fashion.
The 25 resectoscope sheath was introduced per urethra into the bladder and the entire length of the urethra
inspected and there were no urethral strictures. I proceeded to inspect the bladder neck and it showed a large
median lobe. The bladder was trabeculated with cellular formation and there were no tumor or stones. I
proceeded to resect the median lobe down to the capsule and the lateral lobes were likewise resected. The most
prominent finding was that of a median lobe obstruction. At the completion of this, the bleeders were
fulgurated and a #22 catheter was inserted and left indwelling. The patient returned to the recovery room in
good condition.

D: 8/21
T: 8/22

_____

Yuri Retention, MD

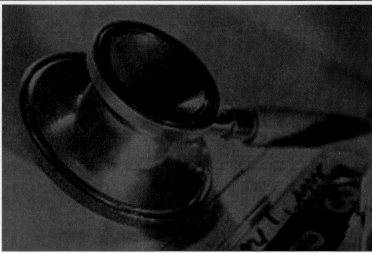

CHAPTER 6

Surgery

Chapter Outline

Surgery Guidelines
Surgery Subsections
Summary
Testing Your Comprehension
Coding Practice I: Review
Coding Practice II: Case Studies

Chapter Objectives

▶ Describe the format of the CPT Surgery section.
▶ Correctly locate surgery codes in the alphabetical index and tabular section of CPT.
▶ Recognize terminology used in operative reports for correct CPT code selection.
▶ Understand the concept of the surgical package.
▶ Correctly assign CPT codes and modifiers to surgical procedures using the Guidelines, notes, and other resources.

Continuous advancements in technology have great significance in terms of health-care quality, especially in regard to surgical procedures. From a coding perspective, these advances and changes result in ongoing additions, deletions, and modifications to CPT codes. Precise coding is critical for appropriate reimbursement for services and as part of medical research. Research on the outcomes of applying new surgical procedures helps determine the actual benefits of the new technology. For example, studying trends using both diagnostic and procedural coding information allows experts to determine to what extent a new endoscopic or laser surgery reduces risk, improves outcomes, and minimizes recovery time when compared with the traditional open surgery. These code-based studies are important in many social, economic, and scientific aspects of surgery. As a result, professional coders play a vital role in improving the quality of health care.

Word Parts and Meanings of Medical Terms Related to Surgical Procedures

Word Part	Meaning	Example	Definition
all/o	other	allograft	Tissue for a graft is taken from a human donor (cadaver, living relative or living nonrelative) other than the patient—same species, different genotype
aut/o	self	autograft	Tissue for a graft is taken from a site on the patient's (recipient's) **own** body
caus/o or cauter/o	burn, burning, heat	cauterization	Use of heat or burning—a hot instrument, a caustic substance, an electrical current—in the destruction of diseased or undesirable tissue
-centesis	surgical puncture to remove fluid	paracentesis	Surgical puncture of a body cavity with a hollow instrument for aspiration of fluid used for diagnosis or for relief of symptoms caused by excessive fluid in a cavity
cry/o	cold	cryosurgery	Destruction of tissue using the application of extreme cold
-dilation or -ectasia/-ectasis	widening, stretching, expanding	dilate	To stretch an opening beyond its normal dimensions
-fusion; fusion	to come together	spinal fusion	Operative immobilization of two or more vertebrae (e.g., laminectomy or diskectomy procedures)
heter/o	different	heterograft	Tissue for a graft is derived from a different species such as a pig; this is also called a xenograft
-lysis	breakdown, separation, destruction	litholysis	The dissolution of a stone such as a kidney stone
-pexy	fixation; put in place	colpopexy	Suture of a prolapsed vagina to a surrounding structure such as the abdominal wall
-plasty	surgical repair	rhinoplasty	Reconstructive, restorative, or cosmetic surgery of the nose
-stasis or -static	to stop or control; controlling	epistasis	Suppression of a secretion such as blood
-stomy	creation of an artificial opening into a hollow structure or new opening between two structures	colostomy/ colosigmoidostomy	Surgical creation of an artificial opening into the colon and the surface of the body; surgical creation of an artificial opening between the sigmoid and the proximal portion of the colon
-tripsy	to crush	lithotripsy	Process of crushing a stone—usually in the urinary system or gallbladder—either surgically or by the use of noninvasive procedures

Surgery Guidelines

The Surgery section is the largest section within the CPT manual and covers the code range from 10021 to 69990. As with other sections of CPT, Guidelines are presented at the beginning of the section. Surgery Guidelines provide definitions or descriptions of terms and concepts that assist with accurate coding, along with the official guidelines for reporting CPT codes. Students should become very familiar with the following Guidelines.

Surgical Package

After reviewing a medical record, beginning coding students have a tendency to overcode by assigning more codes than necessary. This happens because often, many minor procedures are an integral part of a major procedure, and are therefore not coded. These minor procedures are often designated as "separate procedure" in their code description (e.g., 49000). For example, for a laparotomy with appendectomy, you would only code the appendectomy. There is a separate code for a laparotomy because sometimes it can be the only procedure performed, but when it is the operative approach, it is not coded.

The concept of a **surgical package** is similar to a value meal or combination plate at a fast food restaurant. The reason a restaurant can offer a discount for a combination plate (for example, a taco, burrito, chips, and a drink) when all items are ordered at the same time by the same customer is because the cost to the restaurant is less—reduced staff time, one napkin, one take-out bag, etc. Even though each of these items has a separate price, the restaurant can afford to offer a discount when they are purchased as a package. The same is true for many surgical procedures.

The amount that CMS (Medicare and Medicaid) or other payers allow for most surgical CPT codes is based on the assumption that certain services are typically performed in conjunction with most surgeries—**bundled** into one surgical package. Reimbursement for the following services provided by the surgeon is covered under one surgical procedure code and not coded separately:

- Local, topical or metacarpal/metatarsal/digital block anesthesia
- E&M encounter on the date immediately before or on the date of the procedure (including history and physical)
- Immediate postoperative care (dictation of procedure, progress notes, talking with family members, etc.)
- Writing orders
- Evaluating the patient in the postanesthesia recovery area
- Postoperative follow-up care (follow-up E&M services)

Follow-Up Care for Diagnostic and Therapeutic Procedures

Unlike invasive surgical procedures, there is no surgical package for the follow-up care related to diagnostic services such as endoscopic or arthroscopic procedures or injection procedures for radiography or therapeutic surgical procedures. Because of the variability of diagnostic procedures, all services related to the condition for which the diagnostic procedure was performed may be listed using separate CPT codes. Likewise, for therapeutic surgical procedures, only the care that is usually a part of the surgical service itself is included in the CPT code—all other services are listed separately.

Reporting More Than One Procedure or Service

Under the same concept as the surgical package, it is also less expensive and more efficient for a physician to perform more than one surgical procedure at the same session on the same patient. This is because the surgical suite, with any needed supplies and equipment, is already set up and ready to go. There is a cost savings in time and resources when more than one procedure is done at the same time on the same patient, and there are several modifiers that apply to this concept. There are modifiers that reduce the provider's payment for a secondary procedure performed at the same time as the primary procedure. There are also modifiers to justify why a procedure or service that is normally included in the surgical package should be reimbursed at the full amount in addition to the most significant procedure.

Modifiers Used With Surgery Codes

The modifiers shown in the following Quick Reference table are those most commonly appended to codes listed in the Surgery section of CPT. Full descriptions of these modifiers may be found in Appendix A of the CPT manual.

Do not confuse modifier -58 with modifier -78, which is for an UNSCHEDULED return to the operating room during the postoperative period.

Most hospital encoders (software used for coding) do not consistently prompt for modifiers to be appended, so coding personnel must always consider whether or not a modifier should be used. For example, a surgeon performs a colonoscopy and removes tissue for biopsy from three areas of the rectum and colon. The Chargemaster generally has three identical surgical pathology codes. So the coder would need to edit those charges by adding modifier -59 (distinct procedural service) to two of the three surgical pathology CPT codes.

Not using the appropriate modifier may result in overpayment or underpayment to a physician or facility. Overpayments related to coding, intentional or not, are considered to be fraud or abuse and may result in the provider being fined or subject to other penalties such as Medicare exclusion or imprisonment. Underpayments deprive the provider of the full amount of money to which the provider is legally and ethically entitled. Inappropriate use of any modifier may cause the provider to be out of compliance with correct billing.

In the case of a true bilateral procedure, CMS (Medicare/Medicaid) requires that the procedure code be listed once with a modifier -50 appended (e.g., 69020-50) while some other payers require that you list the code twice: the first time without a modifier and the second time with the modifier appended (e.g., 69020, 69020-50). Be aware of the payer's requirements in each case.

Category III Temporary Codes

Category III temporary codes that describe new technologies and procedures are presented immediately after the Medicine section of CPT. These codes are alphanumeric codes with four numbers and a T as the fifth character (e.g., 0016T). AMA lists these codes for up to 5 years. After 5 years, if these codes have not been reassigned to Category I codes, they are archived. Category III codes should always be reported before unlisted CPT codes from Category I are assigned. These codes are located in the CPT alphabetical index with Category I codes.

Unlisted Service or Procedure

If a procedure or service code is not listed in either the main Surgery section or in Category III temporary codes, it may appear as an "unlisted service or procedure." Most subsections of Surgery have codes ending in a 9 or 99 that are specifically defined as "unlisted procedures."

EXAMPLE   *Unlisted laparoscopy procedure, appendix: 44979.*

Quick Reference: Surgery Modifiers

HCPCS II/CPT Modifier	Description	Explanation
27	Multiple encounters on the same date	Used for multiple outpatient hospital evaluation and management services on the same date.
50	Procedure performed on both sides	Used to report a procedure that was performed on both sides of a paired organ or both sides of a single organ when a procedure is distinctly performed twice, such as excision of a nasal polyp from the right nostril and another from the left nostril during the same operative session. Not used when the term "bilateral" or the statement "unilateral or bilateral" is included in the description of the CPT code.
LT and RT	Procedure performed on one side (left or right)	Used when a procedure is performed on only one side of a *paired organ*. For example, an arthroscopic procedure to the right shoulder would have -RT appended because the shoulder is a paired organ.
51	Multiple procedures performed by the same physician during the same session	Added to the code or codes representing the least resource-intensive of the surgical procedures performed on the same patient at the same operative session by the same physician. The most resource-intensive procedure is listed first without a modifier and then the other procedure(s) follow with modifier -51 appended to each. Only used for professional services. (Hospitals do not use modifier -51 for outpatient services.) Never appended to an add-on code (plus sign [+] in front of the code) or with a modifier -51 exempt symbol (circle with a diagonal line through it).
58	Scheduled return for surgery during postoperative period	Used only when the physician who performs a surgery knows at the time of the surgery that the patient must return for a planned, related procedure during the postoperative period. For example, a surgeon performs a repair of a complicated wound on one day and plans to follow up a few days later with reconstructive skin surgery after the wound site has had a chance to start healing and is no longer in danger of becoming infected.
59	Distinct procedural service, independent from other, non-E&M procedures performed on the same day by the same physician when the procedures are not normally reported together and no other modifier is more appropriate	Used when the same or similar procedure is performed on the same patient on the same day, to indicate that the same procedure was done in a different area of the body, done during a different operative session, or done on a separate lesion (and bilateral modifier -50 is not appropriate). The procedure code is paid once at the full amount and once or more at a 50% discount. For example, placing a stent in the internal iliac artery and one in the external iliac artery both code to CPT 35473, so this code would be paid once at 100% and once with a modifier -59 at 50%.
76	Same procedure performed on same patient in separate operative session on the same day	Indicates the same procedure was repeated at a separate operative session on the same day. Because a separate operative session does require full resources for both sessions, the code would be submitted once by itself and once with modifier -76 which will result in both procedures being reimbursed in full (100%) without a multiple procedure discount.

(continued)

Quick Reference: Surgery Modifiers (Continued)		
HCPCS II/CPT Modifier	Description	Explanation
77	Same procedure performed on same patient in separate operative session with different physician on the same day	Used to indicate that the second time the procedure was performed, a different physician did the surgery.
78	Unscheduled return for surgery during postoperative period	Used for a related but unplanned surgical procedure by the same physician during the postoperative period. For example, a patient has an abdominal surgery and the site of the internal stitches becomes infected. The physician may do a separate operation to drain a fistula and remove the stitches.
79	Surgery on same patient during postoperative period for a different, unrelated cause	Used when a surgeon operates on the same patient during a postoperative period but for a reason completely unrelated to the initial procedure. For example, a patient who had been in a car accident had to have open fracture care and then developed acute appendicitis requiring surgery during the postoperative period.
91	Repeated laboratory tests on same patient on same day	Used for repeated clinical diagnostic laboratory tests on the same patient on the same day.

SPECIAL REPORT

When an unlisted service or procedure is performed, the provider must submit a special report along with the claim for this procedure to the payer. Whether the coder or a billing specialist completes this report is determined by the staffing in each medical office. The report must adequately describe the nature, extent, and need for the procedure including time, effort, and equipment necessary to perform the procedure. This information is needed to substantiate the medical necessity for the claim. The report also should indicate the complexity of symptoms, final diagnosis, pertinent physical findings, diagnostic and therapeutic procedures, concurrent problems, and follow-up care. Special reports provide data to help the AMA determine whether a Category III temporary code may be needed in a subsequent edition of CPT or whether an existing code meets the criteria based on the special report.

Surgical Destruction

Surgical destruction of tissue is generally an integral part of a larger surgical procedure regardless of how the destruction is performed. Separate codes are not usually acceptable to describe surgical destruction as part of a more comprehensive surgery. However, if the technique substantially alters the standard management of a problem or condition, there may be exceptions to this rule. In this case, the coder may report a surgical destruction code separately (in addition to the code for the major procedure), using the appropriate modifier (e.g., -59).

Surgery Subsections

Generally speaking, the subsections of the CPT Surgery section are sequenced anatomically starting from the outer layer of the body (skin or integumentary system procedures start with a 1; musculoskeletal system procedures start with a 2) and moving inward within the body. If multiple CPT codes are derived from a medical record, they are sequenced in order of most resource intensive to least resource intensive. It is imperative for coders to be aware of the notes preceding the various subsections and headings. The Guidelines list every subsection within the Surgery section that contains special notes.

Table 6.1 shows the Surgery subsections and the code ranges that apply to each subsection.

 TIP After looking up a CPT code in the alphabetic index and locating the code in the tabular listing, it is important to go to the beginning of a subsection to determine whether special notes apply. Cross-reference notes can be listed at the beginning of a range of codes, after the description of the applicable code, or at the end of a range of codes.

Coders should have reference materials containing anatomic and surgical procedure illustrations and a good medical dictionary on hand. Sometimes the distinction between codes is very fine and only makes sense when the coder thoroughly understands the medical terminology in the operative report and in the code description, notes, and references. Complete,

TABLE 6.1 Surgery Subsections and Code Ranges	
Surgery Subsection	**Code Range**
General surgery	10021–10022
Integumentary system	10040–19499
Musculoskeletal system	20000–29999
Respiratory system	30000–32999
Cardiovascular system	33010–37799
Hemic and lymphatic systems	38100–38999
Mediastinum and diaphragm	39000–39599
Digestive system	40490–49999
Urinary system	50010–53899
Male genital system	54000–55899
Reproductive system procedures	55920
Intersex surgery	55970–55980
Female genital system	56405–58999
Maternity care and delivery	59000–59899
Endocrine system	60000–60699
Nervous system	61000–64999
Eye and ocular adnexa	65091–68899
Auditory system	69000–69979
Operating microscope	+69990

accurate reporting depends on the coder being a detective willing to track down all necessary information.

General Surgery

Procedures that may be performed in any body system are listed in the General Surgery subsection. There are two General Surgery codes: 10021 and 10022. Fine-needle aspiration is the process of using a long, fine needle to withdraw fluids or gasses for drainage or examination of cells.

EXAMPLE	*Fine-needle aspiration without imaging guidance: 10021.* *Fine-needle aspiration with imaging guidance: 10022.*

References following the General Surgery code descriptions provide a list of codes from the Radiology section used to report radiologic supervision and interpretation and clarify that biopsies other than fine-needle aspiration can be found in the applicable anatomic subsection.

Integumentary System

The integumentary system includes skin (consisting of the outer epidermis layer, inner dermis layer, and subcutaneous tissue or superficial fascia) and accessory organs such as hair, nails, and certain glands (e.g., sweat). Figure 6.1 shows the structure of the skin. The integumentary system is the largest body system. Note that modifiers LT and RT are not used for procedures on the skin because it is all part of one body system.

Integumentary System codes range from 10040 to 19499. This subsection contains many notes, definitions, and clarifications as well as instructions and references. It is important for a coder to become familiar with all notes and to be aware that there are also various cross-references found under the description of some individual codes or range of codes.

EXAMPLE	*Incision and removal of foreign body, subcutaneous tissues; complicated: 10121.*
	   To report wound exploration as a result of penetrating trauma without laparotomy or
	    thoracotomy, see 20100–20103.
	   To report debridement associated with open fracture(s) or dislocation(s), use
	    11010–11012 as appropriate.

INCISION AND DRAINAGE (10040–10180)

Incision and drainage (I&D) codes require both incision (cutting into) and drainage be performed, because drainage alone can also be accomplished using fine-needle aspiration. The terms "simple" and "complicated" are used with some of the I&D code descriptions. The coder must look closely at the physician's documentation in the medical record to determine the degree of complexity to select the most appropriate code.

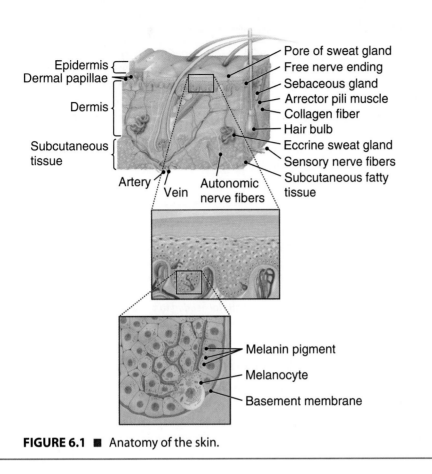

FIGURE 6.1 ■ Anatomy of the skin.

EXAMPLE

For code 10060 I&D of abscess, the choices are simple OR single; for 10061, the choices are complicated OR multiple. This means that simple I&D of more than one abscess is reported using code 10061.

EXCISION-DEBRIDEMENT (11000–11044)

Excision-debridement codes document the removal of dead tissue or foreign material from any type of wound. Debridement of wounds associated with open fractures are assigned to range 11010–11012. Regular skin debridements are reported using range 11040–11044 based on the type of tissue debrided (skin or muscle). Debridement is usually an integral part of wound repair and is not coded separately. However, when one of the following criteria is documented in the medical record, debridement is coded separately from wound repairs:

▶ Gross contamination of an area requiring extensive cleaning
▶ Substantive areas of devitalized or contaminated tissue needing removal
▶ When the debridement is performed as a separate procedure without concurrent wound repair

EXAMPLE

Between code 11008 and code 11010, you will find the following reference: When insertion of mesh is used for closure, use 49568. This reference pertains back to procedure codes 11004–11006, which describe excisional debridement of the abdominal wall. Code 49568 is an add-on code with the description, "Implantation of mesh or other prosthesis for incisional or ventral hernia repair." The appropriate debridement code would be listed first, followed by the add-on code for the mesh (11004, 49568).

A CMS audit in 2004 determined debridement codes for the range **11040–11044** were coded incorrectly 64% of the time for a total overpayment of approximately $64 million. Of these coding errors, 33% were because of incorrect modifier assignment. Using a debridement CPT code with modifier -59 when either the debridement service should have been included in the code for wound repair or when the debridement code should have been used with a different modifier was one of the commonly misused modifiers in this audit.

EXAMPLE

A physician performed a simple repair of a 2.6 cm wound (12002) and also a full-thickness skin debridement of another site on the same extremity (11041). In this case, the correct coding is 12002 and 11041-59. However, if the debridement had been done at the same site as the wound repair, the debridement would not be coded at all unless gross contamination or significant revitalized material needed to be debrided, in which case 11041 with a modifier -22 would be appropriate.

Paring and Cutting (11055–11057)

Paring lesions, like paring an apple, means peeling or scraping away using a blade or other sharp device. The appropriate code for paring and cutting includes control of bleeding. Code 11055 is paring or cutting of benign hyperkeratotic lesion (e.g., corn or callus); single lesion. Code 11056 is for two to four lesions, and 11057 is more than four lesions. Note that 11056 and 11057 are NOT add-on codes. Only one code is ever reported for paring and cutting, regardless of the number of lesions.

EXAMPLE

Paring of 7 corns. Report only code number 11057. DO NOT report 11055 for the first lesion and 11057 for the other 6.

Biopsies (11100–11101)

These biopsy codes are used only to report biopsies that were taken separately from excision or other removal of lesions.

EXAMPLE

Patient had a 1.0 cm benign lesion excised from his upper arm with the lesion being sent to obtain a biopsy, plus tissue from a separate lesion of the lower arm was removed for biopsy.
Code 11401 (excision of lesion of upper arm includes biopsy of the excised tissue in the excision code) plus 11100-59 (biopsy 1 lesion) to report biopsy of tissue from the lower arm with a modifier to indicate this is a distinctly different lesion than the first one.

Removal of Skin Tags (11200–11201)

This procedure is defined as removal by scissoring or any sharp method, ligature strangulation, electrosurgical destruction, or combination of treatment modalities including chemical or electrocauterization of wound, with or without local anesthesia. Code selection includes 11200 for the first 15 lesions and add-on code 11201 for each additional 10 lesions. The add-on code is used for lesions 16–25 and again for each group of 10 lesions. The standard billing form contains a field for reporting units of service, and it is appropriate to use

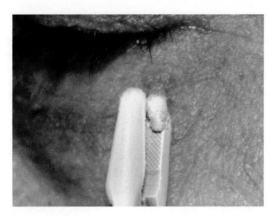

FIGURE 6.2 ■ Removal of a skin tag using liquid nitrogen.

this field to report the number of lesions each time the add-on code is reported. The size of the skin tags do not influence code selection. Figure 6.2 shows the removal of a skin tag using liquid nitrogen.

Patient had skin tags that were causing irritation where her clothing rubbed against the tags; 14 large skin tags were removed from the neck area, and 8 smaller tags were removed from the area around her lower back near her waist. Code 11200 for the first 15 tags plus 11201 for the remaining 7 tags, with 070 in the units of service field of the claim form.

EXAMPLE

SHAVING OF EPIDERMAL OR DERMAL LESIONS (11300–11313)

This procedure is defined as the sharp removal by transverse incision or horizontal slicing to remove epidermal and dermal lesions without a full-thickness dermal excision. It includes local anesthesia and chemical or electrocauterization of the wound. The wound does not require suture closure. Code selection is based on body area and size. The documentation in the medical record includes the measurement in centimeters.

EXCISION OF BENIGN LESIONS (11400–11471) AND MALIGNANT (11600–11646) LESIONS

Excision is defined as the full-thickness (through dermis) removal of a lesion, including margins. Codes are based on morphology (benign versus malignant), then location on the body, and finally by size in centimeters. Each lesion excised is reported separately. Simple closure of a skin lesion and local anesthesia are included in the appropriate code for the excision. Intermediate or complex repair is reported separately.

The appropriate code for each excision is determined by measuring the greatest diameter of the lesion itself plus the narrowest margin of tissue surrounding the lesion that is required to completely remove the lesion and any tissue that may contain cancerous cells (if the lesion turns out to be malignant). The measurement is made before excision and is the same regardless of whether the repair of the surgical site is linear or reconstructed for skin graft. Because the excised lesion is subsequently sent to the laboratory for a pathologist to biopsy, and code selection in the excision range must be identified as either malignant or benign, these codes are not assigned until the surgical pathology report is available in the medical record.

The surgical pathology report is NOT used to code the actual measurement of the excised lesion because shrinkage occurs after removal of tissue.

Once the biopsy results from an excised lesion indicate a malignancy, it is common protocol to re-excise more tissue from the margins to make sure all of the cancerous tissue is removed. Even if the second pathology report demonstrates benign tissue, the re-excision is still coded as malignant because it is the continuance of the original protocol for cancer. When the re-excision is done during the same operative session, just one code is used with the final measurement including additional margins. If the re-excision is done at a subsequent operative session during the postoperative period, the appropriate excision code is used and appended with modifier -58.

EXAMPLES

1. *60-year-old female patient presents for removal of two skin lesions in one session. The first lesion measuring 0.5 cm including margins is excised from the skin of the upper left arm. Surgical pathology results report basal cell carcinoma. The second lesion measures 2.0 cm, including margins and is on her lower back. Surgical pathology results report benign nevus. 11402 (benign lesion); 11600-51 (basal cell lesion). Modifier -51 would be added to the lesser procedure (the smallest lesion), but the hospital coder would not add modifier -59 because the procedures are, by definition, distinct.*
2. *Using local anesthesia, a physician removes a benign neoplasm from the skin of the upper arm of a 45-year-old female patient. The neoplasm measured 1.0 cm in diameter. The physician closed the site with simple sutures: 11400 (no additional codes, no modifiers).*
3. *Using local anesthesia, a physician excises a 2.5 cm malignant melanoma from the stomach area of a 46-year-old male patient. The repair of the wound requires layered closure: 11603; 12031-51.*
4. *Using local anesthesia, a physician excises a 0.50 cm lesion from the upper back of a 63-year-old female patient. Surgical pathology done while the patient was still prepped revealed unclear margins. The physician then excised an additional 0.2 cm of adjacent tissue (margins). The area only required suturing and not a layered closure. Code 11601 is used because the combined measurement is 0.7 cm, and the re-excision was in the same operative session.*

Do NOT add up the total of multiple lesions to report under one code. Because laceration repair requires the coder to add all repairs of the same category and same anatomic grouping together under one code, it is a common mistake to assume the same rule applies to excision of lesions, but it does not. Each excised lesion is coded separately.

Simple (12001–12021), Intermediate (12031–12057), and Complex (13100–13160) Repair (Closure)

See the subsection notes for detailed definitions of each level of repair procedures. To summarize:

▶ Simple repair involves single-layer suturing of a superficial wound (i.e., "simple closure").
▶ Intermediate repair involves the deeper skin and fascia or single-layer closure of a contaminated wound (i.e., "layered closure").
▶ Complex repair involves division, debridement, stents, or retention sutures (i.e., "reconstructive repair" often involving jagged cuts).

TIP The repair procedure codes are provided in centimeters. If the measurement in the medical record is given in inches, the coder must convert inches to centimeters at 2.54 cm per inch.

The CPT manual includes instructions for listing services performed at the time of wound repairs in terms of measurement criteria; multiple wound rules; debridement coding; simple ligation of vessels; and simple exploration of nerves, vessels, or tendons. When multiple wounds are repaired, the coder adds together the lengths of those wounds in the same classification (simple, intermediate, or complex) and the same anatomic sites that are grouped together into the same code descriptor (scalp, axillae, trunk, or extremities). When multiple codes are required, the codes are sequenced from most complex to least complex.

A 59-year-old female patient presents for repair of a deep surgical wound status postexcision of a melanoma, located below her left ear. The defect measures 1.9 cm × 1.4 cm: 12052.

EXAMPLE

ADJACENT TISSUE TRANSFER OR REARRANGEMENT (14000–14350)

The subsection notes refer the coder to the respective anatomic subsections for full-thickness repair of the lip or eyelid. The use of these codes require the surgeon to develop one of the following procedures versus performing a direct closure or rearrangement of traumatic wounds that incidentally results in the same configuration: Z-plasty, W-plasty, V-Y plasty, rotation flap, advancement flap, and double-pedicle flap.

TIP Codes for adjacent tissue transfer or rearrangement include any removal of lesions, so do not code separately.

For procedures in this range, skin is moved or rotated while it is still attached to the main area of skin. The skin is measured in square centimeters. Both primary and secondary defects are added together to determine size. Skin grafts are reported separately. A skin graft necessary to close a secondary defect is considered an additional procedure. In selecting the proper code, the term defect includes the primary and secondary defects. The primary defect resulting from the excision and the secondary defect resulting from flap design to perform the reconstruction are measured together to determine the code.

A 75-year-old female patient presents with a defect status postexcision of a large melanoma. The 2.0 cm defect is located on and beneath her lower right eyelid. It extends subcutaneously. Adjacent tissue transfer is used to repair the defect and ensure the eye does not droop: 14040.

EXAMPLE

SKIN REPLACEMENT SURGERY AND SKIN SUBSTITUTES (15002–15431)

These codes are used to report the preparation of the recipient site and the skin graft or skin substitute, not the primary procedure that results in the need for a graft. For example, if a deep tumor removal requires skin graft for definitive closure, the removal of the tumor is reported under the appropriate anatomic subsection. Then a code (or codes if an add-on code is required) is used from 15002 to 15005 to report the preparation of the recipient site based on body area and size. Finally, the appropriate code(s) from 15040 to 15431 are used to report the actual graft procedure.

These graft procedures do not include excision of lesions when performed, so the excision must be reported separately. The codes vary by type of graft or skin substitute, by body area, and by the size of the area. Codes that use a measurement of 100 cm^2 (squared centimeters) are applicable to patients 10 years of age or older, but 1% of body area is used instead for patients younger than 10 years of age, including infants.

EXAMPLE	*A burn victim required site preparation before undergoing skin grafting. The third-degree, full-thickness burns of the upper legs and torso were excised through the dermis and into the subcutaneous tissue. The area involved measured a total of 148 cm^2: 15002, 15003. Each additional 100 cm^2 is reported as an add-on code for any amount over the first 100 cm^2. If the area was more than 200 cm^2, the add-on code would be used twice.*

FLAPS: SKIN OR DEEP TISSUES (15570–15738) AND OTHER FLAPS AND GRAFTS (15740–15776)

Excision of lesions is reported separately. When repair of the donor site requires skin graft or local flaps, the repair is considered an additional separate procedure. The codes in the 15570–15738 range do not include immobilizations such as large plaster casts, so these are reported as additional, separate procedures when used.

BURNS (16000–16036)

Codes in this range pertain only to the treatment of the burned body surfaces. Application of skin grafts or skin substitutes (15100–15650) are reported separately. Codes 16020–16030 are used to report the application of materials not listed in skin replacement and skin substitute code descriptions. Code 16035 (first incision) and add-on 16036 (each subsequent incision) are for reporting escharotomies. **Escharotomy** is a surgical incision of the necrotic (dead) tissue known as **eschar** that is produced by a limb that has been burned around the circumference. The incision allows the blood flow to reach the unburned tissue beyond the injury.

The most important aspect of coding the treatment of burned body surface areas is the documentation and calculation of the total body surface area (TBSA). For adults, the body is divided into multiples of 9%—the "rule of nines" (except genitals are 1%). The head and each arm represent 9% each, and the front trunk of the body, the back trunk of the body, and each leg represent 18% each. For infants and children, there is an exception to the "rule of nines" to allow for the fact that the head is bigger in proportion to the rest of the body. Therefore, infants and children are measured with 9% for each arm, 18% of the body surface for the head and neck, 18% each for the front and back trunk, and 14% for each leg. The coder must determine the total percentage of body area treated based on these rules. Figure 6.3 shows how the body surface area burned is determined on an adult burn victim.

EXAMPLE	*An adult burn victim was treated for debridement and dressings for partial-thickness burns covering most of the patient's face and scalp: 16025.*

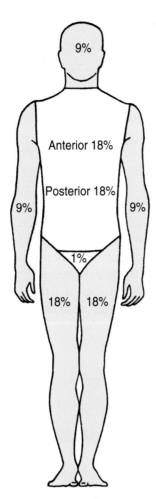

FIGURE 6.3 ■ The Rule of Nines. Used to determine estimated percentage of body surface area.

DESTRUCTION OF BENIGN, PREMALIGNANT (17000–17250) OR MALIGNANT (17260–17286) LESIONS

These code ranges refer to the destruction or ablation of lesion tissue by electrosurgery, cryosurgery, laser, or chemical processes. The CPT manual lists some common benign lesions including condylomata (viral warts), papillomata, herpetic lesions and warts, any premalignant lesion such as actinic keratoses, and any malignant lesion that is destroyed rather than excised. Destruction codes include curettement (removal of tissue using a spoon-shaped instrument called a curette) and local anesthesia. Destruction of lesions does not usually require closure.

TIP   Destruction of lesions by methods such as electrosurgery or chemical treatment does not leave any viable tissue to biopsy, so the distinction between premalignant, malignant, or benign is only in the physician's notes based on information obtained during previous biopsies—no surgical pathology results would be included in the medical record.

MOHS MICROGRAPHIC SURGERY (17311–17315)

This method for removal of large, complex, recurrent, aggressive, or ill-defined skin cancer requires a physician to act in two integrated but separate capacities: as surgeon and pathologist. The outcome is 100% cancer-free margins, having removed the minimum amount of tissue. The precision with which a physician can determine the exact point at which the margins are clear without having to remove any additional tissue results in the best possible cosmetic outcomes when compared with other methods of removing lesions. Once a tumor has been identified as malignant, the surgeon uses **Mohs micrographic surgery**, a staged procedure, to remove a layer of skin tissue involving the tumor and narrow margins. The physician then maps and divides the tumor specimen into pieces. Each piece is embedded into an individual tissue block for microscopic examination to determine whether there are cancerous cells. If cancerous cells are identified, the physician removes another layer of skin and starts the process over again until there are no more cancerous cells identified in the blocks of tissue. Each time the physician removes skin tissue, it is called a stage, no matter how many blocks of tissue are examined. If both surgery and pathology roles are not performed by the same physician, it is not Mohs surgery.

TIP The codes under Mohs micrographic surgery are reported first on body area, then on number of blocks of tissue, and finally, on number of stages.

If repair is performed, appropriate codes are reported separately, in addition to Mohs. On the rare occasion that a biopsy is performed on the same day as the Mohs procedure, then a diagnostic skin biopsy code with modifier -59 to indicate a distinct procedural service would be reported in addition to codes for the Mohs procedure.

EXAMPLE

A 54-year-old male patient has Mohs surgery performed on melanoma of the calf.
   Stage one: 7 blocks
   Stage two: 4 blocks
   Stage three: 3 blocks
   Stage four: 2 blocks
   Code with 17313, 17314, 17314, 17314, 17315 (add-on for more than 5 blocks in any stage, any body area).

EXCISIONAL BREAST SURGERY (19100–19272)

Codes for excisional breast surgery (in which the entire lesion is removed for biopsy) include biopsies (percutaneous or open); the removal of cysts, benign or malignant lesions or tumors; and surgical treatment of breast and chest wall malignancies. These procedures are generally performed after being identified by preoperative radiologic markers called **localization wires**. Placement of needle localization wires preoperatively are coded separately using 19290 (preoperative placement of needle localization wire, breast) and 19291 (add-on for each additional lesion). Radiology codes are used to report the radiologic supervision and interpretation involved in this procedure.

TIP

When coding mastectomies (19300–19307), it is important to know that a partial mastectomy is the same as a lumpectomy (19301). Under total mastectomies, a radical includes pectoral muscles and axillary lymph nodes (19305), or pectoral muscles, axillary lymph nodes, and internal mammary lymph nodes—also known as an "urban type" (19306). A modified radical includes axillary lymph nodes, with or without pectoralis minor muscle but excluding pectoralis major muscle (19307).

The CPT alphabetical index can be misleading for excisional breast surgery because the terms "biopsy" then "breast" do not refer the coder to excisional biopsy. The biopsy code is included in the excisional surgery code. The proper index protocol is:

Breast

    Excision

        Lesion

            By Needle Localization (radiological marker), if applicable.

Description of operation refers to "bilateral needle localized breast biopsies." The code 19125-50 is reported for the excision of breast lesion identified by preoperative radiologic marker, open, single lesion. Modifier -50 indicates a single lesion was excised from each breast. Then, 19290-50 is used to identify the preoperative placement of needle localization wire, breast, and the modifier again indicates both breasts.

EXAMPLE

Musculoskeletal System (20000–29999)

Various fracture care procedures are found in the Musculoskeletal System subsection. These methods of treatment are:

- ▶ Closed treatment—treatment of a fracture without opening the fractured area of the body. May be accomplished by any combination of manipulation of the bone(s) to reposition them properly, also known as reduction, casting, or traction to "pull" the bone back to its proper position.
- ▶ Open treatment—treatment of a fracture that involves some degree of surgical incision or cutting to make the repair.
- ▶ Percutaneous skeletal fixation—treatment that may be accomplished by the use of either an internal or external device that holds the bone in place while it heals.

TIP

The removal of the external device or hardware subsequent to external, percutaneous skeletal fixation is included in the surgical package for fracture care and cannot be billed separately. Most internal fixation devices, such as pins or plates, remain in the body permanently unless they become infected or dislodged.

The diagnosis code for fracture can be open or closed fracture. The fracture care itself can be open or closed reduction of the fracture. Therefore, it is possible to have a closed fracture diagnosis but a procedure for that same fracture indicating open fracture care. Codes for these fracture treatment procedures include the application and removal of the first cast or traction device only. Subsequent replacement of a cast or traction device may require additional codes.

Modifiers are commonly used in coding musculoskeletal surgical procedures. For example, procedures on the shoulders, hips, knees, and feet require -RT or -LT if not bilateral and modifier -50 if bilateral, with the exception of codes that indicate bilateral as part of the description. Also, procedures involving the fingers and toes require a modifier from -FA to -F9 for fingers and -TA to -T9 for toes. Some of the coding challenges in regard to musculoskeletal procedures are described in detail in the following sections.

WOUND EXPLORATION—TRAUMA (20100–20103)

These codes are used for wounds related to or resulting from penetrating trauma and include all services such as:

▶ Surgical exploration and enlargement of the wound
▶ Extension of dissection to determine penetration
▶ Debridement
▶ Removal of foreign body or bodies
▶ Ligation or coagulation of minor subcutaneous tissue, muscle fascia, or muscle not requiring thoracotomy or laparotomy

If the repair is done to major structures or major blood vessels requiring thoracotomy or laparotomy, then those specific codes would be used instead of 20100–20103. Wound repair that only requires simple, intermediate, or complex repair and not enlargement of the wound, extension of dissection, and so forth are described using codes from the Integumentary System instead of these traumatic wound exploration codes.

SPINE: VERTEBRAL COLUMN (22010–22899)

This subsection includes codes for all procedures on the cervical, thoracic, lumbar, and sacral spine. The range for bone grafts related to the spine is 20930–20938. Bone grafting procedures done after spinal **arthrodesis** (surgical fusion or fixation) are reported separately (in addition to arthrodesis codes). Some of the arthrodesis techniques contain specific notes such as a definition of a bony interspace and how to report single versus multiple interspaces under the Anterior or Anterolateral Approach Technique (22548–22585).

 TIP When arthrodesis is done in addition to another procedure, modifier -51 (multiple procedures) should be appended to the arthrodesis code.

Spinal instrumentation (22840–22865) is defined as fixation at each end of the construct and at least one additional interposed bony attachment. Nonsegmental instrumentation is defined as fixation at each end of the construct and may span several vertebral segments without attachment to the intervening segments. For spinal instrumentation, codes 22840–22848 and 22851 are exempt from modifier -51 when reported in conjunction with definitive vertebral procedures. Bone grafts and spinal instrumentation are never performed without arthrodesis; therefore, the arthrodesis codes are modifier -51 exempt when done in conjunction with these procedures.

When two surgeons perform distinct parts of a procedure reported under the same code(s), modifier -62 should be appended to the definitive procedure code(s), including add-on codes, for each surgeon, except for spinal instrumentation or bone graft procedures. Modifier -62 is NOT used in conjunction with spinal instrumentation or bone graft procedure codes.

APPLICATION OF CASTS AND STRAPPING (29000–29799)

Initial casting application and removal performed by the same physician who provided the initial fracture or dislocation care is included in the fracture care procedure code. The same physician cannot report a code from the casting subheading except for reapplication after the postoperative follow-up period. The subsection notes include instructions on reporting these codes when performed by a different physician or when performed in the absence of any other procedure.

Respiratory System

The main subsections of the Respiratory system in the CPT manual include the nose, sinuses, larynx, trachea and bronchi, and lungs and pleura. Respiratory section surgical codes range from 30000 through 32999. Key points regarding coding for common respiratory system procedures follow.

RHINOPLASTY

Rhinoplasty is the reshaping or repairing of the nose internally, externally, or both. Regardless of whether the procedure is open or closed, it is reported using codes 30400–30420 for primary (the first time procedure is performed). These codes may include fracturing a deviated septum, repositioning the septum, reshaping nasal cartilage, removing fat, and a layered closure. If all of these procedures are performed, assign code 30420 (rhinoplasty, primary; including major septal repair).

ENDOSCOPY

Although knowledge of anatomy and physiology is important to all procedural coding, the intricacies of the sinuses often pose a challenge for coders. See Figure 6.4 for an overview of the nasal cavity and sinuses. A surgical sinus endoscopy includes a **sinusotomy** and a diagnostic **endoscopy.** The code range for diagnostic evaluation (31231–31235) refers to the use of a nasal or sinus endoscope to view the interior of the nasal cavity and the middle and superior meatus, the turbinates, and the sphenoethmoid recess. This means that any diagnostic endoscopy includes inspection of all of these areas, so only one code is applicable.

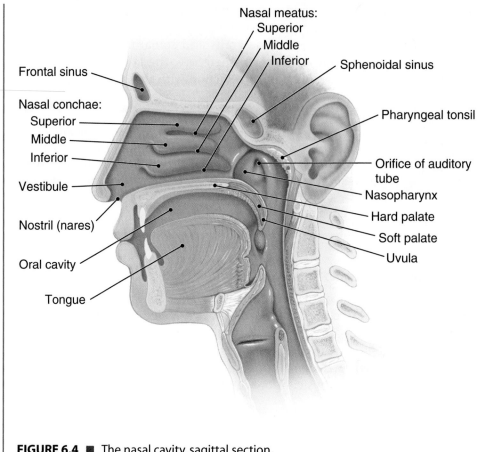

Nasal meatus:
Superior
Middle
Inferior

Frontal sinus

Sphenoidal sinus

Nasal conchae:
Superior
Middle
Inferior

Pharyngeal tonsil

Vestibule

Orifice of auditory tube

Nostril (nares)

Nasopharynx

Hard palate

Oral cavity

Soft palate

Uvula

Tongue

FIGURE 6.4 ■ The nasal cavity, sagittal section.

> ▶ Laryngeal endoscopies (31505–31579). A direct laryngoscopy means an endoscope is passed into the larynx so the physician can view the larynx. An indirect laryngoscopy refers to the use of a tongue depressor to view the epiglottis using a mirror and the vocal cords as the patient says "aahh."
>
> ▶ Tracheal and bronchial endoscopies (31615–31656). For these procedures, code the appropriate endoscope of each anatomic site examined. A surgical bronchoscopy always includes a diagnostic bronchoscopy when performed by the same physician. Codes 31622–31646 include fluoroscopic guidance, when performed. It is important to note that brushings and washings are not biopsies.
>
> ▶ Endoscopies of the lungs and pleura (32601–32665). Surgical thoracoscopy always includes the diagnostic component; therefore a separate code for a diagnostic thoracoscopy should not be assigned. Appropriate codes should be assigned for each anatomic site examined.

TIP When an operating microscope, telescope, or both are used for laryngoscopies, the appropriate code is only to be used *one time* per operative session. (This guideline was recently clarified by both AMA and CMS, which indicates a possible trend in overcoding this procedure.)

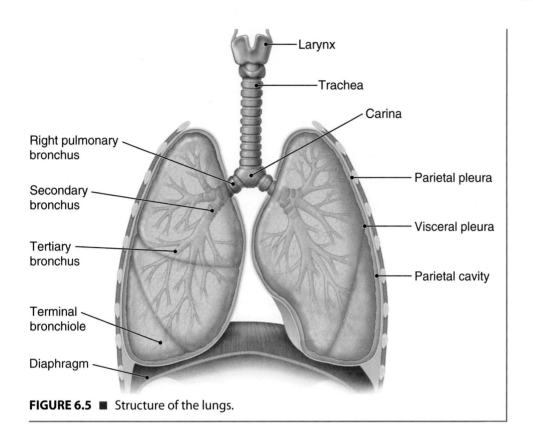

Larynx

Trachea

Carina

Right pulmonary bronchus

Parietal pleura

Secondary bronchus

Visceral pleura

Tertiary bronchus

Parietal cavity

Terminal bronchiole

Diaphragm

FIGURE 6.5 ■ Structure of the lungs.

LUNG TRANSPLANTATION (32850–32856)

See Figure 6.5 for an illustration of the structure of the lungs. Lung **allotransplantation** (human to human) involves three components of physician work:

▶ Cadaver donor pneumonectomy (unilateral or bilateral) entails harvesting the allograft and preserving the allograft. This component is reported using code 32850.

▶ Backbench work is the preparation of a cadaver donor before transplantation and includes the dissection of the allograft from surrounding soft tissues to prepare the pulmonary venous or atrial cuff, pulmonary artery, and bronchus. To report this component of lung transplantation, use code 32855 for a unilateral transplant and code 32856 for bilateral transplant.

▶ Recipient lung allotransplantation includes transplantation of a single or double lung allograft and care of the recipient. This component is reported using codes 32851–32854 depending on whether or not it is a unilateral or bilateral transplantation and whether or not cardiopulmonary bypass is performed.

CONTROL OF NASAL HEMORRHAGE OR EPISTAXIS (30901–30906)

Nasal hemorrhage or epistaxis is commonly referred to as a nosebleed. To select the correct code(s), the following questions must be answered:

▶ Was the hemorrhage anterior or posterior?
▶ If it was anterior, was the hemorrhage described as simple or complex?
▶ If it was posterior, does the record indicate that the control of the bleeding was an initial or a subsequent procedure?

If the physician's documentation for control of nasal hemorrhage is not clear, the coder may assume that if the physician inserts gauze or anterior packing or indicates a cauterization was done, it is most likely an anterior nosebleed. If the physician uses nasal stents, nasal tampons, balloon catheters, or posterior packing, or if the patient is taken into the operating room for ligation of arteries to control bleeding, it is most likely a posterior nosebleed. The diagnosis is helpful in determining whether the procedure was anterior or posterior. A subsequent posterior nosebleed is defined as one subsequent to an initial nosebleed occurring within 1 year.

Cardiovascular System (33010–37799)

The Cardiovascular subsection contains two headings: heart and pericardium, and arteries and veins. Heart and pericardium includes procedures on all coronary arteries and veins in addition to all other procedures related to the heart and the pericardium.

SELECTIVE VASCULAR CATHETERIZATIONS

Because catheterizations can be performed on all vessels, it is important to understand the intricacies of coding selective catheterizations. First, a **catheter** is a tubular instrument that is inserted into a body cavity with the intent of either introducing or withdrawing fluid. The most common cardiovascular catheterization involves inserting a needle into the femoral artery, inserting a guide wire through the needle, withdrawing the needle, and then inserting the catheter over the guide wire so it can be advanced to the heart and, as needed, other arteries branching off the aorta. The catheter used for any vascular surgery contains a contrast medium, which is injected so that the vessels can be visualized. Figure 6.6 shows a catheter inserted into a vessel. Although this chapter is dedicated to codes found in the Surgery section of CPT, the coder should note that many procedures that use a catheter involve codes from Surgery, Radiology, and Medicine. In

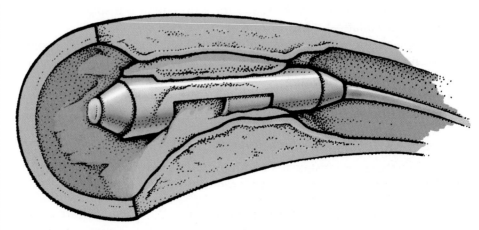

FIGURE 6.6 ■ An endarterectomy catheter for removing obstructions (plaque) from an artery.

fact, most heart catheterizations that do not include access to any non-coronary vessels use only a nonselective catheterization code from the Surgery section and then extensive coding from the Medicine and Radiology sections. All other vascular surgery procedures generally involve more codes from the Surgery and Radiology sections and not as many from the Medicine section.

Selective vascular catheterization codes include introduction and all lesser order selective catheterizations used in the approach. This concept will be discussed in more detail later in this chapter, but basically a **nonselective catheter placement** means the catheter or needle is placed either directly into an artery or a vein without further manipulation or that it is placed only in the aorta from any approach (femoral, and so forth). **Selective catheter placement** means that once the catheter is placed into an artery or vein it is then moved, at a minimum, to another branch off the initial main branch. Each branch of the same vascular family is considered an order.

The main branch of the brachiocephalic family is the brachiocephalic artery, making that artery the first order. The next order, or next smaller branch, from the main branch is the common carotid artery, making it a second-order branch. The third order in this family has more than one artery—the internal and the external carotid arteries branch off the common carotid making them both third orders. If a catheter is placed and then moved through the brachiocephalic artery, the common carotid, and on to the internal carotid artery, the code for third-order selective arterial catheterization of this vascular family—36217 in this case—is the only code reported because this code includes the initial placement and movement of the catheter through the lesser orders. If the catheter was also moved into the external carotid artery, the code 36217 would be reported followed by an add-on code 36218 to report the additional third-order placement in the brachiocephalic artery family.

EXAMPLE

PACEMAKER OR PACING CARDIOVERTER-DEFIBRILLATOR (33202–33249)

Pacemakers and pacing cardioverter-defibrillators are designed to electrically shock the heart so that it returns to and maintains a normal rhythm. Coding pacemaker insertion involves many questions. These include:

▶ Is the pacemaker permanent or temporary?
▶ Approach transverse or via thoracotomy?
▶ Electrodes and pulse generator or other type of device?
▶ Were the electrodes placed in the atria, ventricles, or both?
▶ Was the procedure a revision, a removal, or a replacement?
▶ Was a revision of the skin pocket performed?
▶ Is the current procedure being performed 15 or more days after the initial insertion?

In the past, it was common for the same physician to perform epicardial electrode lead placement and insertion of a generator at the same operative session. More recently, there have been some changes in CPT codes to reflect the current practice trend, in which the generator is placed by the cardiologist at a session other than that of the electrode placement. The codes combining these procedures have been deleted, and new codes for the placement of electrodes (depending on approach) have been added.

> **TIP** If the same physician places both the electrode leads and the generator at the same session, *two codes* must be used, 33202 or 33203 and 33212 or 33213, to accurately reflect these services.

CORONARY ARTERY BYPASS SURGERIES

There are three ways to code coronary artery bypass procedures:

▶ Venous grafting only (33510–33516) procedures are reported using one code from this range depending on how many coronary veins are grafted, from one through six or more. These codes include obtaining the saphenous vein used for grafting, but when an upper extremity vein is harvested, 35500 is reported as an additional code. When a femoropopliteal vein is harvested, 35572 is reported in addition to the appropriate venous grafting code.

▶ Arterial grafting only (33533–33536) procedures are reported using one code from this range depending on how many coronary arteries are grafted. These codes include the use of the internal mammary artery, gastroepiploic artery, epigastric artery, radial artery, and arterial conduits procured from other sites. Obtaining the artery is included in the bypass procedure code except when an upper extremity artery is used or a femoropopliteal vein segment is used. In these cases, the harvesting of the artery or vein segment should be reported separately. For an upper extremity artery, 35600 is reported as an additional code, and the harvesting of the femoropopliteal vein segment is reported separately using code 35572.

▶ Combined arterial-venous grafting (33517–33523; 33533–33536) procedures require a code from each of these ranges. Codes from the range 33517–33523 that describe a coronary artery bypass using both venous and arterial grafts based on the number of grafts (1–6) cannot be reported without a code from the arterial graft range. As is the case with the first two types of coronary artery bypass grafts, harvesting or procurement of the saphenous vein graft and the artery for grafting is included in the graft procedure so it is not reported separately except upper extremity artery (35600), upper extremity vein (35500), or femoropopliteal vein segment (35572).

In coding any of the preceding procedures, if a surgical assistant is involved, the primary code would be used with a modifier -80 on the assistant surgeon's claim for reimbursement. Hospital coders do not report surgical assistants.

> **TIP** Reoperation of a coronary artery bypass procedure or a valve procedure performed more than 1 month after the original operation is reported using the appropriate primary procedure (33400–33496 or 33510–33536 or 33863) plus add-on code 33530.

ENDOVASCULAR REPAIR PROCEDURES

Endovascular repair procedures are reported using what is referred to as a **component coding** method. This method uses multiple codes to fully report complex procedures. There are codes in this component system used to report the open exposure of the iliac or femoral artery, vascular catheterization, deployment or manipulation of surgical devices, and closure of the sites that required puncture of arteries. Codes from the Radiology and Medicine sections are also often required.

The subheadings containing component codes related to endovascular repair procedures include:

▶ Endovascular repair of descending thoracic aorta (33880–33881)
▶ Endovascular repair of abdominal aortic aneurysm (34800–34826 and 34833–34834)
▶ Endovascular repair of iliac aneurysm (34900)

The previously listed codes include placement of an endovascular graft used to repair an aneurysm or to treat a vascular malformation or trauma in the areas listed. The codes include all device introduction, manipulation, positioning, and deployment, including balloon angioplasty and stent deployment within the treatment area both before and after the placement of the endograft itself.

Procedures that are reported separately from the previously listed categories may include initial catheter introduction (36140, 36200, 36245–36248 as appropriate) but not manipulation of the catheter needed to deploy or place the endograft or prosthesis. Extensive repair or replacement of an artery that is not part of the treatment area may be reported separately.

TRANSLUMINAL ANGIOPLASTY—OPEN (35450–35460) AND PERCUTANEOUS (35470–35476)

As is the case with procedures involving catheterizations, **angioplasty** procedures often require the reporting of codes from Surgery, Radiology, and Medicine. Also, when angioplasties are done as part of another procedure, even angiography, modifier -51 or -52 (depending on the exact circumstance) should be appended to the angioplasty code for the physician and modifier -59 for the hospital.

To accurately report angioplasties, the coder must check the documentation to determine the site of the procedure and whether it was done as an open procedure or as a percutaneous procedure. Figure 6.7 illustrates some of the more common treatments to improve blood supply to the heart, including balloon angioplasty.

TIP Percutaneous transluminal coronary angioplasty (PTCA) is coded from the Medicine section using 92982 and 98984.

EXCISION, EXPLORATION, REPAIR, AND REVISION (35700–35907)

Within this range, there are important notes pertaining to both 35879 and 35881. These codes describe open revision of stenoses of a lower extremity arterial bypass graft to avoid blockage in the graft using either vein patch angioplasty or segmental vein interposition. If a **thrombectomy** is used in an arterial revision of the lower extremity, code 35875 is the appropriate code to use. The exception is thrombectomy from hemodialysis grafts or fistulas, which are reported using codes 36831 and 36833.

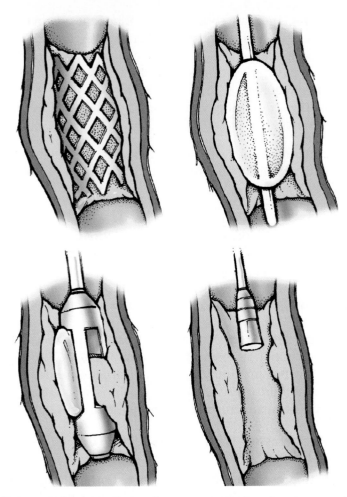

FIGURE 6.7 ■ Close-up views of coronary arteries showing a variety of procedures to improve blood supply to the heart: stent, balloon angiography, atherectomy, laser ablation.

Hemic and Lymphatic Systems

This subsection includes services and procedures involving the spleen, general bone marrow or stem cell transplantation or reinfusion, and lymph nodes and lymphatic channels. Figure 6.8 illustrates the structure of the lymphatic system. Its code range is 38100–38999.

As with most endoscopic procedures, there are notes under surgical laparoscopy of the spleen (38120–38129). Key points are that surgical laparoscopy always includes diagnostic laparoscopy and that diagnostic-only laparoscopy of the spleen using peritoneoscopy uses code 49320, which is in the Digestive subsection.

It can be challenging to master those codes related to bone marrow or stem cell services and procedures. These procedures are reported using 38207–38215 and describe various steps used to preserve, prepare, and purify bone marrow or stem cells before either transplantation or reinfusion. Each code in this range may only be reported once per day, regardless of the quantity of bone marrow or stem cells manipulated.

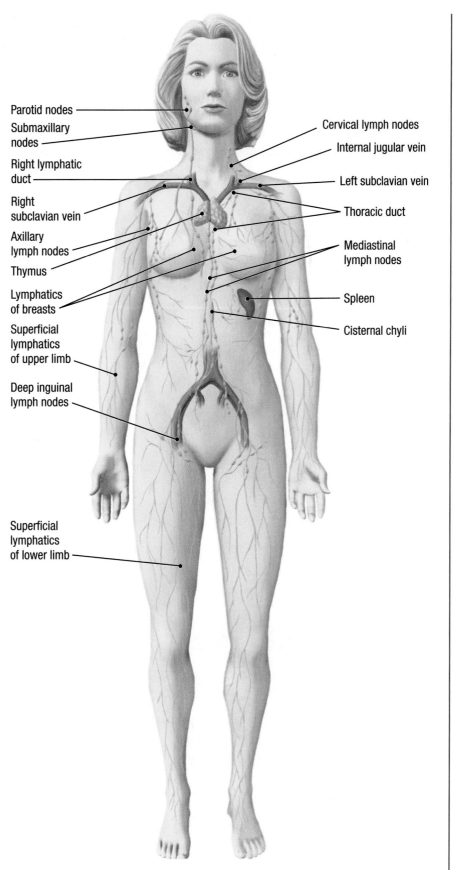

Parotid nodes

Submaxillary nodes

Right lymphatic duct

Right subclavian vein

Axillary lymph nodes

Thymus

Lymphatics of breasts

Superficial lymphatics of upper limb

Deep inguinal lymph nodes

Superficial lymphatics of lower limb

Cervical lymph nodes

Internal jugular vein

Left subclavian vein

Thoracic duct

Mediastinal lymph nodes

Spleen

Cisternal chyli

FIGURE 6.8 ■ Structures and components of the lymphatic system.

Mediastinum and Diaphragm

The mediastinum is the midsection of the thorax and covers all of the thoracic organs except for the lungs. It contains the esophagus, trachea, heart, and the great vessels of the heart such as the superior and inferior vena cava. Only a few procedures are specific to the mediastinum and diaphragm, and these use codes 39000–39599. Mediastinum procedures include mediastinotomy with exploration, drainage, removal of foreign body, or biopsy by either a cervical or transthoracic approach; excision of a cyst or tumor; a mediastinoscopy with or without biopsy; and unlisted procedures. The diaphragm procedures all involve repairs of the diaphragm, most commonly diaphragmatic hernias.

Digestive System

The digestive system breaks down food, processes it into usable substances for the body, and excretes waste products (Fig. 6.9). The code range for digestive system surgical procedures is 40490–49999.

BARIATRIC SURGERY (43770)

Bariatric surgery (for treatment of obesity) may involve the stomach, duodenum, jejunum, or the ileum. The code 49320 is used to report a diagnostic-

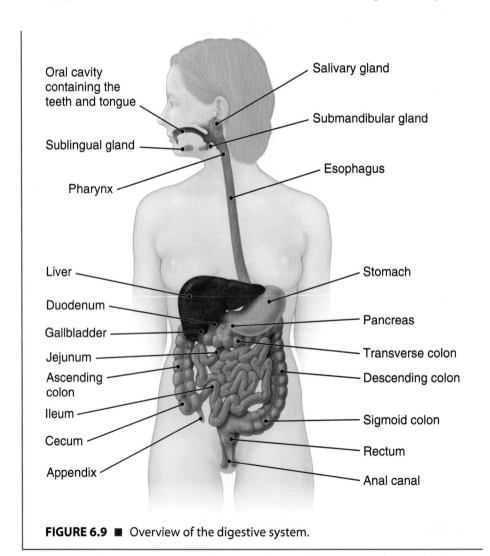

Oral cavity containing the teeth and tongue

Sublingual gland

Pharynx

Salivary gland

Submandibular gland

Esophagus

Liver

Duodenum

Gallbladder

Jejunum

Ascending colon

Ileum

Cecum

Appendix

Stomach

Pancreas

Transverse colon

Descending colon

Sigmoid colon

Rectum

Anal canal

FIGURE 6.9 ■ Overview of the digestive system.

only **laparoscopy.** This code is used for any diagnostic laparoscopic procedure of the abdomen, peritoneum, and omentum. Typical postoperative follow-up care after gastric restriction using the adjustable gastric band technique includes subsequent band adjustments through the postoperative period. Band adjustment is the changing of the gastric band component diameter by injection or aspiration of fluid through the subcutaneous port component.

TRANSPLANTATION

There are three major physician work components involved in allotransplantations. These components are described in detail for lung allotransplantation under the Respiratory subsection. For the digestive system, these areas include:

- ▶ Intestinal allotransplantation (44132–44137 and 44715)
- ▶ Liver allotransplantation (47133–47147)
- ▶ Pancreas allotransplantation (48550–48556)

ENDOSCOPY PROCEDURES ON THE DIGESTIVE SYSTEM (43200–43289)

The upper gastrointestinal endoscopy or **esophagogastroduodenoscopy** is more commonly referred to as an EGD (Fig. 6.10). This procedure is reported using the code range 43234 through 43259. EGDs involve an examination of the esophagus, stomach, and either the duodenum or jejunum. These procedures can be used for injections, placement of tube or catheter, biopsies, excision, or destruction of lesions.

TIP Code only the biopsy, and only one time, if one or more lesions are biopsied and not excised. Code only the excision if a lesion is excised for biopsy. Report both a biopsy code and an excision code when one or more lesions are biopsied without excision *and* one or more different lesions are excised with or without biopsy. If both codes are reported, use modifier -59 for both the physician and the hospital.

There are two endoscopic procedures that are less than a complete EGD. The first is an **esophagoscopy,** which views only the esophagus, and the other is an **esophagogastroscopy,** which views the esophagus and the stomach but not past the stomach.

Lower gastrointestinal endoscopies (45300–45392) can be a little more challenging to code. The lower endoscopy codes specify the instrument used, the purpose for the procedure, and the site in the colon. Multiple codes may be necessary to cover one endoscopic episode. As with all endoscopies, a surgical endoscopy always includes a diagnostic endoscopy, and only the surgical endoscopy is coded. The **colonoscopy** can be one of three types:

- ▶ Proctosigmoidoscopy—examination of the rectum and sigmoid colon (generally between 26 and 60 mm)
- ▶ Sigmoidoscopy—examination of the entire rectum and sigmoid colon, and may include a portion of the descending colon (Fig. 6.11)
- ▶ Colonoscopy—examination of the entire colon from the rectum to the cecum; may include the terminal ileum (greater than 60 mm).

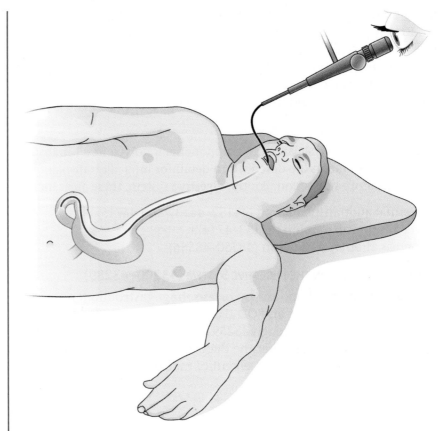

FIGURE 6.10 ■ Esophagogastroduodenoscopy (EGD).

FIGURE 6.11 ■ Sigmoidoscopy.

Colonoscopy with biopsy is only used when tissue is removed for biopsy. If the entire lesion was excised, by any technique or method, the appropriate removal or ablation code would be used and not the biopsy code.

For an incomplete colonoscopy (examination beyond the lower portion of the descending colon but not as far as the cecum), with full preparation for a colonoscopy, the regular colonoscopy code should be used. A modifier must be appended to the colonoscopy code as follows: -52 (reduced services) for the physician's claim; -74 for the hospital's claim if the procedure was discontinued after the administration of anesthesia; and -73 if the procedure was canceled before the administration of anesthesia but after the patient was otherwise prepped for surgery. If the procedure is canceled before the administration of anesthesia, the physician is not allowed to submit a surgical procedure code for reimbursement (not even -52 for reduced services).

The colonoscope was advanced to the cecum. Two polyps measuring 0.5 cm each were removed from the transverse colon using hot biopsy forceps. A third polyp in the descending colon was removed by snare technique. This operative session would be coded using 45384 and 45385. Modifier -59 would be used for both the physician and the hospital to indicate each colonoscopy procedure reported was distinct from the other.

EXAMPLE

HERNIA REPAIR (49491–49611)

Hernia repair codes are categorized primarily by the type of hernia (e.g., inguinal), so the correct reporting of the diagnosis assists the coder in selecting the most appropriate procedure code.

Once the codes for the appropriate type of hernia are located, the coder must determine whether the documentation indicates initial or recurrent (previously repaired at least once). Another distinction with some repair codes involves patient age and clinical presentation as either a reducible hernia (nonobstructive) or incarcerated or strangulated (causing obstruction of the bowels). Hernia repair includes enterolysis unless it is documented as extensive.

TIP In coding hernia repair, assume reducible if not specified in the documentation.

The use of mesh or other hernia repair prostheses is not reported separately except for incisional or ventral hernia repair (49560–49566). In this case, previous surgery has left an abdominal wall defect resulting in a bulging out of contents. When appropriate, add-on code 49568 is used in addition to the primary procedure to report implantation of mesh or other prosthesis for incisional or ventral hernia repair.

TIP Use both an excisional code based on anatomic site (e.g., 54520, orchiectomy) plus a hernia repair code for the excisional repair of strangulated organs or structures such as testes.

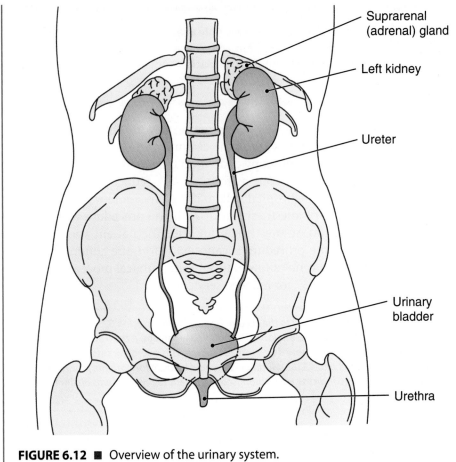

FIGURE 6.12 ■ Overview of the urinary system.

Urinary System

An overview of the urinary system is shown in Figure 6.12. The code range for urinary system surgical procedures is 50010–53899.

KIDNEY SURGERY (50010–50593)

The following definitions are helpful when coding kidney procedures:

▶ Nephrostomy—insertion of a catheter into a kidney for drainage
▶ Nephrotomy—incision of the kidney for exploration only
▶ Nephrolithotomy—incision of the kidney for removal of stones

Extracorporeal shock wave lithotripsy (ESWL) is performed while the patient is under general anesthesia. In this procedure, shock waves target and pulverize stones so the remnants pass through the urinary system.

TIP In general, if an exploratory procedure becomes definitive, code only the definitive procedure.

A **nephrectomy** (kidney excision) can be partial or total. A total nephrectomy is called a radical nephrectomy, and the procedure includes removal of fascia (support tissue) and surrounding fatty tissue, regional lymph nodes, and the adrenal gland. The procedures listed under the heading Kidney and the subheading excision are open procedures.

Although the physician work components for renal allotransplantation (50300–50370) are similar to those covered under lung transplantation, there is also a code for **renal autotransplantation** (50380). Autotransplantation also involves repositioning the kidney in the patient's pelvic area. Renal auto-transplantation includes reimplantation of the autograft as the primary procedure. Secondary extracorporeal procedures such as partial nephrectomy or **nephrolithotomy** are reported separately using a modifier -51 for the physician.

Urodynamics (51725–51797)

It is common for urodynamics codes to be used in various combinations. Modifier-51 should be appended to all additional procedures for reporting the physician's services. Urodynamics procedures are performed by, or under the direct supervision of, a physician. All instruments, equipment, fluids, gases, probes, catheters, technician's fees, medications, gloves, trays, tubing, and other sterile supplies are provided by the physician. When the physician only interprets the results or operates the equipment, the professional component modifier -26 should be appended to identify the physician's professional-only role.

Endoscopy (52000–52010)

Endoscopic procedures include **cystoscopy, urethroscopy,** and **cystourethroscopy.** Note that the endoscopic code descriptions are indented so that the main procedure can be identified without having to list all the minor related functions performed at the same time. Figure 6.13 shows a cystoscopy on a male patient.

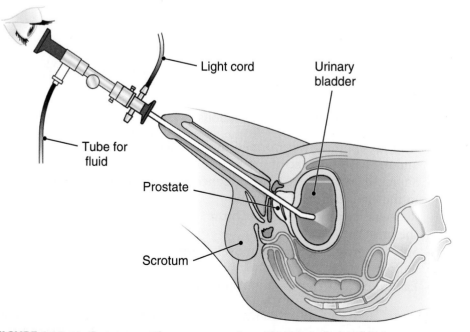

FIGURE 6.13 ■ Cystoscopy. The cystoscope is used to view the bladder.

EXAMPLE

1. The code description for 52601, transurethral electrosurgical resection of prostate (TURP), including control of postoperative bleeding, complete, contains a parenthetical note that vasectomy, meatotomy, cystourethroscopy, urethral calibration or dilation, and internal urethrotomy are included. This means that none of the procedures listed would be coded separately. An exception would be when the secondary procedure requires significant additional time and effort, it may be identified by the addition of a modifier -22, unusual procedural services, on the physician's record (hospital coders do not use this modifier).

   One other situation in which more than one code may be reported is when, owing to the anatomy of the urinary system, one endoscopic procedure must be done before a more extensive endoscopic procedure can be performed.

2. A patient presents for cystourethroscopy and removal of a calculus in the ureter. To remove the calculus, the urethral stricture must be dilated to provide access.

   Code 52352 would be coded for the cystourethroscopy with removal of calculus as the primary procedure.

   Code 52281 with a modifier -51 for the physician would be reported for the cystourethroscopy with dilation of the urethral stricture.

Male Genital System

The code range for male genital system surgical procedures is 54000 through 55980.

Priapism was formerly considered a rare condition brought on by spinal cord injuries or certain penile injuries. It involves a persistent erection not associated with sexual desire and often accompanied by tenderness. The growing use of erectile dysfunction medication such as Viagra is making this condition more prevalent. The treatment is to irrigate or aspirate the blood of the corpora cavernosa (the body of the penis that is surrounded by columns of erectile tissue). This procedure is reported using code 54220.

Orchiectomy (54520–54535), the excision of one (unilateral) or both (bilateral) testes, can be unilateral or bilateral and with or without prosthesis insertion. The operative approach can be scrotal or inguinal. There are codes for simple, partial, and radical.

 TIP A biopsy of the prostate, without other procedures, can be needle or punch and collect single or multiple tissue samples. The code used to report any of these diagnostic biopsies is 55700.

Following are definitions of the various **prostatectomy** procedures:

▸ Perineal approach—performed through the space between the rectum and the base of the scrotum
▸ Suprapubic approach—through the lower abdominal region opening in the bladder neck
▸ Retropubic approach—through the lower abdominal region in front of the prostate
▸ Subtotal prostatectomy—removal of any part of the prostate except the entire prostate
▸ Radical prostatectomy—total removal of the prostate

If lymph nodes are removed the same day as the prostate, there are codes under the various prostatectomy codes to include the **lymphadenectomy**. If the lymphadenectomy is done on a separate day, 38770 is used to report the lymphadenectomy along with the appropriate code for the prostatectomy without lymphadenectomy, such as 55840.

> *55840 is prostatectomy, retropubic radical, with or without nerve sparing.*
> *Code 55845 contains the description for 55840 plus bilateral pelvic lymphadenectomy, including external iliac, hypogastric, and obturator nodes. Therefore, 55845 is the correct way to report the total procedure when performed on the same day. A bilateral modifier is not necessary because the code description states bilateral. If, however, the lymphadenectomy was done on a subsequent date, the code for the prostatectomy would be 55840, and the code for the subsequent lymphadenectomy would be 38770-50 (as this code does not state bilateral in the description).*

EXAMPLE

Reproductive System Procedures

This one-code subsection (55920) was added in 2008 to specifically describe placement of needles or catheters into pelvic organs or genitalia excluding placement in the prostate.

Intersex Surgery

This subsection includes the codes 55970 and 55980 for intersex surgery male to female and female to male, respectively.

Female Genital System

Surgical procedures for the female genital system are covered in the code range 56405–58999. The following definitions of the various **vulvectomy** procedures (56620–56640) will be useful in reporting these procedures accurately based on the degree of the surgery:

- ▶ Simple—removal of skin and superficial subcutaneous tissues
- ▶ Radical—removal of skin and deep subcutaneous tissues
- ▶ Partial—removal of less than 80% of the vulvar area
- ▶ Complete—removal of greater than 80% of the vulvar area

> *Vulvectomy, radical, partial: 56630 is used when the documentation describes removal of less than 80% of the skin and deep subcutaneous tissues of the vulvar area.*

EXAMPLE

A surgical laparoscopy always includes a diagnostic laparoscopy. Diagnostic-only laparoscopies as a separate procedure are coded to peritoneoscopies in the Digestive subsection, 49320.

TIP Use code 53270 (excision or fulguration of Skene's glands) to report destruction or excision of Skene's gland or Skene's gland cyst or abscess because these glands are actually urethral glands (Urinary subsection, urethra heading).

Maternity Care and Delivery

The code range for procedures related to maternity care and delivery is 59000 through 59899. The first rule of maternity care and delivery that must be understood is that total obstetric care is a significant global package when the same physician who provides the antepartum (prenatal) care also delivers the baby or babies and administers the postpartum care. The first code under each delivery subheading includes all routine obstetric care, including antepartum care, delivery, and postpartum care. These inclusive codes are:

▶ Vaginal delivery, antepartum and postpartum care, 59400. This routine vaginal delivery code includes with or without episiotomy and with or without forceps.
▶ Cesarean delivery, 59510.
▶ Delivery after previous cesarean delivery, 59610 (for vaginal delivery after previous cesarean also referred to as VBAC), or 59618 (for cesarean delivery after vaginal delivery was unsuccessfully attempted in a patient who previously had a cesarean delivery).

Each delivery subheading also lists codes for delivery only, delivery with postpartum care, antepartum care only (either 4–6 visits or 7 or more visits), and postpartum care only.

Abortion coding can be tricky. See the following definitions and clarifications:

▶ The terms **incomplete abortion** and **missed abortion** describe the same process (fetus dies but is not expelled).
▶ The terms miscarriage and **spontaneous abortion** have the same meaning.
▶ If a spontaneous abortion occurring in any trimester is also incomplete and it is completed surgically, except by dilation and curettage (D&C), assign code 59812 (treatment of incomplete abortion, any trimester, completed surgically).
▶ If an incomplete or missed abortion (not spontaneous) occurs during the first trimester and is completed surgically, assign code 59820.
▶ For induced abortion, there are different codes depending on method: curettage and evacuation, D&C, curettage only, or evacuation only.

Endocrine System

The code range for endocrine system procedures is 60000 through 60699. Thyroid procedures present the biggest coding challenge. The thyroid has two lobes located on either side of the trachea connected by an isthmus. A thyroid lobectomy (60220) is for a unilateral lobe removal and is defined as total. A total or complete **thyroidectomy** is coded 60240. The definition for this code is the removal of both lobes and the isthmus, so it is bilateral by definition. This means that modifier -50 should not be used.

TIP   There are special codes to report a total or subtotal thyroidectomy for malignancy with either limited (60252) or radical (60254) neck dissection. Neither of these is appropriate if the surgeon simply excises or biopsies a stray lymph node.

Nervous System

The code range for nervous system surgical procedures is 61000 through 64999. In the alphabetic index, there are no entries for procedures using the root myel- such as myelogram. These procedures can be looked up under the Spine entry and also located by the nature of the procedure itself, such as Injection and then Spine.

For procedures related to the skull, meninges, and brain, the codes 61000–61070 are used to describe diagnostic or therapeutic injection, drainage, or aspiration procedures. The coder should see the Radiology section for any radiologic supervision and interpretation codes related to imaging guidance for these procedures.

SURGERY OF SKULL BASE (61580–61619)

Procedures for surgery of the skull base are categorized according to:

- ▸ Approach procedure: anterior, middle, or posterior cranial fossa. The approach is coded separately.
- ▸ Definitive procedure, coded as the first listed procedure, which can be the repair, biopsy, resection, or excision of various lesions of the skull base. When appropriate, the primary closure of the dura, mucous membranes, and skin is reported separately using codes 15732 and 15756–15758.
- ▸ Repair or reconstruction of the defect after the definitive procedure but only if the repair involves extensive dural grafting, cranioplasty, local or regional myocutaneous pedicle flaps, or extensive skin graft.

Skull base procedures often require several surgeons of different specialties working together during the operative session. These operations are not generally staged because definitive closure is necessary to avoid infection. When one surgeon performs the approach, another surgeon performs the definitive procedure, and a third surgeon performs the repair or reconstruction. The coder for each surgeon reports only the applicable code to identify the specific procedure that the surgeon personally performed. If, however, one surgeon performs more than one of the procedures (such as the approach and the definitive procedure), modifier -51 would be appended to the lesser procedure.

STEREOTAXIS (61720–61795) AND NEUROSTIMULATORS (61850–61888)

Stereotaxis code 61793 is used to report stereotactic radiosurgery (the use of three-dimensional coordinates and response to the stimulus of touch to locate the precise site of the brain to be operated on), one or more sessions.

TIP Stereotaxis code 61793 is used *once* regardless of the number of sessions required for a single lesion. If two lesions are treated, this code is reported twice.

Intracranial neurostimulator codes (61850–61888) apply to both simple and complex neurostimulators. Initial or subsequent electronic analysis and programming of neurostimulator pulse generators is reported using codes 95970–95975 in the Medicine section. If microelectrode recording in conjunction with implantation of neurostimulator electrode arrays is performed by the same physician, this service is included and would not be reported separately. If, however, another physician carries out this service during implantation, the service is reported by the second physician using codes 95961–95962 from the Medicine section.

SPINE AND SPINAL CORD

Note that coders need to reference appropriate codes in the Musculoskeletal subsection for application of caliper or tongs and for treatment of fracture or dislocation of spine.

For injection, drainage, or aspiration procedures (62263–62319), the injection of contrast during fluoroscopic guidance and localization is an inclusive component and is not coded separately. Code 62263 reports a catheter-based treatment with targeted injection of substances to dissolve adhesions using an indwelling epidural catheter; this procedure includes percutaneous insertion and removal of the catheter. This code is only used *once* per series of injections or infusions and adhesiolysis treatment spanning 2 or more treatment days. If multiple adhesiolysis procedures are performed all in 1 day, 62264 is the appropriate code.

Common procedures for injection of neurolytic substances such as alcohol, phenol, iced saline, heat, electricity, radio waves, or other type of chemical are reported using codes 62280–62282 depending on how administered. Injections of diagnostic or therapeutic substances such as anesthetic, steroid, antispasmodic, or opioid are coded using 62310–62319.

Based on approach and the condition that resulted in a spinal operation, it is common to have two or more surgeons performing a distinct part or distinct parts of a spinal cord exploration or decompression surgery. Procedures described under the subheadings anterior or anterolateral approach for extradural exploration/decompression (63075-63091) and excision anterior or anterolateral approach, intraspinal lesion (63300–63308) commonly require two or more physicians. Modifier -62 would be added to any procedure code and add-on code in these sections that were performed with two or more surgeons working together as primary surgeons.

Under extracranial nerves, peripheral nerves and autonomic nervous system, subheading neuroplasty (exploration, neurolysis or nerve decompression, 64702–64727), note that **neuroplasty** is defined as the decompression or freeing of intact nerves from scar tissue. External neurolysis and transposition are included in these procedures, but internal neurolysis requiring the use of an operating microscope is reported using code 64727. Facial nerve decompression is reported using code 69720.

Eye and Ocular Adnexa

Eye and ocular adnexa procedures are covered by the code range 65091–68899.

Cataract surgery is very common and sometimes miscoded because the actual code for the appropriate lens extraction from range 66830–66984 includes many procedures that are not coded separately. Codes related to cataract extractions are based on the type of procedure performed. Figure 6.14 illustrates the most common types of cataract surgeries.

When a preliminary iridectomy is performed as part of a cataract extraction or before lens extraction, it is not coded separately because it is included in the code for the lens extraction. Likewise, medication injections such as viscoelastic agents, enzymatic zonulysis, and other pharmacologic products used in conjunction with cataract surgery are included in the extraction procedure and not coded separately. All of the following procedures

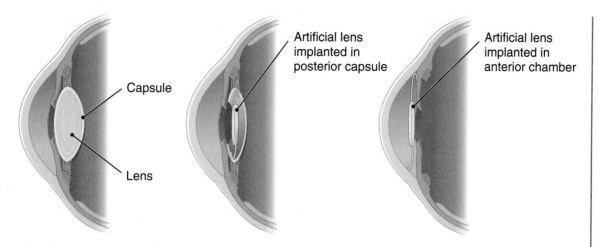

FIGURE 6.14 ■ Cross section of normal eye anatomy (left) and two types of cataract extraction surgeries.

(in addition to those already mentioned) are included when done as part of a cataract extraction and, therefore, not coded separately:

▶ Lateral canthotomy
▶ Iridotomy
▶ Anterior capsulotomy
▶ Posterior capsulotomy

Intracapsular cataract extraction (ICCE) versus extracapsular cataract extraction (ECCE): When a lens is implanted as part of the ICCE or ECCE, it is not coded separately. However, when an intraocular lens prosthesis is not done in conjunction with concurrent cataract removal, it is coded separately under 66985.

An add-on code for use of ophthalmic endoscope, code +66990, should be used in addition to the primary procedure, which must be one of the following:

▶ 65820 (anterior chamber goniotomy)
▶ 65875 (severing adhesions of anterior segment of eye, incisional; posterior synechiae)
▶ 65920 (removal of implanted material, anterior segment of eye)
▶ 66985–66986 (insertion of intraocular lens prosthesis not associated with concurrent cataract removal and exchange of intraocular lens)
▶ 67036 (vitrectomy)
▶ 67038–67040 (vitrectomy with; epiretinal membrane stripping or with focal endolaser photocoagulation or with endolaser panretinal photocoagulation)
▶ 67112 (repair of retinal detachment; by scleral buckling or vitrectomy, on patient having previous ipsilateral retinal detachment repair(s) using scleral buckling or vitrectomy techniques)

TIP Prophylaxis procedures listed under the subheading retina or choroid are often performed in multiple sessions or groups of sessions. Either of the two codes (67141, 67145) are intended to include *all* sessions in a defined treatment period.

Auditory System

Figure 6.15 provides an overview of the structures of the auditory system. The code range for auditory system procedures is 69000–69979.

A simple **mastoidectomy** (excision of mastoid cells or process of the temporal bone in the middle ear) is listed as a transmastoid antrotomy under code 69501. A complete mastoidectomy includes a myringotomy with drain insertion. Apicectomy (excision of the tip of the petrous bone) should only be coded if it is a separate procedure and not part of a radical mastoidectomy.

TIP Do not forget to append modifier -50 if the same procedure is performed on both ears.

A cochlear device implant has two components: a receiver on the outside of the ear and a processor connected to an electrode implanted in the cochlea. The procedure is reported using 69930, regardless of whether or not a mastoidectomy was performed.

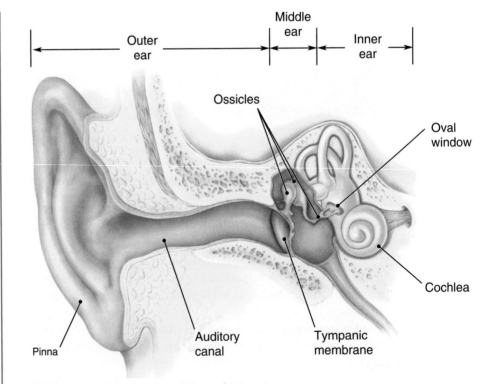

FIGURE 6.15 ■ The outer, middle, and inner ear.

Operating Microscope

Code +69990 is strictly an add-on code for use in addition to the code for the primary procedure. It is used without a modifier -51, as is the case with all add-on codes, and is only assigned when the use of an operating microscope is not already included in the components of the primary code. Notes under the Operating Microscope subsection indicate those codes that do not use the +69990 add-on code.

SUMMARY

The Surgery section of CPT contains 17 subsections. In addition to a subsection for each body system, there are subsections for general and operating microscope procedures and for special procedures such as maternity care and delivery. Coders must be aware of and understand Guidelines, notes, and cross-references located throughout the entire Surgery section to report procedures accurately. It is advisable for coders to have a quick reference to anatomic illustrations and illustrations of surgical procedures and a good medical dictionary on hand while working. Regardless of what type of endoscopy is performed, all surgical endoscopies include diagnostic endoscopies; therefore, a separate code for the diagnostic endoscopy is not reported when a surgical endoscopy was done during the same operative session. Category III codes are to be used, when available, before selecting an unlisted surgical procedure code.

TESTING YOUR COMPREHENSION

1. What type of CPT code can never be reported as a stand-alone code and is used to describe intraservice work associated with a primary procedure?

   _____

2. Which modifier would be the most appropriate for the physician to use to describe an arthroscopy performed in conjunction with an arthrotomy?

   _____

3. In the previous example, which code would have the appropriate modifier appended, the arthroscopy or the arthrotomy?

   _____

4. What are the three kinds of repairs that are listed in the Integumentary System?

   _____

5. Follow-up care for diagnostic services, such as a diagnostic colonoscopy, includes what?

   _____

6. In which subsection of Surgery would you find the code for mastectomy, simple, complete?

   _____

7. In which subsection of Surgery would you find the code for open reduction of vertebral fracture?

   _____

8. In which subsection of Surgery would you find the code for laminectomy for biopsy?

   _____

9. In which subsection of Surgery would you find the code for vulvectomy, simple?

   _____

10. What modifier is used by the physician's coder to identify the physician's role in a surgery as an assistant surgeon but is never used by the hospital coder?

   _____

11. List two ways procedures may be listed in the alphabetic index.

   _____

12. List four procedures that are included when done as part of a cataract extraction and, therefore, not coded separately.

   _____

13. What degree of vulvectomy surgery is described by "removal of skin and deep subcutaneous tissues"?

   _____

14. What type of prostatectomy approach is described as "through the lower abdominal region in front of the prostate"?

   _____

15. What is the name of the procedure that is described as "a surgical incision of the necrotic (dead) tissue that is produced by a limb that has been burned around the circumference"?

   _____

16. What is the name of the type of procedure that describes the excision of one or both testes, with or without prosthesis insertion?

    _____

17. For the procedure described in the previous question, what are the two different operative approaches that may affect code assignment?

    _____

18. What is another way of describing a miscarriage?

    _____

19. Lung allotransplantation (human to human) involves three components of physician work. List each of these components.

    _____

20. What is the term for the physician component of renal transplants described as "involves repositioning the kidney in the patient's pelvic area and includes reimplantation of the autograft as the primary procedure"?

    _____

CODING PRACTICE I   Chapter Review Exercises

Directions

Using the CPT manual, assign all applicable surgical codes and modifiers to the following procedure descriptions:

1. Mastectomy, simple, complete for gynecomastia _____

2. Incision and drainage of abscess; simple _____

3. Layer closure of skin wound, 13.4 cm; arm _____

4. Destruction, by cryosurgery, of 5 flat warts _____

5. Excision, benign lesion, skin, leg, 5.1 cm _____

6. Release of trigger finger _____

7. Hammer toe operation, small toe _____

8. Thoracoscopy of the lungs and pleural space with biopsy _____

9. Pulse generator replacement for dual-chamber pacemaker after removal of old generator _____

10. EGD with placement of gastrostomy tube _____

11. Laparoscopic urethral suspension _____

12. Percutaneous core biopsy of lesion of thyroid _____

13. L2–L3 decompressive laminectomy with medial facetectomies and bilateral L3 foraminotomies _____

14. Extracapsular cataract extraction with insertion of intraocular lens prosthesis _____

15. Bilateral removal of cerumen from the ears _____

16. Excisional debridement of wound including subcutaneous and muscle tissue _____

17. Diagnostic arthroscopy resulting in a complete repair of a torn rotator cuff _____

18. Endotracheal intubation for a patient in anaphylactic shock _____

19. Suture repair of complex right forearm laceration through intramuscular layer _____

20. Excision of 4.1-cm basal cell carcinoma of neck with split-thickness skin graft (45 cm^2) _____

Medical Record Case Studies

Directions

1. Carefully review the operative reports provided for each case study.
2. Research any abbreviations and terms that are unfamiliar or unclear.
3. Identify the postoperative diagnoses and procedures.
4. Because only part of the patient's total record is available, think about what additional documentation you might need.
5. If appropriate, identify any questions you might ask the surgeon to code this case correctly and completely.
6. Complete the appropriate blanks for each case study. Answer questions 1–5 and assign the procedure code(s) for question 6.

Case Study 6.1

Patient: **Patient S**

Patient documentation: **Read Operative Report 6.1**

1. What are the preoperative and postoperative diagnoses (description) that support the medical necessity of this procedure?

   _____

2. Are there any secondary diagnoses present that required additional procedures?

   _____

3. What was the principal or main procedure, and were other secondary procedures performed on this patient?

   _____

4. Do you believe you need additional documentation to correctly assign the surgery codes to this record? If so, what is the additional documentation that you need?

   _____

5. Do you have any additional questions for the surgeon?

   _____

6. What is(are) the procedure code(s) you would assign to this case study?

   _____

   _____

MEDICAL RECORD 6.1

OPERATIVE REPORT

PATIENT NAME:	Patient S
MR#:	111111
DATE OF OPERATION:	03/28/2XXX
PREOPERATIVE DIAGNOSIS:	1. Punctal atresia and imperforate membrane, right lower eyelid, left lower eyelid, left upper eyelid.
	2. Chronic epiphora.
POSTOPERATIVE DIAGNOSIS:	1. Punctal atresia and imperforate membrane, right lower eyelid, left lower eyelid, left upper eyelid.
	2. Chronic epiphora.
OPERATION PERFORMED:	1. Excision of imperforate punctal membrane, right lower lid, left lower lid, left upper lid.
	2. Punctal dilation, nasal lacrimal irrigation and placement of monocanalicular stent, right lower lid, left lower lid, left upper lid.
SURGEON:	Dr. 025
ASSISTANT:	CST 001
ANESTHESIA:	General endotracheal.
COMPLICATIONS:	None.
ESTIMATED BLOOD LOSS:	Minimal.

JUSTIFICATION FOR SURGERY: The patient is a 9-year-old girl who has chronic tearing from both eyes, but was worsening as of late. She was referred to me by an outside ophthalmologist who noted that she had nonpatent puncta in three out of her four puncta, allowing no access to her tear drainage system. My examination confirmed this, with punctual stenosis or atresia in the right lower lid, left upper lid, and left lower lid. The right upper puncta appeared patent. Dye appearance test was positive in both eyes.

She presents for opening of the puncta in the three places noted, with removal of punctual membrane, punctual dilation, nasal lacrimal irrigation and probing to see if the distal nasal lacrimal system is patent, and punctal dilation with placement of temporary punctual stents to prevent re-stenosis and possible DCR surgery if distal occlusion is found.

OPERATIVE PROCEDURE: The patient was taken to the Ophthalmology operating suite where general endotracheal anesthesia was administered. The patient was prepped and draped in a sterile fashion, and lens exposed. After a sterile prep a Vannas scissor was used to incise a membrane over the right lower puncta. The puncta was dilated and probed with a #0 double 00 Bowen's probe. It was noted to be patent into the nose. The probe was introduced into the nasal lacrimal duct, and felt under the inferior turbinate. Nasal lacrimal irrigation also revealed patency following this probing and irrigation, so that the puncta did not re-adhere a mini-monka stent was inserted into the lower puncta, and sutured into position with a single horizontal mattress suture of 7-0 black nylon that was externalized through the skin in the lower lid, approximately 3 mm underneath the puncta. This effectively held the stent in place in appropriate position.

An identical procedure was performed on the left upper lid and left lower lid, first incising the membrane with Vannas scissors, the dilation, probing to reveal patency and insertion of the mini-monka stent in the left upper lid and left lower lid. These were also sutured into position with 7-0 nylon.

Erythromycin ointment was instilled in the eyes and on the operative site. The patient was then allowed to awaken, and was taken to the recovery room in stable condition.

Electronically Signed and Dated

Case Study 6.2

Patient: **Patient T**

Patient documentation: **Read Operative Report 6.2**

1. What are the preoperative and postoperative diagnoses (description) that support the medical necessity of this procedure?

   _____

2. Are there any secondary diagnoses present that required additional procedures?

   _____

3. What was the principal or main procedure, and were other secondary procedures performed on this patient?

   _____

4. Do you believe you need additional documentation to correctly assign the surgery codes to this record? If so, what is the additional documentation that you need?

   _____

5. Do you have any additional questions for the surgeon?

   _____

6. What is(are) the procedure code(s) you would assign to this case study?

   _____

   _____

MEDICAL RECORD 6.2

CARDIAC CATHETERIZATION

PATIENT NAME: Patient T
MR#:   222222
DATE OF PROCEDURE: 11/28/20XX
PHYSICIAN: Dr. 026
REFERRING PHYSICIAN: Dr. 027

REASON FOR STUDY: Severe hypertension. Episodes of dizziness. Patient unable to have stress test. Previous CT scan of the abdomen suggesting severe left renal artery stenosis. To evaluate coronary arteries with heart catheterization and for possible PTA stenting of the left renal artery.

PROCEDURES PERFORMED:

1. Left heart catheterization.
2. Coronary angiography.
3. Left ventriculography.
4. Abdominal aortogram.
5. Bilateral selective renal angiography.

TOTAL AMOUNT OF FLUOROSCOPY TIME: 3.2 minutes.
TOTAL AMOUNT OF CONTRAST: 110 mL of Optiray.
COMPLICATIONS: None.
(Note to Students: Code only the surgery codes)

PROCEDURE IN DETAIL: Informed consent was obtained. Risks of death, myocardial infarction, cerebrovascular accident, allergic reactions, kidney problems, vascular problems, infection, bleeding, need to go to the operating room, limb loss, cholesterol emboli, and others were discussed with the patient and family in detail. The patient and family agreed to proceed with the heart catheterization, peripheral angiography, possible PTA, and stenting. The patient had a degree of dementia. The situation was discussed with the patient's family. Verbal consent from the power-of-attorney, the patient's son.

Technique: The patient's right groin was sterilely prepped and draped and anesthetized with 2% lidocaine. A #6 French introducer was placed in the right femoral artery. A #6 French JL4 catheter was advanced retrogradely and engaged the left main coronary artery. Views were obtained.[a]

The JL4 catheter was exchanged over the wire for a JR4 catheter. The right coronary artery was engaged. Views were obtained. The JR4 catheter was used to cannulate the right renal artery. Views were obtained. The JR4 catheter was used to cannulate the left renal artery. Views were obtained. The left renal artery did not appear to have any significant stenosis. No gradient was noted with engagement. The JR4 catheter was exchanged over the wire for an angled pigtail which was positioned in the left ventricle. Left ventricular pressure was measured. A 30-degree RAO left ventriculogram was obtained. Pullback pressure from the left ventricle into the aorta was recorded. The pigtail catheter was used to obtain abdominal aortogram. The patient appeared to have a secondary right renal artery. We placed again the JR4 catheter to engage the lower pole right renal artery. Views were obtained. The JR4 catheter was removed over the wire. The patient tolerated the procedure well without any complications.

Hemodynamic Findings: Left ventricular pressure 125/35, aortic pressure 160/80.

MEDICAL RECORD 6.2 (CONTINUED)

Renal Artery Aortography: 1. Right renal arteries: Two arteries appeared to be going to the right kidney. The upper pole renal artery appeared medium caliber without significant disease (still medium caliber). **2.** Left renal artery: The left renal artery appeared medium caliber without significant disease. Mild disease is seen at the ostia with a degree of calcification with the degree of stenosis plus/minus 10%–20%. No gradient noted with engagement.

Abdominal Aortogram: The abdominal aorta is tortuous. Appeared mildly diffusely atherosclerotic. No abdominal aortogram aneurysm is noted. Bifurcation of the iliac arteries appears without significant disease.

Left Ventriculography: Left ventriculogram demonstrates normal left ventricular systolic function. No regional wall motion abnormalities, no significant mitral regurgitation, normal-sized ascending aorta.

Coronaries:

Left Main Coronary Artery: The left main coronary artery is large caliber. Appears without significant disease.

Circumflex Coronary Artery: The circumflex coronary artery is a medium to large caliber vessel. Proximal tapers to small caliber in the mid portion. The circumflex artery gives rise to obtuse marginal branch #1, which is a long vessel, small to medium caliber. Obtuse marginal branch #2 is a small caliber vessel. Obtuse marginal branch #3, which is a long vessel, medium caliber, bifurcating to small caliber branches. No obstructive disease of the circumflex system is seen. Luminal irregularities are noted.

Left Anterior Descending Artery: The left anterior descending artery is a medium to larger caliber vessel. Proximally tapers to medium caliber in the mid portion. Small caliber at the apical portion. The left anterior descending wraps around the apex. The proximal mid portion of the left anterior descending has an area with a degree of stenosis plus/minus 40%. The left anterior descending gives rise to diagonal branch #1, which is a tiny caliber vessel. Diagonal branch #2, which is a long vessel, small caliber with 30% ostial disease. Diagonal branches #3, #4, #5, and #6, which are tiny caliber vessels. No significant obstructive disease of the left anterior descending system is seen.

Right Coronary Artery: The right coronary artery is dominant. The right coronary artery is a medium caliber vessel. Appears to have mild atherosclerosis/lumen irregularities. The right coronary artery gives rise to the posterior descending coronary artery, which is a small caliber, and posterolateral branch, which is a slightly longer vessel of small caliber and appears to have a 20% mild disease.

Conclusions:

1. Mild coronary artery disease.
2. No obstructive disease of the renal arteries with minimal atherosclerosis.
3. Atherosclerotic abdominal aorta with no evidence of abdominal aortic aneurysm.
4. Normal left ventricular systolic pressure function without wall motion abnormalities.
5. Systemic arterial hypertension with increased left ventricular end-diastolic pressure.

Recommendations: Will continue medical therapy, risk factor modification of atherosclerotic cardiovascular disease. No intervention is needed at present.

_____

Electronically Signed by Dr. 026

Case Study 6.3

Patient: **Patient U**

Patient documentation: **Read Operative Report 6.3**

1. What are the preoperative and postoperative diagnoses (description) that support the medical necessity of this procedure?

   _____

2. Are there any secondary diagnoses present that required additional procedures?

   _____

3. What was the principal or main procedure, and were other secondary procedures performed on this patient?

   _____

4. Do you believe you need additional documentation to correctly assign the surgery codes to this record? If so, what is the additional documentation that you need?

   _____

5. Do you have any additional questions for the surgeon?

   _____

6. What is(are) the procedure code(s) you would assign to this case study?

   _____

   _____

THE MEDICAL IMAGING
PROFESSIONALS, P.A.

PATIENT NAME: Patient U

MR#:   333333

DATE OF EXAMINATION: 02/23/20XX   10:25

CLINICAL DATA: The patient needs port for chemo. The patient has pancreatic CA.

SUBCUTANEOUS CHEST PORT WITH SUBCUTANEOUS TUNNELING

DESCRIPTION OF PROCEDURE AND FINDINGS: The patient and his wife were fully informed of the risks and benefits, and alternatives to the procedure, and the consent form was signed. IV antibiotics were given. The patient was brought to the angiographic suite and placed upon the table. The patient's neck and chest were prepped and draped in the usual sterile fashion. Next, using ultrasound, the right internal jugular vein was punctured under realtime ultrasound. A wire was subsequently advanced under fluoroscopy.

Next, attention was then turned to the chest wall. A site for the pocket for the port was chosen. This was then anesthetized with Lidocaine, as well as Lidocaine mixed with epinephrine. An incision was made. Using blunt dissection and Bovie cautery, a pocket was created. The underlying fascia was visualized. The wound was then irrigated with antibiotic solution. A small stab incision was then made around the wire at the jugular insertion site. Subcutaneous tunnel was then formed and port was then pulled through the tract. The port was then placed into the pocket. The catheter portion of the port was cut to the appropriate length. The dilator and peel-away sheath was removed. Follow-up fluoroscopy demonstrated excellent positioning of the port. The overlying superficial fascia was then closed with interrupted 2-0 Vicryl sutures. The skin was then closed with interrupted Ethilon 3-0 sutures. The small stab incision in the neck was then closed with 3-0 Ethilon sutures.

The port was accessed. It easily aspirated and flushed. It was flushed with heparinized saline. The port was left accessed as per the request of the oncologist. A sterile dressing was applied. There were no postprocedure complications.

IMPRESSION

Successful placement of a right-sided chest port with subcutaneous tunneling. The port is in excellent position and has excellent function. The port is left accessed and is ready for use.

Thank you for this referral.

Electronically Signed by Dr. 028

Case Study 6.4

Patient: **Patient V**

Patient documentation: **Read Operative Report 6.4**

1. What are the preoperative and postoperative diagnoses (description) that support the medical necessity of this procedure?

   _____

2. Are there any secondary diagnoses present that required additional procedures?

   _____

3. What was the principal or main procedure, and were other secondary procedures performed on this patient?

   _____

4. Do you believe you need additional documentation to correctly assign the surgery codes to this record? If so, what is the additional documentation that you need?

   _____

5. Do you have any additional questions for the surgeon?

   _____

6. What is(are) the procedure code(s) you would assign to this case study?

   _____

   _____

MEDICAL RECORD 6.4

OPERATIVE REPORT

PATIENT NAME:	Patient V
MR#:	444444
DATE OF OPERATION:	03/29/20XX
PREOPERATIVE DIAGNOSIS:	Rectal bleeding.
POSTOPERATIVE DIAGNOSIS:	1. Diverticulosis.
	2. Internal hemorrhoids.
OPERATION PERFORMED:	Colonoscopy.
SURGEON:	Dr. 029

PROCEDURE: Under conscious sedation with 75 mg of IV Demerol and 2.5 mg of IV Versed, in the left lateral decubitus position, digital examination was performed revealing adequate sphincter tone. No palpable masses and no blood. The Olympus CF160Q colonoscopy was inserted and advanced to the terminal ileum and cecum without difficulty. Findings were essentially unremarkable, except for some minimal diverticular changes in the sigmoid and grade 2 internal hemorrhoids that were not actively bleeding. The scope was withdrawn.

The patient tolerated the procedure well.

_____

Electronically Signed: Dr. 029

Case Study 6.5

Patient: **Patient W**

Patient documentation: **Read Operative Report 6.5**

1. What are the preoperative and postoperative diagnoses (description) that support the medical necessity of this procedure?

   _____

2. Are there any secondary diagnoses present that required additional procedures?

   _____

3. What was the principal or main procedure, and were other secondary procedures performed on this patient?

   _____

4. Do you believe you need additional documentation to correctly assign the surgery codes to this record? If so, what is the additional documentation that you need?

   _____

5. Do you have any additional questions for the surgeon?

   _____

6. What is(are) the procedure code(s) you would assign to this case study?

   _____

   _____

MEDICAL RECORD 6.5

OPERATIVE REPORT

PATIENT NAME:	Patient W
MR#:	555555
DATE OF OPERATION:	02/16/20XX
PREOPERATIVE DIAGNOSIS:	Right trigger thumb.
POSTOPERATIVE DIAGNOSIS:	Right trigger thumb.
OPERATION PERFORMED:	Right trigger thumb release; release of Al pulley.
SURGEON:	Dr. 030
ANESTHESIA:	General.
TOURNIQUET TIME:	5 minutes.

PROCEDURE: The patient was given a gram of Ancef preoperatively. After adequate level of anesthesia was obtained, the right upper extremity was prepped and draped in usual sterile fashion. Standard incision over the right volar aspect of the thumb MCP joint was made and carried down to subcutaneous tissues. The flexor tendon sheath, Al pulley was incised, exposing the flexor tendon. No gross abnormalities were noted. The wound was copiously irrigated. Skin was reapproximated with vertical mattress sutures, #4-0 nylon. Fifteen mL of 0.5% Marcaine without epinephrine was infiltrated in the wound. Sterile dressing was placed. Tourniquet was released. The patient was transferred to the recovery room in satisfactory condition.

_____

Electronically Signed: Dr. 030

Case Study 6.6

Patient: **Patient X**

Patient documentation: **Read Operative Report 6.6**

1. What are the preoperative and postoperative diagnoses (description) that support the medical necessity of this procedure?

   _____

2. Are there any secondary diagnoses present that required additional procedures?

   _____

3. What was the principal or main procedure, and were other secondary procedures performed on this patient?

   _____

4. Do you believe you need additional documentation to correctly assign the surgery codes to this record? If so, what is the additional documentation that you need?

   _____

5. Do you have any additional questions for the surgeon?

   _____

6. What is(are) the procedure code(s) you would assign to this case study?

   _____

   _____

MEDICAL RECORD 6.6

OPERATIVE REPORT

PATIENT NAME:	Patient X
MR#:	666666
DATE OF OPERATION:	02/16/20XX
PREOPERATIVE DIAGNOSIS:	Left inguinal hernia/umbilical hernia.
POSTOPERATIVE DIAGNOSIS:	Left inguinal hernia/umbilical hernia.
OPERATION PERFORMED:	Repair of left inguinal hernia, indirect, with mesh/repair of umbilical hernia, with mesh.
SURGEON:	Dr. 031
ANESTHESIA:	General.

FINDINGS: The patient presenting is a 57-year-old male with bulges at both the umbilical area and inguinal area. Plan is for exploration and repair. The procedure, attendant complications, and risks were reviewed, and all questions were answered. The potential for recurrence with the use of mesh was discussed. The patient understands, agrees, and wishes to proceed.

Examination at time of procedure demonstrates an indirect inguinal hernia, moderately large on the left, as well as umbilical hernia, also moderately large, measuring about 5 cm. No incarcerations of content or loss of viability.

PROCEDURE: The patient was placed in the supine position. The area of the abdomen, groin, and genitalia were prepped and draped in the usual sterile fashion. A linear incision was created under the umbilicus and carried into the subcutaneous tissue down the fascia. Fatty tissue surrounding was cleared. The sac was entered at its junction with fascia, and circumferentially incised and excised. The specimen was submitted, fatty tissue reduced. Primary transverse closure of the fascia, with a running stitch of double strength 0 Vicryl. Copious suction lavage of the wound was employed, no evidence of bleeding was noted. Prolene mesh is now placed over the area and anchored circumferentially with interrupted stitches of 0 Prolene suture. Vicryl 3-0 was placed in interrupted stitches to anchor the umbilicus and close the subcutaneous tissue. Surgical staples were applied to the skin for approximation.

Attention was then drawn to the left inguinal area where a curvilinear incision was created in the region of the left groin, carried through the subcutaneous tissue and superficial fascia. External oblique was identified and incised in direction of its fibers. Cord and structures were isolated at the level of the pubic tubercle and placed to Penrose drain traction. Findings as noted above. Identification and preservation of ilioinguinal nerve were accomplished. Sac was dissected free with lipoma and reduced. A large Prolene mesh hernia system was placed to the internal ring and unfurled in the preperitoneal space, after this had been dissected free with a 4 × 4 sponge.

The upper portion of the mesh was now unfurled along the floor, and again, preserving the nerve, anchored with interrupted stitches of 3-0 Vicryl suture at the pubic tubercle, and at the conjoined tendon a T-cut had been created at the level of the ring, with mesh wrapped around the cord to allow this to pass. The mesh was reconnected and anchored to adjacent inguinal ligament. Cord and structures were placed onto the inguinal ligament. Vicryl 3-0 was placed in a running stitch to approximate cut margins, external oblique fascia over cord and structures. Vicryl 3-0 was placed in interrupted stitches to close the subcutaneous tissue. Surgical staples were applied to the skin for approximation.

At the termination of the procedure, Marcaine was injected into the wounds. Sponge, needle, and instrument counts were noted to be correct.

The patient tolerated the procedure well, vital signs were stable, was sent to recovery room in stable and satisfactory condition. Estimated blood loss was approximately 10 mL total throughout.

Electronically Signed: Dr. 031

Case Study 6.7

Patient: **Patient Y**

Patient documentation: **Read Operative Report 6.7**

1. What are the preoperative and postoperative diagnoses (description) that support the medical necessity of this procedure?

   _____

2. Are there any secondary diagnoses present that required additional procedures?

   _____

3. What was the principal or main procedure, and were other secondary procedures performed on this patient?

   _____

4. Do you believe you need additional documentation to correctly assign the surgery codes to this record? If so, what is the additional documentation that you need?

   _____

5. Do you have any additional questions for the surgeon?

   _____

6. What is(are) the procedure code(s) from the surgery section of CPT you would assign to this case study?

   _____

   _____

THE MEDICAL IMAGING PROFESSIONALS, P.A.

PATIENT NAME: Patient Y

MR#: 777777

DATE OF EXAMINATION: 02/23/20XX

CLINICAL DATA: Biopsy, lymph nodes

CT GUIDED BIOPSY OF MESENTERIC LYMPH NODES

Patient was informed of the risks, benefits, and alternatives of the procedure and a consent form was signed.

The patient was brought to the CT suite and placed supine upon the table. Preliminary imaging demonstrated large conglomerate soft tissue mass in the mid abdomen extending to the left most compatible with that of large collection of nodes. Scan was performed after administration of oral contrast to help differentiate loops of bowel. Next, a skin site was chosen. This was prepped and draped in the usual sterile fashion. Local anesthesia was obtained with 1% Xylocaine solution. Next, a 20-guage needle was advanced into the abnormal soft tissue mass. Multiple passes with a cutting needle were made. Good core specimens were obtained. These were sent off for pathology. Preliminary pathology was that of an adequate specimen.

Guiding needle was then removed. Post biopsy scans through the area failed to demonstrate any evidence for hematoma. Patient was sent for observation.

IMPRESSION

Successful CT guided biopsy of the abnormal large mass within the mid abdomen. Final pathology is pending.

Electronically Signed and Dated

Case Study 6.8

Patient: **Patient Z**

Patient documentation: **Read Operative Report 6.8**

1. What are the preoperative and postoperative diagnoses (description) that support the medical necessity of this procedure?

    _____

2. Are there any secondary diagnoses present that required additional procedures?

    _____

3. What was the principal or main procedure, and were other secondary procedures performed on this patient?

    _____

4. Do you believe you need additional documentation to correctly assign the surgery codes to this record? If so, what is the additional documentation that you need?

    _____

5. Do you have any additional questions for the surgeon?

    _____

6. What is(are) the procedure code(s) you would assign to this case study?

    _____

    _____

MEDICAL RECORD 6.8

OPERATIVE REPORT

PATIENT NAME:	Patient Z
MR#:	888888
DATE OF OPERATION:	02/16/20XX
PREOPERATIVE DIAGNOSIS:	Rectocele
POSTOPERATIVE DIAGNOSIS:	Rectocele
OPERATION PERFORMED:	Rectocele repair
SURGEON:	Dr. 033
ANESTHESIA:	General, with endotracheal intubation
COMPLICATIONS:	None

FINDINGS: The patient had an extremely thin rectovaginal plate. As a matter of fact, the levator muscles and the endopelvic fascia were almost nonexistent.

OPERATIVE PROCEDURE: The patient was brought to the operating room and, after an adequate level of general anesthesia, she was placed in a supine lithotomy position. She was then prepped and draped in the usual fashion. A triangular flap incision was made in the posterior fourchette and perineum. This incision was taken through the midline in the vaginal mucosa. At this time I tried to remove the endopelvic fascia from the vaginal mucosa; however, as mentioned above, it was extremely thin, almost nonexistent. This incision was taken to approximately 2 cm from the cervix. With blunt dissection, the endopelvic fascia was completely dissected free. Multiple #0 Vicryl sutures were placed through the small levator muscle and endopelvic fascial tissue that was found to give good support over the rectum. The excess vaginal mucosa was then removed. The vaginal mucosa was then approximated with a running interlocking suture of 3-0 Vicryl. Several interrupted sutures were placed through the perineal muscle to give good support to the perineum. The skin edges were then approximated with a subcuticular stitch of 3-0 Vicryl. The patient tolerated the procedure well. She left the operating room to the recovery room in satisfactory condition.

_____

Electronically Signed: Dr. 033

Case Study 6.9

Patient: **Patient AA**

Patient documentation: **Read Operative Report 6.9**

1. What are the preoperative and postoperative diagnoses (description) that support the medical necessity of this procedure?

   _____

2. Are there any secondary diagnoses present that required additional procedures?

   _____

3. What was the principal or main procedure, and were other secondary procedures performed on this patient?

   _____

4. Do you believe you need additional documentation to correctly assign the surgery codes to this record? If so, what is the additional documentation that you need?

   _____

5. Do you have any additional questions for the surgeon?

   _____

6. What is(are) the procedure code(s) you would assign to this case study?

   _____

   _____

MEDICAL RECORD 6.9

OPERATIVE REPORT

PATIENT NAME:	Patient AA
MR#:	999999
DATE OF OPERATION:	02/27/2XXX
PREOPERATIVE DIAGNOSIS:	Right thyroid nodule.
POSTOPERATIVE DIAGNOSIS:	On frozen section, benign nodular goiter.
OPERATION PERFORMED:	Right total thyroid lobectomy.
SURGEON:	Dr. 034
ANESTHESIA:	General.
FINDINGS:	Enlarged right thyroid lobe with nodular masses darkly pigmented.

PROCEDURE: The patient was given taken to the operating room and was placed in the supine position on the operating table. The patient was then given general oral endotracheal anesthesia after which she was prepped and draped. She was placed in a slightly reversed Trendelenburg position with the head hyperextended underneath a shoulder roll and a bean-bag. The area in the lower neck was marked with a strand of 3-0 silk. The planned line of incision was then marked with ink along the mark made by the strand of silk. 1% lidocaine with 1:100,000 epinephrine was injected subcutaneously along the line.

With a #15 blade, a semilunar incision was made about two fingerbreadths above the clavicle starting from the anterior border of the sternocleidomastoid muscle on the left side going toward the midline and extending up to the anterior ster-nocleidomastoid muscle border on the right side. The incision was then cut with a #15 blade. Bleeders were controlled with a Bovie. The cervical fascia along the midline was identified. This was then split vertically. The linea alba was identified. This was then cut using a pair of Metzenbaum scissors.

The strap muscles were then teased bluntly off the underlying thyroid lobes on each side. Gelpi retractors were placed in the incision site for retraction. Dissection was then done around the right inferolateral border of the thyroid and ligated. The middle thyroid vein was likewise identified. This was doubly clamped, cut, and ligated and so was the right inferior thy-roid artery. Superiorly the thyroid lobe with a nodular mass was identified. This was dissected out with hemostats and a pair of Metzenbaum scissors. The posterior suspensory ligament was identified. It was also cut with a pair of Metzenbaum scissors. Toward the midline, the isthmus was identified. It was then doubly clamped at its attachment to the left thyroid lobe. It was then cut.

The right thyroid lobe was then retracted inferiorly and laterally away from the superior thyroid vessels, which were pre-served. Superior thyroid artery and vein were doubly clamped, cut, and ligated. The right thyroid lobe together with isth-mus was then taken out of the operative field and was sent for frozen section diagnosis. The operative field was then irri-gated with saline solution. Small bleeders were controlled with the Bovie.

At this time hemostasis was noted to have been attained. Frozen-section diagnosis given by Dr. 035, pathologist, was that of benign nodules. No malignancy was identified. A 0.5-inch Penrose drain was placed in the thyroid bed. The strap mus-cles were then sutured together along the midline with #3-0 chromic in simple interrupted manner. Skin closure was done using 5-0 nylon in simple interrupted manner. Bacitracin ointment was applied along the line of incision. A fluff pressure dressing was placed over the neck and was taped onto the skin in a Queen Anne type of dressing.

The patient was awakened and was extubated. She tolerated the whole procedure well. Her condition at the end was sat-isfactory.

Electronically Signed: Dr. 034

Case Study 6.10

Patient: **Patient BB**

Patient documentation: **Read Operative Report 6.10**

1. What are the preoperative and postoperative diagnoses (description) that support the medical necessity of this procedure?

   _____

2. Are there any secondary diagnoses present that required additional procedures?

   _____

3. What was the principal or main procedure, and were other secondary procedures performed on this patient?

   _____

4. Do you believe you need additional documentation to correctly assign the surgery codes to this record? If so, what is the additional documentation that you need?

   _____

5. Do you have any additional questions for the surgeon?

   _____

6. What is(are) the procedure code(s) from the surgery section of CPT you would assign to this case study?

   _____

   _____

SUNSHINE MEDICAL IMAGING PROFESSIONALS

PATIENT NAME: Patient BB
MR#:   101010
DATE OF EXAMINATION: 03/27/2XXX
CLINICAL DATA: Right upper lobe mass

CT GUIDED LUNG BIOPSY

The previous films were reviewed. Procedure and risks, including bleeding and pneumothorax, were explained to the patient who consented. The patient was placed prone in the CT scanner and localized images were obtained.

Using sterile technique, local anesthesia, and CT guidance, a needle was introduced into the lesion from a posterolateral approach. Attempts were made to avoid the superior segment of the left lower lobe, which was adjacent to the acquired approach to the lesion. Biopsy was obtained using a 20-gauge biopsy device. Three cores were collected. Preliminary report is positive for malignancy. The patient tolerated the procedure well. After needle removal, there was an approximately 10% right apical pneumothorax. The patient remained asymptomatic. Follow-up films will be obtained.

IMPRESSION:

Small pneumothorax post CT-guided right upper lobe biopsy, as above.

Thank you for this referral.

_____

Electronically Signed and Dated

MEDICAL RECORD CASE STUDIES 6.10 (Continued)

(SECOND PROCEDURE—SAME PATIENT, SAME PHYSICIAN NEXT DAY)

SUNSHINE MEDICAL IMAGING PROFESSIONALS

DATE OF EXAMINATION: 03/28/2XXX

CLINICAL DATA: Tube placement

CHEST

A right small caliber chest tube was placed and had a Heimlich valve attached to it. Right pneumothorax is almost completely resolved. Only a small residual apical pneumothorax is seen. The patient remains asymptomatic and will be observed for several hours.

IMPRESSION:

Almost complete resolution right apical pneumothorax post chest tube placement.

_____

Electronically Signed and Dated

CHAPTER 7

Evaluation and Management (E/M)

Chapter Outline

Organization of the E/M Section
Commonly Used E/M Terms
E/M Documentation Guidelines
Assigning E/M Codes
Overview of E/M Categories
Modifiers for E/M Services
Testing Your Comprehension
Coding Practice I: Chapter Review Exercises
Coding Practice II: Medical Record Case Studies
Additional Coding Practice Exercise

Chapter Objectives

▶ Name and define the various types of Evaluation and Management services.
▶ Explain the format of the E/M section (categories and subcategories).
▶ Recognize and understand the terminology used in the E/M section.
▶ Identify the modifiers used in the E/M section.
▶ Correctly assign E/M codes and modifiers for services.

In 1992, the Evaluation and Management section was added to the CPT manual, which now encompasses the code range 99201 through 99499. **Evaluation and management** *codes were primarily developed to report the services performed by physicians in terms of the skill, effort, time, and knowledge required to diagnose and treat a patient's condition or to promote health to receive payment from third-party payers. For the most part, these codes are used to report outpatient services provided in a physician's office. They are also used to report physician services provided in hospitals (which can include admissions, consultations, emergency room, critical care, or observation services) and in other settings such as skilled nursing facilities. Although E/M codes are primarily used for reporting physicians' professional services, one exception to this is that hospitals use E/M codes to report emergency department services to be reimbursed for the technical component of care. Reimbursement for E/M services is dependent on reporting the ICD-9-CM* *diagnosis codes that establish the medical necessity for the service. For example, a physician may report a level 2 E/M code to describe an office visit to "evaluate and manage" a 16-year-old girl (established patient) suffering from allergic rhinitis as a result of pollen. The E/M code reported for the service would be 99212, and the ICD-9-CM diagnosis code reported to support the medical necessity for the service would be 477.0.*

Organization of the E/M Section

Note that E/M section (containing codes that begin with "99") is placed out of numerical order in the beginning of the CPT manual. This is because coders in physicians' offices most often use the codes, and the E/M section was placed at the front of the CPT manual for easy access. Appendix C of the CPT manual highlights various clinical examples to help coders and billers in physicians' offices correctly report and process claims using codes from the E/M section.

The E/M section is divided into broad subsections (categories), that describe:

▶ *Location of service* (such as the physician's office or hospital)
▶ *Type of service* (such as a consultation or critical care services)

The E/M section is further divided into subcategories that describe:

▶ *Type of patient* (new or established patient)
▶ *Specific type of care* within a service category (such as pediatric critical care, comprehensive nursing facility assessment, observation care discharge services).

The five-digit E/M codes begin with "99." They are used to describe the level and extent of services provided by the physician. For example, a comprehensive history was taken, a comprehensive examination performed, and medical decision making of moderate complexity was required. E/M service codes describe the nature of the presenting problem (for example, the patient's presenting problems are of moderate to high severity).The codes also document the time typically required to provide a service.

 TIP Although E/M codes begin with "99," be aware that some codes from the Medicine section also begin with "99."

Evaluation and Management Subsections (Categories) and Subcategories

Table 7.1 shows the E/M subsections and the code ranges that apply to each subsection.

TABLE 7.1   Evaluation and Management Subsections and Code Ranges

E/M Subsections/Subcategories	Code Range
Office or other outpatient services	
▶ New patient	99201–99205
▶ Established patient	99211–99215
Hospital observation services	
▶ Hospital observation discharge services	99217
▶ Inpatient hospital observation services	99218–99220
▶ Hospital observation or inpatient care services (including same day admission and discharge services)	99234–99236
Hospital inpatient services	
▶ Initial hospital care	99221–99223
▶ Subsequent hospital care	99231–99233
▶ Hospital discharge services	99238–99239
Consultations	
▶ Office consultations	99241–99245
▶ Initial inpatient consultations	99251–99255
Emergency department services	99281–99288
Pediatric patient transport	99289–99290
Critical care services	
▶ Adult (> 24 months of age)	99291–99292
▶ Pediatric	99293–99294
▶ Neonatal	99295–99296
Continuing intensive care services	99298–99300
Nursing facility services	
▶ Initial nursing facility care	99304–99306
▶ Subsequent nursing facility care	99307–99310
▶ Nursing facility discharge services	99315–99316
▶ Other nursing facility services	99318
Domiciliary, rest home (e.g., boarding home), or custodial care services	
▶ New patient	99324–99328
▶ Established patient	99334–99337
Domiciliary, rest home (e.g., assisted living facility), or home care plan oversight services	99339–99340
Home services	
▶ New patient	99341–99345
▶ Established patient	99347–99350
Prolonged services	
▶ With direct patient contact	99354–99357
▶ Without direct patient contact	99358–99359
Standby services	99360
Case management services	
▶ Anticoagulant management	99363–99364
▶ Medical team conferences	99366–99368
Care plan oversight services	99374–99380
Preventive medicine services	
▶ New patient	99381–99387
▶ Established patient	99391–99397
▶ Individual counseling	99401–99404
▶ Group counseling	99411–99412
▶ Other	99420–99429
Newborn care	99431–99440
Non-face-to-face physician services	
▶ Telephone services	99441–99443
▶ Online medical evaluation	99444
Special E/M services	99450–99456
Other E/M services	99499

Commonly Used E/M Terms

Effective E/M coding requires an understanding of the most commonly used E/M terms, which include the following:

New patient—A patient who has not received any professional services from the physician or another physician of the same specialty and same physician practice group within the past 3 years.

Established patient—A patient who has received professional services from the physician or another physician of the same specialty and same physician practice group within the past 3 years.

Level of service—E/M codes most often describe from one to five levels of service. The level increases as the physician's work effort and intensity increases. Up to seven components can be used to determine the appropriate service level to assign the proper E/M code. As the physician invests more effort, the code level rises, as does the payment level to the provider. Within the seven components used to determine the code level, the first three components are **key components**; they are essential to assigning the correct E/M code. Key components are:

- History (type)
- Examination (type)
- Medical decision making (type)

The next four components are **contributing components**, which are used when applicable:

- Counseling
- Coordination of care
- Nature of presenting problem
- Time

Concurrent care—Concurrent care includes instances when two or more physicians provide similar services to the same patient on the same day. This often occurs when the physicians are from different specialties. A third-party payer may deny or limit payment to one physician unless it can be determined that the concurrent services by all the involved physicians are medically necessary.

EXAMPLE

A patient is admitted to the hospital for an acute exacerbation of chronic obstructive lung disease (COPD) and newly found atrial fibrillation. Dr. Lung treated the patient's COPD, and Dr. Hart treated the patient's atrial fibrillation. Dr. Lung will report ICD-9-CM diagnosis code 491.21 (acute exacerbation of COPD), and Dr. Hart will report ICD-9-CM diagnosis code 427.31 (atrial fibrillation). Coders for both physicians will also assign the correct E/M code from the hospital inpatient or consultative service category.

Unlisted E/M code—When an E/M service is provided that does not have a corresponding code listed from the E/M section, then code 99499 (unlisted E/M service) is used. This is a code of last resort and should only be used when an adequate E/M code describing the service cannot be located. In the rare instances when the unlisted code is used, a special report must be sent to the payer describing the medical necessity for the unlisted E/M service or procedure.

Unlisted CPT codes end with the digits "99," so they are easy to recognize. However, unlisted codes should be used with caution because insurance carriers will often question their usage. Use of unlisted codes may delay or limit payment or result in a denial of payment to the physician.

E/M Documentation Guidelines

In 1995, CMS implemented a set of documentation guidelines for physicians to follow to substantiate the services provided for payment and reported through E/M codes. This information can be found in the Guidelines at the beginning of the E/M section. In 1997, CMS published a revised set of Guidelines. It is important to note that the 1997 Guidelines did not replace the 1995 version; providers elect to follow one or the other set of E/M Guidelines in reporting their services. A full text reference for both the approved 1995 and 1997 CMS Documentation Guidelines is available for download from: http://www.cms.hhs.gov/MLNProducts/downloads/physicianguide.pdf.

Providers and coders must use *either the 1995 or 1997 Guidelines* to validate the E/M codes selected that report professional services. You *cannot* mix and match within an individual record in an attempt to maximize reimbursement.

In many respects, the 1995 and 1997 Guidelines are similar; however, there are striking differences in the (physical) examination requirements. Special notes are provided in the following sections to highlight the distinct differences between the 1995 and 1997 Guidelines. The itemization of the 1997 examination documentation elements removed the subjectivity that could occur using the 1995 documentation requirements. It became easier to perform an item-by-item audit of the specific documentation requirements needed to substantiate an E/M code level and justify the reimbursement to the physician.

The 1997 documentation guidelines are best applied with the use of various commercially available software or templates (see Fig. 7.1 for a sample template). These automated systems and templates are used to count the data elements present that are necessary for correctly assigning an E/M code level and to help determine the correct code. They also create an audit trail that substantiates the rationale for assigning a particular E/M code level. This is particularly beneficial in light of the complexity of the E/M coding process and the possibility for a CMS audit of coding and billing practices.

Assigning E/M Codes

As noted previously, CPT defines each level of E/M services by basing it on a unique combination of the three key components: the type of history, type of examination, and type of medical decision making. For example, an office

Office Visit, New Patient - 3 Elements must be met

Code	History (Hx)	Exam	Decision Making
99201	Prob Foc Hx	Prob Foc Exam	Straightforward
99202	Expand Prob Foc Hx	Expand Prob Foc Exam	Straightforward
99203	Detailed Hx	Detailed Exam	Low Complex
99204	Comprehensive Hx	Comprehensive Exam	Moderate Complex
99205	Comprehensive Hx	Comprehensive Exam	High Complex

Office Visit, Established Patient - 2 of 3 Elements must be met

Code	History (Hx)	Exam	Decision Making
99211	N/A	N/A	N/A
99212	Prob Foc Hx	Prob Foc Exam	Straightforward
99213	Expand Prob Foc Hx	Expand Prob Foc Exam	Low Complex
99214	Detailed Hx	Detailed Exam	Moderate Complex
99215	Comprehensive Hx	Comprehensive Exam	High Complex

History

Type of Hx	HPI	ROS	PFSH
Prob Foc Hx	Brief 1-3 elements below	N/A	N/A
Expand Prob Foc Hx	Brief 1-3 elements below	Prob Pertinent - System directly related to prob	N/A
Detailed Hx	Extended 4 or more below	Extended - System directly related to prob and 2 to 9 additional sys	Pertinent At least 1 item from any of the 3 hx areas must be documented
Comprehensive	Extended 4 or more below	Complete - System directly related to prob plus at least 10 additional systems	Complete 2 or 3 items from any of the 3 hx areas must be documented * If initial, all 3 must be documented

Elements	ROS	PFSH
Location Quality Severity Duration Timing Context Modifying Factors Assoc. Signs & Symp	Constitutional Symptoms; Eyes; Ears, Nose, Mouth & Throat; Cardiovascular; Respiratory; Gastrointestinal; Genitourinary; Musculoskeletal; Integumentary (skin and/or breast); Neurological; Psychiatric; Endocrine; Hematologic/Lymphatic; Allergic/Immunologic	Past Hx Family Hx Social Hx

Exam

Type of Exam - General	Type of Exam - Single Organ	Medical Decision Making — Type of MDM
Prob Foc Exam 1 to 5 elements identified by a bullet (•) in one or more systems(s) or area(s)	**Prob Foc Exam** 1 to 5 elements identified by a bullet (•)	**Straightforward** DX = Minimal CD = Minimal or none RC = Minimal
Expand Prob Foc Exam at least 6 elements identified by a bullet (•) in one or more systems(s) or area(s)	**Expand Prob Foc Exam** at least 6 elements identified by a bullet (•)	**Low Complex** DX = Limited CD = Limited RC = Low
Detailed Exam at least 6 system(s) or area(s) with at least 2 elements identified by a bullet (•) each, or, at least 12 elements identified by a bullet (•) in 2 or more system(s) or area(s)	**Detailed Exam** at least 12 elements identified by a bullet (•). Eye & Psychiatric - at least 9 elements identified by a bullet (•).	**Moderate Complex** DX = Multiple CD = Moderate RC = Moderate
Comprehensive at least 9 system(s) or area(s). All elements identified by a bullet (•) should be performed. For each sys/area, at least 2 elements is expected.	**Comprehensive Exam** should include all elements identified by a bullet (•).	**High Complex** DX = Extensive CD = Extensive RC = High

System/Body Areas	System/Body Areas	Key for MDM
Constitutional Eyes Ears, Nose, Mouth & Throat Neck Respiratory Cardiovascular Chest (Breasts) Gastrointestinal (Abdomen) Genitourinary Male Female Lymphatic Musculoskeletal Skin Neurologic Psychiatric	Constitutional Eyes Ears, Nose, Mouth & Throat Neck Respiratory Cardiovascular Chest (Breasts) Gastrointestinal (Abdomen) Genitourinary Male Female Lymphatic Musculoskeletal Skin Neurologic Psychiatric	DX = Number of diagnoses or Management options CD = Complexity of Data to be reviewed RC = Risk of Complications and/or morbidity or morality

FIGURE 7.1 ■ Sample evaluation and management documentation guidelines template.

visit for a new patient with a problem-focused history, problem-focused examination, and straightforward medical decision making is coded 99201. Contributing components are used, when applicable (e.g., the assignment of critical care codes 99291–99292 are based on the contributing component of time).

When selecting the appropriate level of service, a coder must first consider the supporting documentation in the patient's record. There must be supporting documentation in the medical record, which remains the final source when reporting a particular level of service code. When necessary, the coder must query the physician to clarify that the code selected provides the best description of the service performed.

When assigning an E/M code, coders should consider the service from the physician's viewpoint and do the following steps:

Step 1—Ask Where am I?

Are the services being provided in the physician's office, other outpatient setting, hospital, or nursing home? This is the first critical step that will help coders locate the correct E/M category. This generally narrows the search from 1 to 5 levels of possible codes within a category (e.g., office visit, consultation, emergency department services). Begin by locating the main term "Evaluation and Management" within the alphabetic index. Then review the subterms and select the appropriate category (location or type of service). The category will lead to a single code or range of codes to review within the tabular list.

Step 2—Ask What am I Dealing With?

After selecting the code or range of codes from the index, locate the appropriate code in the tabular list. (Is the physician dealing with a new patient or an established patient? Is he or she performing a specific type of consultation service?) This will lead to the correct E/M subcategory to find the correct code. Remember, coders should never code from the index alone but should review the code description within the tabular list for more information. This practice ensures precise coding.

Step 3—Define the Type of Service by Key Component

Following the 1995 or 1997 Guidelines, determine the level or extent of service by answering the following questions:

- ▶ What type of history was performed?
- ▶ What type of examination was performed?
- ▶ What type of medical decision making was required?

Step 4—Determine the Number of Key Components

To define the appropriate level of E/M service, refer to the key component requirements:

- ▶ *New patients require three of three matches* of the required key components to select the code.
- ▶ *Established patients require two of three* matches of the required key components.

EXAMPLES

1—To qualify code 99203 for an office visit for a new patient, all three key components *are required and must be supported by documentation. For code 99203, a* detailed history, *a* detailed examination, *and* medical decision making of low complexity *are all required (see Table 7.2). If the service is not qualified for a particular level, then the lower level code that is substantiated by the documentation must be used (e.g., if 99203 is not qualified, assign 99202).*

2—To qualify code 99213 for an office visit for an established patient, at least two of the three components *are required (see Table 7.3). If the service does not qualify for a particular level, a lower level code that is substantiated by the documentation must be selected (e.g., if 99213 is not qualified, assign 99212).*

TABLE 7.2	Key Components: Office Visit, New Patient		
Code	History	Examination	Medical Decision Making
99201	Problem focused	Problem focused	Straightforward
99202	Expanded problem focused	Expanded problem focused	Straightforward
99203	Detailed	Detailed	Low complexity
99204	Comprehensive	Comprehensive	Moderate complexity
99205	Comprehensive	Comprehensive	High complexity

Current Procedural Terminology 2008 © American Medical Association. All rights reserved.

TABLE 7.3	Key Components: Office Visit, Established Patient		
Code	History	Examination	Medical Decision Making
99211	N/A	N/A	N/A
99212	Problem focused	Problem focused	Straightforward
99213	Expanded problem focused	Expanded problem focused	Low complexity
99214	Detailed	Detailed	Moderate complexity
99215	Comprehensive	Comprehensive	High complexity

Current Procedural Terminology 2008 © American Medical Association. All rights reserved.

Note how the codes shown in Tables 7.2 and 7.3 end in the digits 1, 2, 3, 4, or 5. Each higher number denotes the increasing effort and work required by the physician to evaluate and manage the patient. This would be commensurate with increasing payments for the provider's services. Familiar "buzz words" in a physician's practice would be that a "level 2 code" was used, or a "level 4 code" was assigned, to bill for a particular patient's service.

Step 5—Identify Any Applicable Contributing Components

Coders should ask the following questions to gather additional information to support the proper E/M codes.

1. *What is the nature of the presenting problem?*

   The five types of presenting problems include:
   ▶ Minimal
   ▶ Self-limited or minor

- ▶ Low severity
- ▶ Moderate severity
- ▶ High severity

2. *What was the average time spent with the patient?*

Specific times that represent average times for the service are noted within the level of service code. *Face-to-face time* describes the time that the physician spends meeting personally with the patient or family. It applies to the office, other outpatient services, and office consultations.

  Unit/floor time describes the time that the physician is present on the patient's hospital unit and at bedside. It includes the time the physician examines the patient, reviews the medical record, makes notes, and communicates with other clinicians and the patient's family. It applies to inpatient hospital care, observation services, initial and follow-up inpatient consultations, and nursing facility services.

3. *Was counseling or coordination of care part of the service?*

When counseling or coordination of care dominates more than 50% of the face-to-face physician-patient encounter, *time* is considered the key factor to qualify for a particular level of E/M services code. It is important that the total time for the visit and time devoted to counseling and coordination of care is documented in the patient's record.

Step 6—Perform a Common Sense Test

Coders should ask themselves whether the E/M code level seems appropriate to the patient's condition and the amount of time the physician spent with the patient. For example, a patient presenting with a severe problem such as acute chest pain that requires a great deal of the physician's time may have level 3 or 4 code assigned. In contrast, a patient being treated for a minor condition such as a common cold needs less of the physician's time and may have a level 1 or 2 assigned.

Selecting the Type of History Performed

A **history** is the patient's *subjective* statements regarding his or her illness or complaint that are recorded by the physician to begin the process of establishing a definitive diagnosis and initiate an appropriate plan of care (i.e., treatment).

  For the first key component, there are four types of histories:

- ▶ Problem-focused
- ▶ Expanded problem-focused
- ▶ Detailed
- ▶ Comprehensive.

  Table 7.4 outlines which elements must be documented to qualify for a specific history type.

  A **chief complaint** (C/C) is required element for all history types and levels. Stated in the patient's own words, the chief complaint is a concise statement describing the symptom, problem, condition, or other cause for the encounter. Three additional elements must be met to quality for a specific history type: history of present illness (HPI); review of systems (ROS); and past, family, or social history (PFSH).

TABLE 7.4	Elements of a History			
History Type	Chief Complaint	History of Present Illness	Review of Systems	PFSH
Problem focused	Required	Brief	N/A	N/A
Expanded problem focused	Required	Brief	Problem pertinent	N/A
Detailed	Required	Extended	Extended	Pertinent
Comprehensive	Required	Extended	Complete	Complete

Current Procedural Terminology 2008 © American Medical Association. All rights reserved.

 TIP In selecting a history type, a chief complaint is required at all levels.

Stated by the patient, the **history of present illness** (HPI), as an element of the history, is a chronologic description (from the beginning through the present) of the symptoms and signs associated with the current condition, complaint, or problem since the patient's last visit to the physician. See Table 7.5 for examples of HPI elements. The two types of HPI include:

▶ *Brief HPI*—There must be documentation of 1–3 elements.
▶ *Extended HPI*—There must be documentation of 4 or more elements.

TABLE 7.5	Examples of HPI Elements
HPI Element	**Examples**
Location	chest, abdomen, arm, leg, groin, head
Severity	excruciating, unbearable, minimal, mild discomfort (e.g., pain scale 1–10)
Timing	1.5 hours after eating, 1 hour after walking
Quality	sharp, dull, burning, chronic, prolonged, intermittent
Duration	for 1 month, since last visit, started 2–3 days ago
Associated signs/ manifestations	nausea and vomiting, shortness of breath, chest pain, abdominal pain
Context	when resting, when walking, when standing up or sitting down
Modifying factors	improves with rest, worsens after eating, better lying on side

 TIP The 1997 Guidelines revised the extended HPI requirements to state: An extended HPI consists of at least four elements of the HPI or the status of at least three chronic or inactive conditions.

Review of systems (ROS), as an element of the history, is an inventory of body systems obtained by the physician through a series of questions asked of the patient (e.g., How is your breathing? How is your heart? How is your sight and hearing? Have you been going to the bathroom regularly?). These questions are designed to identify signs or symptoms that the patient may be experiencing or has previously experienced.

The three types of ROS include:

▶ *Problem-pertinent ROS*—Review of the system directly related to the problem(s) identified in the HPI. The patient's positive and pertinent negative responses help identify the *one system* that should be documented.

▶ *Extended ROS*—Review of the system directly related to the problem(s) identified in the HPI and a limited number of additional systems. The patient's positive and pertinent negative responses for *two to nine systems* should be documented.

▶ *Complete ROS*—Review of the system directly related to the problem(s) identified in the HPI and all additional body systems. *At least 10 organ systems* must be reviewed.

The 14 systems addressed in the review of systems are:

▶ Constitutional symptoms (fever, weight loss, etc. affecting the whole body)
▶ Eyes
▶ Ears, nose, mouth, throat
▶ Cardiovascular
▶ Respiratory
▶ Gastrointestinal
▶ Genitourinary
▶ Musculoskeletal
▶ Integumentary (skin or breast)
▶ Neurologic
▶ Psychiatric
▶ Endocrine
▶ Hematologic/lymphatic
▶ Allergic/immunologic.

The **past, family, or social history** (PFSH), as an element of the history, documents the patient's past medical issues and treatments; family medical events and status; and lifestyle or environmental conditions and social activities and habits (see Table 7.6). The two types of PFSH are:

▶ *Pertinent PFSH*—At least one history area from any of the three history areas must be documented.

▶ *Complete PFSH*—At least one specific item from two of the three history areas must be documented for the following categories: office or other outpatient services, established patient; emergency department; domiciliary care, established patient; and home care, established patient.

TABLE 7.6	Elements of a PFSH
Past (personal) history	A review of the patient's past experiences with illnesses, injuries, operations, and treatments (including allergies, immunizations, and medications)
Family history	A review of medical events in the patient's family, including hereditary diseases or conditions that may place the patient at added risk, as well as the age (if living) and status (alive or dead) of blood relatives
Social history	An age-appropriate review of past and current social activities and lifestyle aspects (marital status, number of children, education, employment or service history, exposure to environmental agents, hobbies, living conditions, use of caffeine, alcohol, tobacco, or drugs)

TABLE 7.7	History Requirements			
History Type	Problem Focused	Expanded Problem Focused	Detailed	Comprehensive
HPI elements: ✓ Location ✓ Quality ✓ Severity ✓ Duration ✓ Timing ✓ Context ✓ Modifying factors ✓ Associated signs and symptoms	*Brief:* 1–3 elements	*Brief:* 1–3 elements	*Extended:* ≥ 4 elements	*Extended:* ≥ 4 elements
ROS (review of systems): ✓ Constitutional ✓ Eyes ✓ Ears, nose, mouth, throat ✓ Cardiovascular ✓ Respiratory ✓ Gastrointestinal ✓ Genitourinary ✓ Musculoskeletal ✓ Integumentary ✓ Neurologic ✓ Psychiatric ✓ Endocrine ✓ Hematologic/lymphatic ✓ Allergic/immunologic:	*None*	*Pertinent* 1 system	*Extended:* 2–9 systems	*Complete:* ≥ 10 systems
PFSH areas: ✓ Past (personal) medical history ✓ Family history ✓ Social history	*None*	*None*	*Pertinent:* 1 history area	*Complete:* 2–3 history areas

Table 7.7 summarizes the requirements for documenting each history type.

Selecting the Type of Examination Performed

Examination is a physician's *objective* physical examination of the patient's body system(s) or body area(s) to gain further data related to the patient's illness or complaint. Together, the subjective data obtained in the patient's history and the objective data obtained in the patient's examination help the physician establish a provisional diagnosis and begin the appropriate plan of care for the patient. The four types of examinations are:

- ▶ *Problem Focused*—The examination is limited to the affected body area or organ system.
- ▶ *Expanded Problem Focused*—The examination involves the affected body area or organ systems as well as symptomatic or related organ systems.

PHYSICAL EXAMINATIONS

Physical Examinations—Recognized Organ Systems and Body Areas

Cardiovascular	Respiratory
Ears, nose, mouth, and throat	Skin
Eyes	Head, including face
Genitourinary/female	Neck
Genitourinary/male	Chest (breasts, axillae)
Hematologic/lymphatic/immunologic	Gastrointestinal (abdomen)
Musculoskeletal	Genitalia, groin, buttocks
Neurologic	Back
Psychiatric	Each extremity

▶ *Detailed*—An extended examination is performed on the affected body area(s) and other symptomatic or related organ systems.

▶ *Comprehensive*—A general multi-system or complete examination of a single organ system (a general multisystem examination should include eight or more of the recognized organ systems).

Review the table above that lists the recognized organ systems and body are as for a physical examination.

TIP   The 1997 E/M Documentation Guidelines presented major changes to the documentation requirements for selecting a particular examination type. Detailed revisions were made to the data elements required to document a General Multi-System Examination and Single Organ System Examination.

GENERAL MULTI-SYSTEM EXAMINATION

The requirements for General Multi-System Examinations are shown below. Note that elements identified by a bullet (•) refer to bulleted items in the Documentation Guidelines (see Table 7.8).

▶ *Problem Focused*—Examination should include performance and documentation of one to five elements identified by a bullet (•) in one or more organ system(s) or body area(s).

▶ *Expanded Problem Focused*—Examination should include performance and documentation of at least six elements identified by a bullet (•) in one or more organ system(s) or body area(s).

▶ *Detailed*—Examination should include at least six organ systems or body areas. For each system or area selected, performance and documentation of at least two elements identified by a bullet (•) is expected. Alternatively, a detailed examination may include performance and documentation of at least 12 elements identified by a bullet (•) in two or more organ systems or body areas.

▶ *Comprehensive*—Examination should include at least nine organ systems or body areas. For each system or area selected, all elements of the examination identified by a bullet (•) should be performed, unless specific directions limit the content of the examination. For each area or system, documentation of at least two elements identified by a bullet is expected.

TABLE 7.8 General Multi-System Examination

System/Body Area	Elements of Examination
Constitutional	• Measurement of **any three of the following seven** vital signs: (1) sitting or standing blood pressure, (2) supine blood pressure, (3) pulse rate and regularity, (4) respiration, (5) temperature, (6) height, (7) weight (may be measured and recorded by ancillary staff) • General appearance of patient (e.g., development, nutrition, body habitus, deformities, attention to grooming)
Eyes	• Inspection of conjunctivae and lids • Examination of pupils and irises (e.g., reaction to light and accommodation, size and symmetry) • Ophthalmoscopic examination of optic discs (e.g., size, C/D ratio, appearance) and posterior segments (e.g., vessel changes, exudates, hemorrhages)
Ears, nose, mouth, and throat	• External inspection of ears and nose (e.g., overall appearance, scars, lesions, masses) • Otoscopic examination of external auditory canals and tympanic membranes • Assessment of hearing (e.g., whispered voice, finger rub, tuning fork) • Inspection of nasal mucosa, septum, and turbinates • Inspection of lips, teeth, and gums • Examination of oropharynx: oral mucosa, salivary glands, hard and soft palates, tongue, tonsils, and posterior pharynx
Neck	• Examination of neck (e.g., masses, overall appearance, symmetry, tracheal position, crepitus) • Examination of thyroid (e.g., enlargement, tenderness, mass)
Respiratory	• Assessment of respiratory effort (e.g., intercostal retractions, use of accessory muscles, diaphragmatic movement) • Percussion of chest (e.g., dullness, flatness, hyper-resonance) • Palpation of chest (e.g., tactile fremitus) • Auscultation of lungs (e.g., breath sounds, adventitious sounds, rubs)
Cardiovascular	• Palpation of heart (e.g., location, size, thrills) • Auscultation of heart with notation of abnormal sounds and murmurs Examination of: • Carotid arteries (e.g., pulse amplitude, bruits) • Abdominal aorta (e.g., size, bruits) • Femoral arteries (e.g., pulse amplitude, bruits) • Pedal pulses (e.g., pulse amplitude) • Extremities for edema or varicosities
Chest (breasts)	• Inspection of breasts (e.g., symmetry, nipple discharge) • Palpation of breasts and axillae (e.g., masses or lumps, tenderness)
Gastrointestinal (abdomen)	• Examination of abdomen with notation of presence of masses or tenderness • Examination of liver and spleen • Examination for presence or absence of hernia • Examination (when indicated) of anus, perineum, and rectum, including sphincter tone, presence of hemorrhoids, rectal masses • Stool sample for occult blood test when indicated
Genitourinary	**MALE:** • Examination of the scrotal contents (e.g., hydrocele, spermatocele, tenderness of cord, testicular mass) • Examination of the penis • Digital rectal examination of prostate gland (e.g., size, symmetry, nodularity, tenderness) **FEMALE:** Pelvic examination (with or without specimen collection for smears and cultures), including: • Examination of external genitalia (e.g., general appearance, hair distribution, lesions) and vagina (e.g., general appearance, estrogen effect, discharge, lesions, pelvic support, cystocele, rectocele) • Examination of urethra (e.g., masses, tenderness, scarring) • Examination of bladder (e.g., fullness, masses, tenderness) • Cervix (e.g., general appearance, lesions, discharge) • Uterus (e.g., size, contour, position, mobility, tenderness, consistency, descent or support) • Adnexa/parametria (e.g., masses, tenderness, organomegaly, nodularity)

(continued)

TABLE 7.8	General Multi-System Examination (Continued)
System/Body Area	**Elements of Examination**
Lymphatic	Palpation of lymph nodes in **two or more** areas: ● Neck ● Axillae ● Groin ● Other
Musculoskeletal	● Examination of gait and station ● Inspection or palpation of digits and nails (e.g., clubbing, cyanosis, inflammatory conditions, petechiae, ischemia, infections, nodes) Examination of joints, bones, and muscles of **one or more of the following six** areas: (1) head and neck, (2) spine, ribs, and pelvis, (3) right upper extremity, (4) left upper extremity, (5) right lower extremity, and (6) left lower extremity. Examination of a given area includes: ● Inspection or palpation with notation of presence of any misalignment, asymmetry, crepitation, defects, tenderness, masses, effusions ● Assessment of range of motion with notation of any pain, crepitation, or contracture ● Assessment of stability with notation of any dislocation (luxation), subluxation, or laxity ● Assessment of muscle strength and tone (e.g., flaccid, cog wheel, spastic) with notation of any atrophy or abnormal movements
Skin	● Inspection of skin and subcutaneous tissue (e.g., rashes, lesions, ulcers) ● Palpation of skin and subcutaneous tissue (e.g., induration, subcutaneous nodules, tightening)
Neurologic	● Test cranial nerves with notation of any deficits ● Examination of deep tendon reflexes with notation of pathologic reflexes (e.g., Babinski) ● Examination of sensation (e.g., by touch, pin, vibration, proprioception)
Psychiatric	● Description of patient's judgment and insight Brief assessment of mental status including: ● Orientation to time, place, and person ● Recent and remote memory ● Mood and affect (e.g., depression, anxiety, agitation)

(Source: U.S. Department of Health and Human Services, Centers for Medicare and Medicaid Services, Medicare Learning Network http://www.cms.hhs.gov/MLNProducts/downloads/physicianguide.pdf).

SINGLE ORGAN SYSTEM EXAMINATION

The requirements for Single Organ System Examinations are shown below. Note that elements identified by a bullet (•) refer to bulleted items in the Documentation Guidelines (see the example in Table 7.9).

▶ *Problem Focused*—Examination should include performance and documentation of one of five elements identified by a bullet (•), whether in a box with a shaded or unshaded border.

▶ *Expanded Problem Focused*—Examination should include performance and documentation of at least six elements identified by a bullet (•), whether in a box with a shaded or unshaded border.

▶ *Detailed*—Examination other than eye and psychiatric examinations should include performance and documentation of at least 12 elements identified by a bullet (•), whether in a box with a shaded or unshaded border. Eye and psychiatric examinations should include the performance and documentation of at least nine elements identified by a bullet (•), whether in a box with a shaded or unshaded border.

TABLE 7.9   Single Organ System Examination: Ear, Nose, and Throat

System/Body Area	Elements of Examination
Constitutional	• Measurement of **any three of the following seven** vital signs: (1) sitting or standing blood pressure, (2) supine blood pressure,(3) pulse rate and regularity, (4) respiration, (5) temperature, (6) height, (7) weight (may be measured and recorded by ancillary staff) • General appearance of patient (e.g., development, nutrition, body habitus, deformities, attention to grooming) • Assessment of ability to communicate (e.g., use of sign language or other communication aids) and quality of voice
Head and face	• Inspection of head and face (e.g., overall appearance, scars, lesions, and masses) • Palpation or percussion of face with notation of presence or absence of sinus tenderness • Examination of salivary glands • Assessment of facial strength
Eyes	• Test ocular motility including primary gaze alignment
Ears, nose, mouth and throat	• Otoscopic examination of external auditory canals and tympanic membranes including pneumo-otoscopy with notation of mobility of membranes • Assessment of hearing with tuning forks and clinical speech reception thresholds (e.g., whispered voice, finger rub) • External inspection of ears and nose (e.g., overall appearance, scars, lesions, and masses) • Inspection of nasal mucosa, septum, and turbinates • Inspection of lips, teeth, and gums • Examination of oropharynx: oral mucosa, hard and soft palates, tongue, tonsils, and posterior pharynx (e.g., asymmetry, lesions, hydration of mucosal surfaces) • Inspection of pharyngeal walls and pyriform sinuses (e.g., pooling of saliva, asymmetry, lesions) • Examination by mirror of larynx including the condition of the epiglottis, false vocal cords, true vocal cords, and mobility of larynx (use of mirror not required in children) • Examination by mirror of nasopharynx including appearance of the mucosa, adenoids, posterior choanae, and eustachian tubes (use of mirror not required in children)
Neck	• Examination of neck (e.g., masses, overall appearance, symmetry, tracheal position, crepitus) • Examination of thyroid (e.g., enlargement, tenderness, mass)
Respiratory	• Inspection of chest including symmetry, expansion, or assessment of respiratory effort (e.g., intercostal retractions, use of accessory muscles, diaphragmatic movement) • Auscultation of lungs (e.g., breath sounds, adventitious sounds, rubs)
Cardiovascular	• Auscultation of heart with notation of abnormal sounds and murmurs • Examination of peripheral vascular system by observation (e.g., swelling, varicosities) and palpation (e.g., pulses, temperature, edema, tenderness)
Chest (breasts)	
Gastrointestinal (abdomen)	
Genitourinary	
Lymphatic	• Palpation of lymph nodes in neck, axillae, groin, or other location
Musculoskeletal	
Extremities	
Skin	
Neurologic/psychiatric	• Test cranial nerves with notation of any deficits Brief assessment of mental status including • Orientation to time, place, and person • Mood and affect (e.g., depression, anxiety, agitation)

(Source: U.S. Department of Health and Human Services, Centers for Medicare and Medicaid Services, Medicare Learning Network http://www.cms.hhs.gov/MLNProducts/downloads/physicianguide.pdf).

▶ *Comprehensive*—Examination should include performance of all elements identified by a bullet (•), whether in a shaded or unshaded box. Documentation of every element in each box with a shaded border and at least one element in a box with an unshaded border is expected.

Selecting the Type of Medical Decision Making Required

Medical decision making (MDM) involves the complexity of establishing a diagnosis or selecting a management option or treatment plan measured by:

▶ The number of possible diagnoses, or management or treatment options, that must be considered

▶ The total amount or difficulty of the data to be obtained, reviewed, and analyzed (medical records, diagnostic tests, etc.)

▶ The risk of significant complications, morbidity or mortality associated with the patient's presenting condition, diagnostic procedures, or possible treatment plans

There are four types of medical decision making:

▶ Straightforward
▶ Low complexity
▶ Moderate complexity
▶ High complexity

TABLE OF RISK

In contrast to determining the type of history or examination in which elements are well defined and can be counted, the MDM type is one of the more difficult key components to determine because there is an inherent degree of subjectivity in choosing the appropriate element levels. The table of risk (see Table 7.10) can be a helpful guide to narrowing the choices for all three MDM elements. Although the table of risk was intended to only qualify the third MDM element of risk of complications and morbidity or mortality in MDM as minimal, low, or moderate, it can help determine the two other MDM elements as well.

1—*If the coder determines through the table that the risk of complications and morbidity or mortality level are* **minimal**, *then the number of diagnoses or management options and amount or complexity of data to be reviewed should be* **minimal**.
2—*If the coder determines through the table that the risk of complications and morbidity or mortality are* **high**, *then the number of diagnoses or management options and amount or complexity of data to be reviewed should be* **extensive**.

EXAMPLES

Since the table of risk has defined data items to review, it can help qualify the other two MDM elements and eliminate subjectivity in determining the MDM type as straightforward, low complexity, moderate complexity, or high complexity. Two of the three elements presented in Table 7.11 must be met or exceeded before selecting a type of medical decision-making.

TABLE 7.10   Table of Risk

Level of Risk	Presenting Problem(s)	Diagnostic Procedures Ordered	Management Options Selected
Minimal	One self-limited or minor problem, (e.g., cold, insect bite, tinea corporis)	Laboratory tests requiring venipuncture, chest x-rays ECG/EEG, urinalysis, KOH prep, and ultrasound (e.g., echocardiography)	Rest Gargles Elastic bandages Superficial dressings
Low	Two or more self-limited or minor problems. One stable chronic illness (e.g., well-controlled hypertension, non-insulin-dependent diabetes, cataract, BPH) Acute uncomplicated illness or injury (e.g., cystitis, allergic rhinitis, simple sprain)	Physiologic tests not under stress, (e.g., pulmonary function tests) Noncardiovascular imaging studies with contrast (e.g., barium enema, superficial needle biopsies) Clinical laboratory tests requiring arterial puncture Skin biopsies	Over-the-counter drugs Minor surgery with no identified risk factors Physical therapy Occupational therapy IV fluids without additives
Moderate	One or more chronic illnesses with mild exacerbation, progression, or side effects of treatment Two or more stable chronic illnesses Undiagnosed new problem with uncertain prognosis, (e.g., lump in breast) Acute illness with systemic symptoms, (e.g., pyelonephritis, pneumonitis, colitis) Acute complicated injury (e.g., head injury with brief loss of consciousness)	Physiologic tests under stress (e.g., cardiac stress test, fetal contraction stress test) Diagnostic endoscopies with no identified risk factors Deep needle or incisional biopsy Cardiovascular imaging studies with contrast and no identified risk factors (e.g., arteriogram, cardiac catheterization) Fluid from body cavity (e.g., lumbar puncture, thoracentesis, culdocentesis	Minor surgery with identified risk factors Elective major surgery (open, percutaneous, or endoscopic) with no identified risk factors Prescription drug management Therapeutic nuclear medicine IV fluids with additives Closed treatment of fracture or dislocation without manipulation
High	One or more chronic illnesses with severe exacerbation, progression, or side effects of treatment Acute or chronic illnesses or injuries that pose a threat to life or bodily function (e.g., multiple trauma, acute MI, pulmonary embolus, severe respiratory distress, progressive severe rheumatoid arthritis, psychiatric illness with potential threat to self or others, peritonitis, acute renal failure) An abrupt change in neurologic status, (e.g., seizure, TIA, weakness, sensory loss)	Cardiovascular imaging studies with contrast with identified risk factors Cardiac electrophysiological test Diagnostic endoscopies with identified risk factors Discography	Elective major surgery (open, percutaneous, or endoscopic) with identified risk factors Emergency major surgery (open, percutaneous, or endoscopic) Parenteral controlled substances Drug therapy requiring intensive monitoring for toxicity Decision not to resuscitate or to de-escalate care because of poor prognosis

(Source: U.S. Department of Health and Human Services, Centers for Medicare and Medicaid Services, Medicare Learning Network http://www.cms.hhs.gov/MLNProducts/downloads/physicianguide.pdf).

TABLE 7.11 Medical Decision Making Requirements			
Medical Decision Making Type	Number of Diagnoses or Management Options	Amount or Complexity of Data to be Reviewed	Risk of Complications and Morbidity or Mortality
Straightforward	Minimal	Minimal or none	Minimal
Low complexity	Limited	Limited	Low
Moderate complexity	Multiple	Moderate	Moderate
High complexity	Extensive	Extensive	High

Current Procedural Terminology 2008 © American Medical Association. All rights reserved.

Overview of E/M Categories

Patients can be seen by the physician in a variety of settings (e.g., physician's office, hospital, skilled nursing facility, etc.) in which the physician can perform a variety of services (office or hospital consultation, preventive medicine, or critical care service). Therefore, the E/M section is divided into broad categories that describe different locations or types of services that include the following:

Office or Other Outpatient Services (99201–99215)

Office or other outpatient services is divided into two categories for new and established patients. New patients require all three key components, and established patients require two of the three components. This category is used for services provided in the physician's office or in other settings such as outpatient clinics or ambulatory care facilities.

Hospital Observation Services (99217–99220, 99234–99236)

This category is used to report physician services provided to patients admitted or registered into observation status in a hospital. The patient does not have to be placed in a special observation area for this service to apply. Three of three key components are required at each level of service.

Hospital Inpatient Services (99221–99239)

These codes report physician services provided to hospital inpatients. Subcategories are provided to describe initial hospital care, subsequent hospital care, and hospital discharge services. The initial hospital care services codes 99221–99223 require three of three key components, and the subsequent hospital care codes require two of three key components. One hospital discharge service code is used to report the final day of the patient's stay.

TIP If an encounter that takes place at another location (e.g., physician's office, emergency room, observation, nursing facility) results in the patient being admitted to the hospital on the same day, all E/M services provided by the responsible physician are considered part of the initial hospital admission and are not reported separately.

Consultations (99241–99255)

A **consultation** is a service provided by a physician when his or her advice or opinion is requested by another physician (usually the attending physician) to help manage the care of the patient. Consultations are usually requested for the following reasons:

▸ There is an obscure or difficult diagnosis
▸ A presenting condition is outside of the attending physician's specialty
▸ To obtain clearance for surgery
▸ There is some suspicion of criminal activity (e.g., the patient is fraudulently trying to obtain disability benefits).

Two subcategories are provided: office or other outpatient consultations and inpatient consultations. The codes do not distinguish between new or established patients, and three of three key components are required for each level. If a patient or family initiates a consult and it is not requested by a physician, it is coded to the office visit codes and is not considered a consult.

Emergency Department Services (99281–99288)

These E/M codes are used to report a physician's professional services provided in the emergency department of a hospital. The codes do not distinguish between new or established patients, and three of three key components are required at each level.

Hospitals use E/M codes to bill Medicare and Medicaid for the technical services provided in emergency departments to receive reimbursement for providing resources such as the facilities, special equipment, medications, and nurses. Although E/M codes were originally developed to report the professional services provided by physicians, CMS regulations require that each hospital develop a system for mapping their ER services to the different levels of effort described by the E/M codes. Methods used include assigning points for the number of nursing interventions and assigning an E/M code level based on the degree of severity associated with the patient's diagnosis. See an example of level of care documentation for an ER visit on page 274.

Pediatric Patient Transport (99289–99290)

These codes report the face-to-face physical attendance and care provided by a physician during the transport of a critically ill or injured pediatric patient. The code assignment is based on time (e.g., 99289 for first 30–74 minutes of hands-on care during transport, with the add-on code 99290 used for each additional 30 minutes).

Pediatric patient transport codes cannot be used for care provided during pediatric critical transport services of less than 30 minutes.

Critical Care Services (99291–99296)

Critical care services are determined by the patient's condition and are not necessarily determined by the place of service (e.g., intensive care unit, cardiac care unit). Subcategories describe critical services relating to the treatment of adults, pediatric patients (29 days through 24 months of age), and neonatal patients (28 days of age or less). The E/M guidelines must be carefully reviewed for each subcategory because many procedures are an integral part of the overall critical care service and are not coded separately (e.g., interpretation of chest x-ray, pulse oximetry, interpretation of cardiac output measurements, ventilation management, blood gases and information stored in computers, gastric intubation, temporary transcutaneous pacing, vascular access procedures).

For adults, the critical care services code assignment is based on time (e.g., 99291 for first 30–74 minutes, with the add-on code 99292 used for each additional 30 minutes). Pediatric and neonatal critical care reporting are based on the days of service (99293 and 99294 describe the initial and subsequent day for pediatric patients, and 99295 and 99296 describe the initial and subsequent day for neonatal patients).

Continuing Intensive Care Services (99298–99300)

These codes are used to report ongoing care services provided by physicians to low-birth-weight newborns. The codes are reported for subsequent days of care, and different codes are provided that identify the present weight of the infant (code 99298 for body weight less than 1,500 g, code 99299 for body weight of 1,500–2,500 g, and code 99300 for body weight 2, 501–5,000 g).

Nursing Facility Services (99304–99318)

Nursing facility services codes report physician services provided in skilled nursing facilities, intermediate care facilities, and long-term care facilities. Subcategories are provided for initial facility care and subsequent facility care. The responsible physicians must ensure that their patients receive a multidisciplinary **plan of care** and must assist in the assessment of the functional capacity of the patient. This is accomplished by using information from the comprehensive Resident Assessment Instrument (RAI) form derived from the Minimum Data Set (MDS) and the Resident Assessment Protocols (RAPs) to identify special areas of concern called "triggers" (e.g., skin integrity and decubitus ulcers, falling risk, confusion, mobility issues, wandering).

Domiciliary, Rest Home (e.g., Boarding Home), or Custodial Care Services (99324–99337)

These codes report E/M services provided by physicians in residential facilities that provide room and board and long-term personal assistance with the activities of daily living, rest homes, and other assisted living facilities. Subcategories are provided for new and established patients. All three key components are required for new patients, and two of the three components are required for established patients.

Domiciliary, Rest Home (e.g., Assisted Living Facility), or Home Care Plan Oversight Services (99339–99340)

These E/M codes report care plan oversight services (supervision) for a patient in a rest home, assisted living, custodial care, or home setting. The physician services may include revision or review of the patient's care plan or health status, review of laboratory work or other studies, and telephone calls with other health-care professionals or family members to assess the patient's condition or to adjust the patient's medical treatment plan. The codes assigned are based on time (code 99339 for 15–29 minutes within a calendar month; 99340 for 30 minutes or more within a calendar month).

Home Services (99341–99350)

Home services codes document physician services provided in the patient's home or private residence. Subcategories are provided for new and established patients. Three of three key components are required for new patients, and two of three are required for established patients.

Prolonged Services (99354–99359)

These codes are used to report direct patient contact (face-to-face time) that goes beyond the usual E/M service level code assigned. Prolonged services codes are add-on codes that are listed separately in addition to the appropriate E/M service code describing the office or other outpatient or inpatient service. These codes are time based (code 99354 for the first hour beyond the usual service; code 99355 for each additional 30 minutes). The reason (medical necessity) for the prolonged services and time involved must be well documented by the physician.

Standby Services (99360)

These codes are used to report standby services requested by another physician that involve extended physician attendance without direct face-to-face patient contact. The physician cannot provide services to other patients during this time. If the physician performs a procedure during that time that is subject to a surgical package, the standby code cannot be reported separately.

Case Management Services (99363–99368)

These codes are used to report a physician's provision of case management services within a managed care plan or integrated delivery system that can include providing direct patient care services, coordinating and supervising patient care among other providers, and controlling access to various health-care services. Subcategories are provided for team conferences and anticoagulant management.

Care Plan Oversight Services (99374–99380)

These codes are used to report services relating to the ongoing review and revision of a patient's care plan in a home health agency, domiciliary, hospice, or nursing facility. Only one physician may report these codes for an individual patient in a 30-day period.

Preventive Medicine Services (99381–99429); Newborn Care (99431–99440)

These codes report periodic preventive medicine services provided by physicians for infants, children, adolescents, and adults (e.g., wellness care, annual health check-ups). If an abnormal condition is encountered during prevention medicine services, an additional E/M service code (99201–99215) can be reported; however, it must be appended with modifier −25, which identifies it as a separate service. Newborn codes are used to report physician services in different settings (e.g., hospital or birthing center).

Telephone (99441–99443), On-line Medical (99444), and Special E/M Services (99450–99456)

Non-face-to-face physician services include telephone calls and on-line medical evaluations that may be billed under certain situations, and special E/M service codes are used to report administrative evaluative services provided by a physician (e.g., basic life, work-related or medical disability examinations).

Other Evaluation and Management Services (99499)

This code for unlisted E/M services is used to report a provided service that does not have a corresponding code listed in the E/M section. This is a code of last resort and should only be used when an adequate code describing the service cannot be located. When this code is used, a special report must be sent to the payer describing the medical necessity for the unlisted E/M service or procedure.

Modifiers for E/M Services

The following table lists CPT modifiers that are commonly used with E/M codes. These modifiers are appended to the E/M service code when certain conditions exist.

Quick Reference: E/M Modifiers		
CPT Modifier	**Description**	**Explanation**
21	Prolonged E/M management service	Used when the face-to-face time or floor/unit service time is greater than what is usually required for the highest level in a given category
24	Unrelated E/M service by the same physician during the postoperative period	Used to report an E/M service performed during the postoperative period that was unrelated to the original procedure
25	Significant and separately identifiable E/M service by the same physician on the same day of a procedure	Used to report that on the day of a procedure, the patient's condition required a significant, separately identifiable E/M service
32	Mandated service	Used when a service has been mandated by a third-party payer (e.g., second opinion/consultation for surgery)
52	Reduced services	Used when a service or procedure is reduced at the physician's discretion
57	Decision for surgery	Used to report an E/M service that results in the initial decision to perform surgery

SUMMARY

E/M codes were primarily developed to report the services performed by physicians in terms of the skill, effort, time, and knowledge required to diagnose and treat a patient's condition to receive payment from third-party payers. E/M codes are easy to locate and recognize as the section is located at the beginning of the CPT manual and the codes begin with "99." The E/M section in the CPT manual is divided into categories and subcategories based on the type of patient (e.g., new or established), location of service (e.g., office or hospital), and level of E/M service provided (to describe the amount of physician's work required).

Some of the most important concepts that coding students need to remember from the chapter are commonly used terms such as the difference between new patients (patient has *not* received services by the practice within 3 years) versus established patients (patient *has* received services by the practice within 3 years). Also, it is important for the coder to remember that E/M codes most often describe from one to five levels of service, and this would be commensurate with increasing payments for the provider's services from health-care payers for the work they do.

Coders must remember that there are up to seven components that can be used to determine the E/M code level. The first three key components (history, examination, medical decision making) are essential to assigning the correct code. When applicable, four more contributing components (counseling, coordination of care, nature of presenting problem, time) can be considered in the assignment of the proper code. In addition, CPT modifiers are available that are commonly used with E/M codes. These modifiers are appended to the E/M service code when certain conditions exist (e.g., modifier -21 describes a prolonged E/M management service). Lastly, it is important to recognize that in 1995 and revised in 1997, CMS provided a set of documentation guidelines for physicians to follow to substantiate the services provided for payment and reported through E/M codes. Providers and coders must use either the 1995 or 1997 Guidelines to validate the E/M codes selected that report professional services; however, a coder cannot mix and match within an individual record in an attempt to maximize reimbursement.

TESTING YOUR COMPREHENSION

1. What are the three key components that must be considered in selecting a level of E/M services?

2. What are the three questions that must be answered to assign the type of medical decision making?

3. What are the types of history that are recognized in reporting E/M services?

4. What are the types of medical decision making in E/M coding?

5. The E/M section is divided into several broad categories. Name three broad categories.

6. In the E/M section, what is the definition of new patient?

7. In the E/M section, what is the definition of established patient?

8. Why were the E/M codes placed out of numerical order at the beginning of the CPT manual?

9. What is special about Appendix C of the CPT manual?

10. Where can the coder locate the 1995 E/M Documentation Guidelines?

11. When selecting the appropriate level of service, what must a coder do?

12. What is the primary goal of E/M coding?

13. What do E/M codes generally describe?

14. In contrast to determining the type of history or type of examination in which elements are well defined and can be counted, what service type is one of the more difficult key components to determine because there is a degree of subjectivity in choosing the appropriate element levels?

15. What is the most striking difference between the 1995 and 1997 E/M Documentation Guidelines?

CODING PRACTICE I   Chapter Review Exercises

Directions

Use your CPT manual to code the following physician services from the E/M section.

1. Patient CC, a 50-year-old patient, visited her family physician with complaints of sharp intermittent left lower quadrant (LLQ) abdominal pain and dark-colored stools. Dr. 037 obtained a detailed personal and family history from Patient CC and performed a detailed physical examination. The physician ordered several diagnostic tests, including a stool culture and barium enema, upper and lower GI series (x-rays), and a complete blood count (CBC) with white blood cell differential, which was to be performed at St. Charity Hospital. Dr. 037 also scheduled upper (EGD) and lower endoscopies (colonoscopy) to be performed as an outpatient. Her initial assessment was possible colitis versus diverticulosis versus colon cancer.

   Code(s): _____

2. Dr. 038 visited the Lazy Days skilled nursing facility for a routine evaluation of his patient, Patient DD, who suffers from Parkinson's disease with visible hand tremors and gait disturbances. Dr. 038 reviews the medical records and signs orders. Dr. 038 performs an examination of Patient DD, which reveals that her condition is stable with no notable change in status since the last visit. With this visit, Dr. 038 spent about 15 minutes examining Patient DD and reviewing her records.

   Code(s): _____

3. Patient EE, an established patient, was seen in Dr. 039's office because of a sore throat, fever, and difficulty swallowing. The patient's temperature was 101 degrees. The final diagnosis was strep throat infection. An initial IM antibiotic was administered and oral antibiotics were prescribed.

   Code(s): _____

4. On referral from his family doctor for a finding of guaiac-positive stools, Patient FF, a 55-year-old patient, was seen by a gastroenterologist, Dr. 040. The consultant conducted a comprehensive history noting the patient's dietary and bowel habits and current medications, as well as a positive family history of colon cancer. A complete physical examination was performed including a digital rectal exam (DRE). Dr. 040 ordered a stool culture, barium enema, repeat stool guaiac, CBC, and colonoscopy to be performed as an outpatient at Happy Trails Hospital. Dr. 040 spent nearly an hour with the patient.

   Code(s): _____

5. Patient GG presents to Dr. 039's office for the first time to bring in her 4-year-old son, who has been crying off and on for the past few days and stating, "Mommy, my ears hurt!" After an expanded problem-focused history and physical examination and review of the patient's medical records record from his previous physician, Dr. 039 prescribed a medication for bilateral otitis media for the child.

   Code(s): _____

6. Dr. 039 saw one of his patients, 89-year-old Patient HH, in the critical care unit of St. Charity Hospital. Patient HH was critically ill and in multisystem organ failure (heart, lungs, liver, and kidneys). The patient needed Dr. 039's constant attention for 1.5 hours.

   Code(s): _____

7. Patient II was recently prescribed a new medicine by his family physician, Dr. 041, for treatment of his essential hypertension. Patient II has a scheduled visit to the doctor's office today for a routine blood pressure check. His blood pressure is recorded at 140/70, which is within borderline to normal limits. Dr. 041's office nurse conducted the blood pressure check under the doctor's supervision.

   Code(s): _____

8. Patient JJ recently moved to Orlando with her 5-year-old son. She presents to Dr. 038's office for the first time because she is concerned that her son may have the flu. He has been running a slight fever, seems

lethargic, and has a runny nose and decreased appetite. Dr. 038 performs an expanded problem-focused history and physical examination taking a nasal culture and reviews the patient's health record from his previous doctor. Dr 038 prescribed the appropriate medication for a suspected RSV upper respiratory infection (URI).

Code(s): _____

9. Dr. 042 conducted a yearly nursing facility assessment on his patient, Patient KK, at the Solitaire Intermediate Nursing Facility. Patient KK has a status post multiple cerebrovascular accident (CVA) history with residual right-sided hemiplegia, expressive aphasia, and dysphagia.

Code(s): _____

10. At the request of Dr. 039, Dr. 038 was asked to see Patient LL at St. Charity Hospital. Patient LL suffers from emphysema secondary to a 60-pack-a-year history of smoking. Dr. 038 reviewed Patient LL's medical record, obtained a comprehensive history, performed a thorough comprehensive examination, and recommended a new medical treatment for her worsening emphysema. A written report of Dr. 038's findings and treatment recommendation was completed and sent to Dr. 039. Assign the appropriate consultation code for the services of Dr. 038.

Code(s): _____

11. Dr. 038 telephoned Patient MM to report on the test results of her laboratory work and tests that included SMA-12, lipid panel, TSH, complete blood count, chest x-ray, and ECG. The call lasted 12 minutes.

Code(s): _____

12. Patient NN, a 60-year-old established patient, was seen by Dr. 043 for an annual routine preventive medicine examination. A comprehensive history and physical examination were conducted. Results of the physical examination were normal. Dr. 043 ordered routine laboratory work, chest x-ray, and ECG to be performed as an outpatient the next day at St. Charity Hospital.

Code(s): _____

CODING PRACTICE II   Medical Record Case Studies

Directions

Part 1: Assigning E/M Codes for Professional Services of Physicians.

Case studies 7.1 through 7.3 represent various physicians involved in an episode of care that started with a patient admitted to the hospital through the emergency department. Because the admission occurred within 72 hours of the ED visit, the hospital will be reimbursed under Medicare-Severity DRG system (MS-DRG) for an inpatient stay; however, each individual physician (emergency room physician, attending physician, and consulting physician) will be paid under the resource-based relative value scale (RBRVS) Medicare Fee Schedule. It is interesting to note the differences in documentation between the emergency physician, the attending, and the consultant.

1. Carefully review the medical records provided for each case study.

2. Research any abbreviations and terms that are unfamiliar or unclear.

3. Identify as many diagnoses and E/M services as possible.

4. Because only part of the patient's total record is available, think about what additional documentation you might need.

5. If appropriate, identify any questions you might ask the physician to code this case correctly and completely.

6. Complete the appropriate blanks below for each case study. Explain (in writing) questions 1–5 and assign the E/M procedure code(s) for question 6.

Case Study 7.1

You are coding for the professional services of the emergency department physician.

Patient: Patient OO

Patient documentation: **Read ED Record 7.1**

1. What is the diagnosis (description) that supports the medical necessity for this E/M service?

   _____

2. Are there any secondary diagnoses present?

   _____

3. What is the description of the E/M service(s) that was provided?

   _____

4. Do you believe you need additional documentation to correctly assign the E/M code(s) to this record? If so, what is the additional documentation that you need?

   _____

5. Do you have any additional questions for the ED physician?

   _____

6. What is(are) the E/M service code(s) you would assign to this case study?

   _____

   _____

MEDICAL REPORT 7.1 ED RECORD

CHARITY HOSPITAL EMERGENCY DEPARTMENT RECORD

PATIENT NAME: Patient OO

MR#: 111111

DATE OF SERVICE: 05/03/20XX

CHIEF COMPLAINT Vaginal Bleeding

I HAVE REVIEWED THE NURSING NOTES AND CONCUR

HISTORY OF PRESENT ILLNESS: The patient is a 33-year-old female who is ambulatory into the emergency department complaining of vaginal bleeding with clots. The patient is feeling heart palpitations and short of breath and very symptomatic. This emergency department on April 26 of this year had seen the patient. An ultrasound at that time showed an enlarged uterus and some right ovarian cysts. Her hemoglobin was 10.4, beta was negative, and she was given a prescription for Ovral q.i.d. for one week and advised to see Dr. 044. The patient tells me she did see Dr. 044 on Monday in his office at which time she said he placed her on progesterone. She has been using about 1–2 pads per day over the last few days and having large clots and now is very symptomatic.

PAST MEDICAL HISTORY: Hypertension, obesity. Prior episodes of vaginal bleeding with prior episodes of palpitations.

OBSTETRICAL/GYNECOLOGICAL HISTORY: D&C. Tubal ligation. Two pregnancies, two live births.

SOCIAL HISTORY: Denies cigarettes or alcohol. She is employed as a clerk at a local grocery store.

MEDICATIONS: Dyazide and iron. Hormones.

ALLERGIES: None.

PHYSICAL EXAMINATION: Vital signs: Initial temperature 97.5 tympanic, pulse 109, respiration 20, and blood pressure 135/66. Repeat orthostatic supine blood pressure 130/72 with pulse 109, standing 125/83 with pulse 148, symptomatic diaphoresis and pallor.

EXAMINATION

LUNGS: Clear.

HEART: Sounds normal, no murmurs.

ABDOMEN: Tender. Externally somewhat enlarged uterus was palpated through the abdomen, due to the obesity it was hard to assess clearly.

GYN: Deferred as she has had prior exams and the etiology is clear as to the bleeding.

LABORATORY DATA: Hemoglobin 7.2, MCV 73, RDW 18. Electrolytes normal. Beta negative.

ED COURSE: IV saline 1 L wide open. Two units of RBCs transfused in the emergency department.

DIAGNOSIS: Acute severe dysfunctional uterine bleeding with symptomatic anemia.

PLAN: I spoke to Dr. 044 on the phone. After some discussion, he finally agreed to admit the patient and agreed to transfuse as well. Once the patient is on the floor, the doctor will be called by the nursing staff for further orders.

DISPOSITION: Admitted.

Electronically Signed and Dated

Case Study 7.2

You are coding for Day 1 of the professional services of the attending physician.

Patient: Patient OO

Patient documentation: **Read Admit H&P 7.2**

1. What is the diagnosis (description) that supports the medical necessity for this E/M service?

    _____

2. Are there any secondary diagnoses present?

    _____

3. What is the description of the E/M service(s) that was provided?

    _____

4. Do you believe you need additional documentation to correctly assign the E/M codes to this record? If so, what is the additional documentation that you need?

    _____

5. Do you have any additional questions for the attending physician?

    _____

6. What is(are) the E/M service code(s) you would assign to this case study?

    _____

    _____

MEDICAL REPORT 7.2 H&P RECORD

CHARITY HOSPITAL

PATIENT NAME:	Patient OO
MR#:	111111
HISTORY AND PHYSICAL:	
DATE OF ADMISSION:	05/03/20XX
CHIEF COMPLAINT:	Vaginal Bleeding

HISTORY OF PRESENT ILLNESS: This 33-year-old female has a past history of anovulatory bleeding, which has never been fully evaluated. On April 26 of this year, the patient presented to Charity Hospital's emergency room with bleeding and was referred to my office where she was seen on April 27 and placed on medroxyprogesterone acetate and ferrous sulfate. Endometrial biopsy was performed. She returned to the emergency room today because of continued bleeding and shortness of breath. Hemoglobin 1 week ago was 10.4 g and this evening is 7.2 g. She is admitted from ED for transfusion and observation.

REVIEW OF SYSTEMS: The patient is short of breath when active but not when lying quietly. She has had some dizziness and nausea once earlier today. She ate breakfast this morning without difficulty. She denies headache, difficulty with micturition and defecation.

PAST SURGICAL HISTORY: Cholecystectomy in 1985, tubal ligation in 1996, and a dilatation and curettage for evaluation of menorrhagia in 1997.

OBSTETRIC HISTORY: Gravida 2, para 2.

HABITS: Denies using cigarettes, alcohol, and drugs.

MEDICATIONS: Present medication includes medroxyprogesterone acetate, which she completed today, and ferrous sulfate.

ALLERGIES: The patient has no known allergies.

FAMILY HISTORY: Mother is hypertensive. Father is hypertensive and an insulin-dependent diabetic. Both children are well. She has one brother who is well.

PHYSICAL EXAMINATION

GENERAL APPEARANCE: Pleasant cooperative female who is large and moderately obese.

VITAL SIGNS: Blood pressure 119/57, resting pulse 86, sitting pulse 102.

HEENT: Eyes—sclerae white. Pupils reactive to light. Fundi membranes appear normal. Mouth—teeth and tongue appear normal. Throat not well visualized. Nose—oxygen by nasal prongs.

NECK: Supple. Thyroid is normal.

LUNGS: Clear to auscultation.

HEART: Regular rhythm without audible murmur.

ABDOMEN: Obese. There is no tenderness.

PELVIC: Deferred.

EXTREMITIES: Warm. Radial pulses are present. Dorsal pedal pulses are not palpable.

MEDICAL REPORT 7.2 H&P RECORD (CONTINUED)

NEUROLOGICAL: The patient is oriented. Gait and strength were not evaluated.

BREASTS: Not examined.

SKIN: Appears normal.

IMPRESSION ON ADMISSION

1. Dysfunctional uterine bleeding.

2. Blood loss anemia secondary to #1, both acute and chronic.

PLAN: Transfusion and continue medical evaluation and treatment.

_____

Electronically Signed and Dated

Case Study 7.3

You are coding for the professional services of the consulting physician.

Patient: Patient OO

Patient documentation: **Read Consultation 7.3**

1. What is the diagnosis (description) that supports the medical necessity of this E/M service?

   _____

2. Are there any secondary diagnoses present?

   _____

3. What is the description of the E/M service(s) that was provided?

   _____

4. Do you believe you need additional documentation to correctly assign the E/M codes to this record? If so, what is the additional documentation that you need?

   _____

5. Do you have any additional questions for the consulting physician?

   _____

6. What is(are) the E/M service code(s) you would assign to this case study?

   _____

   _____

MEDICAL REPORT 7.3 CONSULTATION

CHARITY HOSPITAL

PATIENT NAME:	Patient OO
MR#:	111111
CONSULTATION	
DATE OF ADMISSION:	05/03/20XX **ATTENDING:** Dr. 044
DATE OF CONSULTATION	05/05/20XX **CONSULTANT:** DR. 046

Thank you for the consultation. Patient OO is 33-year-old female who was admitted on May 3 for dysfunctional uterine bleeding, with severe anemia secondary to the uterine bleeding. There is some concern about the shortness of breath that the patient has been developing for the past 2 days. The patient states that she has been having some stuffy nose, associated with some shortness of breath whenever she moves around the room. This has not been associated with fever, chills, cough, or other constitutional symptoms. The patient states that she has shortness of breath whenever she is active but not when lying down. She did have some dizziness and palpitations prior to admission, and I believe those symptoms were related to her anemia. She denies headaches, difficulty on urination or defecation.

PAST SURGICAL HISTORY: Status post cholecystectomy in 1985, tubal ligation in 1996, dilatation and curettage for evaluation of menometrorrhagia in 1997.

HABITS: She denies using cigarettes, alcohol, or drugs.

MEDICATIONS: The patient is taking medroxyprogesterone acetate and ferrous sulfate.

ALLERGIES: No known allergies.

FAMILY HISTORY: Her mother is hypertensive. Her father is hypertensive and insulin-dependent diabetes mellitus. No history of hemophilia, thrombocytopenia, coagulopathy, or blood disorder in the family.

PHYSICAL EXAMINATION:

GENERAL APPEARANCE: Awake, alert, and oriented $\times$ 3. Obese. In no acute distress.

VITAL SIGNS: The patient has remained afebrile with stable vital signs.

HEENT: Within normal limits.

NECK: Supple. No jugular venous distension.

LUNGS: Clear to auscultation.

CARDIAC: Regular rate and rhythm. Normal S1, S2. No S3 or S4.

ABDOMEN: Obese. Soft. Without mass. No hepatosplenomegaly. Positive bowel sounds.

EXTREMITIES: No cyanosis, clubbing, or edema.

DIAGNOSTIC STUDIES: Electrocardiogram done on 5/4 shows normal sinus rhythm with normal electrical axis. Normal P-R and Q-R-S. No ischemic changes. Chest x-ray done in the emergency room was reportedly normal.

LAB DATA: Pertinent labs show arterial blood gasses on room air with pH 7.42, PO_2 92, PCO_2 39.7, bicarbonate 25.3, and saturation of 97.6. Hemoglobin 7.7 and she has already received a blood transfusion. At last report, hemoglobin was 10.

MEDICAL REPORT 7.3 CONSULTATION (CONTINUED)

ASSESSMENT AND PLAN

1. Dysfunctional uterine bleeding.

2. Anemia due to dysfunctional uterine bleeding.

3. Sinusitis.

I believe this patient is having some shortness of breath secondary to the sinus problems and for that, I am going to start her on Claritin 10 mg one p.o., q.d. She should continue having hemoglobin and hematocrit monitoring as per gynecology.

_____

Electronically Signed and Dated

Directions

Part 2: Assigning E/M Codes for the Technical Services of the Hospital
Unlike the previous case studies where you coded for the professional services of physicians, in Case Study 7.4, you will assign the correct E/M code to bill for the technical service of a hospital emergency department.

1. Carefully review the medical record provided for the case study.

2. Research any abbreviations and terms that are unfamiliar or unclear.

3. Identify any ICD-9-CM diagnosis or CPT procedure codes given, and any E/M service(s).

4. Because only part of the patient's total record is available, think about what additional documentation you might need.

5. If appropriate, identify any questions you might ask the hospital's emergency room personnel to code this case correctly and completely.

6. Review Figure 7.2, Charity Hospital's Emergency Department Level of Care form. Add up the points, and assign the appropriate E/M service level.

7. Complete the appropriate blanks for the case study. Explain (in writing) questions 1–5 and assign the E/M procedure code(s) for question 6.

Case Study 7.4

You are coding for the hospital, for the technical services provided within the emergency department.

Patient: Patient PP

Patient documentation: **Read ED Record 7.4 and see sample Emergency Department Level of Care documentation that follows.**

1. What is the diagnosis (description) that supports the medical necessity for this E/M service?

   _____

2. Are there any secondary diagnoses present?

   _____

3. What is the description of the E/M service(s) that was provided?

   _____

4. Do you believe you need additional documentation to correctly assign the E/M code(s) to this record? If so, what is the additional documentation that you need?

   _____

5. Do you have any additional questions for the hospital's ED staff?

   _____

6. After reviewing the Emergency Department Level of Care form, add up the points and assign the appropriate E/M service level.

   What is(are) the E/M service code level you would assign to this case study?

   _____

   _____

MEDICAL REPORT 7.4 ED RECORD

CHARITY HOSPITAL EMERGENCY DEPARTMENT

PATIENT ID:	999999
PATIENT NAME:	Patient PP
REGISTRATION DATE:	8/10/20XX
CHIEF COMPLAINT:	FB IN EYE
MEDICAL RECORD NUMBER:	888888
TIME SEEN BY CLINICIAN:	12:35

The patient arrived via private automobile.

The patient's condition upon arrival was stable.

HPI: The patient presents with a possible foreign body in the right eye that has been present since yesterday prior to arrival. There is some pain. There has been some redness of the right eye. There has been some tearing in the eye. There has been no discharge in the eye. There has been no apparent vision loss. The patient's tetanus status is not current. A Td was given today.

PMH: Negative for significant medical problems contributing to this complaint.

PRIOR SURGERY: No previous significant surgical procedures.

CURRENT MEDICATIONS: The nursing notes were reviewed.

ALLERGIES: There are no reported significant allergies.

PFSH: The patient lives with his family. The patient lives in the local area. The patient is a non-smoker. The patient has no history of alcohol abuse.

REVIEW OF SYSTEMS: See HPI for pertinent systems.

All other systems negative; except as noted.

PHYSICAL EXAM: Vital signs: The nursing notes were reviewed.

Visual Acuity:

O.D. 20/20

O.S. 20/20

O.U. 20/20

Visual acuity performed without glasses. The patient is alert.

EYE(S): Pupils: equal, round and reactive. EOM normal. There is no discharge from either eye. There is some injection.

FUNDOSCOPIC EXAM: No papilledema, hemorrhage, or exudates. There is not a foreign body of the eyelid(s) with lid eversion. Cornea: There is a foreign body noted. The cornea is clear, without hyphema. The foreign-body is embedded and is unable to be removed with Q-tip so the foreign body was removed with a brush with excellent results and the eye was subsequently irrigated. Gentamicin ophthalmic was applied along with double eye patch. Vicodin was given.

DIFFERENTIAL DIAGNOSIS

INTERVENTION

FOREIGN BODY REMOVAL: A "rust ring" identified.

DIAGNOSIS: Foreign Body in the Cornea(s), 930.0 Removal of Corneal Foreign Body without Slit Lamp, 65220

PRESCRIBED MEDICATIONS

Vicodin- ES 7.5 mg/750 mg Tablet, Disp: 6 (six), 1 tab(s) by mouth every 4–6 hours as needed for pain, DO NOT TAKE MORE THAN 8 TABLETS IN 24 HOURS

DISPOSITION

DISCHARGED: The patient was discharged home at 2:20 pm. He was accompanied by his family. The patient's condition upon discharge was stable.

_____

Electronically Signed and Dated

SAMPLE EMERGENCY DEPARTMENT LEVEL OF CARE DOCUMENTATION

CHARITY HOSPITAL – Emergency Department Level of Care

Section I – Select applicable items once per visit

Skip section I for any of the following:
Physician Requested F/U visit – DOA – Visit for removal/adj of device/cath only – Visit for suture/staple removal only – OR Critical Care
(critical condition & critical interventions & 1-on-1 MD/DO Care, unless patient expires <30 min after arrival)

ED Care – Select ONE for every visit

✓ Points
- ☑ (25) Basic ED Care – vital signs/assessment recorded up to 2 times
- ☐ (45) Intermediate ED Care – vital signs/assessment recorded 3 to 4 times
- ☐ (75) Extensive ED Care – vital signs/assessment recorded 5+ times
- ☐ (100) Resuscitative ED Care (resuscitation attempt in ED 6–29 minutes

Medications

✓ Points
- ☑ (15) 1-3 Medications – PO, suppository, topical, inhalants
- ☐ (25) 4+ Medications – PO, suppository, topical, inhalants

Select applicable charge items for medication/fluids/vaccines administered via injection or infusion

Arrival/Disposition

✓ Points
- ☐ (10) Arrival via medical Transport Unit (not for intra-hospital transport)
- ☐ (10) Depart via medical Transport Unit (not for intra-hospital transport)
- ☐ (20) AMA (Against Medical Advice)
- ☐ (25) Transfer out intra-hospital outpatient OR other institution
- ☐ (40) Intra-hospital Inpatient Admission (not for OP observation)
- ☐ (40) Transfer w/Nurse to Other Facility

Additional Patient Needs:

✓ Points
- ☐ (15) Assist patient: dressing, to bathroom, other
- ☐ (15) Poison Control/Animal Control
- ☐ (15) Fax/Call – prescriptions, suppliers, other institutions, police department, caregiver/family (do use for consult call/fax)
- ☐ (15) Consult – nutritionist/dietician/physician specialist/Psych
- ☐ (20) Isolation
- ☐ (20) Bedpan, Incontinence, Ostomy Maintenance (includes any specimens collected)
- ☐ (25) Emotional or Uncooperative Patient
- ☐ (25) Additional staff used
- ☐ (40) Violent /Aggressive

Interventions

✓ Points
- ☑ (5) Visual Acuity
- ☐ (10) **Traction Assist***
- ☐ (10) Doppler
- ☐ (10) Photography (consent form required)
- ☐ (10) Place urine collection bag(s) (includes specimen)
- ☐ (15) Oral/Nasal Collection(s) for lab
- ☐ (15) Piercing(s) removal without cutting
- ☐ (15) **Suture/staple removal***
- ☐ (15) **Stabilization of Body Temperature***
- ☐ (20) Pelvic/Rectal/Perineal Exam (includes any specimens collected)
- ☐ (20) Ring(s)/Piercing(s) removal by cutting
- ☐ (20) Fetal Heart Tones
- ☐ (25) **Enema Administration***
- ☐ (30) **Lens Procedure(s)***
- ☐ (40) Pre-hospital delivery
- ☐ (45) Decontamination
- ☐ (60) **Sexual Assault/Rape Exam***

Only select items below if no related chargeable item is performed

✓ Points
- ☐ (10) Wound specimen collection without procedure
- ☐ (15) Foreign body removal(s) without incision   *N/A*
- ☐ (15) **Removal/Adjustment of Device/Cath without incision***
- ☐ (20) **Tubes: Naso- or oro-gastric***
- ☐ (20) Cleansing and/or Dressing Wound(s) (includes topical agents)
- ☐ (20) Suction/Irrigation 1-3 episodes
- ☐ (30) Suction/Irrigation 4+ episodes

* Asterisk indicates Physician Order Required

Section II – Assign E/M Level

Total Points Assigned in Section I: _____

Points	Description		Code	Charge Code #
N/A	Suture Recheck/Suture Removal	☐	99281	SRECSREM
N/A	DOA	☐	99281	
N/A	Visit for Rem/Adj Device/Cath	☐	99281	RECK
N/A	Physician requested Follow Up	☐	99281	RECK
0-25	Level 1	☐	99281	
30-45	Level 2	☐	99281	LEV1
50-75	Level 3	☐	99282	LEV2
80-105	Level 4	☐	99283	LEV3
110+	Level 5	☐	99284	LEV4
N/A	Critical Care – Critical condition & critical interventions & MD/DO 1-on-1 care (Do not select critical care if patient expires <30 minutes after arrival; Assign points for E/M level instead)	☐	99285	LEV5
		☐	99291	CRTLEVL

ED Physician/PA: *Dr. 047*
Consulting: —
E/M Assigned by: _____

Patient Name: *Patient PP*
Account #: *999999*
Visit Date: *8/10*

Not part of the permanent medical record

Medicine

Chapter Objectives

▶ Describe the format of the CPT Medicine section.
▶ Recognize terminology used in the Medicine section.
▶ Correctly assign CPT codes and modifiers to medicine procedures and services.
▶ Recognize the elements required for complete injection and infusion CPT code assignment.
▶ Understand the various noninvasive and invasive cardiology procedures and correctly assign the applicable CPT Medicine codes.

Services listed in the Medicine section represent a wide variety of diagnostic, therapeutic, and miscellaneous procedures and services for many different specialties. For example, injections and infusions of various substances commonly performed to prevent and treat many conditions are included in the Medicine section. Although rules set by individual payers will govern code selection for certain substances that are injected or infused, the procedure itself must be coded. In addition, the Medicine section contains specialty-specific codes such as those for psychiatry, ophthalmology, and otorhinolaryngology. Codes for services performed by health-care providers other than physicians (physical therapy, occupational therapy, and nutritional counseling) are also included in this section, as are codes for special services by physicians and other services that do not fit neatly into other CPT sections.

Word Parts and Meanings of Medical Terms Related to Medicine			
Word Part	Meaning	Example	Definition
a-	without	aphakia	State of being without a lens
audi/o	hearing	audiometry	Measurement of hearing
chir/o	hand	chiropractic	Pertaining to use of the hands to treat
dia-	through, complete	dialysis	Complete separation such as when nitrogenous waste products in urine are removed from the bloodstream
encephal/o	brain	electroencephalogram	Record of electricity in the brain
nas/o	nose	nasopharyngoscopy	Visual examination of the nose and throat
ocul/o	eye	electro-oculography	Process of recording electrical signals of the eyes
somn/o	sleep	polysomnography	Process of recording many aspects of sleep
spir/o	breathing	spirometry	Measurement of breathing

Organization of the Medicine Section

Within the CPT manual, the Medicine Guidelines and subsections contain specific notes on how to assign the codes. Coders should read the information carefully before code selection. As with all sections of CPT, it is recommended that the coder review all the choices available in the Medicine section to become familiar with its wide variety of services and codes. Table 8.1 shows the Medicine subsections and the code ranges that apply to each subsection.

Common Medicine Modifiers

Modifier -25 is assigned for a separately identifiable evaluation and management (E/M) service by the same physician on the same day as the procedure. This modifier is needed if E/M services, such as a physical exam, are billed in addition to administration of a vaccine at an office visit. The modifier is appended to the E/M code, and all the key components required to justify the selection of the E/M code must be documented in the patient's medical record. A chiropractor or osteopathic physician would also need to use this modifier if an E/M code is submitted on the same date as manipulative treatment. The CPT codes provided for manipulative treatment include assessment of the patient before and after the treatment. Some third-party payers do not recognize modifier -25, so inclusion of the modifier will not guarantee reimbursement for the service(s). Documentation verifying that the patient's condition required additional services must be included in the medical record.

Modifier -50 is applied if a service described as unilateral is provided bilaterally. Codes located in the ophthalmology and otorhinolaryngology subsections may require this modifier. However, the coder should carefully look for terminology such as "unilateral or bilateral" or "both eyes" within the CPT code descriptions and in the medical record to verify the selected code correctly describes the procedure.

TABLE 8.1 Medicine Subsections and Code Ranges	
Medicine Subsection	**Code Range**
Immune globulins	90281–90399
Immunization administration for vaccines/toxoids	90465–90474
Vaccines, toxoids	90476–90749
Hydration, therapeutic, prophylactic, and diagnostic injections and infusions (excludes chemotherapy)	90760–90779
Psychiatry	90801–90899
Biofeedback	90901–90911
Dialysis	90918–90999
Gastroenterology	91000–91299
Ophthalmology	92002–92499
Special otorhinolaryngologic services	92502–92700
Cardiovascular	92950–93799
Noninvasive vascular diagnostic studies	93875–93990
Pulmonary	94002–94799
Allergy and clinical immunology	95004–95199
Endocrinology	95250–95251
Neurology and neuromuscular procedures	95805–96020
Medical genetics and genetic counseling services	94040
Central nervous system assessments/tests	96101–96125
Health and behavior assessment/intervention	96150–96155
Chemotherapy administration	96401–96549
Photodynamic therapy	96567–96571
Special dermatological procedures	96900–96999
Physical medicine and rehabilitation	97001–97799
Medical nutrition therapy	97802–97804
Acupuncture	97810–97814
Osteopathic manipulative treatment	98925–98929
Chiropractic manipulative treatment	98940–98943
Education and training for patient self-management	98960–98962
Non-face-to-face nonphysician services	98966–98969
Special services, procedures, and reports	99000–99091
Qualifying circumstances for anesthesia	99100–99140
Moderate (conscious) sedation	99143–99150
Other services and procedures	99170–99199
Home health procedures/services	99500–99602
Medication therapy management services	99605–99607

Modifier -52 is used if services provided are less than those described by the code. As mentioned above, many services in ophthalmology and otorhinolaryngology are performed bilaterally, so modifier -52 should be used if a procedure noted as bilateral is done on only one eye or one ear.

TIP CPT specifically states that codes for hearing tests are bilateral procedures and that modifier -52 should be used if only one ear is tested.

Modifier -59 is appended if a distinct (separate) encounter occurs on the same day. This may be appended to drug administration codes if a distinct drug administration service was provided earlier in the same day and the codes have already been billed for those services. This modifier is not used if infusions are given in more than one site or if the infusion is stopped and then restarted.

Quick Reference

HCPCS II/ CPT Modifier	Description	Explanation
25	Separately identifiable evaluation and management service by the same physician on the same day of the procedure or other service	Appended to the E/M code. Medical record must include documentation of all key components required to justify the selection of the E/M code and the patient's condition that required the additional services.
50	Bilateral procedure	Used if a procedure described as unilateral is provided bilaterally.
52	Reduced services	Used if services provided are less than the full code describes.
59	Distinct procedural service	Used if a distinct encounter occurs on the same day.

Injections and Infusions

Injection is the process of introducing a fluid (such as a vaccine in liquid form) into the body's tissues using a needle. See Figure 8.1 for various angles used for injections. **Infusion** is the process of introducing a fluid other than blood (such as saline solution) into a vein. These methods are used for a wide range of medical treatments.

Immune Globulins (90281–90399)

Immune globulins are substances produced from immunoglobulins in human blood. Immunoglobulins (antibodies) travel in the blood or lymph and provide protection against certain diseases. Immune globulin products are individually listed with the appropriate CPT codes. They may be administered by the following routes:

▶ Intramuscular (IM)—into a muscle
▶ Subcutaneous (SQ)—into subcutaneous tissue
▶ Intravenous (IV)—into a vein

The coder must assign a code from 90765 to 90779 for the specific administration route in addition to coding the specific immune globulin product (90281–90399).

EXAMPLE	*Miscarriage of pregnancy at 10 weeks, requiring RhoGAM intramuscular administration (mini-dose): 90385, 90772.*

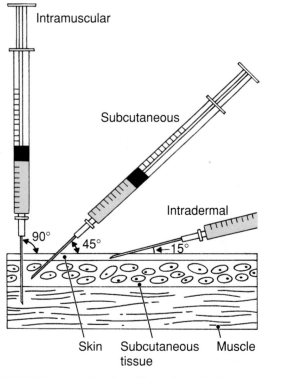

FIGURE 8.1 ■ Angles of insertion of injections.

Vaccines and Toxoids (90476–90749)

Immunity is acquired when the body produces antibodies in response to antigen exposure. Immunity can be acquired from having the active disease or receiving a vaccination. An antigen is a *foreign* substance that can attack the body and cause illness. Antigens may be bacteria, viruses, fungi, or other types of germs. Vaccines (viruses) and toxoids (bacteria) that are attenuated (weakened) can be injected in small amounts to enable the body to form antibodies, resulting in an immune (antigen/antibody) response. The immune response provides protection against the antigen if a subsequent exposure occurs.

Vaccination and toxoid administration codes are divided by route of administration, age of patient, and number of administrations. Routes include:

- ▶ Percutaneous—through the skin (absorption)
- ▶ Intradermal—into the skin
- ▶ Intramuscular—into a muscle
- ▶ Subcutaneous—into subcutaneous tissue (beneath the skin)
- ▶ Intranasal—into the nasal cavity
- ▶ Oral—into the mouth

Vaccination codes are specific for patients younger than 8 years of age and for age 8 and older. Add-on codes are provided for each additional administration. The coder should remember that *each additional* means the add-on code will be assigned for each additional injection or administration after the initial one.

TIP
Complete coding of vaccination and toxoid injection services requires that each injection or administration be coded separately. Two codes are required for each administration: one for the injection or administration procedure and one for the vaccine or toxoid product.

Coders should read the guidelines carefully to ensure the correct code choice. If the physician is present at the time of vaccine administration and provides face-to-face counseling to the patient and family, codes 90465 or 90467 are assigned along with applicable add-on code(s). If the physician is not present to provide counseling, the proper code selection is 90471 for the first injection and 90472 for each additional vaccine or toxoid administration. To separately code for E/M services at the time of immunization administration, the -25 modifier is appended to the E/M code. Physician office visits must meet the documentation requirements for key components (see details in the Evaluation and Management chapter of this textbook).

Some payers may not recognize the use of modifier -25. The E/M services should be documented thoroughly in the medical record. However, E/M service provided on the same day as an injection or infusion may not be reimbursable.

Hydration (90760–90761)

Hydration codes are used for reporting intravenous (IV) administration of prepackaged fluid and electrolytes. These codes are not applicable to infusion of drugs or other substances and should not be reported if concurrently administered with chemotherapy or infusions of other drugs. Hydration is typically not a high-risk procedure, and once the IV line is in place, the patient requires little monitoring. Documentation of start and stop times is needed to allow the coder to choose the correct code(s). The codes are based on time, with 90760 for the initial hour and an add-on code of 90761 used for each additional hour.

Supply codes (substance/drug and amount administered) for injections and infusions are documented using a "J" code from HCPCS Level II, such as J7030 for infusion of normal saline solution, 1,000 mL. Some commercial payers do not accept the HCPCS Level II supply codes and will not reimburse for them. In this case, CPT provides a general supply code, 99070, that is submitted along with the name(s) of the product(s) used. To avoid repeating the code for a particular product (e.g., drug), the number of units can be reported in an additional field on the billing form/abstract.

EXAMPLE

A dehydrated patient is infused with one unit of a 5% dextrose/normal saline solution, which takes approximately 50 minutes: 90760, J7042.
Alternatively, supply code 99070 can be used for the product administered if required by the payer (in place of J7042).

Therapeutic, Prophylactic, and Diagnostic Injections and Infusions (90765–90779)

Therapeutic, prophylactic, and diagnostic injections and infusions are used for various medicinal substances. These codes are *not* used for hydration or the administration of chemotherapy. Assignment of the codes describes the route of administration and length of time given, with one code for the first hour and an add-on code for each additional hour. The add-on code for 1 hour may be applied if the time is greater than 30 minutes beyond the 1-hour increment.

When administering multiple injections or infusions, the code for initial services is assigned just once unless a separate IV site is required for different substances per protocol. Modifier -59 should be used with the second initial services code to indicate it is a distinct service. The initial service should be identified as the most significant or key service provided.

> **TIP** The initial hydration code of 90760 should not be used to report initial services if *any* other drug is administered. Even if hydration is listed as the first service received, the coder should report this service using 90761 with the drug administration code as the initial service.

The following services are included in the CPT codes for injections and infusions and are not reported separately:

▶ Local anesthesia
▶ Starting the IV
▶ Establishing access to the IV, catheter, or port
▶ Flushing of the line at the conclusion of the infusion
▶ Supplies
▶ Preparation of the substance(s) to be infused

Concurrent infusions in which multiple substances are administered simultaneously through one IV site can occur. The IV line receives additional fluids concurrently through one or more ports that are part of the IV tubing. For example, a patient is receiving fluids through an IV line. Based on the laboratory work, it is determined that this patient requires a second medication, such as potassium. A second bag of fluid containing potassium is hung on the IV pole, and the potassium IV line is connected to the port on the tubing of the original bag of fluids. This is commonly called **piggybacking** (see Fig. 8.2). Either infusion pump or gravity drip methods are typically used.

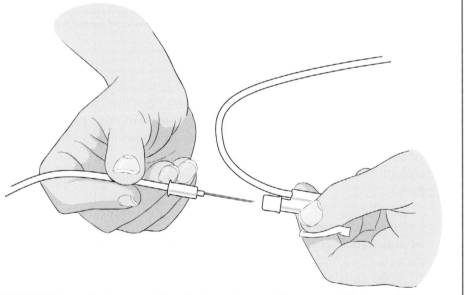

FIGURE 8.2 ■ IV piggyback. Needle being inserted into secondary port of IV set.

A separate CPT add-on code is provided for concurrent infusions, and this should be reported only once per encounter. If a second encounter occurs on the same day and it is clearly documented in the medical record, the concurrent infusion code may be reported a second time with modifier -59 (distinct and separate service; same day) appended.

EXAMPLE   *Laboratory work for a patient receiving 2-hour IV Lasix returns and shows hypokalemia. Patient receives piggybacking of potassium with IV Lasix fluids: 90765, 90766, 90768. Report the following "J" codes from HCPCS Level II for the products administered: J1940, J3480. (Alternatively, supply code 99070 can be used for the products administered, if required by the payer.)*

CPT provides codes for **intravenous push** and **intra-arterial push**. A substance that is pushed is injected directly into an existing IV line that is in use. To use these push codes, the provider must be present for the administration of the substance, or the infusion must take less than 16 minutes to complete. If a push is given subsequent to starting a separate infusion, then the push is coded as subsequent, *not* as an initial service. If a total infusion lasts less than 16 minutes, the push code is assigned for the service. Push codes cannot be assigned for infusion services that do not meet the time requirements for add-on codes. For instance, if a patient receives an (initial) infusion for 1 hour 10 minutes, only the initial code of 90765 would be assigned. No add-on or push code can be assigned for the 10 minutes past 1 hour of services.

EXAMPLE   *Patient presents with severe vomiting and dehydration. IV infusion of normal saline, 1,000 mL for 2 hours. Phenergan IV push given. Report code 90774 for IV push, 90761, 90761 for administration of hydration (normal saline), and the following "J" codes from HCPCS Level II for the products administered: J2550, J7030. (Some payers do not recognize "J" codes, and then the supply code 99070 can be used for the products administered.)*

Note in the preceding example that 90760 is *not assigned* for the initial hydration services. Recall that the initial service does not necessarily mean the first treatment provided to the patient. Instead, the initial service describes the primary reason for the encounter. In this example, Phenergan is provided to stop the nausea and vomiting.

Coders must keep in mind the following key points for coding injections and infusions:

▶ Vaccine and toxoid administration services require two codes, one for administration and one for supply—both codes are found in the CPT manual.
▶ To report clearly separate E/M services with vaccine and toxoid administration codes, key components must be clearly documented and modifier -25 appended to the E/M code.

▶ Hydration codes for prepackaged fluids and electrolytes are based on the time of infusion. The initial code is for first hour, with an add-on code for each additional hour.

▶ Hydration codes are not reported if fluids are administered with chemotherapy or other drugs.

▶ Supply of infusion products for hydration codes is found in the "J" codes of HCPCS Level II or use 99070 for supply and specify product.

▶ Therapeutic, prophylactic, and diagnostic injections are based on route and time. Initial code is for first hour; add-on code for each additional hour.

▶ Initial service reported is for the most significant or key service provided, i.e., sequence first.

▶ Supply of injection products for therapeutic, prophylactic, and diagnostic injections is found in the "J" codes of HCPCS Level II. If the payer does not allow submission of "J" codes, use 99070 and specify the product(s).

▶ Sequential infusions or injections are those given after the initial infusion.

▶ Concurrent infusions must be in separate bags, through the same IV line.

▶ Push codes are assigned when a substance is injected directly into an existing IV line.

▶ Push codes require the presence of provider or an infusion requiring less than 16 minutes to complete.

The following examples are provided as further explanation of CPT administration codes only. Supply codes were intentionally omitted.

EXAMPLES

1—Pediatric patient presents to the emergency room with a kidney stone:
Started 12:10 ended 13:20 Normal saline bolus 1 liter IV: 90761
12:25 Toradol 30 mg IV push—note this is reported as the initial service: 90774
12:40 Zofran 4 mg IV push: 90775
13:05 Dilaudid 4 mg IV push: 90775
13:05 Benadryl 50 mg IV push: 90775
14:00 to 15:10 D5-1/2 NS with 20 meq KCl 150 mL/hr: 90761
*16:25 to 16:55 Dilaudid 2 mg IV NOT CODED: Dilaudid was administered at 13:05, and the
    second infusion at 16:25 cannot also be reported.*
2—Pediatric patient presents to the emergency room with bloody diarrhea:
03:40 Claforan 50 mg/kg IV: 90765
04:19 Ampicillin 30 mg/kg IV: 90766
3—Pediatric patient presents to the emergency room with testicular pain:
Started 21:55 ended 22:55 20 mg/kg bolus normal saline: 90761
22:22 4 mg morphine IV push—note this is reported as the initial service: 90774
*23:34 2 mg morphine IV push NOT CODED: morphine was administered at 22:22 and
    cannot be reported a second or third time.*
23:52 10 mg ketorolac IV push: 90775
*00:40 2 mg morphine IV NOT CODED: morphine was administered at 22:22 and cannot
    be reported a second or third time.*

Psychiatry (90801–90899)

Psychiatry is the medical specialty concerned with the diagnosis and treatment of mental disorders. Psychiatric codes are provided for inpatient and outpatient services. Psychiatric consultations may be requested by the patient's primary care provider. This service requires a thorough review of the patient's history and a lengthy psychiatric examination. Results are then reported back to the requesting physician and a written report is completed. An appropriate code from the Evaluation and Management (E/M) section of CPT is assigned for this service.

Psychotherapy is the treatment of emotional, behavioral, personality, and psychiatric disorders based primarily on verbal or nonverbal communication and interventions with the patient. Medical E/M services for a health assessment and medication monitoring can be provided in conjunction with psychotherapy visits. These codes are used to report services by the psychiatrist, nurse practitioner, or physician assistant. Family practitioners, obstetricians, and other medical doctors may also assign these codes if a patient's visit is for psychotherapy or other psychiatric services. It is recommended that psychotherapy be provided either before or after the E/M services to ensure correct code selection for timing of psychotherapy services. Codes for individual psychotherapy are based on time spent face-to-face with the patient. Interactive psychotherapy is usually provided to children and includes play therapy and nonverbal communication. Psychotherapy services other than medical E/M services may be reported by psychologists, social workers, and counselors.

EXAMPLE	*Patient with depression presents to the psychiatric office for medication management and psychotherapy. Psychiatrist spends 10 minutes reviewing history and physical changes and response to new medication. Twenty minutes of face-to-face psychotherapy is then provided with the patient: 90805.*

Family psychotherapy may be provided with or without the patient present. In either case, the code selected is applied to the patient's record. If a child is seen alone, and then the parents are seen alone for information about the child's condition or treatment, the total time of the services may be added for a single psychotherapy visit code with the child.

Dialysis (90918–90999)

End-stage renal disease (ESRD) is also called chronic kidney disease (CKD). When a patient has stage 5 CKD, only 15% of kidney function remains. This is insufficient to adequately remove waste products of metabolism (nitrogenous wastes; urea) from the bloodstream, and **hemodialysis** is then necessary to cleanse the blood. The procedure is usually performed three to four times a week.

CPT provides codes for ESRD management in the outpatient setting based on one full month or per day of services. The codes are further delineated by patient age ranges of younger than 2 years, 2 to 11 years, 12 to 19 years, and older than 20 years of age. These codes include initiation of the dialysis cycle, care provided during dialysis visits, all E/M services provided at the time of dialysis, and telephone calls relating to this care. For patients younger than 20 years of age, the ESRD codes also include nutritional assessment and review, growth monitoring, and parental counseling and support. These ESRD management codes also include the actual hemodialysis procedure (i.e., don't code separately).

EXAMPLE	*A 12-year-old patient with chronic kidney disease receives 1 month of hemodialysis services on an outpatient basis: 90920.*

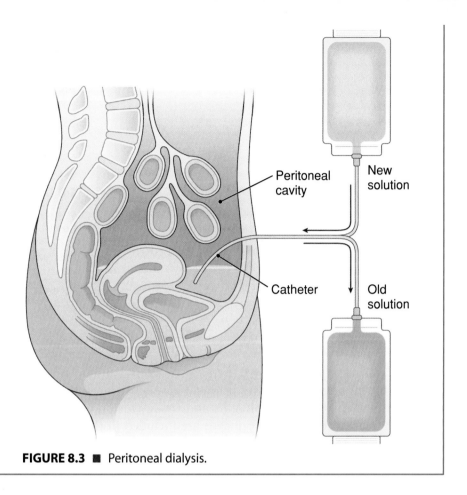

FIGURE 8.3 ■ Peritoneal dialysis.

If an ESRD patient is admitted to the hospital, then appropriate inpatient care codes from the E/M section are submitted for the time of hospitalization. ESRD codes for services provided to inpatients if the physician is physically present during hemodialysis will include codes from 90935 to 90940. If the physician visits the patient at a time other than during hemodialysis, the appropriate E/M code would be assigned. For outpatient ESRD services of less than 1 month (where an inpatient stay occurred), ESRD per-day codes are applied.

Hemodialysis procedure codes 90935 and 90937 are also used for patients without ESRD for inpatient *and* outpatient settings (e.g., patient has reversible acute renal failure). If the patient receives peritoneal dialysis (see Fig. 8.3) or dialysis services other than hemodialysis, separate codes are provided in the 90945–90999 range. The coder should look carefully for documentation of repeated evaluations by the physician during the dialysis cycle for adjustments in the dialysis prescription. Codes are available for these repeated evaluations versus a single physician evaluation.

Gastroenterology (91000–91299)

Gastroenterology is the medical specialty concerned with treating disorders of the gastrointestinal tract, including the esophagus, stomach, intestines, and associated organs.

Gastroesophageal reflux disease (GERD) causes stomach acid to flow back up (reflux) into the esophagus. GERD is often associated with hiatal hernia. The

FOCUS ON MEDICAL NECESSITY

Test (CPT Code)	Possible Diagnosis	ICD-9-CM Code
Gastrointestinal tract imaging, intraluminal (e.g., capsule endoscopy), esophagus through ileum, with physician interpretation and report (91110)	Iron deficiency anemia secondary to blood loss (chronic)	280.0
	Iron deficiency anemia unspecified	280.9
	Regional enteritis of small intestine	555.0
	Regional enteritis of small intestine with large intestine	555.2
	Regional enteritis of unspecified site	555.9
	Diverticulosis of small intestine with hemorrhage	562.02
	Diverticulitis of small intestine with hemorrhage	562.03
	Angiodysplasia of intestine with hemorrhage	569.85
	Hemorrhage of gastrointestinal tract unspecified	578.9
Gastrointestinal tract imaging, intraluminal (e.g., capsule endoscopy), esophagus, with physician interpretation and report (91111)	Portal hypertension AND one of the following:	572.3
	(1) Esophageal varices in diseases classified elsewhere with bleeding, or	456.20
	(2) Esophageal varices in diseases classified elsewhere without bleeding	456.21

presence of this acid changes the pH (acid-base balance) of the fluids in the esophagus and may cause esophagitis and tissue erosion over time. Tests to measure the pH levels in the esophagus are included in the gastroenterology subsection of CPT. In addition, motility studies for the esophagus, stomach, and duodenum are provided. These studies are called manometric studies and they measure movement.

EXAMPLE   *Patient with gastroparesis receives electrogastrography, diagnostic, transcutaneous: 91132.*

Capsule endoscopy is a procedure in which the patient swallows a "camera pill," and images captured by the camera are interpreted by the physician. Codes are reported for the esophagus only or for the esophagus through the ileum. The above Focus on Medical Necessity table provides ICD-9-CM codes for diagnoses related to the capsule endoscopy procedures. This is an example of a local coverage determination (LCD) for First Coast Service Options, Inc., of Florida, provided on the CMS Web site. All procedure codes in CPT require a diagnosis code to prove medical necessity. See Chapter 3 for further discussion of medical necessity.

Ophthalmology (92002–92499)

Ophthalmology is the medical specialty concerned with the eye, its diseases, and refractive errors. Ophthalmologists and optometrists are "eye doctors" who assess refractive errors and treat disorders of the eye. Ophthalmologists are medical doctors (M.D.) trained to perform eye surgery in addition to providing medical care. CPT provides specific codes for services provided to new and established ophthalmologic patients. If the services provided are less than those described in codes 92002–92014, the coder should assign an appropriate code from the E/M section of CPT.

Routine ophthalmoscopy along with mydriasis (dilation of pupils) is considered part of either general or special services and is not coded separately

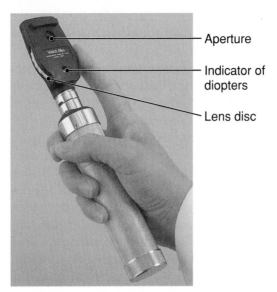

Aperture

Indicator of diopters

Lens disc

FIGURE 8.4 ■ Ophthalmoscope. A device used to examine the interior of the eye through the pupil.

(see Fig. 8.4). Specific tests that are coded separately include fluorescein angioscopy to determine the blood supply to the retina (e.g., in diabetes) and tonometry to determine the pressure within the eye to test for glaucoma, for example. Glaucoma occurs when fluid (aqueous humor) within the eye is unable to drain properly, causing a buildup of pressure within the eye and eventual peripheral vision loss if untreated.

Visual field (VF) testing is performed to determine defects in the field of vision. Codes are assigned based on whether the testing is limited, intermediate, or extended. This is determined by the type of equipment and complexity of the studies. Drooping eyelids (blepharoptosis) often occur with aging. A surgical repair of the eyelid can be done; this procedure is called blepharoplasty and is usually not covered by health insurance or Medicare unless significant vision obstruction can be demonstrated. If VF testing is done to determine medical necessity for blepharoplasty, two tests may be run. In the first test, the patient's eyes are taped, and in the second test, the eyes are not taped to determine the degree of visual obstruction. A modifier -76 is required on the second test to explain the need for two VF tests on the same date by the same provider.

Established patient with a family history of glaucoma receives provocative tests with interpretation and report, without tonography, as part of an intermediate level office visit: 92012, 92140.

EXAMPLE

Codes are provided for supply and fitting of contact lenses and fitting of glasses. A special type of contact lens is used for treatment of corneal pathology such as abrasions, ulcers, and dry eyes. The code is 92070 and this is assigned per eye treated. Spectacle services include prosthetic services for aphakia. Aphakia is absence of the lens of the eye, which is removed surgically, usually because of cataracts.

The coder should also be aware of two codes for visual acuity testing by technicians, done as part of a screening test: 99172 and 99173. These screening codes would only be used to report an ophthalmologist's services if they are performed as part of a school screening program.

Special Otorhinolaryngologic Services (92502–92700)

Services listed in the special otorhinolaryngologic services subsection include a medical evaluation. Therefore, these services are not usually performed as part of a comprehensive office visit with an otorhinolaryngologist, whose practice involves diagnosis and treatment of diseases of the ear, nose, and throat (including the pharynx, larynx, tracheobronchial tree, and esophagus). Routine E/M services for otorhinolaryngology include procedures such as otoscopy, rhinoscopy, and hearing tests using whispered voice or tuning forks, and therefore are not coded separately. If calibrated electronic equipment is used to test hearing, CPT does provide codes for these services.

Auditory rehabilitation codes are included in this subsection and include testing for hearing loss and speech understanding. Codes for these services are based on time, with the first code accounting for 1 hour and the add-on code representing each additional 15 minutes spent with the patient. Services include obtaining a history, describing the procedures to the patient, assessing the patient, and making recommendations. As with all timed services, start and stop times are required to allow the coder to perform correct code selection. The clinician must go at least 8 minutes past the initial hour to assign the add-on code for 15 minutes of service time.

Auditory rehabilitation codes are also provided for patients with hearing loss before learning to speak. This is usually assigned to children with the assumption that a hearing aid or cochlear implant is not enough for the child to understand speech. Additional training is necessary to teach these patients how to process the auditory stimuli they are receiving with the new aids. A CPT code of 92633 is available if the patient loses hearing after learning speech, or postlingual.

EXAMPLE	*Level 2 follow-up office visit with otorhinolaryngologist, examination includes a tuning fork test: 99212.*

Cardiovascular Services (92950–93990)

Electrocardiography provides a tracing record of the electrical activity in the heart (Fig. 8.5). If this service is provided in a physician's office, the coder should be aware of the code choices for the entire procedure, including interpretation and report; provision of a tracing only; or, provision of interpretation and report only. A Holter monitor is a portable device for providing 24-hour (or more) continuous tracings of heart's electrical activity. A Holter is used to detect transient or insidious arrhythmias that are not readily seen on routine (short) electrocardiogram tracings such as those done in the physician's office. Codes in the range of 93224–93237 are assigned based on the specific technology used for the monitor.

Echocardiography is ultrasound of the heart chambers and valves and the great vessels, including the aorta and venae cavae. The images may be two dimensional or Doppler. Complete studies provide information about the structure (as noted above) and function of the heart, including direction and velocity of blood flow, intracardiac pressures, stroke volume and cardiac output, valve

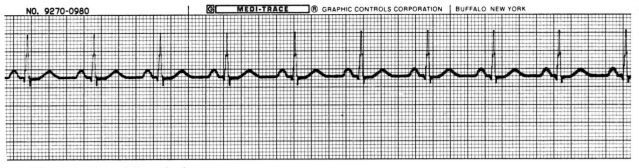

FIGURE 8.5 ■ Normal sinus rhythm.

formation, and ventricular function during both systole and diastole. Limited studies provide a thorough evaluation of a limited area.

Two approaches are transthoracic and transesophageal echocardiogram. Transthoracic is performed by passing the transducer directly over the chest wall externally. Transesophageal echocardiogram (TEE) requires a probe with a transducer to be passed through the mouth into the esophagus, where special expertise is necessary to place the transesophageal probe endoscopically. CPT provides codes for only this portion of the procedure if necessary, 93313 and 93316. Separate codes are then assigned to report the services of the physician who completes the TEE procedure, interprets the findings, and prepares a report.

Cardiac catheterization requires **component coding**, which was introduced in the Surgery chapter of this textbook. This method uses multiple codes to fully report complex procedures and account for all the work involved. There are three components to cardiac catheterization procedures: 1) catheter placement code, 2) all applicable injection procedure codes but only once in a given area, and 3) imaging supervision and interpretation codes that match up with the injection code(s). Cardiac catheterizations include the following procedures, which may not be coded separately:

▶ Catheter insertion, type should be documented as percutaneous or cutdown
▶ Positioning and repositioning of catheters, this includes fluoroscopic guidance
▶ Injection of dyes, which should be documented as to site of angiography such as coronary arteries, aorta, atria, ventricles, bypass grafts, renal and femoral vessels
▶ Recording of intracardiac and intravascular pressures
▶ Obtaining blood samples for blood gas analysis or dilution curves
▶ Cardiac output measurements
▶ Pharmacologic administration

For correct code assignment, in addition to the preceding items, the report should contain the side(s) of the heart evaluated, the method of accessing the left side of the heart, presence of congenital anomalies, and insertion of a closure device.

If the cardiologist discovers significant blockage of coronary vessels during cardiac catheterization, he or she may elect to perform percutaneous transluminal coronary angioplasty (PTCA). PTCA (see Fig. 8.6) is now

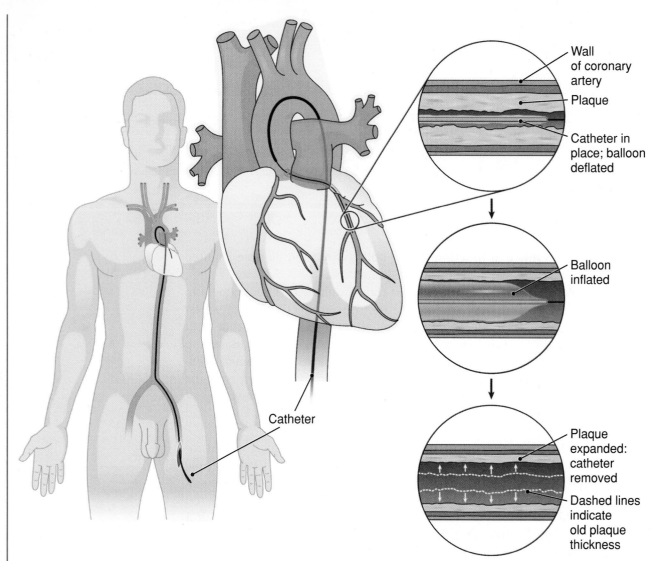

FIGURE 8.6 ■ Coronary angioplasty. A guide catheter is threaded into the coronary artery. A balloon catheter is inserted through the occlusion, and the balloon is inflated and deflated until plaque is flattened and the vessel is opened.

commonly referred to as percutaneous coronary intervention (PCI), and these terms and abbreviations may be used interchangeably. PTCA is performed at the same episode as cardiac catheterization, and both procedures are coded.

During PTCA, the cardiologist may elect to place stents in narrowed vessels in addition to balloon angioplasty. If stent placement is performed, the PTCA is not coded separately, as this is an integral part of the stenting procedure. Stenting codes are assigned for each vessel treated, but multiple stents in one vessel are reported as one stenting. Cardiac catheterization is coded in addition to the stenting procedure.

Atherectomy may also occur in conjunction with cardiac catheterization. In this procedure, a tiny instrument is used to remove the plaque from the

FOCUS ON MEDICAL NECESSITY

Test (CPT Code)	Possible Diagnosis	ICD-9-CM Code
Intracardiac catheter ablation of atrioventricular node function, atrioventricular conduction for creation or complete heart block, with or without temporary pacemaker placement (93650)	Anomalous atrioventricular excitation	426.7
	Lown-Ganong-Levine syndrome	426.81
	Other specified conduction disorders	426.89
	Paroxysmal supraventricular tachycardia	427.0
	Paroxysmal ventricular tachycardia	427.1
	Atrial fibrillation	427.31
	Atrial flutter	427.32
	Other specified cardiac dysrhythmias	427.89
Intracardiac catheter ablation of arrhythmogenic focus; for treatment of supraventricular tachycardia by ablation of fast or slow atrioventricular pathways, accessory atrioventricular connections or other atrial foci, singly or in combination (93651)	Same as for 93650	Same
Intracardiac catheter ablation of arrhythmogenic focus; for treatment of ventricular tachycardia (93652)	Same as for 93650	Same

inner walls of the narrowed vessel. PTCA is not coded separately with atherectomy, as the code description includes the statement "with or without balloon angioplasty." Cardiac catheterization is coded in addition to atherectomy.

Electrophysiologic studies (EPS) and mapping are diagnostic procedures performed to determine areas of damaged tissue in the heart that cause severe arrhythmias, such as atrial fibrillation, ventricular tachycardia, and/or ventricular fibrillation. Intracardiac catheter ablation is then performed to destroy the focus of aberrant tissue. The patient will typically receive these services on the same date, beginning with the EPS, then the mapping or measuring of EPS events with the patient in a resting state, and finally the ablation or destruction of the area of ectopic tissue (localized area of irritated or diseased tissue) in the area of the atrioventricular node. The Focus on Medical Necessity table above provides ICD-9-CM codes for diagnoses related to cardiac procedures from the local coverage determination for Highmark Medicare Services Pennsylvania Carrier, provided on the CMS Web site. Local coverage determinations are often provided by a state for specificity in determining medical necessity.

Pulmonary Services (94002–94799)

A mechanical ventilator is a device used to assist the patient with breathing. Ventilator management codes are provided for inpatient services as well as nursing home, rest home, and assisting living. The codes are based on initial day or subsequent day(s). Codes from this subsection cannot be used in conjunction with E/M codes. For home health visits for mechanical ventilator care, assign code 99504.

FIGURE 8.7 ■ Spirometer. Used to measure lung volumes and capacities.

Pulmonary function testing includes spirometry, which is a measurement of breathing mechanics (Fig. 8.7). The patient takes a maximal inhalation and then performs maximal exhalation as fast and hard as possible into a spirometer, a device that measures lung volume and intrapulmonary pressure. Data are plotted on both a volume-time curve and a flow-volume curve. CPT provides a code for spirometry performed before and after bronchodilator treatment. Code 94060 is assigned if multiple increasing dosages of a treatment are administered to determine the effects of the treatment in increments.

EXAMPLE	*Before and after bronchodilator test using aerosolized Alupent: 94060, J7669 or 99070.*

Allergy and Clinical Immunology (95004–95199)

CPT provides codes for allergy testing by percutaneous, intradermal, patch, inhalation, and ingestion methods. (See Fig. 8.8 for an example of a patch test.) Once sensitivities have been determined, the patient may be treated by immunotherapy. Professional services may include only the injection. Codes include services of patient observation and patient education. A separate E/M code is not assigned.

EXAMPLE	*A college student provides a vial of serum to the health center for periodic allergy shots by the health center nurse. Student presents for a single injection: 95115.*

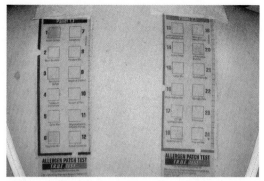

FIGURE 8.8 ■ Allergy test patches. Patches will be removed after 48 hours.

Professional services may also include the physician who prepares and provides the antigen. The comprehensive codes (95120–95134) include both services and are described as either single or two or more injections for the allergenic extracts. Additional codes are provided for single, two, three, four, or five insect venoms. An E/M code is not submitted on the day of allergen injections unless a separate service is provided.

Neurology (95805–96020)

Neurology is the medical specialty concerned with diagnosis and treatment of disorders of the neuromuscular system. A variety of tests are included in this section of CPT, including tests of the central and peripheral nervous systems (CNS and PNS).

Sleep studies are usually performed at a hospital or in a specialized facility designed for the evaluation of sleep disorders. The patient may or may not be attended by a technologist. Ventilation, respiratory effort, electrocardiogram (or heart rate), and oxygen saturation are measured. Polysomnography testing includes electroencephalography (EEG), electrooculography (EOG), and electromyography (EMG). Sleep staging (Fig. 8.9) is performed with these three measures and one to three additional factors including:

▶ Electrocardiogram
▶ Airflow
▶ Respiratory effort
▶ Gas exchange
▶ Limb muscle activity
▶ Extended EEG
▶ Penile tumescence
▶ Gastroesophageal reflux
▶ Continuous blood pressure monitoring

Codes are assigned based on the number of additional factors and whether or not continuous positive airway pressure (CPAP) is used. CPAP delivers a stream of compressed air that keeps the airway open and allows unobstructed breathing.

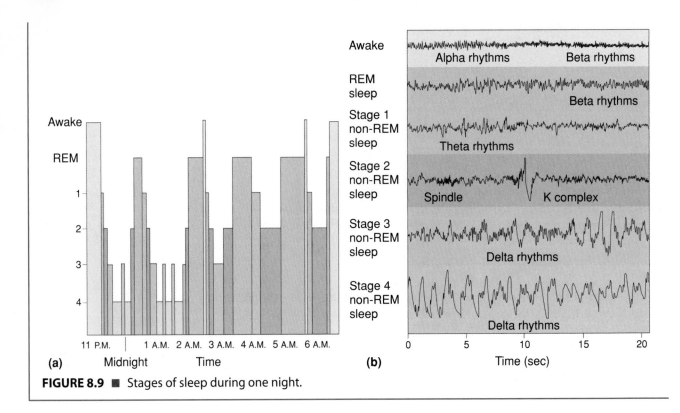

FIGURE 8.9 ■ Stages of sleep during one night.

> **TIP** Code 95811 is assigned only if four or more additional factors are measured, and CPAP is initiated with 6 hours of continuous use.

If the patient is intolerant of the CPAP and it is removed before the 6 hours required, modifier -52 is appended to signify the provision of a reduced service.

Electroencephalography (EEG) is the recording of electrical activity of the brain derived from electrodes attached to the scalp. As previously mentioned, this is an important component of a sleep study. An EEG may be done as a diagnostic tool in other settings, such as to determine a possible diagnosis of epilepsy. As a routine test, it can be coded for 20 to 40 minutes of recording (95816), 41–60 minutes of recording (95812), or greater than 1 hour (95813). EEG is also performed for determination of cerebral death evaluation (i.e., "brain death").

Special EEG tests are performed for identification of seizure focus in the cerebrum with the use of 8, 16, or more channel telemetry. The electroencephalographic recording may be done with or without video recording. Codes for these procedures are for each 24 hours and include both the recording and the physician interpretation. Code 95953 is assigned when a portable unit is used for EEG monitoring and recording.

Electromyography (EMG) is the recording of electrical activity generated in muscle for diagnostic purposes, such as evaluation for spinal cord injury or muscular dystrophy. These tests are commonly done on the extremities and four successive codes are available, depending on how many extremities are tested. Codes are also provided for EMG testing of the larynx and the hemidiaphragm.

Chemotherapy Administration (96401–96549)

Chemotherapy is the treatment of a disease, usually cancer, by means of chemical substances or drugs. Chemotherapy services are complex and require physician supervision. The following services are included in chemotherapy codes: local anesthesia, IV beginning and maintenance, supplies, and preparation of chemotherapy agent(s). Timing of services is important for correct administration code assignment. The first hour is assigned code 96413, and each additional hour is assigned the add-on code 96415. Separate codes are reported for each method of administration. Administration of additional medications, such as those to control nausea or vomiting (antiemetic), are coded separately. As mentioned earlier, incidental hydration administered in conjunction with chemotherapy is not coded separately.

TIP "J" codes are provided in HCPCS Level II for specific chemotherapeutic substances. These codes should be reported in addition to the administration services to fully explain the chemotherapy. For carriers that do not accept "J" codes for payment, use the supply code 99070 and specify the chemotherapeutic agent(s) the patient received.

Prolonged chemotherapy regimens may require the use of an **infusion pump.** If the regimen calls for 1 day of prolonged administration followed by a refill and second day of prolonged infusion, a code is provided for the refill services, 96521. When the regimen calls for continuous infusion for several days, including infusion pump initiation, infusions for several days, and then disconnection of the pump, codes 96416 and 99211 are reported. This is assuming no refill of chemotherapy agents is required. The final service of having the pump unhooked by a nurse is a Level 1 E/M code. If the patient returns periodically to repeat this same regimen, each treatment regimen is coded separately.

Physical Medicine and Rehabilitation (97001–97799)

Physical therapy, occupational therapy, and athletic training sessions are provided codes for evaluation and re-evaluation. Codes in the range of 97001–97006 may be reported only one time per date of service. Specific treatment codes are also available for the therapy provided. Supervised modalities do not require direct contact with the provider and may include application of hot or cold packs, mechanical traction, electrical stimulation, vasopneumatic devices, paraffin baths, whirlpool, diathermy, infrared, and ultraviolet. These services may only be reported one time per date of service, even if they are applied to multiple body areas. However, multiple different modalities may be reported on the same date.

Patient suffering from lumbar strain has application of hot packs and unattended electrical stimulation: 97010 and 97014.   EXAMPLE

Constant attendance **modalities** require direct patient contact by the provider. This means that the provider cannot assign the patient a set of exercises to complete while the provider works with another patient. Each of the codes represents 15 minutes of treatment time with the modality. These services should be given in increments of no more than two per day. Iontophoresis is the application of electrical current to the tissue to enhance delivery of ionized medications. This service must be performed by a physical therapist to qualify for reimbursement under Medicare. Therapeutic procedures are also given in 15-minute increments. A physician or therapist must have direct patient contact for these services. If more than two patients are being supervised simultaneously, code 97150 is assigned. This would require constant attendance but not one-to-one patient contact. For physical and occupational therapy, Medicare does not consider more than 1 hour of therapeutic services medically necessary. Because of this rule, more than four 15-minute units of service submitted on a claim are likely to be denied.

EXAMPLE	*Two or more postoperative total hip replacement patients using treadmills for endurance training: code 97150.*

Training for activities of daily living (ADL) includes activities such as getting dressed, transfer techniques for getting on and off the toilet, in and out of the shower or tub, in and out of the bed to a chair, and use of equipment for meal preparation. These services are coded in 15-minute increments.

Medical Nutrition Therapy, Acupuncture, and Chiropractic Manipulative Treatment (97802–98943)

Nutritional counseling must be ordered by a physician and provided by a registered dietician. The visits are timed, in 15-minute increments. Initial assessment and intervention is coded twice if the time spent with the patient is 30 minutes on the initial visit. If a physician provides nutritional counseling or therapy, a code should be assigned from the E/M section.

Acupuncture is a type of alternative, nontraditional treatment for conditions such as pain management, in which long, fine needles are inserted under the skin at particular points on the body. This therapy is of Asian origin and is becoming an accepted method in the United States. Codes are provided for the initial 15 minutes with or without electrical stimulation. Each additional 15 minutes may be coded with an add-on code, based on whether or not electrical stimulation was provided. Only one initial code may be reported for each treatment session. Evaluation and management services may be reported separately with modifier -25 if the patient presents with a separately identifiable condition that is not treated with the services included in acupuncture treatment.

Chiropractic manipulative services are provided to regions of the spine. CPT defines these as the cervical region, thoracic region, lumbar region, sacral region, and pelvic region. If manipulation is performed on more than one segment in a region, it is coded as one region adjusted.

EXAMPLE	*Patient who suffered an iliosacral rotation requires chiropractic manipulative treatment to the pelvic region, sacrum, and L5: 98941 (for three to four regions).*

Special Services, Procedures, and Reports (99000–99091)

This subsection of CPT serves as a catchall for miscellaneous services not listed under other categories. Coders are encouraged to read all the special services codes to become familiar with the choices available there.

As discussed in the Pathology and Laboratory chapter, handling of a specimen that is sent to an outside laboratory for testing is coded 99000. Other miscellaneous codes include those used to document shipping of orthotics and prosthetics for adjustments. The miscellaneous supply code for injectables and infusion products is 99070. Other services such as medical testimony, group educational services, completion of special insurance forms, and escort of patient for treatment are also included in this CPT subsection.

Physician services may include codes for services provided after hours or on weekends or holidays. If a patient is seen emergently in the office, disrupting the schedule of patients for the day, code 99058 may be added to the applicable E/M code for the service. If a patient is seen in the office on a weekend when the office is normally closed, 99050 is assigned in addition to the E/M code. If a physician's normal business hours include being open for a portion of the day on Saturday, it would not be appropriate to include code 99050 in billing for services. In this case, code 99051 is assigned to designate that the visit occurred on a Saturday during regularly scheduled office hours. Whether or not this service code is reimbursed, third-party payers do recognize that services provided in the office are less expensive than those provided in a hospital emergency room.

SUMMARY

The Medicine section of CPT contains codes for many services (e.g., injections and infusions) that do not fit adequately or exclusively into other sections of the CPT manual, such as Surgery of Radiology. Many specialties are represented in the Medicine section, and accordingly the codes include rules and guidelines applicable to the varied services provided. Reading through the choices available in this section will help coders become familiar with all the procedures and services listed. For example, understanding the difference between concurrent, subsequent, push, and other techniques for injections and infusions, along with proper documentation of start and stop times for services, will ensure correct code selection.

TESTING YOUR COMPREHENSION

1. Why is a Holter monitor used?

   _____

2. What condition is tonometry performed to test for?

   _____

3. Why would a psychiatrist report medical E/M codes?

   _____

4. Which modifier is used if separate E/M services are provided on the same date as a vaccination administration?

   _____

5. What services are included in the CPT codes for injections and infusions?

   _____

6. What is the supply code provided by CPT if a carrier will not accept HCPCS Level II "J" codes?

   _____

7. What are the three tests included in polysomnography?

   _____

8. Which type of therapy service requires direct patient contact by the provider?

   _____

9. When can a physician bill using 99050 for seeing a patient on a Saturday?

   _____

10. What changes the pH of fluids in the esophagus?

    _____

11. Why is hemodialysis used in patients with ESRD?

    _____

12. What might be an advantage of using capsule endoscopy over traditional endoscopy?

    _____

13. What are the three components of cardiac catheterization coding?

    _____

14. If a physician discovers blockage of coronary vessels during cardiac catheterization, what treatment options might be undertaken (nonsurgical)?

    _____

15. What type of activities are the following: getting in and out of the shower or tub, getting in and out of the bed to a chair, and use of equipment for meal preparation?

    _____

CODING PRACTICE I Chapter Review Exercises

Directions

Use your CPT manual to code the following tests using codes from the Medicine section.

1. Vitamin B_{12} intramuscular injection _____

2. Electroconvulsive therapy _____

3. Patient with *Pneumocystis carinii* pneumonia is treated with aerosol pentamidine _____

4. EEG all night _____

5. Prosthetic training, leg, 35 minutes _____

6. Physical therapist provides gait training _____

7. IM injection of Penicillin _____

8. Physical therapist provides 3-D kinetic analysis of stride characteristics _____

9. 15 patch tests _____

10. Actinotherapy (ultraviolet light) _____

11. One-year-old patient receives ESRD services for 1 month including parental counseling _____

12. Patient receives Ig IM _____

13. Rhinomanometry _____

14. 12-lead ECG tracing only _____

15. Genetics counseling, 30 minutes _____

16. IM injection of testosterone _____

17. Closure of ventricular septal defect _____

18. Dermatologic treatment with ultraviolet light _____

19. Group nutritional counseling, 30 minutes _____

20. Home health care for ADL assistance _____

21. Chemotherapy treatment with 5FU for 55 minutes and subsequent hydration with D5W for 47 minutes

_____

22. Chemotherapy treatment with Taxotere 60 mg mixed with fluids, 5 hours of continuous infusion time

_____

23. Hydration for dehydration, 6 hours _____

24. Acupuncture without electrical stimulation, 35 minutes _____

25. Dr. 048 provides outpatient cardiac rehabilitation services with continuous ECG monitoring _____

CODING PRACTICE II   Medical Record Case Studies

Directions

1. Carefully review the medical reports provided for each case study.
2. Research any abbreviations and terms that are unfamiliar or unclear.
3. Identify as many diagnoses and procedures as possible.
4. Because only part of the patient's total record is available, think about any additional documentation that you might need.
5. If appropriate, identify any questions you might ask the physician or other health-care provider to code this case correctly and completely.
6. Complete the appropriate blanks below for each case study. Explain (in writing) questions 1–5 and assign the Medicine code(s) for question 6.

Case Study 8.1

Patient: **Patient QQ**

Patient documentation: **Read Medical Report 8.1.**

1. What is the diagnosis (description) that supports the medical necessity of this procedure?

   _____

2. Are there any secondary diagnoses present that required additional procedures?

   _____

3. What was the principal or main procedure, and were other secondary procedures performed on this patient?

   _____

4. Do you believe you need additional documentation to correctly assign the Medicine codes to this record? If so, what is the additional documentation that you need?

   _____

5. Do you have any additional questions for the physician or other health-care provider?

   _____

6. What is(are) the procedure code(s) you would assign to this case study?

   _____

   _____

GENERAL HOSPITAL
DEPARTMENT OF RADIOLOGY

PATIENT'S NAME:	**Patient QQ**	DATE OF BIRTH:	**7/20**
DATE EXAM PERFORMED:	**8/11/20XX**	HOSPITAL ROOM NO.:	**OP**
RADIOLOGY FILE NO.:	**22957833**	REFERRING PHYSICIAN:	**Dr. 049**

2D ECHO COMPLETE STUDY

INDICATION: Syncope

FINDINGS: The technical quality of the study was fair to good. Overall left ventricular chamber size appeared normal. Global left ventricular systolic function appeared normal. The estimated ejection fraction was 50 to 55%. No segmental wall motion abnormalities were detected. The left atrium and aortic root were of normal dimensions. The right-sided chambers appeared normal. No pericardial effusion was demonstrated. The cardiac valves appeared normal. Doppler is performed to monitor blood flow through the chambers and may have revealed a trace of mitral insufficiency.

Electronically Signed and Dated

Case Study 8.2

Patient: **Patient RR**

Patient documentation: **Read Medical Report 8.2**

1. What is the diagnosis (description) that supports the medical necessity of this procedure?

   _____

2. Are there any secondary diagnoses present that required additional procedures?

   _____

3. What was the principal or main procedure, and were other secondary procedures performed on this patient?

   _____

4. Do you believe you need additional documentation to correctly assign the Medicine codes to this record? If so, what is the additional documentation that you need?

   _____

5. Do you have any additional questions for the physician or other health-care provider?

   _____

6. What is(are) the procedure code(s) you would assign to this case study?

   _____

   _____

MEDICAL REPORT 8.2

Patient Name: **PATIENT RR**   Smoker: **No**

Age: 87 Diagnosis: **DYSPNEA**

Physician: **DR. 050**

COMPLETE PULMONARY FUNCTION ANALYSIS

SPIROMETRY	Ref	Pre	% Ref	Post	% Ref	% Chg
FVC Liters	3.00	1.69	56	1.67	56	−1
FEV1 Liters	1.83	1.24	68	1.20	65	−1
FEV1/FVC%	78	73		72		
FEF 25-75% L/sec	1.02	0.91	89	0.80	78	−12
FEF 50% L/sec	1.84	1.45	78	1.33	72	−8
FEF 75% L/sec	0.40	0.37	92	0.30	75	−18
PEF L/sec	6.05	3.55	59	3.81	63	7
FIVC Liters	3.00	1.40	47	1.32	44	−6
FIF50% L/sec		2.60		0.95		−64
PIF L/sec		2.68		2.02		−24
FEF/FIF50		0.56		1.41		153
MVV L/min	71	41	58			
F BPM		50				
LUNG VOLUMES						
TLC Liters	6.29	5.36	85			
VC Liters	3.00	1.69	56			
IC Liters	2.35	1.11	47			
FRC N2 Liters	3.94	4.25	108			
ERV Liters	1.18	0.43	37			
RV Liters	2.74	3.67	134			
RV/TLC %	45	69				
DIFFUSING CAPACITY						
DLCO mL/mmHg/min	18.4	11.1	61			
DL Adj mL/mmHg/min	18.4	11.1	61			
DLCO/VA mL/mHg/min/L	3.25	3.97	122			
VA Liters	6.35	2.81	44			
IVC Liters	1.69	1.34	80			

PFT Result: Forced vital capacity is mildly reduced to 56% of predicted. FEV1 is mildly reduced to 1.24 liters, which is 68% of predicted. FEV1:FVC ratio is normal at 0.73. Postbronchodilator there is a paradoxical 4% decrement in FEV1. Total lung capacity is normal at 85% of predicted. Diffusion capacity is preserved at 122% of predicted when corrected for alveolar volume of measurement.

Impression: No obstruction, mild restriction with paradoxical response to bronchodilator and preserved diffusion capacity. Clinical correlation suggested.

Case Study 8.3

Patient: **Patient SS**

Patient documentation: **Read Medical Report 8.3**

1. What is the diagnosis (description) that supports the medical necessity of this procedure?

   _____

2. Are there any secondary diagnoses present that required additional procedures?

   _____

3. What was the principal or main procedure, and were other secondary procedures performed on this patient?

   _____

4. Do you believe you need additional documentation to correctly assign the Medicine codes to this record? If so, what is the additional documentation that you need?

   _____

5. Do you have any additional questions for the physician or other health-care provider?

   _____

6. What is(are) the procedure code(s) you would assign to this case study?

   _____

   _____

GENERAL HOSPITAL
DEPARTMENT OF RADIOLOGY

PATIENT'S NAME:	Patient SS	DATE OF BIRTH:	7/20
DATE EXAM PERFORMED:	10/1/20XX	HOSPITAL ROOM NO.:	OP
RADIOLOGY FILE NO.:	257833	REFERRING PHYSICIAN:	Dr. 051

Ultrasound Carotids, Complete, Bilateral

INDICATION: Dizziness, floaters in vision

FINDINGS: Gray-scale, color, and spectral Doppler imaging was used to examine the bilateral carotid and vertebrobasilar arterial systems. There is no evidence of significant plaquing. Incidental note is made of a tortuous left ICA with a high bifurcation. However, there is no evidence for a hemodynamically significant stenosis. The spectral Doppler values are as follows:

	Right	Left
CCA (PSV)	72	67
ICA (PSV)	94	98
ICA (EDV)	44	46
ICA/CCA ratio	1.3	1.5

The vertebral artery flow was shown to be antegrade bilaterally.

IMPRESSION: No ultrasound evidence for a hemodynamically significant carotid artery stenosis by NASCET criteria.

Electronically Signed and Dated

Case Study 8.4

Patient: **Patient TT**

Patient documentation: **Read Medical Report 8.4**

1. What is the diagnosis (description) that supports the medical necessity of this procedure?

   _____

2. Are there any secondary diagnoses present that required additional procedures?

   _____

3. What was the principal or main procedure, and were other secondary procedures performed on this patient?

   _____

4. Do you believe you need additional documentation to correctly assign the Medicine codes to this record? If so, what is the additional documentation that you need?

   _____

5. Do you have any additional questions for the physician or other health-care provider?

   _____

6. What is(are) the procedure code(s) you would assign to this case study?

   _____

   _____

GENERAL HOSPITAL
DEPARTMENT OF CARDIOLOGY

PATIENT'S NAME:	Patient TT	DATE OF BIRTH:	6/1
DATE EXAM PERFORMED:	10/1/20XX	HOSPITAL ROOM NO.:	OP
MEDICAL RECORD NO.:	157833	REFERRING PHYSICIAN:	Dr. 052

Cardiac stress test

INDICATION: Syncopal episode, dizziness

The patient was stressed today using the modified Bruce protocol. The patient was able to exercise for a total of 7 minutes and 59 seconds. Maximum heart rate was 153 bpm, which is 89% of the maximum predicted heart rate. Maximum blood pressure was 130/78. The patient was asymptomatic through the whole test. She had no chest pain, no shortness of breath, and no dizziness. There were no arrhythmias and no ischemic changes.

IMPRESSION: Negative treadmill exercise test.

Electronically Signed and Dated

Case Study 8.5

Patient: **Patient UU**

Patient documentation: **Read Medical Report 8.5**

1. What is the diagnosis (description) that supports the medical necessity of this procedure?

   _____

2. Are there any secondary diagnoses present that required additional procedures?

   _____

3. What was the principal or main procedure, and were other secondary procedures performed on this patient?

   _____

4. Do you believe you need additional documentation to correctly assign the Medicine codes to this record? If so, what is the additional documentation that you need?

   _____

5. Do you have any additional questions for the physician or other health-care provider?

   _____

6. What is(are) the procedure code(s) you would assign to this case study?

   _____

   _____

MEDICAL REPORT 8.5

GENERAL HOSPITAL
DEPARTMENT OF CARDIOLOGY

PATIENT'S NAME:	Patient UU	**DATE OF BIRTH:**	7/31
DATE EXAM PERFORMED:	1/19/20XX	**HOSPITAL ROOM NO.:**	OP
FILE NO.:	257833	**REFERRING PHYSICIAN:**	Dr. 053

Tilt table test

INDICATION: Syncope

HISTORY OF THE PRESENT ILLNESS

The patient is a 48-year-old woman with long history of fainting spells in young adulthood and then no fainting spells for about 20 years until her late 40s. She then began to have slight episodes of lightheadedness after working out at the gym. These occurred during the cool-down period. She did not actually faint but was able to abort the episode by going and lying down in the changing room. She then was at a dinner party at her friend's house and had a syncopal event preceded by lightheadedness and flushing. She lost consciousness for about 5 seconds. Subsequent echocardiogram and stress test were totally normal.

DESCRIPTION OF PROCEDURE

The patient was brought to the electrophysiology laboratory in a stable fasting condition. IV access was obtained. Blood pressure was intermittently monitored using a standard cuff. ECG was continuously monitored. The patient was watched in the supine position for a 10-minute equilibration phase and then was tilted to a 70-degree head up tilt position. About 3 minutes into the tilt, she began to complain of lightheadedness, became pale and diaphoretic, and then lost consciousness. The tilt table was rapidly removed back to the supine position, and the patient was re-equilibrated for about 10 minutes. When she was back to baseline, the electrodes and IV were removed. She was observed until fully alert and comfortable and then left the laboratory in good condition.

RESULTS

Baseline blood pressure in the lying position was 108/70 with a heart rate of 52 beats per minute. The standing blood pressure before getting on the tilt table was 120/70 with a heart rate in the 50s. Upon tilting, the blood pressure was stable initially at 116/80 with a pulse rate of 62 beats per minute. After she began to complain of lightheadedness, the blood pressure was palpated to a systolic of 70 and the pulse rate was 69 beats per minute. After the tilt table was lowered back to the supine position, the systolic blood pressure persisted in the 80s for 1 or 2 minutes and then slowly rose back to her baseline level of 115/64. The heart rate gradually declined down to the mid 40s after the supine position was reestablished and then gradually climbed again into the 50s, which had been her baseline heart rate.

The baseline ECG showed sinus bradycardia at a rate of 56 beats per minute, and it was basically totally within normal limits. During her syncopal event, the ECG showed sinus bradycardia at a rate of 46 beats per minute and was otherwise unchanged.

CONCLUSION

Positive tilt table test for neurocardiogenic syncope with a predominantly vasoactive component and a delayed bradycardic component. The onset of the symptoms was very rapid with a very quick prodrome of lightheadedness lasting only a few seconds.

Case Study 8.6

Patient: **Patient VV**

Patient documentation: **Read Medical Report 8.6**

1. What is the diagnosis (description) that supports the medical necessity of this procedure?

   _____

2. Are there any secondary diagnoses present that required additional procedures?

   _____

3. What was the principal or main procedure, and were other secondary procedures performed on this patient?

   _____

4. Do you believe you need additional documentation to correctly assign the Medicine codes to this record? If so, what is the additional documentation that you need?

   _____

5. Do you have any additional questions for the physician or other health-care provider?

   _____

6. What is(are) the procedure code(s) you would assign to this case study?

   _____

   _____

MEDICAL REPORT 8.6

GENERAL HOSPITAL
SLEEP LAB

PATIENT'S NAME:	Patient V V	**DATE OF BIRTH:**	4/14
DATE EXAM PERFORMED:	3/18/20XX	**HOSPITAL ROOM NO.:**	SL2
MEDICAL RECORD NO.:	157621	**REFERRING PHYSICIAN:**	Dr. 054

Polysomnogram sleep study

HISTORY: The patient is being placed in the sleep study for an evaluation to rule out obstructive sleep apnea or other sleep-related problems because she was noted on a 24-hour Holter monitor to have significant bradycardia and sinus pauses during sleep. She did describe some symptoms of EDS, insomnia, and some restlessness. Her Epworth sleepiness scale was 7 consistent with moderate sleepiness.

AGE: 48 **HEIGHT:** 5'5" **WEIGHT:** 145 lb

ALCOHOL: She drinks about one alcoholic drink per week.

CAFFEINE: She drinks about three cups of coffee per day.

MEDICATIONS: Synthroid and fludrocortisone.

SLEEP TIME STATISTICS: Time in bed, 411 minutes. Total sleep time, 256 minutes. Total nonREM sleep, 20 minutes. Total REM sleep, 46 minutes. Sleep onset, 10 minutes. Sleep efficiency, 62%.

SLEEP DISRUPTION EVENTS: She had 20 arousals, 19 awakenings, for a total of 39.

SLEEP STAGE STATISTICS: The patient was awake for 27.2% of the study. Stage I, 0.4%. Stage II, 42.8%. Stage III, 11.9%. Stage IV, 4.6%. REM sleep, 13.1%.

She had a total of two apneas, both central in origin for an apnea-hypopnea index of 0.5%.

OXYGEN SATURATION: Mean, 98% awake. Her minimum saturation during sleep was 91%. Her range was 91% to 98%. Oxygen saturations were greater than 89%, 100% of the time.

CARDIAC EVALUATION: ECG statistics showed her wakefulness heart rate average 53. Her sleep average was 48. She did not have any significant cardiac dysrhythmias noted.

As stated previously, there were a total of two apneas throughout the entire night, both central in origin, the longest lasting 16 seconds. They both occurred when the patient was in a nonsupine position.

FINDINGS

1. As stated above, the two central apneas throughout the entire night.
2. ECG was notably bradycardic but no other sinus pauses were noted.
3. There were no periodic leg movements or myoclonus.
4. Snoring was light.
5. The lowest oxygen saturation was 91%.

SUMMARY

1. This is an essentially normal sleep study record. It was an adequate study. The sleep efficiency was 62%, which is an adequate study, and the patient did reach REM sleep 13.1%, which is adequate.
2. While there was bradycardia, there were no significant dysrhythmias or pauses noted.
3. Clinical correlation suggested, but there appears to be no sleep-related disorders accounting for her bradycardia during sleep.

Case Study 8.7

Patient: **Patient WW**

Patient documentation: **Read Medical Report 8.7**

1. What is the diagnosis (description) that supports the medical necessity of this procedure?

    _____

2. Are there any secondary diagnoses present that required additional procedures?

    _____

3. What was the principal or main procedure, and were other secondary procedures performed on this patient?

    _____

4. Do you believe you need additional documentation to correctly assign the Medicine codes to this record? If so, what is the additional documentation that you need?

    _____

5. Do you have any additional questions for the physician or other health-care provider?

    _____

6. What is(are) the procedure code(s) you would assign to this case study?

    _____

    _____

GENERAL HOSPITAL
PHYSICAL THERAPY DEPARTMENT

PATIENT'S NAME:	Patient WW	**DATE OF BIRTH:**	5/14
DATE EXAM PERFORMED:	2/16/20XX	**HOSPITAL ROOM NO.:**	OP
MEDICAL RECORD NO.:	142980	**REFERRING PHYSICIAN:**	Dr. 055

PROGRESS NOTE

S: "My back has been bothering me a lot."

O: Rode bicycle 15 minutes in exercise room to warm up. Back massage 12 minutes.

Cervical traction 20 minutes 8# to 30#, with moist heat to low back 20 minutes.
Diagonal/lateral chest passive stretches. Lateral trunk stretches. Core stability exercises. Active stretch knee to chest unilateral and bilateral. 17 minutes.

A: Tolerated well.

P: Continue three times a week.

Electronically Signed and Dated

Case Study 8.8

Patient: **Patient XX**

Patient documentation: **Read Medical Report 8.8**

1. What is the diagnosis (description) that supports the medical necessity of this procedure?

   _____

2. Are there any secondary diagnoses present that required additional procedures?

   _____

3. What was the principal or main procedure, and were other secondary procedures performed on this patient?

   _____

4. Do you believe you need additional documentation to correctly assign the Medicine codes to this record? If so, what is the additional documentation that you need?

   _____

5. Do you have any additional questions for the physician or other health-care provider?

   _____

6. What is(are) the procedure code(s) you would assign to this case study?

   _____

   _____

FOLLOWUP OFFICE VISIT

PATIENT'S NAME:	Patient XX	**DATE OF BIRTH:**	3/31
DATE EXAM PERFORMED:	6/6/20XX	**MEDICAL RECORD NO.:**	1101

CHART NOTE

SUBJECTIVE: This 77-year-old female comes in today for an eye check. She has newly diagnosed diabetes mellitus and complaints of impaired vision.

OBJECTIVE: BP 220/114, checked twice. Pulse rate 72 beats per minute. Snellen test without glasses showed visual acuity 20/40 left and right. Pupils were equal, round, reactive to light and accommodation. Cranial nerves intact. Mature cataracts noted bilaterally. Evaluation of the disks of her eyes was hampered by constriction of the pupils; however, some mild arteriolar narrowing could be detected. Funduscopy was inadequate because of the brisk papillary constriction.

ASSESSMENT

1. Impaired visual acuity secondary to cataracts and possibly effects from diabetes mellitus.
2. Markedly elevated hypertension.

PLAN: She was advised to seek medical attention for the hypertension. Following a medical workup, we will evaluate the cataracts further and possibly consider surgery.

_____

Electronically Signed and Dated

CHAPTER 9

HCPCS Level II and Advanced Coding Concepts

Chapter Outline

HCPCS Level II Codes and Modifiers

Using CPT and HCPCS Level II Codes to Report Advanced Cardiovascular Services and Procedures

Using CPT and HCPCS Level II Codes to Report Advanced Oncology Services and Procedures

CPT Category II Codes

CPT Category III Codes

Testing Your Comprehension

Coding Practice I: Chapter Review Exercises

Coding Practice II: Medical Record Case Studies

Chapter Objectives

▶ Describe the purpose and format of HCPCS Level II codes.

▶ Recognize terminology used in medical records for complex cardiovascular and oncology procedures.

▶ Differentiate between HCPCS Level II codes and modifiers for reporting physician services versus hospital services.

▶ Assign appropriate HCPCS and CPT codes and modifiers to report complex cardiovascular services and procedures.

▶ Assign appropriate HCPCS and CPT codes and modifiers to report complex oncology services and procedures.

▶ Describe the purpose and format of CPT Category II tracking codes.

▶ Describe the purpose and format of CPT Category III temporary codes.

In 1966, the American Medical Association (AMA) published the Current Procedural Terminology (CPT) coding system to reflect services and procedures provided by physicians. In 1986, the Health Care Financing Administration (now known as the Centers for Medicare and Medicaid Services or CMS) determined that CPT codes were not adequate to reflect the level of detail needed to describe certain services and supplies payable under Medicare. To meet this need, the federal government created the **Healthcare Common Procedure Coding System** (abbreviated as HCPCS and pronounced hick-picks). This coding system is also referred to as National Level II. CMS considers CPT as HCPCS Level I; therefore, the HCPCS is a combination of CPT and National Level II codes.

Word Parts and Meanings of Medical Terms Related to Equipment, Supplies, and Cardiovascular and Oncology Services

Word Part	Meaning	Example	Definition
ather/o	fatty, yellowish plaque	atherectomy	Removing fatty tissue from an artery either surgically or by use of heat (cauterization)
-ectomy	cut out; remove	endarterectomy	Removing the inner lining of an artery by incision to eliminate blockage
fulgur/o	lightening	fulguration	Tissue destruction by use of an electrical current
-opsy	visualization	biopsy	Visual examination of tissue
ortho-	straight or correct	orthosis	Orthopedic device used to correct or improve function of a movable body part
prosthe-	an addition; to place	prosthesis	Artificial replacement of a part of the body
-plasty	surgical repair	angioplasty	Surgical repair of a vessel
-tomy	surgical incision	angiotomy	Incision into a blood vessel
-rrhaphy	to suture	cardiorrhaphy	Suturing the heart muscle
thromb/o	clot	thrombectomy	Removal of a blood clot

HCPCS comprises two levels of coding.

▶ Level I—Consists of the CPT codes, maintained by the AMA.
▶ Level II—Consists of the National Level II HCPCS codes, which are alphanumeric codes containing one alphabetic character (A through V) and four numbers.

HCPCS Level II codes identify equipment, products, supplies, and services not included in CPT. Medicare, Medicaid, and many private insurers cover items not detailed in CPT so the Level II alphanumeric codes were created to enable submission of claims for reimbursement of these medical services and supplies. In 2003, CMS was authorized under earlier HIPAA legislation to officially maintain and distribute HCPCS Level II codes as part of the requirement for standardized coding systems. HCPCS Level II codes are maintained and published by a CMS HCPCS Workgroup that includes representatives from CMS, private insurers, state Medicaid agencies, and Medicare contractors.

In addition to explaining how to use HCPCS Level II codes and modifiers, this chapter provides instructions and practice in coding advanced surgical procedures that require coding from multiple sections of CPT/HCPCS. The differences between codes and modifiers used by the hospital under the outpatient prospective payment system (OPPS) for complex situations versus the codes and modifiers used to report the roles of various professional providers are discussed. Because comprehensive cardiovascular procedures and complex oncology procedures commonly require advanced coding across CPT/HCPCS sections, these specialties are the focus of this chapter. Finally, the format and purpose of CPT Category II tracking codes and CPT Category III temporary codes are covered.

HCPCS Level II Codes and Modifiers

The HCPCS Level II code manual consists of 22 sections. Codes in these sections range from A0000 to V5999. There is an alphabetic index at the back of the book that first lists the main term of the item that requires a code, and subterms (indented under the main term) show a code or range of codes that may be appropriate. The coder should next review each choice in the alphanumeric-ordered listing (i.e., from the tabular section of the manual) to make the final code selection. HCPCS Level II also contains Guidelines at the beginning of each section that define the items needed to report the supplies, services, or procedures listed in the section.

HCPCS Level II codes also have modifiers. Each Guideline contains modifiers that are common to that section. A complete list of all modifiers is located in Appendix B of the Medicare Part B Reference Manual and may also be found in the HCPCS code manual appendix that includes the complete listing of HCPCS codes and modifiers.

TIP Some HCPCS Level II modifiers may be appended to CPT codes, but CPT numeric modifiers are NOT appended to Level II alphanumeric codes.

Durable Medical Equipment

Another feature of HCPCS Level II is a description of **Durable Medical Equipment Medicare Administrative Contractors** (DME MACs), formerly known as Durable Medical Equipment Regional Carriers (DMERCs). These contractors process all Medicare claims for **durable medical equipment** (DME) used outside the physician's office, such as a wheelchairs, hospital beds, walkers, and portable oxygen equipment. DME MACs are also responsible for processing claims for **prostheses** (such as an artificial hip joint, Fig. 9.1), **orthoses**, and supplies. There are four DME MACs in the United States. Each is responsible for processing claims submitted from a particular region. Providers must obtain a supplier number to submit claims to the appropriate DME MAC. The CMS website describes the DME MAC contracts in detail: http://www.cms.hhs.gov/MedicareContractingReform/Downloads/DME_MAC_Awards_General_Fact_Sheet.pdf.

The manufacturers of durable medical equipment and other materials and supplies generally provide wholesale and resale medical equipment and supply companies with the appropriate HCPCS code for each product. Obtaining the appropriate code from CMS is part of the application process for getting a product approved for Medicare reimbursement. Standardized software for retail stores also expedites the correct billing process using HCPCS Level II codes.

Coverage Restrictions and Code Ranges

Within HCPCS Level II, there are various coverage restrictions:

- ▶ Not valid for Medicare use (example: A0225 Ambulance service; neonatal transport, base rate, emergency transport, one-way)
- ▶ Non-covered by Medicare (example: J7304 Contraceptive supply, hormone-containing patch, each)
- ▶ Special coverage instructions (example: L8600 Implantable breast prosthesis, silicone or equal)
- ▶ Carrier discretion (example: K0001 Standard wheelchair)

HCPCS Level II contains several types of codes. Some of these types are payer- or provider-specific, whereas others are used by many types of

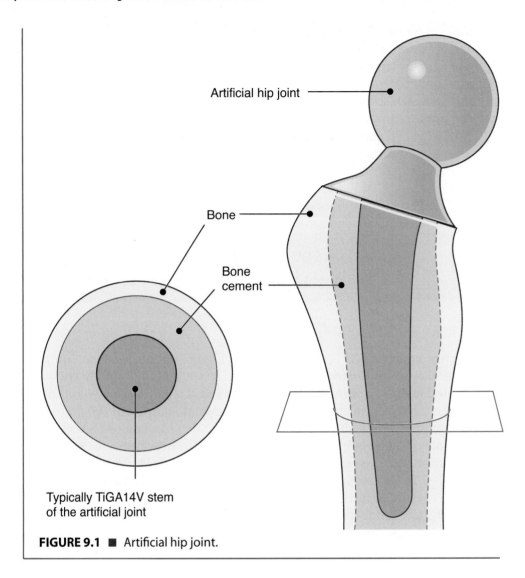

Artificial hip joint

Bone

Bone cement

Typically TiGA14V stem of the artificial joint

FIGURE 9.1 ■ Artificial hip joint.

providers and insurers. Table 9.1 represents codes classified as Permanent National Codes and the code ranges for each section.

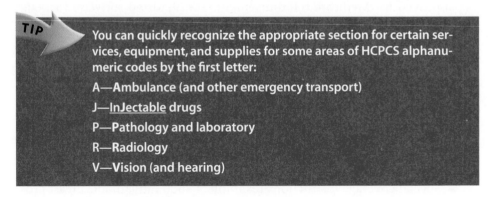

TIP

You can quickly recognize the appropriate section for certain services, equipment, and supplies for some areas of HCPCS alphanumeric codes by the first letter:

A—Ambulance (and other emergency transport)

J—<u>InJectable</u> drugs

P—Pathology and laboratory

R—Radiology

V—Vision (and hearing)

Dental Codes (D0000–D9999)

Dental codes (beginning with a "D") represent another section of HCPCS Level II codes. Dental codes are published by the American Dental Association

TABLE 9.1   HCPCS Level II Permanent National Code Ranges

HCPCS Level II Section Name	Code Range	Example
Transportation services	A0000–A0999	A0429—Ambulance service, basic life support, emergency transport
Medical and surgical supplies	A4000–A7509	A4357—Bedside urinary drainage bag, day or night, with or without anti-reflux device, with or without tube, each
Enteral and parenteral therapy	B0000–B9999	B4164—Parenteral nutrition solution; carbohydrates (dextrose), 50% or less (500 mL = 1 unit)—home mix
Durable medical equipment	E0000–E9999	E0250—Hospital bed, fixed height, with any type side rails; with mattress
Drugs administered other than oral method	J0000–J8999	J1460—Injection, gamma globulin; intramuscular 1 mL
Chemotherapy drugs	J9000–J9999	J9055—Injection cetuximab, 10 mg
Orthotic procedures	L0000–L4999	L1800—Knee orthosis; elastic with stays, prefabricated, includes fitting and adjustment
Prosthetic procedures	L5000–L9999	L5702—Replacement, socket, hip disarticulation, includes hip joint
Medical services	M0000–M9999	M0064—Brief office visit for the sole purpose of monitoring or changing drug prescriptions used in the treatment of mental psychoneurotic and personality disorders
Pathology and laboratory	P0000–P9999	P9010—Blood (whole) for transfusion per unit
Diagnostic radiology services	R0000–R9999	R0076—Transportation of portable ECG to facility or location; per patient
Vision services	V0000–V29999	V2020—Frames, purchases
Hearing services	V5000–V5999	V5170—Hearing aid, in the ear

(ADA) and include **Current Dental Terminology** (CDT) codes to report dental procedures and supplies. CMS has a contract with the American Medical Association to use CPT codes as HCPCS Level I and has a similar agreement with the ADA to use CDT codes as part of HCPCS Level II dental codes.

Crown-indirect resin-based composite: D6710.   **EXAMPLE**

Miscellaneous and Experimental Codes (A9000–A9999)

Miscellaneous and experimental codes allow suppliers and providers to begin submitting claims for reimbursement as soon as the U.S. Food and Drug

Administration (FDA) approves a new service or supply not described by any other code. Data are collected and analyzed by the CMS HCPCS Workgroup during the period in which a request has been submitted to CMS for consideration of a new permanent code. Codes in this range are comparable to CPT Category III codes for emerging technology.

Temporary Codes

There are sections of temporary codes used to represent procedures, services, technology, supplies, and equipment (such as the Sager splint, Fig. 9.2) that have not yet become part of the permanent HCPCS Level II codes. Table 9.2 outlines the sections and code ranges of temporary codes.

Note that Type B hospital-based emergency departments are those meeting one of the following requirements:

▶ Licensed by the state in which it is located as an emergency room or department open less than 24 hours a day, 7 days a week

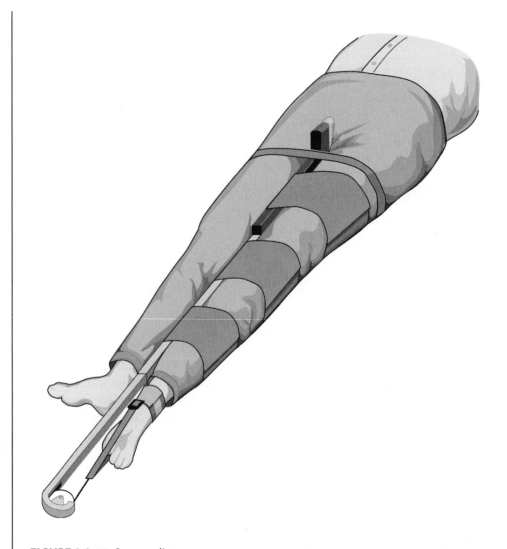

FIGURE 9.2 ■ Sager splint.

TABLE 9.2 HCPCS Level II Temporary Code Ranges			
HCPCS Level II Temporary Code Section Name	**Code Range**	**Purpose**	**Example**
Temporary hospital outpatient PPS	C0000–C9999	Used to report drugs, biologic substances, and devices eligible for transitional pass-through payments and items classified as "new technology" under the OPPS.	**Catheter, suprapubic/cystoscopic** C2627 (in 2008)
Temporary procedures and professional services	G0000–G9999	Used to report professional services or procedures that would normally be reported using CPT codes but for which a detailed CPT code does not exist.	Five temporary G codes were implemented in 2007. G0380 through G0384 describe the level of hospital emergency visits provided in a type B department.
Temporary codes DMERCS	K0000–K99899	Used for durable medical equipment.	**Standard hemi (low seat) wheelchair** K0002 (in 2008)
Temporary codes (other)	Q0000–Q9999	Used for drugs, medical equipment, and services that are not yet described in HCPCS Level II.	Cast supplies, long leg splint, adult, fiberglass Q4042 (in 2008)

▶ Held out to the public as a place that provides care for emergency medical conditions on an urgent basis without requiring a previously scheduled appointment, and it is open less than 24 hours a day, 7 days a week

▶ During the calendar year immediately preceding the calendar year in which a determination under this section is being made, it provides at least one-third of all of its outpatient visits for the treatment of emergency medical conditions on an urgent basis without requiring a previously scheduled appointment, regardless of its hours of operation

Special Payer/Service Codes

Table 9.3 shows three code ranges designed to be used in billing certain payers in specific situations.

Most alphanumeric codes for services, procedures, drugs, and supplies administered during an outpatient hospital stay are processed through the Charge Description Master, but in some cases a facility coder must use HCPCS Level II codes for Medicare patients.

Pure screening colonoscopy in the outpatient department of a hospital or an outpatient physician-owned surgery center for a Medicare patient at high risk: G0105.
For a Medicare patient not at high risk: G0121.

EXAMPLES

In the physician's office or clinic setting, the coder routinely reports alphanumeric codes for many drugs and services, such as immunizations, injections, and supplies sent home with the patient (e.g., crutches). It is

TABLE 9.3 HCPCS Level II Special Payer/Service Code Ranges			
HCPCS Level II Code Category	Code Range	Purpose	Example
Select rehabilitative services	H0000–H9999	Used by Medicaid in states that mandate separate codes for identifying mental health services such as alcohol and drug rehabilitative services.	Rehabilitation program, per 1/2 day H2001 (in 2008)
Private payer codes	S0000–S9999	Used by private payers and some Medicaid agencies but NOT used by Medicare.	Spirometer S8190 (in 2008)
State Medicaid agency codes	T0000–T9999	Used by state Medicaid and some private payers to report items for which there are not permanent codes but which are required to meet reporting mandates.	Adult-sized disposable incontinence product, protective underwear, pull-on T4528 (in 2008)

important for all coders to know how and when to report HCPCS Level II codes based on the payer.

Using CPT and HCPCS Level II Codes to Report Advanced Cardiovascular Services and Procedures

As discussed in the Radiology and Medicine chapters, there are many types of diagnostic and treatment procedures for common cardiovascular diseases. Some of these are **noninvasive procedures**, meaning they do not require the insertion of an instrument or device into the patient's body. Noninvasive procedures are diagnostic in nature. There are also certain minimally invasive procedures described in the Medicine section that can be diagnostic or therapeutic.

EXAMPLES

1—*Noninvasive diagnostic procedure: ECG with at least 12 leads; with interpretation and report: 93000.*
2—*Minimally invasive diagnostic procedure: Bundle of His recording: 93600.*
3—*Minimally invasive therapeutic procedure: Intracardiac catheter ablation of arrhythmogenic focus; for treatment of supraventricular tachycardia by ablation of fast or slow atrioventricular pathways, accessory atrioventricular (svt) connections, or other atrial foci, singly or in combination: 93650.*

In many cases, definitive treatment of heart or vascular disease requires surgical intervention. Complicated inpatient cardiovascular surgeries (e.g., see Figs. 9.3 and 9.4) frequently rely on adjuvant procedures during the operative session. To report these advanced surgeries, CPT codes and modifiers may be required from the Surgery, Radiology, and Medicine sections for the professional component of care (physician). Outpatient operative sessions may also require HCPCS Level II codes and modifiers to report the technical component of cardiovascular surgery. Additionally, certain outpatient

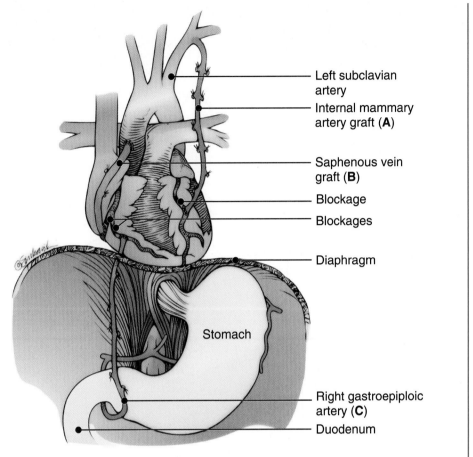

Left subclavian artery

Internal mammary artery graft (**A**)

Saphenous vein graft (**B**)

Blockage

Blockages

Diaphragm

Stomach

Right gastroepiploic artery (**C**)

Duodenum

FIGURE 9.3 ■ Three coronary artery bypass grafts (A, B, and C).

cardiovascular surgeries, such as pacemaker insertion (Fig. 9.6) require HCPCS codes and modifiers to report the technical component.

Coders for hospitals only report CPT codes for surgeries performed in the outpatient department of the facility. Coders for surgeons and other healthcare professionals involved in a surgical episode of care report CPT codes regardless of whether or not the surgery performed was on an inpatient or outpatient basis. The ranges of CPT codes most frequently used to report cardiovascular surgical procedures are:

▶ Surgery: cardiovascular system subsection (33010–37799)
▶ Radiology:
Diagnostic imaging, heart (75552–75556)
Vascular procedures, aorta and arteries (75600–75790)
Radiologic guidance, fluoroscopic guidance (77001–77003)
Computed tomography guidance (77011–77014)
Magnetic resonance guidance (77021–77022)
Nuclear medicine subsection, diagnostic, cardiovascular system (78414–78499). Several diagnostic ultrasound guidance procedures may also be applicable.
▶ Medicine: cardiovascular subsection (92950–93799). Cardiac catheterization codes (93501–93572) include introduction, positioning and repositioning of one or more catheters, recording of intracardiac and

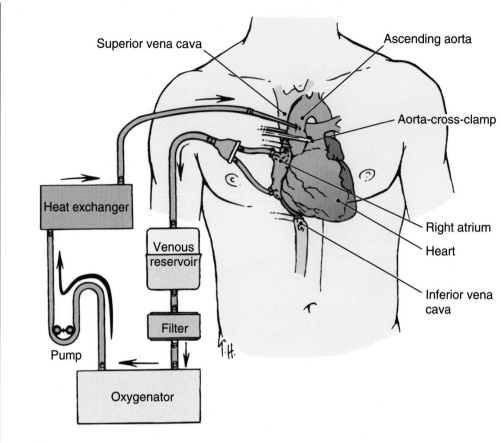

FIGURE 9.4 ■ Cardiopulmonary bypass system.

intravascular pressure, and obtaining blood samples for measurement of blood gases or dilution curves and cardiac output measurements. Most cardiac catheterization procedure codes for the facility are entered into the CDM. The coders have to verify these codes are correct, determine whether modifiers are applicable, and add ICD-9-CM diagnoses codes, but they do not usually have to add a code from the Surgery section of CPT. Coders for the physician must be very careful to ensure that all applicable codes are reported for cardiac catheterization procedures without overcoding.

Cardiovascular procedures require codes from Surgery, Radiology, Medicine, or HCPCS Level II. The following examples demonstrate the need for several codes to correctly report the procedures performed.

EXAMPLES

1—Recall that nonselective catheter placement occurs when the catheter is not advanced beyond the vessel in which it is placed, or the catheter is only advanced to the aorta. Selective placement follows a hierarchy of orders within a vascular family. If a second-order or higher branch is entered within the same vascular family, the nonselective and first-order codes are not used because the second-order code includes the route the catheter had to follow.

A catheter is placed in the right femoral artery and advanced to the abdominal aorta, where contrast material is injected for imaging. The catheter is then advanced into the left common iliac artery for imaging of the left lower extremity. Finally, the catheter is manipulated into the left superficial femoral artery for further imaging and evaluation of the tibial vessels.

Initial third-order or more selective abdominal, pelvic, or lower extremity artery branch: 36247.

Abdominal aorta: 75625.

Extremity: 75710.

Tibial vessels: 75774.

Note that the nonselective (36200) and first-order selective catheter placement code (36245) for the abdominal, pelvic, or lower extremity artery branch are not coded because the code for initial third order or more for that same vascular family include the lesser order and nonselective codes.

2 —*A 64-year-old female patient is brought to the outpatient department of a hospital to have an internal cardioverter-defibrillator inserted to treat sick sinus syndrome (SSS). Using fluoroscopic guidance, a pocket is created. An electrode lead and single-chamber pacing cardioverter-defibrillator with pulse generator are placed. The same surgeon then performs electrophysiologic evaluation with testing of pulse generator.*

71090 and G0300 (hospital) or 33249 (physician) and 93641.

In coding cardiac procedures (such as catheterization of the femoral artery, Fig. 9.5, or placement of a pacemaker, Fig. 9.6), coders must remember to read the Guidelines in each applicable section and the notes and cross-references found throughout subsections, headings, subheadings, code ranges, and individual codes for assistance in selecting all of the appropriate codes.

EXAMPLES

1—*The cardiac catheterization heading contains a description of cardiac catheterization and notes such as "when selective injection procedures are performed without a preceding cardiac catheterization, these services should be reported using codes in the vascular injection procedures section 36011–36015 and 36215–36218."*

2—*The pacemaker or pacing cardioverter-defibrillator subheading notes have cross-references referring coders to the range of codes in the Medicine section for electronic analysis of internal pacemaker system. The next note refers the coder to a specific code, 71090, for reporting radiologic supervision and interpretation with insertion of pacemaker.*

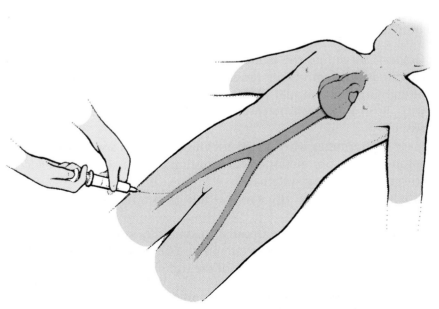

FIGURE 9.5 ■ Catheterization of the right femoral artery for coronary angiography.

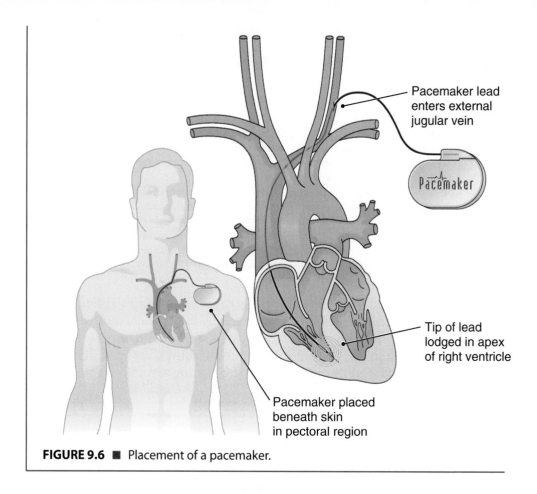

FIGURE 9.6 ■ Placement of a pacemaker.

Using CPT and HCPCS Level II Codes to Report Advanced Oncology Services and Procedures

Cancerous lesions can form in any body system, and at least 200 different types of cancer have been identified. To understand cancer coding, coders should be aware of four factors:

1. Grade—Determines the maturation of the tumor. Under microscopic examination, tumor cells range from well-differentiated, with cells resembling their normal tissue source, to very poorly differentiated, with disorganized cells having little or no resemblance to their source tissue.
2. Stage—Determines whether or not the cancer has spread to adjacent organ structures or metastasized to distant organic sites via the bloodstream or lymphatic system.
3. Prognosis—Estimates the survival rate as determined by grade and stage of the cancer.
4. Protocol—Determines the optimal treatment or combination of treatments (adjuvant therapies) available to obtain the best possible outcome, given the grade and stage of the tumor.

A **malignant** lesion (solid tumor) can be primary or metastatic. For example, a **biopsy** of a lesion excised from the liver can identify whether the diseased cells are liver cells or cells from another organ such as the pancreas. If

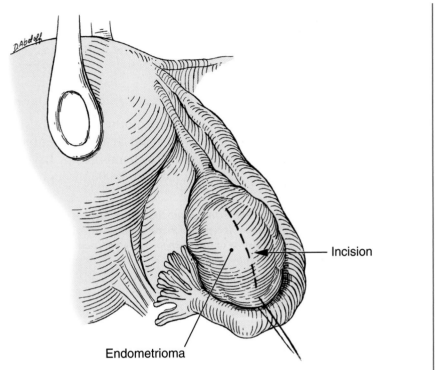

FIGURE 9.7 ■ Excision of ovarian endometrioma through the abdomen. The ovarian cortex is incised longitudinally.

the cells are pancreatic, the primary lesion is in the pancreas, but the cancer has spread from the pancreas to the liver.

All these factors have significant bearing on the treatment. Coding for complex cancer surgery, such as excision of ovarian endometrioma (Fig. 9.7), often includes reporting from the Surgery, Radiology, and Medicine sections of CPT plus HCPCS Level II codes.

1—A mastectomy for breast cancer is reported using codes from the Surgery section, integumentary subsection, breast, excision.

2—An excision for a malignant ovarian lesion is reported using codes from Surgery, female genital system, oviduct/ovary.

EXAMPLES

Other common procedures and services reported in conjunction with any type of cancer surgery are located in both the Radiology and Medicine sections of CPT.

Radiation Oncology

Radiation oncology is a subsection of Radiology (77261–77799). The procedures in this range include services independent of surgery and procedures that may be performed concurrently with or immediately after surgery. (Note that other Radiology procedures frequently performed in conjunction with cancer surgery are not listed in the radiology oncology subsection because the procedures also reflect biopsies of lesions that are not necessarily malignant.)

The code 77032 is listed under the Radiology section, radiologic guidance subsection, but it is used to report the radiologic supervision and interpretation of mammographic guidance for needle placement for biopsy or preparation for excision of a lesion.

Chemotherapy

The Medicine section of CPT contains a chemotherapy administration subsection. Chemotherapy may be administered at the time of surgery and requires an additional code. Drugs specific to chemotherapy have a dedicated section of HCPCS Level II codes that range from J9000 through J9999.

Code 96450, chemotherapy administration into the central nervous system (CNS), requiring and including spinal puncture, is reported in conjunction with a code from the Surgery section such as 61215, insertion of subcutaneous reservoir, pump or continuous infusion system for connection to ventricular catheter.

CPT Category II Codes

Category II codes supplement Category I codes and are used as a performance measurement tracking system designed to collect information on the quality of care. These codes are alphanumeric, consisting of four numbers followed by the letter "F." The Category II codes section immediately follows the Medicine section. CMS publishes the codes twice each year, on January 1 and July 1. Ideally, these codes make the chart abstracting and review process more efficient by allowing the tracking of a quality measure through a practice management system instead of through a full chart review. Category II codes are used by professional providers only and not by hospitals submitting claims under the OPPS.

Chest x-ray results documented and reviewed: 3006F.

In 2006, the Tax Relief and Health Care Act (TRHCA) was enacted, authorizing CMS to establish the **Physician Quality Reporting Initiative** (PQRI). PQRI included a financial incentive program to encourage certain professionals to report, on a voluntary basis, quality measures using Category II codes. CMS collects these data as part of a plan to implement a "pay-for-performance" strategy that will encourage the provision of high-quality, cost-effective care to patients.

In 2007, PQRI listed 74 unique reporting measures. Each measure represents diagnosis and HCPCS codes for services or procedures that are commonly submitted to CMS under a fee-for-service reimbursement program. Examples of the reporting measures include, but are not limited to:

▶ Preventive care
▶ Efficient managing of chronic conditions
▶ Management of acute conditions
▶ Utilization of various resources

Use of Category II codes with specific modifiers, as appropriate, indicates that a requirement was or was not met. If not met, the reason is noted. The modifiers are unique to Category II codes and indicate when a performance measure was taken into consideration but is excluded because of medical, patient, or system reasons.

> *The code 1000F-2P indicates that the quality measure "tobacco use assessed" was considered but was excluded because the patient refused to participate.*

EXAMPLE

CPT Category III Codes

Category III codes are temporary and are updated annually. They consist of four numbers followed by the letter "T." These codes are designed for reporting emerging technology services and procedures. Category III codes allow data capture and analysis of new procedures until a decision is made to delete the temporary code and add a permanent Category I code, change the description of the code, or delete the code without a new Category I code to replace it. The CPT alphabetic index includes these codes under appropriate main terms.

TIP Coders should always choose a Category III code if one is appropriate before reporting an unlisted Category I CPT code. If a Category III code description matches a HCPCS Level II code description, Medicare always requires the use of the HCPCS Level II code instead of the Category III temporary code.

A temporary code is always deleted if it has not been assigned a Category I code within 5 years. Category III codes are released by AMA each year on January 1 and July 1.

> *As of 2008, the code 0090T was used to represent total disc arthroplasty (artificial disc), anterior approach, including discectomy to prepare interspace (other than for decompression) cervical; single interspace. (alphabetic index: replacement, intervertebral disc, cervical interspace).*

EXAMPLE

SUMMARY

In addition to the individual sections that comprise the main body of the CPT manual, coders must also learn to use the supplemental sections covering:

▶ CPT Category II codes—to track and measure performance for quality improvement strategies
▶ CPT Category III codes—temporary codes that reflect emerging technologies, services, and procedures

Coders must also learn to use the HCPCS Level II National (alphanumeric) code manual to report certain medical supplies, services, procedures, durable medical equipment, drugs, orthoses, and prostheses not listed in the CPT manual. It is important for students and beginning coders to practice coding from multiple sections of CPT and HCPCS to report all appropriate codes for complex surgical procedures and other advanced services.

TESTING YOUR COMPREHENSION

1. HCPCS Level II codes are also known as _____.

2. HCPCS Level I codes are maintained by _____.

3. HCPCS Regular Level II codes are maintained by _____ based on a workgroup with representatives from other agencies and organizations.

4. HCPCS Level II codes that start with a letter D are maintained by _____.

5. In the Medicare Part B Reference Manual, a complete list of HCPCS Level II modifiers is located in Appendix _____.

6. HCPCS Level II codes in the range L5000–L9999 represent _____.

7. Durable Medical Equipment (DME) codes are in range _____.

8. Codes beginning with a J are used for drugs administered other than _____ method.

9. Codes beginning with a G are used as part of the reimbursement methodology known as Hospital _____.

10. In what subsection of Radiology in CPT would you find the range 75552–75556? _____

11. Grading of cancer refers to the _____ of the lesion.

12. A stage IV malignant lesion has poorly _____ tissue cells.

13. What section of CPT contains codes for a mastectomy? _____

14. Chemotherapy administration codes are found in the _____ section of CPT.

15. CPT Category II codes are used to report quality measures under what CMS initiative? _____

Chapter Review Exercises

CODING PRACTICE I

Directions

Use your CPT manual to code the following excerpts from medical source documents. For those labeled as HCPCS Level II, students who do not have a National Level II manual or access to an encoder can access CMS online HCPCS codes at http://www.cms.hhs.gov/hcpcsreleasecodesets/anhcpcslist.asp

1. Optiray contrast material for coronary angiography 350 mg/mL (HCPCS Level II) _____

2. Injection, 10 mg Imuran for cancer treatment (HCPCS Level II) _____

3. Self-contained monitor with digital check systems for a pacemaker (HCPCS Level II) _____

4. Permanent saline breast implant (Mentor style 2700 contoured profile) (HCPCS Level II) _____

5. Excision of a 3-cm melanoma of the neck. This area requires extensive undermining to close an approximate 5-cm closure. Additionally, an excision of a sentinel node of the neck is performed _____, _____, _____

6. A venous femoral–popliteal bypass using vein _____

7. Repair of malfunctioning two-electrode transvenous dual-chamber pacemaker _____

8. Insertion of an implantable venous-access port (Groshong catheter) _____

9. Removal of a right-sided Port-A-Cath _____

10. Excision of squamous cell carcinoma on left cheek with 5 cm by 6 cm split skin graft reconstruction _____, _____,_____

11. Transperineal placement of catheters into the prostate for four-source radioelement application with cystoscopy _____

12. Partial removal of the large intestine with end-to-end anastomosis of the remaining colon with ileum owing to colon cancer _____

13. A total unilateral thyroid lobectomy with contralateral subtotal lobectomy including isthmectomy _____

14. Catheter introduced into the right femoral artery and advanced to the ascending aorta. The catheter is advanced into the right common carotid, and contrast material is injected for imaging of the neck _____, _____, _____

15. List the two codes needed to describe both the surgery and the radiographic supervision of a CT-guided aspiration and removal of patient's abdominal wall fluid _____, _____

CODING PRACTICE II   Medical Record Case Studies

Directions

1. For each case study, carefully review the medical reports of complex cardiovascular and oncology surgeries performed in the outpatient department of a hospital.

2. Research any abbreviations and terms that are unfamiliar or unclear.

3. Identify as many diagnoses and procedures as possible.

4. Because only part of the patient's total record is available, think about any additional documentation that you might need.

5. If appropriate, identify any questions you might ask the surgeon or other health-care provider to code this case correctly and completely.

6. Complete the appropriate blanks below for each case study. Explain (in writing) questions 1–5 and assign the code(s) for question 6.

Note: HCPCS Level II codes can be located with either an HCPCS manual or access to an encoder. Also, CMS provides online access to HCPCS Level II codes each year. The link is: http://www.cms.hhs.gov/hcpcsreleasecodesets/anhcpcs/list.asp

Case Study 9.1

Patient: **Patient YY**

Patient documentation: **Read Operative Report 9.1**

1. What are the preoperative and postoperative diagnoses (description) that support the medical necessity of this procedure?

   _____

2. Are there any secondary diagnoses present that required additional procedures?

   _____

3. What was the principal or main procedure, and were other secondary procedures performed on this patient?

   _____

4. Do you believe you need additional documentation to correctly assign the surgery codes to this record? If so, what is the additional documentation that you need?

   _____

5. Do you have any additional questions for the surgeon?

   _____

6. What is(are) the procedure code(s) you would assign to this case study?

   _____

   _____

MEDICAL REPORT 9.1

SUNSHINE MEDICAL CENTER
REPORT OF OPERATION

DATE: 01/12/20XX

PATIENT NAME: Patient YY

PREOPERATIVE DIAGNOSIS: Skin lesion of left lower eyelid

POSTOPERATIVE DIAGNOSIS: Squamous cell carcinoma of left lower eyelid

SURGEON: Dr. 056

OPERATION:

1. Excision of 1.5 × 1.3 cm squamous cell carcinoma of the left lower eyelid.

2. Wound closure with rhomboid skin flap (adjacent tissue transfer).

ANESTHESIA: Monitored anesthesia care.

INDICATIONS AND CONSENT: This is a 34-year-old white male who presents with a large skin lesion over the left lower eyelid. He now presents for excision of this skin lesion with intraoperative frozen sections followed by reconstruction. The benefits and risks have been explained to the patient thoroughly and he wishes to proceed at this time.

PROCEDURE: The patient was prepped and draped in the usual sterile fashion after successful monitored anesthesia care was administered. A #15 blade scalpel was used to excise the large skin lesion over the left lower eyelid after infiltration of the tissues with lidocaine with epinephrine solution. The resection was carried out involving full-thickness skin down to the orbicularis oculi muscle fibers. This was promptly tagged at the 12 o'clock margin and sent for intraoperative frozen sections. The intraoperative frozen sections came back with clear margins; however, very close to the deep margin. Therefore, additional deep tissue was resected and sent for permanent pathology. Hemostasis was achieved with electrocautery.

Our attention was now directed toward reconstruction of the left lower eyelid. A rhomboid skin flap was designed and dissected out using a #15 blade scalpel. The flap was rotated medially and inset into the wound defect. The donor site was approximated primarily. The deep dermal layers were approximated using 5-0 Vicryl sutures in an interrupted fashion. The skin edges were then approximated using 5-0 plain gut sutures in an interrupted fashion. The wound was finally dressed with Neosporin ointment. At the end of the case, the patient did not have any evidence of ectropion of the left lower eyelid.

He tolerated the procedure well without any complications. Estimated blood loss was minimal. Fluids: 500 mL crystalloid. The patient was taken to the PACU in stable condition.

_____
Electronically Signed and Dated

SURGICAL PATHOLOGY: A. Skin, left lower eyelid, excision: invasive squamous cell carcinoma, well differentiated with keratoacanthomatous features extending to 0.1 cm away from the deep inked margin. B. Left lower eyelid, new deep margin, excision, skeletal muscle and benign fibroadipose tissue. No evidence of malignancy.

Case Study 9.2

Please note for this case study that the patient was treated originally by a surgeon for a right modified radical mastectomy and subsequently, Dr. 057 performed a left breast reduction mammoplasty and right breast delayed reconstruction using tissue expander—until wound healed—500 mL. For Medical Report 9.2, it is 6 months later and Dr. 057 is now doing this second-stage procedure. (The tissue expander would have required an HCPCS Level II code at the time it was inserted.)

Patient: **Patient ZZ**

Patient documentation: **Read Operative Report 9.2.**

1. What are the preoperative and postoperative diagnoses (description) that support the medical necessity of this procedure?

   _____

2. Are there any secondary diagnoses present that required additional procedures?

   _____

3. What was the principal or main procedure, and were other secondary procedures performed on this patient?

   _____

4. Do you believe you need additional documentation to correctly assign the surgery codes to this record? If so, what is the additional documentation that you need?

   _____

5. Do you have any additional questions for the surgeon?

   _____

6. What is(are) the procedure code(s) you would assign to this case study?

   _____

   _____

MEDICAL REPORT 9.2

SUNSHINE MEDICAL CENTER
REPORT OF OPERATION

DATE: 07/11/20XX

PATIENT NAME: Patient ZZ

PREOPERATIVE DIAGNOSIS: Right breast cancer, status post first-stage breast reconstruction with tissue expander

POSTOPERATIVE DIAGNOSIS: Right breast cancer, status post first-stage breast reconstruction with tissue expander

SURGEON: Dr. 057

OPERATION: Second-stage right breast reconstruction with removal of tissue expander and replacement with a permanent saline-filled implant.

ANESTHESIA: General

PROCEDURE: The patient was prepped and draped in the usual sterile fashion after successful induction of general anesthesia. The lateral aspect of the transverse scar over the right chest was incised using a #15 blade scalpel. This dissection was carried down through the subcutaneous tissue until the muscle envelope was identified. The muscle envelope was then incised approximately 2 cm inferior to the skin incision to stairstep the entry of the two incisions. The capsule was opened and the tissue expander was removed. It was felt to be intact and free of infection. Preoperatively, the patient was found to have a superior malposition of the tissue expander as compared to her left breast reduction. Therefore, the inferior aspect of the breast capsule was then incised using electrocautery, and this dissection was carried down further approximately 3 cm, separating the subcutaneous tissue from the rectus fascia in order to obtain a more inferior breast mound. After this was accomplished, a 7-mm Jackson-Pratt drain was placed into the pocket after a stab incision was placed in the axilla. The pocket was irrigated with dilute Betadine solution. The permanent saline implant (Mentor style 2700 contoured profile), 500-mL implant, was then placed into the pocket and was filled with 500 mL of normal saline. The skin edges were reapproximated with skin staples and the patient was placed in an upright position to assess symmetry. After this was accomplished, the fill tube was removed and the wound was reapproximated in multiple layers using 3-0 PDS sutures in interrupted fashion. The skin edges were then reapproximated using 4-0 PDS sutures in a running subcuticular fashion. The 7-mm Jacson-Pratt drain was secured using a 3-0 nylon suture. The wound was then dressed with Mastisol and Steri-Strips followed by ABD pads and Ace wraps. The patient tolerated the procedure well without any complications. Estimated blood loss minimal. Fluids were 500 mL crystalloid. The patient was extubated and taken to the recovery room in stable condition.

Electronically Signed and Dated

Case Study 9.3

Patient: **Patient AAA**

Patient documentation: **Read Operative Report 9.3**

1. What are the preoperative and postoperative diagnoses (description) that support the medical necessity of this procedure?

   _____

2. Are there any secondary diagnoses present that required additional procedures?

   _____

3. What was the principal or main procedure, and were other secondary procedures performed on this patient?

   _____

4. Do you believe you need additional documentation to correctly assign the surgery codes to this record? If so, what is the additional documentation that you need?

   _____

5. Do you have any additional questions for the surgeon?

   _____

6. What is(are) the procedure code(s), including Level II HCPCS, you would assign to this case study?

   _____

   _____

Note: HCPCS codes would be added as follows: Visipaque contrast materials injected into vesselsx3; four different C-codes for catheterization supplies including introducer/sheath, other than guiding, other than intracardiac, catheter, transluminal angioplasty, non-laser (may include guidance, guide wire, and closure device, vascular (implantable/insertable); and fentanyl citrate 50 mcg/mL.)

MEDICAL REPORT 9.3

SUNSHINE MEDICAL CENTER
CARDIAC CATHETERIZATION REPORT

DATE: 07/11/20XX
PATIENT NAME: Patient AAA
PHYSICIAN: Dr. 058

INDICATION FOR STUDY: The patient is a 68-y/o male, with a dx of coronary artery disease of native and grafted vessels; hypertension and hyperlipidemia.

PROCEDURES

1. Left heart catheterization.
2. Left coronary artery angiography (right coronary angiography not performed, as the right coronary artery was totally occluded on previous catheterization).
3. Left ventriculography.
4. Right femoral angiography.
5. Saphenous vein graft/stub injections times three.
6. Left internal mammary artery angiography.
7. Ascending aortography.

TECHNIQUE: The patient's right groin was sterilely prepped and draped and anesthetized with 2% lidocaine. A 6 French introducer was placed in the right femoral artery. The JL4 catheter was used for selective angiography of the left coronary artery. The right coronary artery was not imaged, as it was totally occluded on the patient's previous catheterization. The JR4 catheter was unsuccessful in cannulating; however, the JR4 catheter was advanced into the ascending aorta and attempts to use this to cannulate the saphenous vein grafts were unsuccessful. The JR4 catheter was then placed in the left subclavian artery, and left internal mammary artery angiography was performed. Left internal mammary artery graft noted to be supplying the diagonal artery. The LCB catheter was then advanced into the ascending aorta, and selective angiography of the saphenous vein graft to the obtuse marginal branch 2 and the posterolateral artery were performed. The LCB catheter was unsuccessful to cannulate the saphenous vein graft to the left descending. However, a suggestion of a stub seemed to be present. The pigtail catheter was advanced to the aortic valve and manipulated into the ventricle. Left ventricular pressures were recorded and left ventriculography performed. The pigtail catheter was then pulled back into the ascending aorta, and aortography was performed in two views, failing to demonstrate a third saphenous vein graft. The 3DRC catheter was then advanced into the ascending aorta, and cannulation of the stub of the saphenous vein graft to the left anterior descending was identified. Right femoral artery angiography was then performed to evaluate for extent of peripheral vascular disease. The patient tolerated the procedure well. Hemostasis was obtained utilizing Angio-Seal. The patient was taken to the recovery room in satisfactory condition.

COMPLICATION: None

MEDICAL REPORT 9.3 (Continued)

HEMODYNAMIC FINDINGS

1. Left ventricular pressure 135/22.
2. Aortic pressure 135/41 with a mean of 83.
3. Heart rate 69 beats per minute.
4. Body surface area 1.72 meters squared.

ANGIOGRAPHIC FINDINGS

LEFT MAIN CORONARY ARTERY: The left main coronary artery originates normally in the left sinus of Valsalva. It is subtotally occluded throughout its course.

LEFT ANTERIOR DESCENDING ARTERY: The left anterior descending artery courses normally in the interventricular groove. The first diagonal artery is totally occluded at its origin. A small second diagonal artery is present. The left anterior descending demonstrates a proximal 80% eccentric lesion. Remnants of the distal anastomosis are seen in the distal left anterior descending. No competitive flow is seen in the distal left anterior descending or retrograde flow seen in the remnants of the saphenous vein graft to the left anterior descending.

CIRCUMFLEX CORONARY ARTERY: The circumflex coronary artery is moderate to severely diseased in its proximal to mid segment and totally occluded in its mid to distal segment. One obtuse marginal artery is seen arising in the proximal portion. The first obtuse marginal artery demonstrates an ostial 90% concentric lesion. The obtuse marginal artery is a small caliber vessel.

RIGHT CORONARY ARTERY: The right coronary artery was not visualized on this study as it was totally occluded on the patient's previous catheterization.

SAPHENOUS VEIN GRAFT TO THE POSTEROLATERAL ARTERY: Widely patent with good flow into the native vessel. Retrograde flow into the distal circumflex and down into the second posterolateral artery is appreciated. Faint collateral circulation to the distal right is noted.

SAPHENOUS VEIN GRAFT/STUB TO THE LEFT ANTERIOR DESCENDING: The saphenous vein graft to the left anterior descending is totally occluded in its ostial segment.

ASCENDING AORTOGRAPHY: Ascending aortography was performed in two views, demonstrating only two saphenous vein grafts arising from the ascending aorta. The ascending aorta demonstrates normal caliber. No aortic insufficiency appreciated.

LEFT VENTRICULOGRAPHY: Normal left ventricular size, no regional wall motion abnormalities, normal systolic function, ejection fraction of 66%. No evidence of mitral valve prolapse or mitral insufficiency.

RIGHT FEMORAL ARTERY ANGIOGRAPHY: The CFA demonstrates mid-luminal irregularities. The SFA and profunda were not visualized on this study due to a low takeoff. The introducer was noted to be inserted well above the bifurcation. Calcification of the iliac vessels is also appreciated.

CONCLUSIONS

1. Severe left main coronary artery disease.

2. Severe three-vessel coronary artery disease.

3. Totally occluded saphenous vein graft to the left anterior descending.

4. Native left anterior descending with 80% proximal lesion. Obtuse marginal #1 not previously bypassed with ostial 90% lesion.

5. Patent saphenous vein grafts to the obtuse marginal #2 and posterolateral artery #1.

6. Patent left internal mammary artery graft to the left anterior descending.

7. Right coronary artery not visualized on this study, as on previous catheterization was totally occluded.

8. Normal systolic pressure.

9. Elevated left ventricular end-diastolic pressure.

10. Normal systolic function.

RECOMMENDATIONS: Will have catheterization film evaluated for possible catheter-based intervention versus re-do coronary artery bypass surgery.

_____

Electronically Signed and Dated

Case Study 9.4

Patient: **Patient BBB**

Patient documentation: **Read Operative Report 9.4**

1. What are the preoperative and postoperative diagnoses (description) that support the medical necessity of this procedure?

   _____

2. Are there any secondary diagnoses present that required additional procedures?

   _____

3. What was the principal or main procedure, and were other secondary procedures performed on this patient?

   _____

4. Do you believe you need additional documentation to correctly assign the surgery codes to this record? If so, what is the additional documentation that you need?

   _____

5. Do you have any additional questions for the surgeon?

   _____

6. What is(are) the procedure code(s) you would assign to this case study?

   _____

   _____

SUNSHINE MEDICAL CENTER
OPERATIVE AND SURG PATH REPORTS

DATE: 09/12/20XX
PATIENT NAME: Patient BBB
PHYSICIAN: Dr. 059
ASSISTANT: Dr. 060

ANESTHESIA: General

PREOPERATIVE DIAGNOSIS: Multiple skin lesions, suspicious for malignancy

POSTOPERATIVE DIAGNOSIS: Malignancies (basal cell carcinoma) of skin of face, ear, and scalp; multiple facial lesions, right and left preauricular lesion.

OPERATIONS PERFORMED

1. Excision malignant skin lesion of nasal tip—3.0 cm—repaired with paramedian forehead flap.
2. Excision of right postauricular malignant skin lesion—3.8 cm—with advancement flap with reconstruction.
3. Excision of malignant neoplasm of the left preauricular skin, 1.3 cm.
4. Excision of left scalp malignant neoplasm, 1.8 cm.
5. Excision of benign lesion of the left cheek, 1.9 cm.

PROCEDURE IN DETAIL: The patient was taken to the operating room where general endotracheal anesthesia was administered. After successful induction of anesthesia, the patient was prepped and draped in the standard sterile fashion. The skin lesions in question were then outlined with a marking pen. The lesions were injected with 1% lidocaine and epinephrine.

The nasal tip lesion was excised circumferentially using a #15 blade scalpel. This was oriented for the pathologist and sent for frozen-section examination. The frozen-section reports confirmed positive margins initially. The margins were re-excised twice. The final margins were clear. At this point the defect size was 3.0 cm. The alar cartilage was exposed; the overlying perichondrium was intact.

The right postauricular skin lesion was then excised with a #15 blade scalpel. This was sent for frozen-section examination. The initial margins were positive. After re-excision of the margins, the final frozen-section report was that the margins were clear.

The left periauricular lesion was then excised using a #15 blade scalpel. It was oriented for the pathologist and sent for frozen-section examination. The initial margin was clear. The wound edges were undermined. The Burrows triangles were then excised superiorly and inferiorly. The skin edges were reapproximated with 5-0 nylon suture.

The left scalp lesion was then excised circumferentially using a #15 blade scalpel. It was sent for frozen-section examination. The margins were initially positive. After re-excision the new margins were clear and the wound edges were undermined with tenotomy scissors. The wound edges were then reapproximated with 3-0 nylon suture.

The right postauricular defect was then inspected. The defect diameter was 3.8 cm. The postauricular skin was generously undermined using tenotomy scissors. An advancement flap was designed with a marking pen. The undermined skin was advanced anteriorly. The anterior edge was sutured to the posterior aspect of the helix. Nylon 5-0 suture was used to secure the advancement flap into place.

The nose was then inspected. The defect of the right nasal tip and ala measured 3.0 cm. The decision was made to perform a paramedian forehead flap. A Doppler was brought into the room and used to identify the supratrochlear and supraorbital

MEDICAL REPORT 9.4 (Continued)

arteries. These were outlined with a marking pen. The pedicle was then designed with incisions lateral to the arterial supply. The flap length was determined using a ruler. The flap length was designed to be 4.0 cm. The donor site was outlined with a marking pen. A template was designed by placing a dry sterile piece of paper on the defect. An imprint was made and outlined with marking pen. This was then inverted and placed at the top of the designed pedicle. The donor site and pedicle were then incised with a #15 blade scalpel. The flap was then very carefully elevated with liberal use of the Doppler to confirm intact blood supply. After the flap was adequately elevated, it was rotated and placed into position on the nasal tip. The flap was then sutured to the nasal tip using 5-0 nylon suture.

The pedicle incisions were then reapproximated. First the skin was undermined carefully on the left and the right. Nylon 4-0 was used to reapproximate the skin. The donor defect was then inspected. The edges were undermined. Nylon 3-0 was used to reapproximate the edges. A small Burrows triangle was removed superiorly. Mattress sutures were used to reapproximate the edges. A small 3 × 3 cm area of tissue was left to heal by secondary intention, right in the center of the donor site.

The wounds were all cleaned and dressed with triple antibiotic ointment. A small piece of Xeroform was placed on the pedicle. No pressure dressing was applied across the nose. A pressure dressing was applied to the right postauricular skin region.

The patient was awakened and extubated in the operating room. He was taken to the recovery room in good condition. There were no complications. All counts were correct. Subsequently determined an overnight stay for observation was medically justified.

———————————

Electronically Signed and Dated

ABSTRACT FROM SURGICAL PATH REPORT

A. Skin, nasal lesion excision, basal cell carcinoma tumor present at peripheral 12 to 8 o'clock margin; all other margins appear free of tumor.

B. Skin, right posterior auricular, excision: basal cell carcinoma.

C. Skin, left preauricular excision; basal cell carcinoma.

D. Skin, left scalp excision; basal cell carcinoma.

E. Skin, nasal lesion, re-excision; basal cell carcinoma; tumor present at 8 to 9 o'clock margin; all other margins appear free of tumor.

F. Skin, right posterior auricular re-excision; basal cell carcinoma.

G. Skin, left scalp re-excision; no evidence of malignancy.

H. Skin, nasal 8 to 9 o'clock margin excision; margins of second excision appear free of tumor.

I. Skin, right posterior auricular; basal cell carcinoma; margins of excision appear free of tumor.

J. Skin, left cheek excision; early invasive well-differentiated squamous cell carcinoma arising in a background of squamous cell carcinoma in-situ. Squamous cell carcinoma in-situ focally present at peripheral margin.

Case Study 9.5

Patient: **Patient CCC**

Patient documentation: **Read Operative Report 9.5**

1. What are the preoperative and postoperative diagnoses (description) that support the medical necessity of this procedure?

   _____

2. Are there any secondary diagnoses present that required additional procedures?

   _____

3. What was the principal or main procedure, and were other secondary procedures performed on this patient?

   _____

4. Do you believe you need additional documentation to correctly assign the surgery codes to this record? If so, what is the additional documentation that you need?

   _____

5. Do you have any additional questions for the physician?

   _____

6. What is(are) the procedure code(s), including HCPCS Level II, you would assign to this case study?

   _____

   _____

   (Note: To code the HCPCS Level II codes, the supplies used included a "guidewire used as a vascular starter and an introducer sheath, other than guiding for endovascular intervention.")

SUNSHINE MEDICAL CENTER

REASON FOR EXAM:	Renal failure
PATIENT NAME:	Patient CCC
ORDERING PHYSICIAN:	Dr. 061
CLINICAL DATA:	Renal failure, swollen arm
PROCEDURE:	Fistulogram × 2/left upper extremity venogram/angioplasty of distal left brachiocephalic vein and left subclavian vein
DATE OF OPERATION:	1/11/20XX
RADIOLOGIST:	Dr. 062

COMPLICATIONS: No immediate complications, status post fistulogram × 2/left upper extremity venogram/angioplasty of distal left brachiocephalic vein and left subclavian vein.

MEDICATIONS: Ancef 1 gm IV piggyback preop/heparin 2000 units IV/Versed 2 mg IV total/fentanyl 100 mcg IV

CONTRAST: 75 mL nonionic

PROCEDURE/FINDINGS: After the risks, benefits, and alternatives of the procedure were explained to the patient who demonstrated full understanding with all questions answered, written informed consent was obtained and placed in the chart.

The left arm was prepped and draped in the usual sterile fashion. 1% lidocaine was used to anesthetize the skin. A small skin nick was performed near the arterial anastomosis aimed centrally. A 6-French short vascular sheath was placed. A left upper extremity venogram was performed demonstrating a widely patent left AV fistula centrally. Outflow is noted via the left subclavian vein. As seen on prior studies, there is stenosis of the proximal left subclavian vein measuring up to 40%. There is stenosis at entry of the pacemaker wires measuring up to 60–70% and there is stenosis of the distal left brachiocephalic vein at the origin of the superior vena cava measuring up to 70%.

An 8-mm balloon was placed over the wire and inflated for 2 minutes each insufflation twice at each site up to 15 atmospheres. Follow-up contrast injection demonstrated improvement with significant decreased amount of forward flow into collateral vessels. It was decided at this time not to increase the balloon size since the wires appeared to have minimal motion when moving the balloon and I did not want to displace the wires. The wires remained intact.

Contrast injection was performed demonstrating the arterial anastomosis, which is widely patent without significant disease of the visualized arteries within the elbow and forearm.

The sheaths were removed and pressure held manually for hemostasis. There was no bleeding or hematoma. The hand remained warm. Sterile dressings were applied. The left radial pulse was only Dopplerable prior to exam and remained so.

IMPRESSION

Status post angioplasty of the two venous stenoses with improvement and decreased amount of collateral flow.

Electronically Signed and Dated

Case Study 9.6

Patient: **Patient DDD**

Patient documentation: **Read Operative Report 9.6**

1. What are the preoperative and postoperative diagnoses (description) that support the medical necessity of this procedure?

   _____

2. Are there any secondary diagnoses present that required additional procedures?

   _____

3. What was the principal or main procedure, and were other secondary procedures performed on this patient?

   _____

4. Do you believe you need additional documentation to correctly assign the surgery codes to this record? If so, what is the additional documentation that you need?

   _____

5. Do you have any additional questions for the physician?

   _____

6. What is(are) the procedure code(s), including HCPCS Level II, you would assign to this case study?

   _____

   _____

[Note: HCPCS Level II used in this record but not presented on previous medical record examples include Heparin NA (porcine) 10000 units/10 mL injection to thin the blood at the site of the clot.]

MEDICAL REPORT 9.6

SUNSHINE MEDICAL CENTER

REASON FOR EXAM: Clotted dialysis graft

PATIENT NAME: PATIENT DDD

CLINICAL DATA: The patient with clotted AV graft

PROCEDURE: Left arm AV graft/mechanical thrombectomy/fistulogram and angioplasty

DATE OF OPERATION: 12/13/20XX

Prior to beginning the procedure, the case was discussed with the referring physician. Attending nephrologist wishes interventional therapy for this patient's clotted graft rather than surgical revision. The patient was fully informed of the risks and benefits, and alternatives to the procedure. The patient is familiar with the procedure. Potential risks, including that of bleeding, infection, embolization, and limb loss, were discussed. All of the patient's questions were answered and a consent form was signed. IV antibiotics were given. The patient was brought to the angiographic suite and placed upon the table. IV conscious sedation was provided with Versed and fentanyl. The patient's left arm was prepped and draped in the usual sterile fashion. Local anesthesia was obtained with Xylocaine solution. Next, the clotted graft was punctured with a micropuncture needle, with the needle tip pointing toward the venous outflow. Subsequently, a sheath was placed. Via the sheath, an 8 mm × 4 cm Conquest angio balloon was advanced over the wire. Using this catheter as a diagnostic catheter, central venograms were performed which demonstrated the axillary, subclavian, brachiocephalic veins, as well as the superior vena cava to the patient. The catheter was positioned at the level of the venous anastomosis, where there is stricturing seen on venograms, as well as on prior studies. The balloon was then inflated and a waist was seen within the balloon. Multiple high-pressure inflations were performed. The balloon was then deflated and removed. Next, an Arrow-Trerotola device was advanced to the venous limb of the graft. Previously, IV heparin had been given. Next, the device was activated and mechanical thrombectomy of the venous side of the graft was performed. It was noted there was now a thrill within the graft. Follow-up venograms demonstrated flow through the venous side of the graft with only minimal residual narrowing involving the venous anastomosis.

In order to ensure there was no clot on the arterial side, the graft was once again punctured with a micropuncture needle with the stent pointing toward the arterial anastomosis. A second sheath was then placed. Next a C2 catheter was then advanced over the wire into the graft and then placed across the arterial anastomosis. An injection was performed, which demonstrated the arterial anastomosis to be widely patent. No residual thrombus was seen within the graft. There was brisk flow seen through the graft, as well as within the more distal artery.

The patient tolerated the procedure well. The patient is without complaint. Both sheaths were then pulled.

IMPRESSION

1. Successful mechanical thrombectomy with angioplasty venous anastomosis.

2. There were no postprocedure complications.

3. At the end of the procedure, there was a good thrill within the graft.

Electronically Signed and Dated

PART III

THE IMPACT OF CODING ON REIMBURSEMENT, AND MANAGED HEALTH CARE

Coding, Reimbursement, and Managed Care

Chapter Outline

Landmark Health-Care Legislation
Shift to Integrated Delivery Systems and Managed Care
Medical Coding, Managed Care, and Quality Improvement
Data Quality and Managed Care
Testing Your Comprehension

Chapter Objectives

▶ Explain the vital link, emerging role, and financial impact of medical coding as it relates to health-care reimbursement and managed care.

▶ Describe the evolution of coding and health-care reimbursement systems.

▶ Define the data requirements needed to support provider reimbursement, communication among diverse providers, and research.

▶ Identify landmark federal legislation that resulted in alternative health-care settings and prospective payment systems.

▶ Define managed care and the various types of managed-care organizations.

▶ Recognize the significance the inpatient prospective payment system had on outpatient services and on the use of CPT coding.

▶ Understand and explain the difference between the MS-DRG, ASC, APG, APC, and RBRVS reimbursement systems.

▶ Describe reasons for the shift from inpatient to outpatient services that occurred during the 1980s and 1990s.

▶ Recognize the significance of "upcoding."

▶ Identify the major obstacles to precise coding.

Medical coding plays a significant role in health-care reimbursement and today's managed care environment. The importance of precise coding cannot be emphasized enough. Health information managers and health-care administrators must be fully knowledgeable of the inpatient and outpatient data requirements needed for the survival and growth of their institutions to continue their mission of providing quality patient care. The current U.S. health-care system is a data-driven industry. Medical coding systems, including ICD-9-CM and CPT, are fundamental communication tools that support this complex infrastructure.

Medical (clinical) coding represents the data requirements needed to support the following key functions and processes:

▶ Provider reimbursement from Medicare, Medicaid, and other third-party payers for inpatient and outpatient services

▶ Sharing of clinical data across a network of providers in various settings to provide for continuity of patient care

▶ Research designed to improve, standardize, and optimize the quality of patient care while controlling health-care costs

▶ The merging of traditional facility management (by health-care administrators) and clinical patient management (by physicians) into clinical process management to meet the demands of third-party payer reimbursement formulas linked to the quality of work performed and the patient outcomes achieved by the provider (i.e., pay-for-performance systems)

From its origins in the first half of the 20th century, the primary purpose of coding medical diagnoses and procedures was to retrieve health record data for research. As time passed, the business of health-care delivery grew, and the information obtained from classifying and retrieving health record data through medical coding proved to be helpful in health-care administration as part of planning, delivering, and marketing services to meet the needs of communities and the nation. Moreover, coded medical data became increasingly useful in extracting information to evaluate and improve the quality of patient care services (e.g., using coded data to promote evidence-based medicine and outcome management).

As medical coding systems evolved, providers realized that codes made it easier for them to report their services to third-party payers for reimbursement. In place of long narrative descriptions of diagnoses and procedures, medical codes (ICD-9-CM, CPT) could be quickly entered into computerized billing systems to transmit patient information to third-party payers. This, in turn, expedited payments to hospitals, physicians, and other providers for the work they performed. Medical codes allow payers of health-care services (government programs and commercial insurers) to know exactly what they are paying for, why the patient sought the services, whether or not the services provided were medically necessary, and whether the charges from the provider are fair and reasonable.

Landmark Health-Care Legislation

In the 1960s, legislation was enacted to provide payment for health-care services for the nation's elderly, poor, and disabled. From that base, other legislation has evolved designed to increase the availability and affordability of care for America's citizens.

1965 Amendments to the 1935 Social Security Act

In 1965, federal amendments to the 1935 Social Security Act established Title 19 Medicare, Health Insurance for the Elderly, and Title 18 Medicaid, the Medical Assistance Program for the Indigent. With this legislation, the federal government became the health-care payer or insurer for a substantial segment of the U.S. population. However, at the time of the initial passage of the legislation that created the Medicare program, it was not realized how this landmark legislation would ultimately drive the importance of:

- ▶ Medical coding, including ICD-9-CM and CPT
- ▶ Proliferation of managed-care organizations and integrated delivery systems
- ▶ Computer networking (intranets, LAN) in health care
- ▶ Subsequent federal health-care legislation, including the Health Insurance Portability and Accountability Act of 1996
- ▶ Continuous quality improvement processes increasingly applied to health care
- ▶ The movement of health-care services from cottage industries (marked by provider autonomy and control) to corporate industrial models (the "industrialization" of health care)
- ▶ Pay-for-performance provider reimbursement systems that promote high-quality services

The initial payments to providers under the Medicare and Medicaid programs were based on **retrospective reimbursement.** Payment was provided after the health-care services were rendered, and reimbursement was calculated based on the provider's usual charge for the service. From 1966 to 1983, under a retrospective reimbursement formula, hospitals were paid for the services they provided and billed, and there was little interest in reducing or controlling the costs of those services.[1] However, Medicare's 1966 Conditions of Participation mandated that hospitals establish a plan for **utilization review** (UR) as well as a permanent UR committee. The goal of the UR process was to ensure that services provided to Medicare beneficiaries were medically necessary.[2] The initial UR function under Medicare was an internal process in which physicians within the same hospital reviewed the services provided by their peers to certify whether or not those services were medical necessary. The original UR process was commonly known for the 14-day inpatient re-certifications by a peer physician. Today, an inpatient **length of stay** (LOS) of 14 days or more is rare. Eventually, this internal utilization review process was deemed inadequate because physicians serving on the same medical staff were hesitant to question their peers regarding the need for patient admissions and continued patient stays.

Without an effective UR process or strong link to the quality of patient care, health-care costs throughout the 1970s and 1980s quickly spiraled because of increasing physician and hospital fees that threatened to bankrupt the Medicare Trust Fund (the repository for payroll tax contributions to Medicare). Under Medicare's retrospective payment formula, providers' charge-based reimbursement system, a **fee-for-service** indemnity plan, came to be known as the "blank check." This system ensured that provider revenue exceeded operational expenditures, resulting in the unrestrained inflation of health-care costs. As this could not be sustained indefinitely, cost-containment efforts at the national level provided the momentum for control of resource utilization at the provider level. In the 1970s, the first major attempts at federal cost containment for health-care services were initiated.

1972 Bennett Amendment to the Social Security Act

By 1972, the Medicare Trust Fund was in serious financial trouble, and in an effort to reduce Medicare and Medicaid spending, additional amendments to the Social Security Act were enacted through Public Law 92-603. This law established the **Professional Standards Review Organization** (PSRO) program to implement concurrent utilization review. Through provisions within the law, the federal government moved the previous internal utilization review function of hospitals to the PSRO, an independent external agency managed by physicians. Contracted by the Health Care Finance Administration (now CMS), the PSRO's scope of work was to review patient care with the goal of protecting the Medicare Trust Fund. Their duties included an external review of the appropriateness of care given to Medicare and Medicaid patients for hospital inpatient services. The significance of the PSRO was that it marked the beginning of health-care utilization review processes as we know them today. Primarily through a review of medical records, the focus of the PSRO reviews included:

▶ Ensuring that quality care was provided
▶ Verifying the medical necessity for inpatient care based on the patient's condition
▶ Ensuring that the care provided was efficient and effective

To determine whether or not aspects of a patient's care were medically necessary, appropriately delivered, and in compliance with professionally recognized standards of quality care, the PSRO (reviewers) used objective clinical screening criteria (e.g., intensity of service, severity of illness criteria by InterQual®). If clinical screening criteria were not met, the PSRO concluded that the patient's medical necessity did not warrant an inpatient admission. A common PSRO finding was that the patient's condition could have been treated more appropriately in a less expensive nonacute setting; this introduced the concept of denying payment for care deemed unnecessary.[3]

1973 Health Maintenance Organization Act

Espoused by President Nixon, the Health Maintenance Organization Act of 1973 (P.L. 93-222) was driven by a growing concern for the rising costs of employee health benefits. It established federal loans and grants for developing and implementing health-care delivery organizations called **health maintenance organizations** (HMOs). An HMO is a prepaid voluntary health plan that provides an umbrella of various health-care services to enrollees in return for a fixed monthly **premium** (i.e., capitation). HMO premiums shared by employers and enrollees are lower than the premiums for other types of health-care plans.[4] As a result, the HMO Act of 1973 funded the development of alternative health-care delivery systems incorporating multiple settings and services.

1974 Employee Retirement Income Security Act

The Employee Retirement Income Security Act (ERISA) regulated the corporate use of pension funds to protect employees from misuse or fraud that could result in the loss of retirement funds. ERISA also allowed large employers (national corporations) to establish their own self-funded health plans that were not subject to state regulations (that were disparate and in some cases, cost prohibitive). In place of state oversight, the self-funded health plans were subject to federal review. Employer organizations designed health plans using alternative delivery systems and cost-containment strategies such as utilization review and wellness care.

1982 Tax Equity and Fiscal Responsibility Act

By early 1982, Congress recognized that the cost of health care had reached critical dimensions; the Medicare Trust Fund was nearly depleted.[5] In an attempt to correct this situation, Congress passed the Tax Equity and Fiscal Responsibility Act (TEFRA), which set overall limits on Medicare spending and required the development of a **prospective payment system** (PPS) for inpatient hospitalizations. Unlike the retrospective reimbursement formula where providers billed "usual and customary charges" for provided services, TEFRA controlled hospital inpatient payments based on a PPS in which the amount of payment for a patient case is established before services are rendered.

Under TEFRA, the reimbursement method called **Diagnosis Related Groups** (DRGs) assigns fixed (prospective) payments to hospitals for inpatient services based on the average cost of treating the patient's condition. Patient health-care services are reported using ICD-9-CM diagnosis and procedure codes. Beginning in 1983, DRG payments to hospitals for inpatient services were phased in over 3 years. Coinciding with the federal fiscal year (FY) that begins on October 1, regulations with respect to the system are revised and updated annually. The proposed and final regulations are printed in the *Federal Register*, a newsletter that documents federal legislation. Hospital inpatient payment rates are based on DRGs, which for FY 2008 were renamed **Medicare Severity-DRGs** (MS-DRGs). MS-DRGs establish a **relative weight** and prospective payment that reflects the average resources and procedures required to treat a particular condition. The actual amount the hospital is paid for each Medicare inpatient is based on the national relative weight for a particular MS-DRG times the hospital's individual **base rate** (also called blended rate). A base rate provides a monetary adjustment to the hospital's final payment by factoring in individual characteristics (e.g., geographic location; urban, rural, or teaching status; local labor costs). The MS-DRG weight multiplied against the base rate converts the hospital payment to dollars.

EXAMPLE

MS-DRG prospective payment formula

MS-DRG 690—Kidney and urinary tract infections w/o MCC
CMS weight 0.8000
A/LOS 4.3
G/LOS 3.6
Medicare inpatient reimbursement
Hospital A's individual base (blended) rate = $4,000.
Hospital B's individual base (blended) rate = $4,096.
MS-DRG reimbursement formula for Hospital A = CMS weight 0.8000 × Hospital A's base rate $4,000. = Total payment: $3,200.00
MS-DRG reimbursement formula for Hospital B = CMS weight 0.8000 × Hospital B's base rate $4,096. = Total payment: $3,276.80
MDC 011 Diseases and disorders of the kidney and urinary tract
Principal diagnosis
Urinary tract infection NOS 599.0
Secondary diagnoses
Hyponatremia 276.1
Intractable nausea and vomiting 536.2

MS-DRG = Medicare severity-diagnosis related groups
w/o MCC = without major complication and/or comorbidity
A/LOS = average length of stay
G/LOS = geometric mean length of stay
MDC = major diagnostic category
NOS = not otherwise specified

1982 Peer Review Improvement Act

Linked to TEFRA, the Peer Review Improvement Act of 1982 renamed the PSRO to become the **Peer Review Organization** (PRO). The PROs had a similar function to the PSRO in that they reviewed the medical necessity for patient admission and continued stay. The new law added coding and DRG validation and preadmission reviews to the responsibilities of the PROs. Because the reported ICD-9-CM medical codes established the payment rates to hospitals, coding and DRG validation was necessary to determine whether the payments were appropriate. PROs needed to be wary that medical coders can knowingly (fraud) or unknowingly (abuse) report codes to payers that are not representative of the diagnoses and services given to patients, therefore generating higher payments to the providers. This is an unethical and fraudulent practice called **upcoding**.[6] The PROs continued to use clinical screening criteria and issued denials for hospital payment if the patient's admission was determined to be not medically necessary.

In 2002, the PROs were renamed the **Quality Improvement Organizations** (QIOs). Within each state, CMS continues to contract with QIOs, which are private administrative organizations that include physician staff, to oversee the Medicare and Medicaid programs. The QIO contracts are called the Statement or Scope of Work and are awarded for 3-year periods through competitive bidding. The QIO's main role is to review and improve the care for Medicare or Medicaid patients. Similar to its predecessor the PRO, the QIO performs a utilization review function but plays a more collaborative role in quality-improvement activities with providers.

1989 Omnibus Reconciliation Act

The Omnibus Reconciliation Act (OBRA) of 1989 led to the development of the Resource-Based Relative Value Scale (RBRVS) that phased in the Medicare Fee Schedule (MFS) for prospective payments to physicians for their services. RBRVS values are published annually in the *Federal Register*. Implemented in 1992 and phased in over 5 years, RBRVS uses the MFS fixed-payment system to reimburse physicians' practice expenses based on the relative value for:

▶ The physician's work
▶ Practice expense (overhead)
▶ Malpractice expense related to a service or procedure reported by CPT codes

The three components of the code are further adjusted by a geographic practice cost index (GPCI). The GPCI serves to adjust payments to physicians according to work, overhead, and malpractice costs specific to different areas of the country. To receive reimbursement under Medicare and Medicaid, physicians must report CPT/HCPCS procedure or service codes and report ICD-9-CM diagnoses codes that describe the medical necessity for the services performed. Based on the federal RBRVS model, most third-party payers or commercial insurers also structure fee schedules to assign payments to physicians.

| EXAMPLE | *RBRVS Prospective Payment Formula*
CPT Code 99204—Level 4 Office Visit, new patient
Orlando, Florida |

Relative Value Units (RVUs) Geographic Practice Cost Index (GPCIs)

RVUw = 2.30	GPCIw = 1.0
RVUpe = 1.50	GPCIpe = 0.936
RVUm = 0.12	GPCIm = 1.251

Conversion Factor (CF) = $37.90

RBRVS formula: (RVUw × GPCIw) + (RVUpe × GPCIpe) + (RVUm × GPCIm) × CF = payment to physician

Therefore, (2.30 × 1.0) + (1.50 × 0.936) + (0.12 × 1.251) = 3.854 (total adjusted RBRVS weight) × $37.90 (CF) = $146.07 fee to the physician

RBRVS = Resource-based relative value scale
RVU = relative value for the procedure
GPCI = geographic practice cost index value
w = physician work
pe = practice expense
m = malpractice expense
CF = conversion factor

1996 Health Insurance Portability and Accountability Act

The Health Insurance Portability and Accountability Act (HIPAA) of 1996 was passed as an amendment to ERISA and the Public Health Services Act. Goals of HIPAA included provisions to:

▶ Ensure health insurance portability by allowing employees to maintain coverage when changing jobs
▶ Simplify health-care administration through electronic claims submission
▶ Reduce health-care fraud and abuse
▶ Ensure the privacy and security of **protected health information** (PHI)

The Title II Administrative Simplification component of HIPAA standardizes the electronic exchange of health and financial data to all providers, payers, and clearinghouses that use **electronic data interchange** (EDI) for the communication of health-care information. The resulting standardized electronic transactions through code sets (ICD-9-CM and CPT), minimum data sets (UB-04 [formerly UB-92], CMS 1500), transmission standards (e.g., HL7, ANSI), and national provider and health plan identifiers now allow for the sharing of clinical data from provider-to-provider across various health-care settings that encompass the continuum of care.

1997 Balanced Budget Act

The Balanced Budget Act of 1997 required the Department of Health and Human Services to implement an outpatient prospective payment system (OPPS) for reimbursing hospitals for outpatient services delivered to Medicare patients. This was implemented on August 1, 2000, as Ambulatory Payment Classifications (APCs). Based on the 3M Ambulatory Patient Groups (APG) that were a prospective payment system for facility-based ambulatory care, APCs apply predetermined payment rates to hospitals for both medical and surgical outpatient services. The APC payment rates are based on the CPT/HCPCS codes reported. Although ICD-9-CM diagnosis codes do not establish the APC payment rate, a provider's claim can be denied for payment if the reported diagnosis codes do not establish medical necessity for the procedures coded in CPT/HCPCS. Several APCs may be assigned for one patient visit for each CPT/HCPCS code submitted. Accurate and timely charge entry (at the point of patient service) and procedure and diagnosis coding are crucial for a hospital to receive the full payment for each claim. APCs use complex discounting formulas that group multiple APCs together to calculate a single reimbursement to the hospital. The OPPS using APCs is conceptually comparable to the Inpatient Prospective Payment System (IPPS) program using Medicare Severity-Diagnosis Related Groups. Unlike the inpatient MS-DRG system where a single MS-DRG is assigned at patient discharge, multiple APCs may be assigned to a single outpatient visit.

The first step in calculating the APC payment is to identify the **status indicator**, relative weight, and unadjusted payment rate for each APC related to the reported CPT/HCPCS code. For example, a status indicator "T" identifies surgical procedures that are subject to discounting (see Table 10.1 for additional examples).

TABLE 10.1 Sample Portion of APC Status Indicator

Indicator	Service	Status
N	Items and services packaged into APC rate	Paid under OPPS, payment packaged into payment for other services
P	Partial hospitalization	Paid under OPPS, per diem APC
S	Significant procedure, not discounted when multiple	Paid under OPPS, separate APC
T	Significant procedure, multiple-procedure reduction applies	Paid under OPPS, separate APC
V	Visit to clinic or emergency department	Paid under OPPS, separate APC
X	Ancillary service	Paid under OPPS, separate APC

For status T, the full APC amount is computed for the surgical procedure with the highest weight, and 50% of the APC amount is computed for any other surgical procedures performed during the same operative episode. The payment method applied to status "T" indicators acknowledges that in instances when more than one surgery was being performed during a single operative episode, the additional procedures would not require the additional expenses that would be incurred if the patient were returned to the operating room for each separate surgical procedure. The hospital's individual wage index amount is also used to adjust payments for wage variances that occur across different geographic areas in the country.

EXAMPLE

APC Prospective Payment Formula
DX: 211.2 Benign neoplasm of duodenum/jejunum/ileum
535.40 Gastritis w/o mention of hemorrhage
535.60 Duodenitis w/o mention of hemorrhage
578.9 GI hemorrhage, unspecified
530.89 D/O of esophagus (irregular z-line)
43258 EGD; other ablation lesion
APC: 00141—Level I Upper GI Procedure
Status: T—Significant procedure subject to multiple procedure discounting

AND

43239-59 EGD; bx, single/multiple; (-59 Distinct procedural service)

APC: 00141—Level I Upper GI Procedure

Status: T—Significant procedure subject to multiple procedure discounting

REIMB MEDICARE APC

TOTAL: $741.54

CMS: $533.58

Copay: $207.96

TOT ADJ WT: 12.48

OPPS $741.54

APC 1: 00141 43258 TOT $494.36 H $305.72 C $$138.64 U 1 W 8.32 P 1.00 OPPS

APC 2: 00141 43239 TOT $247.18 H $177.86 C $69.32 U 1 W 8.32 P 0.50 OPPS (50% of regular price because of multiple procedure discounting)

APC = Ambulatory Payment Classifications

DX = diagnosis

GI = gastrointestinal

D/O = disorder of

EGD =esophagogastroduodenoscopy

bx = biopsy

REIMB = reimbursement

TOT ADJ WT = total adjusted weight

OPPS = Outpatient Prospective Payment System

Shift to Integrated Delivery Systems and Managed Care

The 1980s and 1990s were marked by a shift from inpatient services, which had been the primary mode of care, to a proliferation of outpatient services provided within various settings. Those settings included hospital observation units, step-down units, home health-care agencies, ambulatory surgery centers, medical clinics, and physician group practices. The principal reasons for this shift included:

▶ Hospitals' response to inpatient denials resulting from the PSRO and PRO utilization review process

▶ Rapidly emerging new technologies that afforded less invasive procedures (e.g., laparoscopic surgeries) performed on an outpatient basis

▶ Consumer demand for shorter hospital stays

▶ Providers' attempts to escape the cost controls imposed under the inpatient prospective payment system DRGs

▶ Federal legislation (e.g., 1973 HMO Act, ERISA) that supported the shift from inpatient to outpatient and other alternative health-care settings

There were many reasons to account for this rapid shift from inpatient to outpatient services, but most importantly, it set the stage for an increasing spectrum of health-care services that rocketed the **managed care** environment. Generally, managed care represents a type of health-care delivery system that attempts to manage the access, delivery, quality, and cost of care to a particular population. The flourishing managed care environment revealed other needs such as increased computer networking requirements, federal privacy laws set forth in HIPAA regulations, and utilization review or case management and **continuous quality improvement** (CQI) processes at all levels of care (Fig. 10.1).

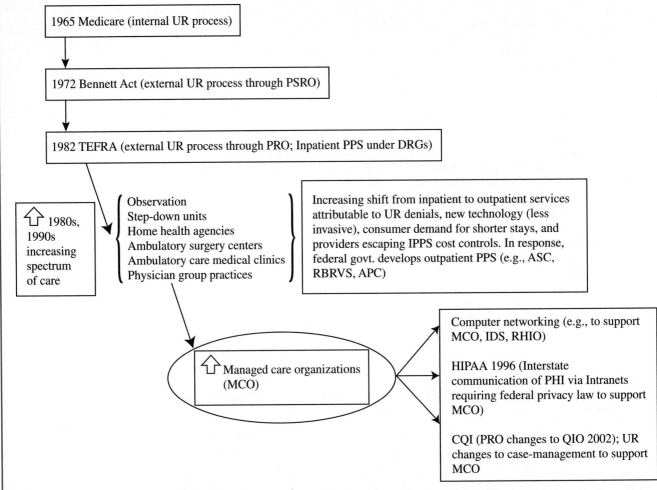

FIGURE 10.1 ■ Major landmarks on the path to managed care. There were many reasons to account for the rapid shift from inpatient to outpatient services (e.g., federal laws, the UR process, prospective payment systems, new technologies, consumer demand) that set the stage for the managed care environment. The managed care environment revealed other needs such as increased computer networking requirements, federal privacy laws set forth in HIPAA regulations, and utilization review or case management and continuous quality improvement processes at all levels of care.

Transition to Managed Care

The concept of managed care is not a new phenomenon; it can be traced back to the mid-1800s. Plantation owners in Hawaii, mining companies in Pennsylvania and Minnesota, and lumber companies in Washington, Wisconsin, and Michigan tried to attract and keep immigrant workers by offering medical care. The companies contracted with local physicians and hospitals for a set number of beds. Some of the companies even built medical clinics and hospitals.[7]

A consequence of the initial Medicare legislation has been a paradigm shift in the provision of health care, with a rapid transition to managed care. Before the 1980s, the emphasis was on acute care and the treatment of individual illnesses. Hospital services functioned as cottage industries, and the goal was to fill beds and gain market share by maintaining a high patient occupancy rate. Beginning in the 1970s with the enactment of federal cost-containment laws (PPS), new technologies, and increased consumer demand, the emphasis shifted to the provision of care to maintain wellness and manage the diseases of

TABLE 10.2 Most Common Types of MCOs

Organization Type	Description	Payment	Operations
Health Maintenance Organization (HMO)	Manages the delivery of health-care services to an enrolled population. Can include staff models (physicians as employees) and network models that contract with multiple physician groups and provider organizations.	Capitation: per-member-per-month (PMPM) fixed payment structure.	Wellness and preventive screening to maximize profits. Utilization review of all services. Use of a primary care provider (PCP) "gatekeeper" to coordinate patient access to care. Non-coverage of services outside of HMO network (except for emergencies).
Preferred Provider Organization (PPO)	Network of participating physicians limited to the plan.	Discounted fee-for-service: Negotiates a discounted rate (e.g., 20%) from the provider's usual and customary fee.	Financial penalties or reduced coverage if enrollee seeks care from a nonnetwork provider.
Point of Service (POS) Plan (Open Access)	Combines an HMO plan with traditional indemnity insurance.	Combines capitation with increasing financial penalties (deductibles and co-pays) for enrollees who receive care from nonparticipating providers.	Allows more choices and flexibility for enrollees who may opt to receive services from participating or nonparticipating physicians.

defined populations (groups) through **managed care organizations** (MCOs) and integrated delivery systems. With this trend came the new health-care focus: to provide quality care at reduced cost as a strategic corporate necessity at all levels. Managed care methods were primarily instituted in an effort to control health-care costs by coordinating care through a spectrum of settings, while evaluating its appropriateness and medical necessity at all levels through utilization review, case management, and disease management processes. In short, managed care simply changes the way health care is managed.

The most common types of managed care organizations are shown in Table 10.2.

The fundamental change accompanying the transition to managed care is that the locus of control for technological decision making in health services has moved from the individual professional to the organization.[8] This creates greater responsibility for the managed care organization to apply CQI methods to improve the provision of care while containing costs for the patient population it serves across all levels and settings within the system.

Medical Coding, Managed Care, and Quality Improvement

In the managed care environment (an integrated delivery system), precise coding is required on all levels of care in every setting to support provider reimbursement, communication of clinical information through a network of providers, research, and clinical process management.

Research involves using the coded data for a wide range of quality improvement activities that relate to:

▶ Development of treatment protocols (evidence-based best practices)
▶ Marketing

- ▶ Case-mix analyses (of types of patients treated)
- ▶ Outcomes management and benchmarking
- ▶ Utilization review
- ▶ Case and disease management.

The mix of activities (products and services) in health-care organizations is so varied that classification (coding) systems become extremely important components of any comparative analysis of health-care quality issues. It is no accident that the field of quality improvement in health care moved very slowly until the widespread adoption of the Diagnosis Related Groups (DRG) system for quality purposes.[9] For example, the various DRG systems offer nearly 500 categories to describe health-care products. These rather loose product designations have been the basis of managed care and disease management because they allow researchers to collect and compare outcomes and costs across organizations and processes for many purposes, including process enhancement.[10] These same analyses can be performed using the APC groupings and RBRVS service levels to compare outcomes and costs relating to outpatient services.

Provider Documentation

Documentation is the basis of coding, and coding is the basis for collecting and transferring accurate data within the health-care system. Clear, concise documentation is essential. Clinicians' illegible handwriting and insufficient or poor-quality documentation are major sources for error; the benefits of great initiatives such as ICD-10-CM and HIPAA will not be fully realized unless their use is commensurate with improved physician documentation systems. Inadequate documentation will corrupt coded data at all levels of the managed care environment (i.e., reimbursement, sharing clinical data, and research).

ICD-10-CM

Although it is widely accepted among health information professionals that ICD-10-CM is a better classification to capture more clinical detail, ICD-10-CM's success depends on a corresponding increase in the level of detail within physicians' documentation. Although it can be argued that the increased specificity resulting from the addition of thousands of additional ICD-10-CM codes may capture physician documentation more accurately, there is an even stronger argument that if physician documentation remains dormant at ICD-9-CM levels, the gap preventing full ICD-10-CM utilization as a result of insufficient physician documentation will widen significantly (Fig. 10.2). In effect, the application of ICD-10-CM would not be as efficient or cost effective as intended.

HIPAA

One of the primary goals of HIPAA legislation is for providers to share patient data electronically across a continuum of health-care settings to improve the coordination of patient care and decisions relating to care, reduce administrative costs, and reduce the waste and inefficiency associated with repeated and unnecessary tests and procedures. Although individual settings such as hospitals, physician offices, and clinics have demonstrated increasing success in developing cost-efficient processes using CQI methods, these successes have been compartmentalized and represent a vertical alignment of "best practice"

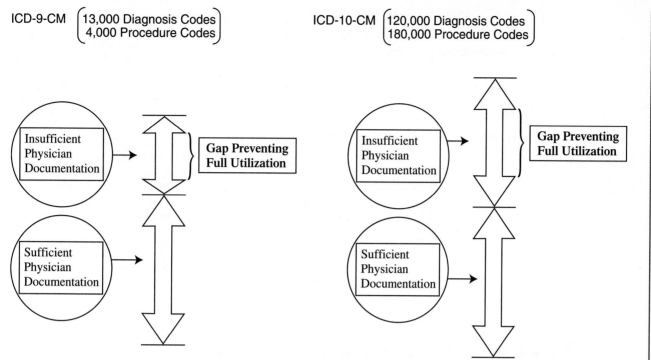

FIGURE 10.2 ■ Comparison of ICD-9-CM and ICD-10-CM coding systems. If physician documentation remains dormant at ICD-9-CM levels, the gap preventing full ICD-10-CM utilization as a result of insufficient physician documentation will widen significantly.

protocols limited to each facility. The horizontal flow of patients' clinical data within a provider network over time (from "womb to tomb") is currently not of sufficient quality to reduce the number of tests and procedures or to assist in making more sound medical decisions as aspired to by HIPAA (Fig. 10.3).

Also, poor data affect the electronic transfer of patient information that is critical to the success of Regional Health Information Organizations (RHIOs). RHIOs are groups of organizations with a business stake in improving the quality, safety, and efficiency of health-care delivery by sharing health-care data across a common platform. They include providers, purchasers of care, manufacturers, vendors, and other stakeholders within a given region. RHIOs are the building blocks of the proposed National Health Information Network initiative.

Data Quality and Managed Care

Data quality is of critical importance to the administrative decisions that must be made within a managed care environment. If the underlying coded data are unreliable, the information and decisions that drive reimbursement, communication of clinical information through a network of providers, and research will be adversely affected throughout the entire health-care system. Currently, coded health-care data (the data that drive managed care) are often not of good quality.

For example, Section 306 of the Medicare Modernization Act directed CMS to investigate Medicare claims payments using Recovery Audit Contractors

HIPAA Framework (Title II, Administrative Simplification)

Standardized	Unique Identifiers	Privacy	Security	Sanctions (Monetary and Imprisonment)
Code Sets (ICD-9-CM, CPT) Minimum Data Sets (MDS) Transmission Protocols (ANSI, HL7)	Physician Hospital Other Healthcare Facility Patient Plan Clearing House	PHI Training Policies & Procedures Patient Privacy Notice Secure PHI Designate Responsible Individual	Passwords Firewalls Audits Data Backup Disaster Recovery Access Control Encryption/Decryption	HIPAA Offense ✓ $100 – single violation of provision ✓ Up to $25,000 Multiple violations/same requirement during calendar year ✓ Up to $50,000 Wrongful disclosure PHI; Up to one year ✓ Up to $100,000 Wrongful disclosure of PHI committed under false pretenses; Up to five years ✓ Up to $250,000 Wrongful disclosure of PHI committed under false pretenses with intent to sell, transfer, use for commercial advantage, personal gain, or malicious harm; Up to 10 years

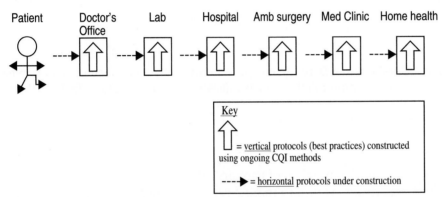

Key

⬆ = vertical protocols (best practices) constructed using ongoing CQI methods

----▶ = horizontal protocols under construction

FIGURE 10.3 ■ Data flow. Providers use coded data to obtain information for improvement efforts and making decisions. There is a vertical way to look at the use of data within an individual organization and a horizontal way to look at the use of data across organizations. Internally, within individual settings such as hospitals and physician offices, providers have demonstrated increasing success at using (and improving) the data needed to develop cost-efficient processes (best-care practices). However, externally, the shared horizontal flow of patients' clinical data is currently of inadequate quality to assist in making sound medical decisions across provider networks.

(RACs) under a 3-year demonstration project. RAC investigations commonly target high-risk and high-volume DRGs and high-volume operative services, which often reveal improper coding practices. The FY 2006 RAC Status Report describes that the Medicare Fee for Service (FFS) Payments Report for November 2006 shows that 4.4% of the Medicare dollars paid did not comply with one or more Medicare coverage, coding, billing, and payment rules. This equates to $10.8 billion in Medicare overpayments and underpayments [fiscal year 2006].[11]

If incorrect coding relating to reimbursement is significant, then it logically follows that using the same data for other purposes will produce results that are compromised and inaccurate. Worst case, the sharing of inaccurate clinical information among providers can potentially result in life-threatening consequences for the patient. And yet, providing complete and accurate documentation can be a challenge in settings in which physicians are time-pressed and sometimes fatigued. In general, the managed care system is dependent on excellent documentation to support proper coding, which in turn, supports the infrastructure of provider payment, provider communication, and research.

Electronic Health Record and Standard Documentation

There are many current hospital-based initiatives to develop the **electronic health record** (EHR) as a panacea to inadequate documentation by the clinician. However, these hospital information systems are often forced on physicians who may interpret this effort as another attempt to usurp their autonomy and control of patient care. Federal initiatives to develop frontline projects that promote standardized electronic physician documentation systems can serve as a foundation to a national health-care informatics system. This core system can be designed to correct deficiencies commonly occurring in physician documentation in "real time." The system can be programmed to mimic the attributes of a good physician documenter, in a sense, forcing every physician to document well. As individuals, clinicians will usually accept and support office systems that simultaneously improve their work life and patient care.[12]

Although many physicians use commercially available electronic medical office systems (e.g., practice management systems that incorporate medical record dictation, coding, and billing), these are usually disparate systems tailored to meet the needs of a specific physician's practice or specialty; they may or may not have online connections to local hospitals or health-care networks. A federally subsidized initiative to find a universal concept and **minimum data set** (MDS) and format to standardize physician documentation following a good model can correct insufficient documentation at its originating source. Physician documentation systems will still be available through commercial vendors that develop products tailored to specialties such as endocrinology, pathology, urology, neurology, plastic surgery, psychiatry, or cardiology; however, these systems must adhere to an open documentation architecture that uniformly collects, corrects, and meets a common core of universal data requirements that serve established national informatic needs (i.e., a national standard for the electronic medical record).

Many current federal health-care initiatives involve retrospective analyses, and these studies require results reporting after the process of care has occurred. Significant savings can be realized through a frontline standard documentation process. These initiatives include RACs, Core Measures reporting, retrospective QIO reviews, present-on-admission indicators (POA), fraud and abuse, and outcomes reporting, to name a few. The cost of administrating these back-end processes is enormous and includes the cost of government administration and enforcement of regulations and the cost to providers to adhere to the regulations; these costs are passed down to patients and all taxpayers and contribute to the titanic cost of health care. An accepted national electronic standard for physician documentation can reduce medical errors and the cost of those errors at all levels.

Reshaping health-care communication at its base (the physician) allows change in the assessment process at the individual physician–patient level. This can be achieved through mandatory data requirements, clinical triggers, alerts, and cues. Physicians are well aware that the lack of adequate assessment of the patient can result in poor quality care. Instituting core documentation changes provides a mechanism to shape patient assessment in a consistent manner that allows precise data to be collected that will filter upward through all levels of the health-care system. Each success of the process at the individual physician–patient level adds to the collective success of the entire health-care system. A standardized physician documentation system does not practice medicine but influences physicians' practice behaviors by consistently requiring data input that will aid in the assessment, diagnosis, and treatment of patients. Good data are needed to make good decisions, and physicians will accept documentation systems as breakthrough technology that assists them in performing their jobs, as opposed to dictating to them how to do their jobs.

A large portion of data collected for quality purposes continues to be collected passively through claims reporting systems (UB-04 and CMS 1500) as required by CMS. A national effort to improve clinical reporting systems for claims submission and obtain the information necessary to improve the efficiency and effectiveness of care at all levels is warranted. This need is evidenced by the new application of Medicare Severity-DRGs that continue to be reported through a financial system (UB-04 claims submission).

Coders and billers routinely assign codes that are reported through the MDS requirements set forth in the UB-04 and CMS 1500 claim forms. In this process, coders must review and interpret physician documentation to correctly assign codes. The lack of precision in this process is well evidenced by the widespread use of Physician/Coder Query forms that are routed to physicians to request documentation clarifications needed to correctly assign codes. Supported by an electronic standard documentation system, the responsibility for documentation precision is rightly delegated at the physician level, whereas the responsibility for data quality remains at the coder or biller level (and can be supported through the use of encoders).

The benefits of developing a national standard for an electronic physician documentation system include:

▶ Assurance of consistent, complete, and comprehensive patient assessments by physicians that lead to the establishment of definitive diagnoses, appropriate provision of care, and reduction of medical errors

▶ Support for the full utility of the ICD-10-CM coding system to increase the granularity of clinical information throughout the health-care system

▶ Support for the further application of HIPAA provisions to communicate accurate clinical data through a health network to study and improve the vertical (facility-specific) and horizontal components of care across time and through a network of providers

▶ Support for CQI methods focused on prevention rather than improvement after the fact

▶ Support for the potential to reduce health-care costs related to monitoring inefficiencies that occur at the back end of services (costs attributed to government administration and enforcement of regulations and the cost to providers to adhere to the regulations, which is passed down to the patients and all taxpayers)

SUMMARY

Medical coding creates the vital link from the provision of health-care services to reimbursement and managed care. Landmark health legislation such as Title 19 Medicare and Title 18 Medicaid, the HMO Act of 1973, and TEFRA of

1982 drove the creation of alternative care delivery systems and prospective payment systems in an attempt to contain skyrocketing health-care costs. The primary modality of care has shifted from inpatient care to a proliferation of outpatient services, thereby shaping integrated delivery systems and the U.S. health-care market under managed care. Medical coding plays a key role in providing the data required for provider reimbursement, sharing of clinical information within a provider network, and research across all levels (administrative and clinical) and health-care settings (inpatient and outpatient) to promote quality care at reduced cost. As medical documentation is the basis of all coding, there is a critical need to standardize physician documentation systems to ensure the accuracy of coding at its originating source.

TESTING YOUR COMPREHENSION

1. What four functions does medical (clinical) coding support?

   _____

2. What individuals must be especially knowledgeable in inpatient and outpatient data requirements needed to promote the survival of their health-care institutions to continue to grow and meet their mission of providing high-quality patient care?

   _____

3. The passage of what federal law ultimately drove the importance of medical coding, managed care and integrated delivery systems, computer networking, HIPAA, CQI processes, and the movement of health-care services from cottage industries to corporate industrial models?

   _____

4. What did Medicare's 1966 Conditions of Participation mandate that hospitals do?

   _____

5. What is the main goal of the UR process under Medicare?

   _____

6. What was the main focus of PSRO and PRO reviews?

   _____

7. What was the major significance of TEFRA legislation?

   _____

8. Hospital inpatient payment rates are based on Diagnosis Related Groups (DRGs), which were renamed what in FY 2008?

   _____

9. What was the major significance of the Balanced Budget Act of 1997?

   _____

10. What were the reasons for the shift from the provision of inpatient to outpatient services that occurred throughout the 1980s and 1990s?

    _____

11. Identify a major obstacle to precise coding.

    _____

12. Can incorrect coding affect patient care?

    _____

13. What are the five benefits of developing a national standard for an electronic physician documentation system?

    _____

14. What is the basis of all coding?

    _____

Glossary

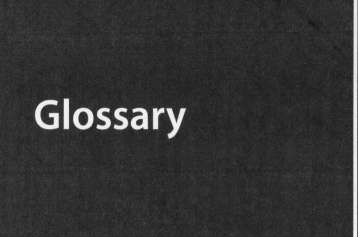

Advance Beneficiary Notice (ABN)	A form signed by the patient that states that the patient is responsible for payment if the service is denied by Medicare, and it may only be obtained for specific services. Without an ABN, the Medicare patient cannot be billed for a test.
agglutination	1. The process by which suspended bacteria, cells, or other particles are caused to adhere and form into clumps; similar to precipitation, but the particles are larger and are in suspension rather than being in solution. For specific agglutination reactions in the various blood groups, see Blood Groups Appendix. 2. Adhesion of the surfaces of a wound. 3. The process of adhering.
allotransplantation	Transplantation of an allograft.
amniocentesis	Transabdominal aspiration of fluid from the amniotic sac.
anatomic position	The erect position of the body with the face and gaze directed anteriorly (cranium aligned in orbitomeatal or Frankfort plane), the upper limbs at the side, and the palms of the hands directed anteriorly; terms of spatial relation such as posterior, anterior, lateral, and medial, are applied to the parts as they stand related to each other and to the axis of the body when in this position.
anesthesiologist	1. A physician specializing solely in anesthesiology and related areas. 2. A person with a doctoral degree who is board certified and legally qualified to administer anesthetics and related techniques.
anesthesiology	The medical specialty concerned with the pharmacologic, physiologic, and clinical bases of anesthesia and related fields, including resuscitation, intensive care, and acute and chronic pain.
anesthetic	1. A compound that reversibly depresses neuronal function, which produces loss of ability to perceive pain and/or other sensations. 2. Collective designation for anesthetizing agents administered to a person at a particular time.

3. Characterized by loss of sensation or capable of producing loss of sensation.
4. Associated with or owing to the state of anesthesia.

angiography	Radiography of vessels after the injection of a radiopaque contrast material; usually requires percutaneous insertion of a radiopaque catheter and positioning under fluoroscopic control.
angioplasty	Reconstitution or recanalization of a blood vessel; may involve balloon dilation, mechanical stripping of intima, forceful injection of fibrinolytics, or placement of a stent.
anteroposterior	1. Relating to both front and rear. 2. In x-ray imaging, describing the direction of the beam through the patient (projection) from anterior to posterior, e.g., an A-P projection of the abdomen; or the direction of view (A-P view) when a film is viewed as if one is facing the patient (anterior to posterior) regardless of projection.
antibody	An immunoglobulin molecule produced by B-lymphoid cells that combine specifically with an immunogen or antigen. Antibodies may be present naturally, their specificity is determined through gene rearrangement or somatic replacement or may be synthesized in response to stimulus provided by the introduction of an antigen; antibodies are found in the blood and body fluids, although the basic structure of the molecule consists of two light and two heavy chains, antibodies may also be found as dimers, trimers, or pentamers. After binding antigen, some antibodies may fix, complement, bind to surface receptors on immune cells, and in some cases may neutralize microorganisms.
antigen	Any substance that, as a result of coming in contact with appropriate cells, induces a state of sensitivity or immune responsiveness and that reacts in a demonstrable way with antibodies or immune cells of the sensitized subject in vivo or in vitro. Modern usage tends to retain the broad meaning of antigen, employing the terms "antigenic determinant" or "determinant group" for the particular chemical group of a molecule that confers antigenic specificity.
arthrodesis	The stiffening of a joint by operative means.
arthrography	Act of making an arthrogram. Imaging of a joint following the introduction of a contrast agent into the joint capsule to enhance visualization of the intraarticular structures.
assay	1. The quantitative or qualitative evaluation of a substance for impurities, toxicity, or other characteristics; the results of such an evaluation. 2. To examine; to subject to analysis. 3. Test of purity; trial.
autopsy	An examination of the organs of a dead body to determine the cause of death or to study the pathologic changes present.
base unit	The fundamental units of length, mass, time, electric current, thermodynamic temperature, amount of substance, and luminous intensity in the International System of Units (SI); the names and symbols of the units for these quantities are meter (m), kilogram (kg), second (s), ampere (A), kelvin (K), mole (mol), and candela (cd).

best care practices	Advance standard treatment protocols that represent the most recent, efficient, and effective means of treating diseases.
Bethesda method (Bethesda System)	The standard format for reporting cervical cytology findings according to the Bethesda system comprises three elements: 1. a statement of the adequacy of the specimen for examination (satisfactory or unsatisfactory); 2. general categorization (negative for intraepithelial lesion or malignancy; epithelial cell abnormality; or other); and 3. descriptive diagnosis, elaborating on the general categorization and including mention of all significant abnormalities, as well as of the patients hormonal status (when vaginal cells are present in the smear).
biopsy	Process of removing tissue from a living body to examine microscopically to determine the presence or absence of disease or to precisely diagnose a disease.
block (of tissue)	A piece of tissue.
body planes	1. A two-dimensional flat surface. 2. An imaginary surface formed by extension of a point through any axis or two definite points.
brachytherapy	Radiotherapy in which the source of irradiation is placed close to the surface of the body or within a body cavity; e.g., application of radium to the cervix.
bundled	A set of services covered under the main procedure code (e.g., a surgical package). Submitting separate codes for services that are part of the main procedure code is considered unbundling and is illegal, even though there are separate codes available for certain services.
capitation	A system of medical reimbursement wherein the provider is paid an annual fee per covered patient by an insurer or other financial source, which aggregate fees are intended to reimburse all provided services.
carrier	The insurance company, payer, or third-party payer.
catheter	A tubular instrument inserted into a body cavity to introduce or withdraw fluid.
certified registered nurse anesthetist (CRNA)	A registered professional nurse with additional education in the administration of anesthetics. Certification achieved through a program of study recognized by the American Association of Nurse Anesthetists.
Chargemaster	A computerized comprehensive list of service codes for laboratory, pathology, radiology, and other services used to expedite claims to third-party payers that is used by hospitals.
chemistry test	Quantitative and specific component levels of various substances are measured of blood, urine, feces, or other body fluids.
chemotherapy	Treatment of disease by means of chemical substances or drugs; usually used in reference to neoplastic disease.
chief complaint	The primary symptom that a patient states as the reason for seeking medical care.

Clinical Laboratory Improvement Act (CLIA)	The government regulation of laboratories that established the standards for processing laboratory studies. All providers must have CLIA certification to provide any laboratory tests and this Certificate Number must be included on the CMS 1500 billing form.
colonoscopy	Visual examination of the inner surface of the colon by means of a colonoscope.
comorbidity	A preexisting condition that affects the patient's care or length of stay.
complete blood count (CBC)	A combination of the following determinations: red blood cell count, white blood cell count, erythrocyte indices, hematocrit, differential blood count, and sometimes platelet count.
complication	A condition that occurs after admission that affects the patient's care or length of stay.
component coding	A method that uses multiple codes to fully report complex procedures. Codes are often from different sections of CPT, such as Surgery, Radiology, and Medicine.
computed tomography (CT)	Imaging anatomic information from a cross-sectional plane of the body, each image generated by a computer synthesis of x-ray transmission data obtained in many different directions in a given plane.
concurrent care	Instances when two or more physicians provide similar services to the same patient on the same day.
concurrent infusions	Multiple substances are administered simultaneously through one IV site.
consultation	Meeting of two or more physicians or surgeons to evaluate the nature and progress of disease in a particular patient and to establish diagnosis, prognosis, and therapy.
continuous quality improvement (CQI)	A data-driven process for improving performance in products or services. The CQI management philosophy accepts the view that products and services can always be improved through ongoing assessment and process improvement methods and that each error, defect or complaint, no matter how small, represents an opportunity for improvement.
contributing component	Four additional components that are used to determine level of service when applicable. They are: counseling, coordination of care, nature of presenting problem, and time.
conversion factor	A number assigned to convert a relative value for the anesthesia service to the payment in dollars based on the geographic location in which services are provided.
crossmatch	1. A test for incompatibility between donor and recipient blood, carried out before a transfusion to avoid potentially lethal hemolytic reactions between the donor's red blood cells and antibodies in the recipient's plasma, or the reverse; performed by mixing a sample of red blood cells of the donor with plasma of the recipient (major crossmatch) and the red blood cells of the recipient with the plasma of the donor (minor crossmatch). Incompatibility is indicated by clumping of red blood cells and contraindicates use of the donor's blood. 2. In allotransplantation of solid organs (e.g., kidney), a test for identification of antibody in the serum of potential allograft

recipients that reacts directly with the lymphocytes or other cells of a potential allograft donor; presence of these antibodies usually, if not always, contraindicates the performance of the transplantation because virtually all such grafts are subject to a hyperacute type of rejection.

culture and sensitivity	A specimen is cultured and grown and the isolated bacteria's susceptibility (sensitivity) to particular antibiotics is determined.
Current Dental Terminology (CDT)	Standardized coding system used to document dental treatment procedures and services to payers; generally updated every two years by the American Dental Association.
cystoscopy	The inspection of the interior of the bladder by means of a cystoscope.
cystourethroscopy	The inspection of the interior of the bladder by means of a cystourethroscope.
cytogenic study	Complex tests used to identify genetic disorders through analysis of tissue, cells, and/or chromosomes. They usually require multiple CPT codes to fully explain the services rendered.
cytology	The study of the anatomy, physiology, pathology, and chemistry of the cell.
cytopathology	The study of disease changes within individual cells or cell types.
Diagnosis-Related Groups (DRGs)	A disease classification system that relates the type of inpatients a hospital treats (case mix) to the costs incurred by the hospital.
diagnostic mammography	Radiologic examination of the female breast with equipment and techniques designed to screen, diagnosis, and/or confirm cancer.
diagnostic ultrasound	The use of ultrasound to obtain images for medical diagnostic purposes, employing frequencies ranging from 1.6 to about 10 MHz.
dipstick test	A specific methodology used in various laboratory studies; a small plastic stick has various pads with special reagents that react in specific ways to body fluids.
dosimetry	Measurement of radiation exposure, especially x-rays or gamma rays; calculation of radiation dose from internally administered radionuclides.
durable medical equipment	Medical equipment designed to be used more than once, such as crutches, a hospital bed, or a wheelchair.
Durable Medical Equipment Medicare Administrative Contractor (DME MAC)	Companies that have a Medicare contract to serve as the single pointof contact for suppliers within a designated region for claims-related business for durable medical equipment, prosthetics, and orthotics.
electronic data interchange (EDI)	The process used for communication via electronic means between providers, payers, and clearinghouses for processing insurance claims.
electronic health record (EHR)	A computerized medical record system that uses a specific software program to record and store all aspects of a patient's health record.
encounter	The meeting between the patient and healthcare provider for which medical assistance is being requested by the patient.
endoscopy	Visualization of any body cavity using an endoscope. Some endoscopic procedures have specific names, such as arthroscopy, which is viewing the inside of a joint.

epidural	On (or outside) the dura mater. [Usage note: epidural and extradural are nearly synonymous, with the exception that epidural implies immediate proximity to the dura mater, and extradural may be unconnected with it.]
erythrocytes	A mature red blood cell.
eschar	Necrotic (dead) tissue produced by a limb that has been burned around the circumference.
escharotomy	A surgical incision of necrotic (dead) tissue that is produced by a limb that has been burned around the circumference. The incision allows blood flow to reach the non-burned tissue beyond the injury.
esophagogastroduodenoscopy (EDG)	Endoscopic examination of the esophagus, stomach, and duodenum usually performed using a fiberoptic instrument.
esophagogastroscopy	Endoscopic examination of the esophagus and stomach usually performed using a fiberoptic instrument.
esophagoscopy	Inspection of the interior of the esophagus by means of an endoscope.
established patient	A patient who has received professional services from the physician or another physician of the same specialty and same physician practice group within the past three years.
evaluation and management	Codes that were developed to report the services performed by physicians in terms of the skill, effort, time, and knowledge required to diagnose and treat a patient's condition or to promote health to receive payment from third-party payers. For the most part, these codes are used to report outpatinet services provided in a physician's office.
evocative/suppression test	Component levels of a substance are measured after the administration of an evoking/suppressing agent. The results can confirm or rule out certain disorders.
examination	1. Any investigation or inspection made for the purpose of diagnosis; usually qualified by the method used. 2. A method of evaluation of skills or knowledge after receiving instruction in a given field.
extracorporeal shock wave lithotripsy (ESWL)	Breaking up of renal or ureteral calculi by focused sound energy.
fee-for-service (FFS)	Insurance coverage that reimburses participants and providers following submission of a claim. Participants have few if any restrictions on which hospitals or doctors to use.
fine needle aspiration	The aspiration and removal of tissue or suspensions of cells through a small needle.
fiscal intermediary	The government contractor that processes claims for government programs.
frontal plane	A vertical plane at right angles to a sagittal plane, dividing the body into anterior and posterior portions, or any plane parallel to the central coronal plane.
general anesthesia	Loss of ability to perceive pain associated with loss of consciousness produced by intravenous or inhalation anesthetic agents; may include amnesia and musle relaxation.

grouper	A software application used to input the principal diagnosis and other critical information about a patient and then provide the correct DRG code.
health maintenance organization (HMO)	A comprehensive prepaid system of health care intended to have emphasis on the prevention and early detection of disease, and continuity of care; often used synonymously with "managed care plan."
Healthcare Common Procedure Coding System (HCPCS)	Medical procedure coding system made up of two levels: Level I consists of the CPT codes; Level II consists of the national codes used to document services not represented in the Level I CPT codes.
hematology	The medical specialty that pertains to the anatomy, physiology, pathology, symptomatology, and therapeutics related to the blood and blood-forming tissues.
hemodialysis	Dialysis of soluble substances and water from the blood by diffusion through a semipermeable membrane; separation of cellular elements and colloids from soluble substances is achieved by pore size in the membrane and rates of diffusion.
highest level of certainty	For inpatients, when final diagnoses are documented as "possible," "probable," likely," "questionable," "rule-out," or "suspected," the conditions should be coded as though the diagnoses were established or definitive. However, this rule does not apply for diagnosis coding for outpatient services, which are coded only to the "highest level of certainty." In contrast to inpatient coding rules, outpatient coding rules often require sign or symptom coding because encounters are short and definitive test results are not always available; and therefore, definitive diagnoses are not established by patient discharge. For example, if the physician documented a final diagnosis of "chest pain, possible angina" and it was an inpatient stay, only the angina would be coded; however, for an outpatient encounter, only the chest pain would be coded.
history	1. A record of a patient's symptoms, illnesses, and conditions, alterations in development, and significant related life events. 2. A record of earlier events, usually with some sort of analysis and interpretation.
history of present illness (HPI)	The chronological description (from the beginning through the present) of the symptoms and signs associated with the current condition, complaint, or problem since the patient's last visit to the physician.
immune globulins	Substances produced from immunoglobulins in human blood. They contain antibodies that provide protection against certain diseases. Immune glbulin products are individually listed with the appropriate CPT code.
incomplete abortion	Also known as missed abortion. Situation in which the fetus dies but is not expelled.
infusion	1. The process of steeping a substance in water, either cold or hot (below the boiling point), to extract its soluble principles. 2. A medicinal preparation obtained by steeping the crude drug in water. 3. The introduction of fluid other than blood, e.g., saline solution, into a vein.

infusion pump	A device that monitors and controls the flow of IV solutions; commonly used with prolonged chemotherapy regimens.
injection	1. Introduction of a medicinal substance or nutrient material into subcutaneous tissue (i.e., subcutaneous or hypodermic injection), muscular tissue (i.e., intramuscular injection), a vein (i.e., intravenous injection), an artery (i.e., intraarterial injection), the rectum (i.e., rectal injection or enema), the vagina (i.e., vaginal injection or douche), the urethra, or other canals or cavities of the body. 2. An injectable pharmaceutical preparation.
Inpatient Prospective Payment System (IPPS)	Medicare payment system for hospital services; program is based on diagnosis-related groups (DRGs).
intra-arterial push	The procedure when a substance is injected directly into an existing intra-arterial line that is in use. The provider must be present for administration of this substance or the infusion must take less than 16 minutes to complete.
intravenous push	The procedure when a substance is injected directly into an existing IV line that is in use. The provider must be present for administration of this substance or the infusion must take less than 16 minutes to complete.
intravenous regional block	A form of selective intravenous regional anesthesia of the distal arm or leg in which a tourniquet is applied and local anesthesia is injected through a cannula in the distal extremity.
key component	The first three levels that are utilized to determine the level of service. The key components consist of: history, examination, and medical decision making.
laparoscopy	Examination of the contents of the abdominopelvic cavity with a laparoscope passed through the abdominal wall.
length of stay (LOS)	The amount of time a patient is admitted to a medical facility.
leukocytes	A white blood cell.
level of service (LOS)	This identifies the physician's work effort in providing treatment and care to the patient.
local anesthesia	A general term referring to topical, infiltration, field block, or nerve block anesthesia but usually not to spinal or epidural anesthesia; may also refer to pharmacologic agents used to achieve local anesthesia
localization wire	A radiological marker used to identify tissue targeted for treatment or removal. Markers are placed prior to the surgery and are coded separately from the excision.
lymphadenectomy	Excision of lymph nodes.
magnetic resonance imaging (MRI)	A diagnostic radiologic modality, using nuclear magnetic resonance technology, in which the magnetic nuclei (especially protons) of a patient are aligned in a strong, uniform magnetic field, absorb energy from tuned radiofrequency pulses, and emit radiofrequency signals as their excitation decays. These signals, which vary in intensity according to nuclear abundance and molecular chemical environment, are converted into sets of tomographic images by using field gradients in the magnetic field, which permits 3-dimensional localization of the point sources of the signals.

malignant	Condition that progressively worsens and that may be fatal (such as cancer); in regard to a neoplasm, refers to locally invasive and destructive growth and metastasis.
managed care	A contractual arrangement whereby a third-party payer (e.g., insurance company, government agency, or corporation) mediates between physicians and patients, negotiating fees for service and overseeing the types of treatment given.
managed care organization (MCO)	An organization with the goal of controlling health care costs by coordinating care through a spectrum of settings, while evaluating its appropriateness and medical necessity at all levels through utilization review, case management, and disease management processes.
mastoidectomy	A group of operations on the mastoid process of the temporal bone and middle ear to drain, expose, or remove an infectious, inflammatory, or neoplastic lesion.
medical coding	The process of assigning a numerical or alphanumerical code to a procedure; used for insurance and billing purposes.
medical decision making (MDM)	Involves the complexity of establishing a diagnosis and/or selecting a management option or treatment plan. There are four types: straightforward, low complexity, moderate complexity, and high complexity.
medical necessity	The criterion that requires medical treatments to be appropriate and provided in accordance with generally accepted standards of medical practice; the procedure must match the diagnosis.
medical record (MR)	The detailed chronicle of a patient's encounter with any health care provider; includes progress notes, laboratory results, radiology results, consultations, and other forms of reports.
Medicare Severity DRG (MS-DRG)	The new name for the program implemented by the Centers for Medicare and Medicaid Services to better account for the differences in patient severity so that hospitals will be paid more for treating complicated cases.
metastatic	Condition in which a disease or diseased cells have spread from one body organ or system to another.
microbiology	The science concerned with microorganisms, including fungi, protozoa, bacteria, and viruses.
midsagittal plane	A plane vertical in the anatomic position, through the midline of the body that divides the body into right and left halves. (obsolete term for median plane)
minimum data set	Often referenced as the MDS required for Long Term Care, MDS can also be used as a generic term that describes the minimum core of data that must be reported by providers to insurers including Medicare to receive reimbursement.
missed abortion	Also known as incomplete abortion. Situation in which the fetus dies but is not expelled.
modality	1. A form of application or employment of a therapeutic agent or regimen. 2. Various forms of sensation, e.g., touch, vision, etc.

Mohs micrographic surgery	A technique for removal of skin tumors with a minimum of normal tissue, by prior necrosis with zinc chloride paste, mapping of the tumor site, and excision and microscopic examination of frozen section of thin horizontal layers of tissue, until all of the tumor is removed. More recently, the preliminary step of chemical necrosis has been omitted.
monitored anesthesia care (MAC)	The use of sedatives and other agents, however the dosage is low enough that patients remain responsive and breathe without assistance.
multi-axial system	Procedures can be looked up in the CPT manual in different ways. This provides for more flexibility to search for the correct code.
National Correct Coding Initiative (NCCI)	An initiative to develop correct coding methodologies to improve the appropriate payment of Medicare claims.
nephrectomy	Removal of a kidney.
nephrolithotomy	Incision into the kidney for the removal of a renal calculus.
neuroplasty	Decompression or freeing of intact nerves from scar tissue.
new patient	A patient who has not received any professional services from the physician or another physician of the same specialty and same physician practice group within the past three years.
noninvasive procedure	Procedure that does not require insertion of an instrument or device through the skin or a body orifice for diagnosis or treatment.
non-selective catheter placement	The catheter is placed either directly into an artery or a vein without further manipulation or placed only in the aorta from any approach.
nuclear medicine	The clinical discipline concerned with the diagnostic and therapeutic uses of radionuclides, including sealed radiation sources.
orchiectomy	Removal of one or both testes.
orthoses (plural, singular is orthosis)	Specialized mechanical devices (such as braces or splints) that support supplement or help straighten weakened joints or limbs.
outpatient code editor	As part of the CMS' 1996 National Correct Coding Initiative (NCCI), the Outpatient Code Editor (OCE) uses pre-programmed (software) edits that identify procedures and services described by combinations of HCPCS/CPT codes that cannot be billed together on the same day of service for a particular patient. All Medicare outpatient claims are scrutinized by the NCCI/OCE edits and coding errors can result in claim denials. In addition, the inappropriate billing of certain services separately rather than globally (packaged) in order to receive higher reimbursement is called "unbundling" and is considered an fraudulent and unethical practice that can result in charges and prosecution of the offending health care provider.
Outpatient Prospective Payment System (OPPS)	The payment system established by the federal government to control the costs of patient care received in ambulatory care settings.
panel	Groups of laboratory tests commonly performed together and assigned one code.
past medical, family, and/or social history (PFSH)	An element of the history, which documents the patient's past medical issues and treatments; family medical events and status; and lifestyle/environmental conditions and social activites/habits.

Peer Review Organization (PRO)	They review the medical necessity for patient adminssion and continued stay.
Physician Quality Reporting Initiative (PQRI)	Financial incentive program to encourage certain health-care professionals to voluntarily report quality measures using Category II codes. CMS collects this data as part of a plan to implement a "pay-for-performance" strategy that will encourage the provision of high-quality cost-effective care.
piggybacking	The common practice of hanging a second smaller IV bag on the IV pole and connecting the tubing to a port on the tubing of the original bag of fluids.
plan of care (care plan)	Establishing the treatment plan for a patient that involves all medical providers and ancillary services to ensure the patient receives the best care possible. It is used to assist in the assessment of the functional capacity of the patient.
positron emission tomography (PET)	Creation of tomographic images revealing certain biochemical properties of tissue by computer analysis of positrons emitted when radioactively tagged substances are incorporated into the tissue.
posteroanterior	A term denoting the direction of view or progression, from posterior to anterior, through a part.
premium	The amount paid monthly by individuals to their carrier for health insurance.
primary diagnosis	The term commonly used to describe the first diagnosis sequenced for outpatient reporting.
Professional component	The physician-based care.
Professional Standards Review Organization (PSRO)	An independent external agency managed by physicians that perform external reviews of patient care with the goal of protecting the Medicare Trust Fund. Their duties included an external review of the appropriateness of care given to Medicare and Medicaid pateints for hospital inpatient services.
Prospective payment system (PPS)	A program established by the federal government; limits reimbursements to healthcare providers by assigning fixed-payment rates that are based on the average cost of treating the patient's condition or providing a specific service.
prostatectomy	Removal of a part or all of the prostate.
prostheses (plural, singular is prosthesis)	Fabricated substitutes (such as artificial legs or hip joints) for damaged or missing body parts.
protected health information (PHI)	Specific information that is identified by HIPAA as confidential and must be handled in very specific ways; name, DOB, address, insurance information, diagnoses, etc.
qualitative testing	Determination of the nature, as opposed to the quantity, of each of the elements composing a substance.
Quality Improvement Organization (QIO)	In 2002, the PROs were renamed QIOs; CMS continues to contract with them. They are private administrative organizations that include physician staff, to oversee the Medicare and Medicaid programs.
quantitative testing	Determination of the amount, as well as the nature, of each element comprising a substance.

radiation oncology	1. The medical specialty concerned with the use of ionizing radiation in the treatment of disease. 2. The medical specialty of radiation therapy. 3. The use of radiation in the treatment of neoplasms.
radiolucent	Relatively penetrable by x-rays or other forms of radiation.
radiopaque	Exhibiting relative opacity to, or impenetrability by, x-rays or any other form of radiation.
regional anesthesia	Use of local anesthetic solution(s) to produce circumscribed areas of loss of sensation; a generic term including conduction, nerve block, spinal, epidural, field block, infiltration, and topical anesthesia.
Regional Healthcare Information Organization (RHIO)	An organization that serves a particular population of healthcare consumers to coordinate, manage, and improve patient care.
relative weight	A mathematical measurement that represents the work and resources required to treat a patient's condition or provide a service. Medicare's nationally assigned relative weight for a condition or service is multiplied times a conversion factor or blended rate to convert the relative weight to dollars. The relative weight is essentially part of a third-party payer's reimbursement formula.
renal autotransplantation	The transfer of an organ or other tissue (skin, bone, muscle, tendon, nerve, arterial or venous segments) as grafts or vascularized (by pedicle or microanastomosis) structures from one location to another in the same person (e.g., a kidney moved from its original position to the pelvis, where the iliac vessels provide vascular supply).
retrospective reimbursement systems	A system of payment where the healthcare providers were paid for services based on the prevailing charge for rendering service.
review of systems (ROS)	An inventory of body systems obtained by the physician through a series of questions asked of the patient. These questions are designed to identify signs and/or symptoms that the patient may be experiencing or has previously experienced.
rhinoplasty	Reshaping or repairing of the nose internally, externally, or both.
sagittal plane	Plane parallel to the median plane; sagittal planes are vertical planes in the anatomic position.
screening mammography	Radiologic examination of the female breast with equipment and techniques designed to screen for cancer.
section (of tissue)	A thin slice of the tissue block that has been prepared for examination.
selective catheter placement	Once the catheter is placed into an artery or vein, it is then moved, at a minimum, to another branch off the initial main branch.
sentinel node scan	The first lymph node to receive lymphatic drainage from a malignant tumor; the sentinel nodes are identified as the first to take on a radionuclide or dye injected into the tumor.
serum	1. A clear, watery fluid, especially that moistening the surface of serous membranes, or exuded in inflammation of any of those membranes. 2. The fluid portion of the blood obtained after removal of the fibrin clot and blood cells, distinguished from the plasma in circulating blood. Sometimes used as a synonym for antiserum or antitoxin.

single photon emission computed tomography (SPECT)	Tomographic imaging of metabolic and physiologic functions in tissues, the image being formed by computer synthesis of photons of a single energy emitted by radionuclides administered in suitable form to the patient.
sinusotomy	An incision into a sinus for medical or surgical treatment
SOAPing	The format used in the problem-oriented MR for recording progress notes: Subjective (data), Objective (data), Assessment (of diagnoses), and Plan (for care).
source document	The document used to find the names of the procedures to properly assign the CPT code.
specimen	A small part, or sample, of any substance or material obtained for testing.
spontaneous abortion	Spontaneous expulsion of the fetus, also known as a miscarriage.
status indicator	Medicare has assigned alphabetic payment status indicator (PSIs) codes to HCPCS/CPT codes to indicate whether or not particular procedure or service is covered (reimbursed) under Medicare's outpatient prospective payment system (OPPS) (e.g., PSI code "V" describes a clinic or emergency department visit paid under OPPS).
stereotaxis	1. Three-dimensional arrangement. 2. Stereotropism, but applied more exactly where the organism as a whole, rather than a part only, reacts.
Superbill	Another name for encounter form, used in physician offices, contains a checklist of tests and other procedures.
supine	1. Denoting the body when lying face upward. 2. Supination of the forearm or of the foot.
surgical package	Reimbursement for typical services provided by the same surgeon for a given procedure, covered under one surgical procedure code (not coded separately). Services include: local anesthesia, encounter on the date immediately prior to or on the date of the procedure (including history and physical), immediate postoperative care, writing orders, evaluating the patient in the post-anesthesia recovery area, and post-operative follow-up care (follow-up E&M services).
Technical component	Facility-based care (e.g., hospital).
third-party payer	An organization or person (other than the patient) who furnishes the money to pay for the provision of health care services.
thrombectomy	The excision of a thrombus.
thrombocytes	An irregularly shaped, disclike cytoplasmic fragment of a megakaryocyte that is shed in the marrow sinus and subsequently found in the peripheral blood, where it functions in clotting. A platelet contains granules in its central part (granulomere) and, peripherally, clear protoplasm (hyalomere), but no nucleus, is about one third to one half the size of an erythrocyte, and contains no hemoglobin. Syn: platelet.
thyroidectomy	Removal of the thyroid gland.
transcutaneous	Denoting the passage of substances through unbroken skin, as in absorption by inunction; also passage through the skin by needle puncture, including introduction of wires and catheters by Seldinger technique. Syn: transcutaneous.

transfusion	Transfer of blood or blood component from one person (donor) to another person (receptor).
transverse plane	A plane across the body at right angles to the coronal and sagittal planes; transverse planes are perpendicular to the long axis of the body or limbs, regardless of the position of the body or limb; in the anatomic position, transverse planes are horizontal planes; otherwise the two terms are not synonymous.
ultrasound	The use of ultrasound to obtain images for medical diagnostic purposes, employing frequencies ranging from 1.6 to about 10 MHz.
unbundling	Assigning multiple CPT codes when one CPT code would fully describe the service or procedure.
upcoding	The use of a procedure code that provides a higher payment than the code for the service actually provided.
urethroscopy	Inspection of the urethra with a urethroscope.
usual and customary charge	Setting fees by comparing the usual fee the provider charges for the service as well as the customary fee charged by most providers in the community.
utilization review	The process of reviewing the patient's records to ensure that services provided to Medicare beneficiaries were medically necessary.
vulvectomy	Excision (either partial, complete, or radical) of the vulva.

References

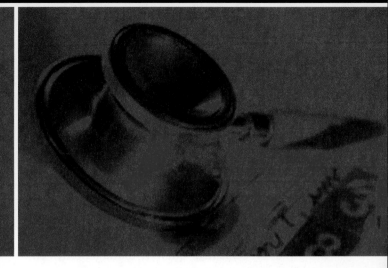

CHAPTER 1

1. Slee A, Slee V, Schmidt HJ. Slee's Health Care Terms, 5th Ed. Sudbury, MA: Jones and Barlett Publishers, 2008:436–437.
2. Greene M, Fenton S. Clinical classifications and terminologies. In: LaTour K, Eichenwald S, eds. Health Information Management: Concepts, Principles, and Practice. Chicago: American Health Information Management Association, 2006:311.
3. Hazelwood A, Venable C. Reimbursement methodologies. In: LaTour K, Eichenwald S, eds. Health Information Management: Concepts, Principles, and Practice. Chicago: American Health Information Management Association, 2006:383.
4. LaTour K. Healthcare information standards. In: LaTour K, Eichenwald S, eds. Health Information Management: Concepts, Principles, and Practice. Chicago: American Health Information Management Association, 2006:156.

CHAPTER 2

1. Russo R, Russo JJ. Health care compliance plans: good business practice for the new millennium. J AHIMA 1998;69:24, 26–28, 30–31; quiz 33–34.

CHAPTER 3

1. May 1999. *CPT Assistant*, as taken from 1999 *College of American Pathologists Professional Relations Manual* (p. 158, Pathologist Professional Component Billing for Clinical Laboratory Services).

CHAPTER 4

1. Buck SL. Coding for mammography services. J AHIMA 2007;78:86–88.
2. The ASTRO/ACR Guide to Radiation Oncology Coding, 2007. Chicago: American Medical Association, 2006.

CHAPTER 5

1. Nguyen A-T. Monitored anesthesia care. Internet J Health 2000;1(1). http://www.ispub.com/ostia/index.php?xmlFilePath=journals/ijh/vol1n1/mac.xml. Accessed August 6, 2007.

2. Teslow M. Health data concepts. In: Abdelhak M, et al., eds. Health Information: Management of a Strategic Resource, 3rd Ed. St. Louis: Saunders Elsevier, 2007:110.

CHAPTER 10

1. Falen T. U.S. health care policy and the rising uninsured: an alternative solution. J Health Soc Policy 2004;19:1–25.

2. Cassidy B. Health care delivery systems. In: LaTour K, Eichenwald S, eds. Health Information Management: Concepts, Principles, and Practice, 2nd Ed. Chicago: American Health Information Management Association, 2006:15.

3. Zeman V. Clinical quality management. In: LaTour K, Eichenwald S, eds. Health Information Management: Concepts, Principles, and Practice, 2nd Ed. Chicago: American Health Information Management Association, 2006:510.

4. Hazelwood A, Venable C. Reimbursement methodologies. In: LaTour K, Eichenwald S, eds. Health Information Management: Concepts, Principles, and Practice, 2nd ed. Chicago: American Health Information Management Association, 2007:358.

5. Huffman E. Health Information in Reimbursement. In: Cofer J, ed. Health Information Management. Chicago: Physicians' Record Co, 1994:459.

6. Falen T, Liberman A. Learning to Code with ICD-9-CM for Health Information Management and Health Services Administration. Baltimore: Lippincott Williams & Wilkins, 2007:14.

7. Ray M. Health care systems. In: Abdelhak M, Cole S, Odell C, eds. Health Information: Management of a Strategic Resource, 3rd Ed. St. Louis, Saunders Elsevier, 2007:6.

8. Upshaw V, Kaluzny A, McLaughlin C. CQI, transformation, and the "learning" organization. In: McLaughlin C, Kaluzny A, eds. Continuous Quality Improvement in Health Care: Theory, Implementation, and Applications. Sudbury, MA: Jones and Bartlett Publishers, 2006:192.

9. Savitz L, Bernard S. Measuring and assessing adverse medical events to promote patient safety. In: McLaughlin C, Kaluzny A, eds. Continuous Quality Improvement in Health Care: Theory, Implementation, and Applications. Sudbury, MA: Jones and Bartlett Publishers, 2006:229.

10. McLaughlin C, Kaluzny A. Continuous Quality Improvement in Health Care: Theory, Implementation, and Applications. Sudbury, MA: Jones and Bartlett Publishers, 2006:15.

11. FY 2006 RAC Status Report November 2006. Accessed 9/15/2007 at http://www.cms.hhs.gov/RAC/Downloads/RACStatusDocument–FY2006.pdf.

12. Solberg L, Kottke T, Brekke M. Quality improvement in primary care: the role of organization, collaboratives, and managed care. In: McLaughlin C, Kaluzny A, eds. Continuous Quality Improvement in Health Care: Theory, Implementation, and Applications. Sudbury, MA: Jones and Bartlett Publishers, 2006:298.

Index

CD-ROM(s) available at Reference Desk.

W 80 F187La 2009
Learning to code with
 CPT/HCPCS
(CD-ROM i

W 80 F187La 2009
Learning to code with
 CPT/HCPCS
(CD-ROM included)

DATE DU

DATE	ISSUED TO
06/27/10	ILL to Kew Gardens